Economics for Lawyers

ECONOMICS FOR LAWYERS

Richard A. Ippolito

Princeton University Press
Princeton and Oxford

Library of Congress Cataloging-in-Publication Data
Ippolito, Richard A.
   Economics for lawyers / Richard A. Ippolito.
      p. cm.
   Includes bibliographical references and index.
   ISBN 0-691-12177-X (cl : alk. paper)
   1. Law and economics. 2. Economics. 3. Law—
   Economic aspects—United States. I. Title.
K487. E3I67 2005
330'.024'34—dc22

                              2004043155

British Library Cataloging-in-Publication Data is
available
This book has been composed in 10/12 Sabon
Printed on acid-free paper. ∞
pup.princeton.edu
Printed in the United States of America
10 9 8 7 6 5 4 3 2 1

Contents

Chapter 7

Externalities

The Coase Theorem   228

Chapter 8

Pollution in the Workplace: Contract or Externality?

An Introduction to the Rules of Law   247

Chapter 9

Lemons Markets and Adverse Selection

Signals, Bonds, Reputation, and Tie-ins as Solutions   282

Introduction

The purpose of this course is to provide the economic foundations for the study of law and economics, and to provide law students with the elementary tools that are required to interact with clients in both a corporate and a government setting. Contracts written in a corporate setting are meant to help the firm attain its business objectives. Corporation counsel can more effectively integrate these goals into legal documents if they understand the underlying rationale and goals of the contracts. Tort actions are integrally involved with the notion of economic damages, and the presentation and cross-examination of expert testimony. Government regulations are part of a broader objective to foster social goals that often involve the trade-off of costs and benefits. Put simply, lawyers are more likely to be successful if they are conversant in economic problems that are the genesis of client legal actions.

The goals are relatively simple: to understand the derivation of demand and supply curves and the economic interpretation of equilibrium in markets, and to be able to portray and understand the social costs of interference with free trade among willing participants. An important feature of this discussion is the concept of equilibrium, and an appreciation for the role of profit in directing resources toward their most valuable uses.

The tendency for resources to flow to profitable ventures is an important theme in the course. If incentives are properly erected, then this free flow of capital and other resources will ensure that the economy produces the goods and services most valued by consumers. We shall see that perverse outcomes can arise under some circumstances. An example is contracting under duress. If these contracts are upheld, large amounts of social waste can result. Similarly, and perhaps counterintuitively in the area of patent law, if innovators are allowed to capture the entire benefits of their ideas, then the value added by new innovations can be nearly zero. These issues give rise to a need to think about optimal reward structures in contracting.

We will spend considerable time studying various instances where market conditions are less than ideal to produce optimal economic outcomes. Market imperfections are one important factor that gives rise to demand for lawyers. We will discuss problems raised when markets are monopolized, and show the extent of social harm that results when firms perceive the possibility of earning extraordinary profits by raising prices above competitive levels. Antitrust enforcement and corporation defenses use large amounts of legal time in the United States, and an appreciation for these issues will prove useful for law students who gravitate toward this area of the law. We also will spend a great deal of time discussing the problems of imperfect information.

In a world in which perfect information was freely available, the need for contracting would be sharply diminished. But information is neither free nor perfect. We are not entirely sure that the products we purchase are the promised quality. Firms are unsure that the workers they hire will work as hard as they promise. Neither are participants in market deals sure that their counterparts will deliver their parts of the bargain. Various market mechanisms arise to ensure honesty in market transactions, many of which do not require contracting.

We will spend time talking about the concepts of "reputation," "signals," 'sorting," and various ways in which contracts in the labor markets can be arranged to ensure desired behavior by workers. Lawyers who understand these concepts will be better able to help corporate clients achieve their various goals while still protecting them from inadvertently violating various discrimination laws that can carry substantial penalties.

We also will spend considerable time dealing with externalities, and in particular, we will discuss the problem of airport noise in some detail. What is the most efficient way to deal with an external negative "product" like noise that adversely affects homeowners around an airport? Here, we will discuss the notion of the Coase theorem and illustrate how airport authorities can determine the "optimal" amount of noise. These issues abound in the law surrounding property rights, zoning ordinances, and the like, and they highlight the problems that arise when certain resources, like airspace, are not privately owned.

Game theory, which is the last subject covered in this book, is a framework to help you think about strategy when faced with decisions when outcomes also depend on other players' decisions (who do not share their intentions with you). Lawyers involved in litigation and many in commercial transactions spend much of their careers in situations in which some "player" is trying to get an advantage on their client. Your client's optimal response often depends on trying to anticipate the options facing your adversary, and then choosing the strategy that is most likely to give your client the more profitable result.

Broadly, this book can be interpreted as the study of the benefits that flow from well-defined property rights, inclusive of the freedom to earn income from this property, and to use either the property itself, or the income it generates, to make beneficial trades with other willing market participants.

What Makes This Book Different

Most textbooks do not give the right amount of detail that is important for legal applications. In price theory, for example, most books devote lots of space to the discussion of special cases to the general rules, a practice that has little application and serves to distract and discourage students trying to learn the basics of economics, often for the first time. Similarly, many topics that are important for legal applications are either ignored or treated too skimpily to provide the proper background for further study.

In place of price theory textbooks, most law students are given various articles to read, are asked to learn applications from the study of various cases, or are assigned a chatty book that soft-pedals the basic concepts in price theory. This approach might be suitable for those who already have a good background in the principles of economics, but otherwise, the hodgepodge approach is too unsystematic for most students. It leaves them with no foundation in the economic concepts that are required to understand the applications that arise in various cases they encounter along the way.

I skip the extraneous material in price theory and present the topics that serve as a basis for most applications later on. The book comprises perhaps one-half of materials found in most price theory books, but also spends more time discussing issues not typically found in most textbooks. While the principles are presented in general terms, the book leans heavily on learning by doing. Most of the concepts are developed through application to illustrative problems, some in considerable detail. The book assumes no prior knowledge of economics or mathematics beyond algebra. Concepts are illustrated through extensive use of charts and diagrams.

Finally, the book takes into account the great variation in economics and quantitative training and ability in a typical entering class to law school. Thus, I try to make each chapter understandable for all students, regardless of background. However, the materials are presented in such a way that students who already know the basics will be suitably challenged along the way. In addition, I use footnotes to occasionally embellish the text by way of explaining some technical points. Footnote materials, especially those involving mathematics, are not candidates for exam questions and thus may be safely ignored by all students. But students looking for some additional technical materials may find what they are looking for in the footnotes and a few more challenging appendices. Also, numerous questions and exercises are presented along the way, where answers usually are given in footnotes.

Recommended Supplementary Reading

For those trying to learn the basics from a first-level book, I recommend N. Gregory Mankiw's *Principles of Microeconomics* 3rd ed. (Hinsdale, IL: Dryden Press, 2004). The first edition (1998) and second edition (2000) are also perfectly fine, and less expensive. I recommend this book for summer reading for all students, but especially for those who have had no prior courses in economics. Past students, and yours truly, give this book excellent reviews.

For those who want a book beyond principles that can serve as a reference book to get a second look at a key concept in price theory, the following price theory books are good choices (and involve very little math). I list the latest editions, but any edition of these books is fine:

Walter Nicholson, *Intermediate Microeconomics and Its Applications,* 7th ed. (Hinsdale, IL: Dryden Press, 1997).
Robert Pindyck and Daniel Rubinfeld, *Microeconomics*, 5th ed. (Englewood Cliffs, NJ: Prentice-Hall, 2000).
Jack and David Hirshleifer, *Price Theory and Its Applications*, 6th ed. (Englewood Cliffs, NJ: Prentice-Hall, 1998).

For those who prefer a mathematical reference book, I recommend Walter Nicholson, *Microeconomic Theory: Basic Principles and Extensions*, 7th ed. (Hinsdale, IL: Dryden Press, 1998).

Other books worth reading *after* you have taken the course:

Adam Smith, *The Wealth of Nations: An Inquiry into the Nature and Causes* (New York: Modern Library, 1994) (or any publisher). All economists can benefit from reading this book ten times, and lawyers will do themselves a favor to read it at least once. It serves to remind us how old and how intuitive most economic ideas really are.

Milton Friedman, *Capitalism and Freedom* (Chicago: University of Chicago Press, 1963). Friedman is, well, Friedman. Everything he ever wrote except for his work on monetary theory is good reading for lawyers. His writing is approachable, intuitive, and insightful.

Paul Heyne, *The Economic Way of Thinking*, 9th ed. (Englewood Cliffs, NJ: Prentice-Hall 1999). This book is an unstructured approach that imparts the ideas of economics in many settings.

Henry Butler, *Economic Analysis for Lawyers* (Durham, NC: Carolina Academic Press, 1998). This book includes many legal cases that incorporate the use of economics.

Economics for Lawyers

Chapter 1

Finding the Optimal Use
of a Limited Income

Main Economic Concepts	1. More is better.
	2. Free choice is a valuable commodity.
	3. Freedom to trade can make everyone better off.
New Terms	1. Indifference curve
	2. Diminishing marginal utility
	3. Budget constraint
	4. Optimal use of a limited income
	5. Pareto efficiency
	6. Pareto optimal allocation
	7. Pareto efficient allocation
	8. Edgeworth box diagram
	9. Contract curve
	10. Compensation principle
	11. Substitution effect
	12. Price effect
	13. Income effect
	14. Corner solution

The best place to start the study of economics is with a model of consumer decisions. Each of us has a limited income and must make choices about how best to allocate it among competing uses. Compared to a bundle of goods and services that are given to us with a market value of $20,000, most of us would prefer to have a $20,000 income to spend as we want. Why? Because each of us has different preferences for different goods and services, and thus, the "value" of a dollar is higher if we have the opportunity to spend it as we please. The value of free choice is a central tenet in economics and provides the basis to understanding the concept of a demand curve.

I. Indifference Curves

I am going to pursue this problem in a simplified way. There are two goods, clothing and housing. There are no other uses of income, no savings and no taxes.

A. THE MAIN QUESTION

A person has $100 to spend during some period. Using the assumptions below, how much does he spend on clothing and housing?

> Assumptions about consumer preferences:
> 1. Each consumer knows his or her preferences and is able to articulate them so that we can portray them in the form of a chart.
> 2. Preferences are consistent. If a consumer tells us that some bundle of goods A is superior to bundle B, and bundle B is superior to bundle C, then it must follow that A is preferred to C.
> 3. More is better. Consumers prefer a bundle of goods that has more of both goods. Likewise, a bundle with fewer of both goods is inferior.

To answer this question, I need to introduce the concept of an **indifference curve**. An indifference curve merely tells us the various combinations of goods that make a particular consumer indifferent. Consider figure 1-1, panel (a). I assume that we can create a homogeneous unit of clothing, like yards of quality-adjusted material. This measure is shown on the horizontal axis. I also assume that we can create a homogeneous unit of housing, like number of quality-adjusted square feet, which I show along the vertical axis. Suppose we consider some combination of clothing and housing labeled B, which corresponds to 25 units of clothing and 50 units of housing. What other combinations of clothing and housing would make this consumer indifferent to this particular allocation?

B. INDIFFERENCE CURVES SLOPE DOWNWARD

We know that any bundle that has both more housing and more clothing must be superior to B, and thus, any such bundle cannot be on the same indifference curve. This inference follows from the axiom "More is better." The combinations of housing and clothing labeled II in the figure denote superior bundles as compared to B. Likewise, our consumer cannot be indifferent between the bundle labeled B and any combination of both less housing *and* less clothing, denoted by area IV in the figure. This means that the indifference curve passing though point B must pass through areas I and III. In other words, the indifference curve must be downsloping from left to right. Panel (b) in figure 1-1 shows one such indifference curve that satisfies this criterion.

This particular indifference curve is unique to some hypothetical person that we are considering. To be concrete, suppose that we are drawing an indifference curve for Jane Smith, who in fact possesses the bundle of goods labeled A. This bundle comprises 100 units of housing and 12.5 units of clothing. And suppose that we quiz her as follows: if we take away some units of housing, leaving her with only 50 instead of 100, how many additional units of clothing would she require in order to be indifferent to bundle A? We suppose that she answers, 12.5 units,

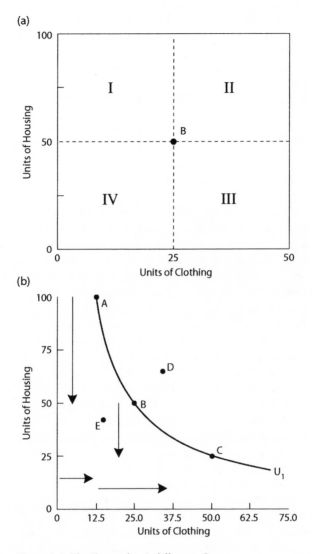

Figure 1-1. The Shape of an Indifference Curve

which I show in the diagram. This corresponds to bundle *B*. Thus, we know that bundles *A* and *B* must lie on the indifference curve. Note that over the relevant range, Jane is willing to give up an average of 4 units of housing for each unit of clothing she obtains.[1]

---

[1]This is the average trade-off of clothes for housing over the relevant range. The trade-off is different for each individual unit.

Assuming that we continue asking her questions like this, we could draw a line through all the points of her indifference curve, which I label as U_1 in panel (b). That is, U_1 describes all the combinations of clothing and housing that make Jane indifferent to bundle A; we can think of all these combinations as yielding the same *utility* to her, which is why I use the letter U to denote the indifference curve.

C. OTHER THINGS TO KNOW ABOUT INDIFFERENCE CURVES

A few other features of indifference curves are important to know: they (a) are convex to the origin, (b) are infinite in number, (c) never cross each other, and (d) different consumers have different indifference curves.

Indifference curves are convex from the origin. This phenomenon is due to the concept of **diminishing marginal utility**, meaning that consumers attach a higher value to the first units of consumption of clothing or housing, and less value to marginal units of clothing or housing once they have an abundance of them. Thus, if Jane has lots of housing and little clothing, as for example at point A in the figure, she is willing to trade 50 units of housing for 12.5 units of clothing to form bundle B. But once she attains this bundle, she attaches less value to obtaining still more clothing and is more reluctant to give up more units of housing.

For example, starting at point B, suppose that we take 25 units of housing from Jane, say from 50 to 25 units in the figure. She requires 25 more units of clothing to make her indifferent to bundle B. Bundle C denotes the new allocation. Over the range B to C, she is willing to sacrifice only 1 unit of housing to receive 1 unit of clothing, on average. Compare this to the move from point A to point B, where she was willing to give up four times as much housing for each unit of additional clothing, on average. The difference is that at point B, she already has a fair amount of clothing and thus is not willing to give up as much housing to obtain even more clothing.

There are an infinite number of indifference curves. Panel (b) in figure 1-1 depicts a single indifference curve for Jane. That is, I started with bundle A and then drew an indifference curve through all the other bundles like B and C that yield the same utility to her. But suppose that Jane started with an allocation of goods labeled D. We know that this bundle of goods cannot be on indifference curve U_1 because in comparison to bundle B, for example, bundle D has both more clothing *and* more housing. Since more is better, then it follows that D must be on a higher indifference curve than B. Following the same reasoning, bundle E must be on a lower indifference curve.

If we pursued the same experiment with Jane starting from bundle D as we did when she had bundle A, we could draw a second indifference curve running through bundle *D* in the figure. If we do, then we have an indifference curve labeled U_2. Similarly, we could draw an indifference curve passing through point *E*, labeled U_0. I show these indifference curves in figure 1-2, panel (*a*). U_2 is a higher indifference curve than U_1, and therefore any combination of housing and clothing on this curve is preferred to U_1. Similarly, U_0 is a lower indifference curve than U_1, and

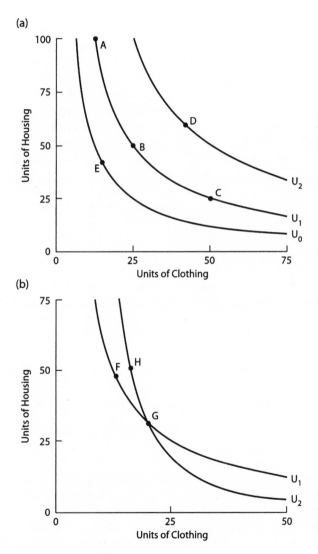

Figure 1-2. An Indifference Curve Map

therefore any combination of clothing and housing on this curve is inferior to U_1. In reality, there are an infinite number of indifference curves. To keep the figures simple, we normally portray only two or three in the relevant range to illustrate a problem.

Indifference curves do not cross. Each indifference curve is uniformly higher than the one below. Why? If they were not depicted this way, they would violate the rule of consistency. Consider panel (*b*) in figure 1-2. In this figure, I have drawn indifference curve U_1 and show points labeled F and G. I also portray indifference curve U_2 passing through point G. In drawing it this way, I am saying that bundle G yields the same amount of utility as bundle F. I also am saying that bundle G is the same as bundle H. But how can this be true, since bundle H has more housing and clothing than bundle F? This conundrum violates the consistency rule. We avoid this problem as long as we ensure that indifference curves never cross.

Note that we can use this same idea to remind ourselves that any bundle on a higher indifference curve is superior to any bundle on a lower indifference curve. Consider panel (*a*) in figure 1-2. How can we be sure that bundle C is inferior to bundle D? We know this because bundle C offers the same utility as bundle B because they are on the same indifference curve. But bundle B clearly is inferior to bundle D because there are fewer units of housing and clothing in bundle B compared to D. Since C is the same as B, it follows that C also must be inferior to D. This is another application of the principle that more is better.

Different consumers have different indifference curves. The indifference curves drawn for Jane are specific to her tastes. Ken Jones would have a different set of indifference curves depending on his tastes for clothing and housing. The basic look of his indifference curves would be similar to Jane's (downsloping, convex, etc.), but his trade-off of clothing and housing very likely would be somewhat different.

II. Gains from Trade Using the Edgeworth Box Diagram

With this small amount of modeling, we already can illustrate an important principle of economics—namely, the gains that result from trade. I demonstrate this concept in the simplest possible way. I assume that there are only two people, Jane and Ken. I have C_{max} units of clothing and H_{max} units of housing. I want to demonstrate the proposition that if I allocate these units in any arbitrary way to Ken and Jane, they almost always will make each other better off by trading. To do this, I need to show Jane and Ken's indifference curves on the same picture. This is done through the use of an **Edgeworth box diagram**.

As a first step, I write Jane's indifference curves in figure 1-3, panel (*a*). I label C_{max} and H_{max} on the vertical and horizontal axis to remind myself that this is the maximum amount of clothing and housing available in the problem. In panel (*b*), I write Ken's indifference curves, but I do it in an odd way: I rotate it 180 degrees, so that his origin is diagonal to Jane's. In this picture, Ken has more clothing and housing as he moves away from his origin, as depicted by the arrows. Note that I also

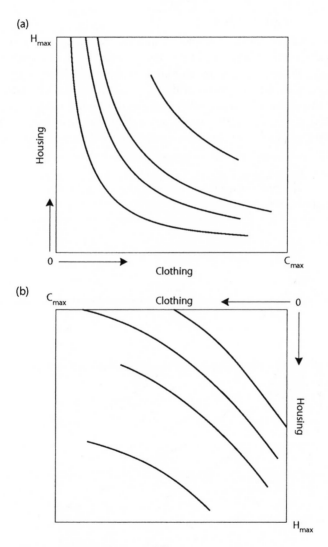

Figure 1-3. Jane's and Ken's Indifference Curve Maps

show C_{max} and H_{max} as the limits in this chart, so that the horizontal and vertical lengths of the axes are the same as Jane's.

EXERCISE:
Step 1: Draw two sets of indifference curves for Ken and Jane, both recognizing the maximum amount of housing and clothing. Draw them in seperate charts, but draw Ken's indifference map upside down.

A. CONSTRUCTION OF THE BOX

To create the "box," simply slide Ken's indifference curve map until it is superimposed onto Jane's. Note that the charts exactly fit together because the lengths of the axes are the same on Jane's and Ken's figures. I show these charts superimposed in figure 1-4. I label Ken's indifference curves K_i and Jane's J_i. Larger subscripts denote higher levels of utility. (Note that it is OK that Ken's and Jane's indifference curves cross each other, as long as Jane's and Ken's own indifference curves do not cross.)

EXERCISE:
Step 2: Slide the two indifference curve maps toward each other until they exactly overlap.

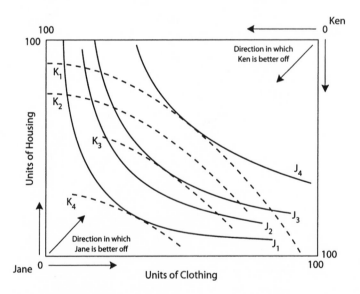

Figure 1-4. Edgeworth Box Diagram

I want to illustrate the initial amount of clothing and housing that Ken and Jane have to start with. I could portray this allocation anywhere in the box, because the axes have been drawn so that no matter where I plot a point, the total amount of clothing and housing must add to the maximum amounts. For illustration, I *arbitrarily* allocate these goods as described by point A as shown in panel (*a*) of figure 1-5. Jane has lots of housing and not much clothing, while Ken has lots of clothing and not much housing.

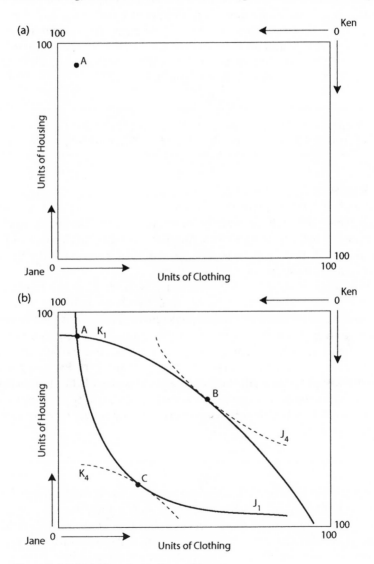

Figure 1-5. Initial Allocation to Ken and Jane

> EXERCISE:
> *Step 3*: Depict the initial allocation of housing and clothing to Ken and Jane. This allocation is arbitrary; it does not matter where in the box we start.

To solve the problem, I reintroduce some indifference curves. Recall that there are an infinite number of indifference curves for both Ken and Jane, and so by definition, we know that each has one curve passing through point A; and so I draw these curves as illustrated in panel (*b*), figure 1-5. Notice that these curves, when superimposed, look like a cigar. Ken's indifference curve is K_1 and Jane's is J_1.

> EXERCISE:
> *Step 4*: Draw Jane's and Ken's indifference curves through point A.

B. PARETO SUPERIOR TRADES

It is immediately apparent that a trade could make either Ken or Jane or both better off without making either worse off. This trade involves Jane giving some housing to Ken, and Ken giving some clothing to Jane, meaning that the allocation moves in a southeast direction in the figure—that is, toward the fat part of the "cigar."

For example, suppose that Ken and Jane trade in a way that moves their allocation from A to B. In this case, Ken is no worse off than at A, because he is on the same indifference curve; but Jane is clearly better off because at B she is on a higher indifference curve compared to point A (compare J_4 to J_1). When a trade makes at least one participant better off and no participant is worse off, then it is said to be **Pareto superior**. Similarly, they could trade so that Jane is no worse off but Ken is better off. Ken gets the best deal without reducing Jane's utility at point C. The move from A to C also is Pareto superior. Many moves starting from A are Pareto superior.

> EXERCISE:
> *Step 5:* Start trading so that the allocation of goods moves toward the center of the "cigar." We do not know how Ken and Jane will work the trade, but we know that both can be better off by some trade. Consider the extreme trades first, that is, those that make one consumer much better off but keep the other one at the same level of utility.

It is not possible to know exactly who is going to get the better deal in a trade. It depends on Jane's and Ken's relative bargaining power. Most likely, however, both will gain, and we can characterize the range of outcomes in which both can be better off compared to point A.

To do this, I add a few more indifference curves in the relevant range in panel (a) of figure 1-6. Consider a move from point A to point D. In

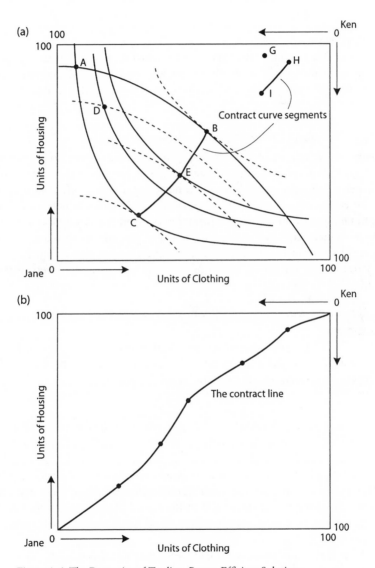

Figure 1-6. The Dynamics of Trading: Pareto Efficient Solutions

comparison to point *A*, both Ken and Jane each are on a higher indifference curve, and thus both have benefited from the trade. Clearly, the move from *A* to *D* represents a Pareto superior move. But at point *D*, both can trade again to further increase their utility. In general, as long as a "smaller cigar" can fit inside a "larger cigar" then in an Edgeworth box diagram, both consumers can be made better off by further trading. When does this process stop?

EXERCISE:
Step 6: Depict some arbitrary move toward the middle of the "cigar." Any such move will show that both Ken and Jane will be better off. Draw Ken's and Jane's indifference curves through this point.

C. THE CONTRACT CURVE: PARETO OPTIMAL ALLOCATIONS

Once they reach a point where their indifference curves no longer form a "cigar" but are just tangent, then it is not possible for one to gain by further trade without making the other person worse off. One such outcome is depicted by point *E*. In general, this condition defines a **Pareto optimal allocation**. A Pareto optimal allocation exists when any possible move reduces the welfare of at least one person. Sometimes, a Pareto optimal solution is referred to as a **Pareto efficient allocation**. Likewise, a Pareto superior move sometimes is referred to as a Pareto efficient trade.

EXERCISE:
Step 7: The process ends when any further trade reduces the utility of at least one of the consumers. This occurs where two indifference curves just touch, or are tangent to, each other.

So far, I have portrayed a solution for one arbitrary initial allocation of clothing and housing, namely *A*. For this allocation, I have shown at least three possible trading outcomes, namely *B*, *C*, and *E* in panel (*a*), figure 1-6, whereby at least one consumer is better off and none is worse off. Depending on how Jane and Ken bargain, we could have a solution anywhere along the segment *CB* in the figure. Any point along this segment has the characteristic that Jane's and Ken's indifference curves are tangent.

What if the allocation we started with was not *A* but some other point in the Edgeworth box, for example, point *G* in panel (*a*)? Repeating the exercise for this allocation would lead us to some solution along the segment *IH*, which also is a segment along the contract curve.

If we completed many such exercises, we could find many solutions in the chart, all of which were characterized by the tangency of Ken's and Jane's indifference curves. I already have shown two segments along this line, namely, *CB* and *IH*. If we draw a line connecting all of these points, we have the **contract curve** in the Edgeworth box, which I show in panel (*b*), figure 1-6, by the diagonal line connecting the origins of Jane's and Ken's indifference curve maps. This line can be smooth or not so smooth, depending on how the participants' indifference curves look.

EXERCISE:

Step 8: Show the contract curve in the Edgeworth box, which depicts the bundles that are Pareto optimal outcomes, regardless of where the original allocation is depicted.

EXERCISE:

To test your understanding of the Edgeworth box, start with a replication of figure 1-5, panel (*a*). Put a dot anywhere in the Edgeworth box designating the initial allocation. Draw Ken's and Jane's indifference curves that pass through that point. Unless you know Ken's and Jane's utility function exactly, there is no way you can exactly represent where these indifference curves lie, but you can draw illustrative indifference curves for them, paying attention to the rules of indifference curves that you have learned. You can then bound the solution (best deal for Jane and best deal for Ken) and show the segment along the contract curve between these points that represents the range of possible solutions.

Finally, while we have not worried about where Ken and Jane end up on the contract curve, given their initial allocation, in reality it makes a difference to each participant. For example, starting from point *A* in panel (*a*), figure 1-6, it matters to Ken where along the segment *CB* he ends up; he is far better off at *C* than *B*. The opposite is true for Jane. The differences in outcomes is one reason why corporations spend large amounts of money trying to sway contracts in ways that are favorable to them, without at the same time making the deal unprofitable for the other party. Put simply, lawyers and other professionals are paid considerable sums to help influence outcomes along the contract curve.

Pareto superior: A trade that makes at least one party better off without making anyone worse off.

Pareto optimal allocation: Any outcome that cannot be altered without making at least one person worse off. Sometimes, a *Pareto optimal solution* is referred to as a *Pareto efficient allocation.* Likewise, a Pareto superior move sometimes is referred to as a *Pareto efficient trade.*

On the contract curve: A shorthand way of describing a Pareto optimum solution; its meaning derives from the Edgeworth box.

GAINS FROM TRADE: LESSONS FROM THE EDGEWORTH BOX

Even though no new production takes place, Ken and Jane both improve their welfare by trading some units of clothing and housing. Both improve the welfare of their trading partner as a by-product of pursuing their own interests.

In reference to figure 1-6, panel (*a*), if the initial allocation is depicted by point *A* and the final allocation after trading by point *E*, then both Ken and Jane walk away from the transaction thinking they got a good deal. That is, trading is not a zero sum game: trading can improve the welfare of all the participants to the trade.

Owing to diminishing marginal utility and the fact that individuals do not all have the same preferences for goods, an arbitrary allocation of goods to individuals usually is not as good as the allocation that individuals choose if given the opportunity to trade.

III. The Budget Line: The Essence of the Economic Problem

In most market settings, individuals are not trading directly with each other but instead are faced with market prices that are beyond their influence. In addition, their income is given and limited. A consumer's problem is to allocate her income among available products and services to attain the highest level of utility. In our simple problem where there are only two goods and no taxes or savings, then we can depict the consumer's budget constraint as follows:

Budget line: $I = P_H H + P_C C$

The variable I is the consumer's income, P_H is the price of each unit of housing, P_C is the price per unit of clothing, and H and C are the units of housing and clothing that the consumer purchases.

Figure 1-7, panel (*a*), illustrates the consumer's budget. To make the example concrete, I assume that the price of housing is $1 per unit,

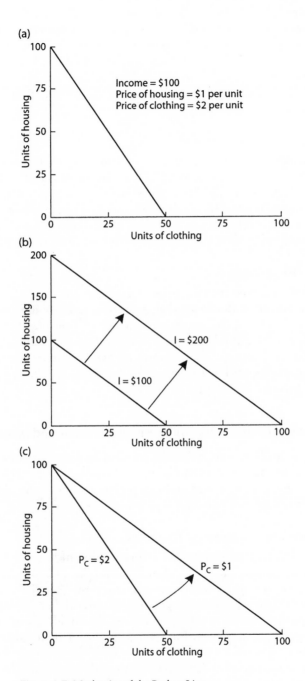

Figure 1-7. Mechanics of the Budget Line

while the price of clothing is $2 per unit. I also suppose that income is $100. The budget constraint tells us that if the consumer spends all of her money on housing, she can purchase 100 units; if she allocates all her money to clothing, then she can purchase 50 units. In addition, the budget constraint describes every other possible allocation of housing and clothing that she can afford. The linear segment in figure 1-7 represents this budget.

A. IMPACT OF INCOME CHANGES

The particular budget shown in figure 1-7 assumes an income of $100. Suppose her income doubles to $200 but that the prices of clothing and housing remain the same. Then the budget line moves parallel to the right, as shown in panel (b). In this case, she now can purchase 200 units of housing and no clothing or 100 units of clothing and no housing, or any combination in between, as shown by the income line $I = \$200$.

B. IMPACT OF PRICE CHANGES

Alternatively, suppose that the price of clothing falls from $2 to $1, but everything else stays the same; that is, income is $100 and the price of housing is $1. Then, the maximum amount of housing that the consumer can purchase still is 100 units. But now she can purchase twice as many units of clothing if she allocates all her income to clothing. This means that the budget line rotates out in the direction of the price reduction, as illustrated in panel (c).

IV. Consumer Choice: The Optimum Use of a Limited Income

We are now ready to put our model together to determine how Jane allocates her income between clothing and housing. We merely superimpose Jane's budget constraint and indifference curves in the same chart, as shown in figure 1-8, panel (a).

A. DETERMINING THE OPTIMAL SOLUTION

We know that Jane must purchase a combination of housing and clothing that is consistent with her budget line; and thus, bundles like A or F in the figure are possible allocations. Suppose that Jane considers allocation F. This allocation is possible because it lies on her budget curve. She enjoys utility level U_1. Similarly, she could choose bundle G that also gives her utility U_1. But she can do better than either of these allocations.

In particular, at point F, Jane is willing to trade a substantial amount of housing to obtain some additional clothing, as depicted by the steepness

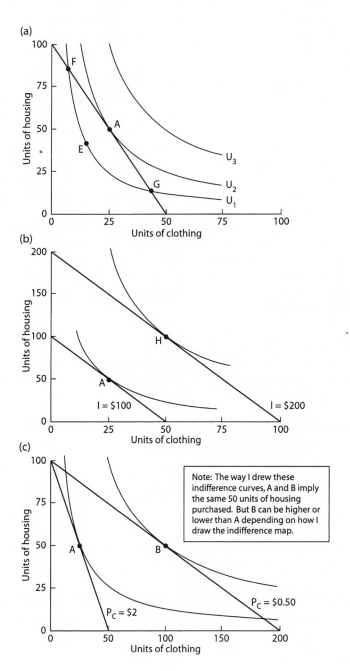

Figure 1-8. Optimal Allocation of Income

of her indifference curve around this point. The budget line is much flatter over this range. More specifically, around point *F*, in order to obtain one more unit of housing, Jane is *willing* to sacrifice about 10 units of housing. But the market prices are such that she is *able* to obtain 1 more unit of clothing in exchange for only 2 units of housing. So it appears like a good deal to continue giving up housing for clothing at these prices.

Alternatively, you can use the shortcut from the Edgeworth box. At point *F*, the area bounded by the indifference curve and the budget line (area *FEG*) looks like a cigar, and *F* is the tip of the cigar. You know that she needs to move toward the center of the cigar. As she trades housing for clothes at market prices, she goes to a higher utility curve and finds herself at the tip of ever-smaller cigars, until she attains the bundle where the budget line and indifference curve are just tangent. Point *A* describes this solution.

More simply still, Jane's optimal allocation is found by moving along her budget line until she attains her highest utility. It is apparent from inspection that this solution is depicted by point *A* in the figure, where Jane's budget line is tangent to her indifference curve. At point *A*, it is not possible for Jane to alter her allocation along her budget line without reducing her level of utility.

B. PORTRAYING AN EXACT SOLUTION

To obtain a specific solution for Jane, I assume that her utility is described by the following mathematical function, which is a common example used for illustration:

> Assume that Jane's utility function is described as follows:
> $$U = \sqrt{C}\sqrt{H}$$

Jane's utility equals the square root of units of clothing consumed times the square root of units of housing consumed. For this utility function then, for any given value of *U*, say U_1, then setting *C* to a series of values from zero to some large number means that *H* must fall according to the shape of the indifference curve U_1.[2]

---

[2]This utility function is $U = C^{1/2} H^{1/2}$. At utility level U_1, then housing *H* and clothing *C* are related as follows $H = U_1^2/C$, which defines one indifference curve. To draw utility curves, you can draw out a 45-degrees curve from the origin using a chart like figure 1-8. For $H = C = 1$ then $U = 1$, which you can label U_1, then this indifference curve is defined by $H = 1/C$. Next, $H = C = 2$ so that $U_2 = 2$, where this indifference curve is defined by $H = 4/C$, and so on.

Assuming a particular utility function for Jane allows me to find exact solutions to Jane's allocation.[3] If I assume that her utility function is somewhat different, then I would find some other particular combination of clothing and housing that would maximize the value of her income. It turns out that given her tastes, Jane's optimum use of her $100 is to buy 25 units of clothing and 50 units of housing.

At the optimal allocation at point A in panel (a), the slope of her indifference curves exactly matches the slope of her budget constraint. In equilibrium, Jane is *willing* to trade housing for clothing at exactly the same rate that she is *able* to at given market prices.[4] Since point A is on her budget curve, 25 units of clothing and 50 units of housing exactly exhaust her income.

Even if he had the same income as Jane, Ken's allocation likely would be different, unless he happened to have the same tastes for housing and clothing as Jane. For example, given his preferences, he might consume 70 units of housing and 15 units of clothing. That is, given the same income, consumers often find the highest value of their money by allocating it differently than other consumers.

C. HOW A CHANGE IN INCOME AFFECTS CHOICE

Now we can reconsider what happens to Jane's consumption if her income increases. Panel (b) in figure 1-8 demonstrates the solution when her income doubles to $200. At the higher level of income, Jane searches for the allocation of clothing and housing that gives her the highest utility. This solution is depicted by bundle H in the figure. Notice that at the higher income level, Jane consumes more units of clothing and housing as compared with bundle A. In general, as long as a good is "normal," consumers will consume more of it at higher income levels.[5]

---

[3]If I maximize her utility function $U = C^\alpha H^\beta$ subject to her income constraint $I = P_C C + P_H H$, then I have the first-order condition $C = H\Phi$, where $\Phi = (P_H/P_C)(\alpha/\beta)$. Substituting for C in her budget constraint, I have $H^* = I/(P_H + \Phi P_C) = I/P_H(1 + \alpha/\beta)$. Thus, Jane consumes more housing the lower the price of housing relative to clothing, and the higher her income. Substituting H^* back into her income constraint, I have $C^* = (I - P_H H^*)/P_C$. Note that when α and β each are ½, then her optimal solution always occurs where she spends 50 percent of her income on each commodity.

[4]Economists sometimes refer to this condition as one where the ratio of the marginal utility of goods equals the ratio of prices, but I do not use this nomenclature in this book.

[5]There are exceptions; for example, perhaps if consumers have sufficient income, they do not purchase hamburger but replace it with steak. But these exceptions are not important for our purposes.

D. THE IMPACT OF A PRICE CHANGE ON THE OPTIMUM SOLUTION

A change in prices also affects Jane's optimum consumption pattern. Suppose that the price of clothing falls from $2 to 50¢ but everything else remains the same. Panel (c) depicts the problem. Point A denotes Jane's original allocation of income. Point B denotes her optimal allocation when the price of clothing falls. Not surprisingly, Jane ends up buying more units of clothing at the lower price, but it is interesting that given her particular utility function, Jane consumes the same 50 units of housing at the lower price of clothings.

If Jane had somewhat different tastes, meaning that her indifference curves looked somewhat different from those I depict in the figure, a reduction in the price of clothing might lead Jane to consume either more or fewer units of housing. It seems odd that if the price of clothing falls, Jane's consumption of both clothing *and* housing could increase; this sounds more like an outcome from an increase in income. This puzzle will be solved when we look more closely at the nature and consequences of the change in the price of clothing.

V. The Compension Principle: The Dollar Value of Changes in Utility

In this section, I want to look more closely at the price change depicted in panel (c), figure 1-8. The price reduction clearly makes Jane better off. Her utility increases as depicted. We know that Jane is better off at the higher utility, but by how much? While we do not know how to quantify "utils," it turns out that we can measure this utility change in dollars.

A. VALUING THE UTILITY CHANGE FROM A PRICE REDUCTION

The most obvious way to measure the dollar value of the price reduction is to reflect on the money Jane saves at the lower price. Jane is purchasing 25 units of clothing at price $2. The price then falls from $2 to 50¢. If she continues to consume 25 units of clothing, she has an additional $37.50 to spend ($1.50 times 25 units). In other words, Jane has to be better off by at least $37.50. It turns out that she is even better off than this. To determine a more precise estimate, ask the following question: What is the maximum amount that Jane would pay Ken if he had the power to reduce the price of clothing from $2 to 50¢?

Figure 1-9 demonstrates the solution. This figure reproduces panel (c) in figure 1-8, except that it adds two new budgets lines, one passing through bundle A and another tangent to bundle C. To determine the dollar value of the utility change, start at the new equilibrium denoted by point B. At this equilibrium, Jane enjoys utility level U_3. Then ask: At the new prices, how much income would Jane require to attain her *old* level of utility, U_1?

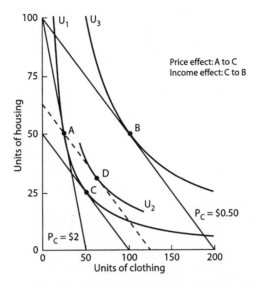

Figure 1-9. Effects from a Change in Price of Clothing

Put differently, how much income would we have to take away from Jane to put her on her old indifference curve? Income changes are represented by parallel shifts in budget lines. Start at point *B*. Drag Jane's budget line leftward in a parallel way until it just touches her old indifference curve—this is the budget line that passes through point *C* shown in the figure. It is tangent to U_1 at point *C*.

We now have sufficient information to obtain a dollar value of the utility change. At point *B*, Jane's income is $100. You can read this income from figure 1-9. The budget line intersects the horizontal axis at 200 units. The price of clothing on this line is 50¢. Ergo, her budget is $100.

Similarly, the budget line that passes through point *C* intersects the horizontal axis at 100 units of clothing. The price of clothing on this budget line also is 50¢. Hence, the income level that defines this budget line is $50.

The dollar value of the increased utility from the price reduction is the difference between these two amounts, $100 − $50. Put differently, if Ken held the power to change the price of clothing, Jane would be willing to pay him an amount up to $50. I obtained this estimate by applying the compensation principle; that is, I searched for that level of income that restores Jane's original level of utility.[6]

---

[6]For small price changes it turns out that we obtain a good approximation to this answer by simply calculating the product of the change in price, times quantity of clothing that Jane was consuming at the original $2 price. For large price changes such as the one I show (from $2 to $0.50), this approximation is too crude. I pursue this issue more carefully in chapter 2.

Compensation principle: A change in utility brought about by either a change in price or other interference to the market can be translated into a dollar value by searching for the increment in income that restores the original level of utility.

Consider two jobs for lawyers. One is in the area of contracts, a job characterized by more or less predictable hours and a relatively low level of anxiety. The other is in the area of litigation, a job that involves tight deadlines, travel to various court venues, and a high degree of anxiety. Most lawyers require some pay premium (a "compensating differential") to do litigation over contracts that makes up for the reduction in utility caused by the rigors of the job. This is an application of the compensation principle.

Consider the situation in which a well-meaning mom forces her daughter, Jane, to attend a ballet performance. Jane does not pay anything for the ticket and wasn't going to do anything that night anyway. She is visibly upset during the performance and cannot describe how much she hated the experience. Upon leaving, in tears, she accuses her mom of "kidnapping" her and threatens legal action (life in the twenty-first century!). Mom knows that she has imposed substantial disutility on Jane and asks how much it would take (in dollars and cents) to make things right. Jane says that had mom asked her ahead of time how much she would have to pay Jane to accompany her to the ballet, Jane would have said $200. Assuming that Jane is honest, we know the dollar value of her reduction in utility. Damages after the fact often are illuminated by asking about the price of a contract that the plaintiff would have required to be exposed to the damages that resulted. This is an application of the compensation principle.

Why is the answer not $37.50? This is the dollar amount in Jane's pocket when the price change is announced. At the old prices, she purchased 25 units at $2 apiece. Now these units cost $12.50. Ergo, she has $37.50 still in her pocket to purchase more clothing and more housing. The reason this answer is incorrect is that if Jane had a budget of $62.50 at the new prices, she could attain a higher level of utility than U_1.

This alternative can be shown in figure 1-9 as follows. Drag Jane's budget line leftward from point B, but instead of continuing to point C, stop at point A as shown by the dotted-line budget schedule in the figure. This is the budget line at the new prices that permits Jane to purchase the bundle of goods that was optimal under the old prices.

It is evident, however, that faced with this budget constraint, Jane would not consume bundle A, but rather would proceed down the budget line to find a higher utility level, U_2. The optimum bundle is depicted at point D. Comparison of this budget line to her \$100 income measures the difference in utility U_2 and U_3. We want the dollar value of the change in utility from U_1 to U_3. To find the true estimate, continue reducing Jane's income until it is just tangent to utility level U_1, which is shown by bundle C in the figure.

B. ANATOMY OF A PRICE CHANGE: INCOME AND "PRICE" EFFECTS

The work we just did to value the change in Jane's utility also serves to illustrate the two components of any price change. First, the price of clothing falls relative to housing, meaning that Jane's new optimum allocation will be more favorable to clothing relative to housing. This is called either the **substitution effect** or, alternatively, the **price effect**, and is reflected by a move along a single indifference curve. Second, the lower price allows Jane to attain a higher level of utility. This is called the **income effect** and is shown by a parallel shift in budget lines between two indifference curves.

In terms of figure 1-9, the movement from bundle A to C describes the sole effect of the change in relative prices without commingling it with the effect of the change in utility. The movement from A to C describes "price effect," or, alternatively, the "substitution effect." More units of clothing are consumed and fewer units of housing, as is apparent from comparing points A and C. The price effect is always negative. That is, a reduction in the price of clothing leads to an increase in quantity consumed, after compensating for the income effect. The move from C to B denotes the income effect. Normally, the income effect is positive for both housing and consumption.

It is apparent by inspection that as a result of the price effect, Jane increases the quantity of clothes she consumes from 25 to 50 units. As a result of the income effect, she purchases an additional 50 units of clothes. In terms of housing, she reduces her quantity consumed from 50 units to 25 units, owing to the substitution effect. But she consumes 25 more units as a result of the income effect. The income effect exactly offsets the substitution effect, which is a result specific to her utility function. Other utility functions could generate situations in which either the substitution effect dominated the income effect or vice versa.

> *Anatomy of a price change*: If the price of X falls, then, owing to the substitution effect (also called the price effect), the quantity of X consumed increases. The price effect is always negative. Owing to the income effect, ruling out exceptions (which I do in this book), more of X is purchased as well as more of everything else.

VI. Applications of the Compensation Principle

A. BUCKLEY'S TULIPS AND MUMS PROBLEM

An illustration of the compensation principle is found in an example of the harm done by "detrimental reliance" from Frank Buckley's Contracts I class. My interpretation of the problem goes something like this. Frank likes to plant tulips and mums in his garden every year. Tulip bulbs are planted in the fall and bloom in the spring. Mum seeds are planted in the spring and bloom in the fall. For simplicity, suppose that Frank has $150 to spend on flowers, that there is no way his wife will give him more flower money, and that there is no chance Frank will spend less than his full budget. The price of mums and tulips is $1 per pot.

I portray Frank's indifference curves in figure 1-10, panel (*a*). Given his particular set of indifference curves, it turns out that if the prices of mums and tulips are the same (which they are in this problem), Frank's optimal flower bundle has an equal number of mums and tulips. I have drawn a 45-degree line from the origin to make sure that I portray his optimal solution along this line (the 45-degree line describes equal numbers of the two kinds of flowers in the garden). Frank's usual allocation is depicted by point *A*, where his garden has 75 tulips and 75 mums.

For Frank's birthday one year (his birthday is in a winter month), Frank's uncle Dick feels generous and promises Frank an extra $100 to finance the planting of more flowers in the coming year. Dick promises to give Frank the gift after he receives his tax refund. Anticipating the extra $100, Frank now has a $250 budget to purchase flowers. I depict the higher budget line in the figure. Naturally, given Frank's preference for symmetry, as reflected in the neat-looking indifference map, he wants to plant 125 mums and 125 tulips with the higher income (point *D*).

Anticipating the gift, Frank orders 125 mums in the winter for spring planting. After he plants them, Uncle Dick calls, saying that on account of an unusually small refund this year, he is changing the amount of Frank's gift from $100 to zero. But since Frank already has committed $125 of his flower budget, he has only $25 to spend on tulips.

Frank immediately threatens to sue his uncle Dick, claiming substantial harm. Dick replies, "How can there be any harm? You still have the $150 you always had." But harm was imposed. *Assuming that we know exactly how to calculate Frank's indifference curves*, we can calculate the amount of the harm. Since I assume a particular utility function for Frank, I can find the answer mathematically. You cannot know the exact

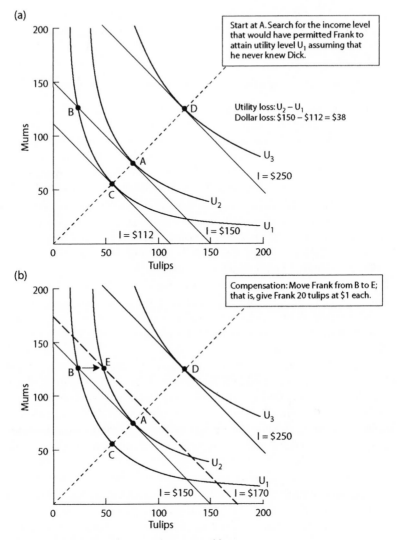

Figure 1-10. Buckley's Tulips and Mums Problem

answer by eyeballing panel (*a*), figure 1-10, but you can show the harm qualitatively.[7]

[7]In the example, I suppose that Frank's utility curve is described by $U = M^{1/2}T^{1/2}$. His budget line is described by $\$150 = P_M M + P_T T$, where P_M and P_T are \$1. Note that this is the same utility function that I assigned to Jane, and thus I can use the derivation in note 3 to show that when prices are equal, Frank always chooses a 50:50 allocation of mums and tulips in his garden.

1. Using the Compensation Principle to Calculate Damages

I suppose that after the flower seasons are over by late fall, Uncle Dick thinks about the harm he imposed on his nephew and decides to make Frank "whole." We need to figure out how much Dick owes Frank to accomplish this outcome. To do this, note that the problem arises because Frank relies on his uncle's promise. But owing to Dick's unreliable character, Frank ends up with 125 mums and 25 tulips; that is, he still has $150 to spend, but he has committed to 125 mums (they cannot be returned after they have been planted), thereby leaving him with only $25 to purchase tulips. This outcome is depicted by point *B* in panel (*a*).

While at first it seems odd that harm has occurred even though no monetary damages are observed ($150 is $150 according to Uncle Dick), it is apparent that harm has been imposed, because consumers are not indifferent to arbitrary allocations of their income. Harm has occurred because Frank's optimal 50-50 allocation of flowers is more valuable than the lopsided look caused by Uncle Dick reneging on his promise.

Frank evaluated point *B* when he decided on the original allocation of his income, but rejected it in favor of point *A*. By choosing point *A*, Frank enjoys U_2 units of utility, whereas point *B* yields only U_1 units of utility. Because of his uncle's promise and subsequent reneging, Frank is stuck at point *B*. This explains why Frank is mad, but does not provide a dollar value of the loss.

We can determine this amount by using the compensation principle. We ask the question: at what level of income could Frank have attained utility level U_1? To find out, simply drag the $150 income budget line parallel to the left until it is tangent to utility level U_1. This solution is found at point *C* (where the budget line is tangent to the indifference curve U_1). Since I have assumed a particular utility function for Frank, it turns out that this budget line is equivalent to $112.[8]

In effect Uncle Dick's unreliability reduced Frank's income from $150 to $112. Put simply, Uncle Dick owes his nephew $38 to compensate him for the harm done by his untrustworthy act.

In reality, we could not know Frank's exact indifference curve mapping. But Frank surely does. And so we could imagine Uncle Dick

---

[8]The solution is easily determined. Because of the special utility curve I assume for Frank (see prior note), we know that $U_1 = 125^{1/2} \, 25^{1/2} = 56$. How much income does Frank need to attain 56 utils? We know that if the prices of mums and tulips are the same, then he always chooses an equal number of tulips and mums. Call this variable x. Solve for the value of x that gives 56 utils: $U_1 = 56 = x^{1/2} x^{1/2}$. Solving for x times the solutions, $x = 56$. Since the price of mums and tulips is $1, then 56 tulips and 56 mums can be obtained with $112. That is, if Frank has $112 he would allocate half to mums and tulips and attain U_1. With $150 in income, we know that Frank attains U_2. The dollar difference in these two utility levels is $38.

asking Frank in September after winning some money at the race-track, "Frank, how much would it take to offset the harm I imposed on you last spring?" Supposing that Frank was totally honest with his uncle, then if his indifference curves are like those drawn in figure 1-10, he would answer "$38." Dick forks over this amount. A family quarrel is settled.

The point is general. *Anytime that a consumer is pushed away from his optimal allocation of income, harm is imposed. In principle, money damages from this harm are calculable.* While it generally is impossible to know this number (since the harmed party might overstate his loss), it explains one reason why your client might be sued for damages even when no dollar loss is visible. Two additional issues, however, must be addressed before leaving this problem. First, there is often more than one way to compensate for harm, and thus, it is worth looking for the cheapest settlement amount. Second, we can at least bound the damages done to Frank, even if we cannot know his indifference curves.

2. A Second Way to Compensate Frank

I have supposed that Uncle Dick procrastinates until late fall to compensate Frank. We have calculated this amount to be $38. Suppose, however, that Uncle Dick understands the harm he has done in August, when there still is time for Frank to plant more tulips in the fall. In this case, it might be cheaper for Uncle Dick to get Frank back onto his utility curve U_2 right away.

Consider panel (b) in figure 1-10. Dick can do this by purchasing enough extra tulips to move Frank from point B to point E. It turns out that given the particular indifference curves that I have assumed for Frank, an additional 20 tulips would accomplish this outcome.[9]

In this case, Uncle Dick makes things right for only $20 instead of $38. This solution is cheaper because Frank attaches some value to the extra 50 mums that Dick induced Frank to purchase, and so adding a few tulips to this burgeoning mums collection is sufficient to make Frank whole right away. In this case, waiting to settle up would cost Uncle Dick an extra $18. If, of course, Frank is so mad at Uncle Dick that he refuses Dick's offer of $20 worth of tulips right away, then

---

[9]Using the particular utility function for Frank as specified in note 7, we know that absent interference from Dick, Frank would have purchased 75 tulips and 75 mums, and thus, would have attained utility level U_2, which equals $U_2 = 75^{1/2}75^{1/2} = 75$. At point B, we know that Frank is at utility level U_1, which as I showed in note 8, equals 56 ($U_1 = 56$). We know that at B, Frank has 125 mums. If he had T tulips, then, together with 125 mums, he could attain utility U_2 as described at point E. We need to solve for T: $U_2 = 75 = 125^{1/2}T^{1/2}$, which implies $T = 45$. Since Frank already has 25 tulips at point B, this means that Dick can get Frank to point E by giving him 20 more tulips.

Frank's claim on Dick is limited to \$20.[10] So, if Frank cools down only next fall, and then demands \$38 from Dick, then Dick should give him only the \$20 he originally offered. Frank's irrational behavior cost him the \$18 difference.

3. Bounding the Solution When Dick Doesn't Know Frank's Utility Function

I have supposed that either I know Frank's indifference curve map or he accurately portrayed it for me. But suppose that I do not know his mapping and he is not volunteering the information. He just demands damages in the amount \$Z. How can I bound a reasonable estimate on harm imposed by Uncle Dick? One way is to assume that Frank is absolutely committed to symmetry in his garden. I defined this condition as follows: Frank always chooses the same number of each flower for his garden, *regardless of the relative prices between tulips and mums*. In this case, an additional tulip is worthless unless it is accompanied by an additional mum and vice versa.[11]

Figure 1-11, panel (a), portrays these indifference curves. Each utility curve is a right angle denoting the idea that given some level of mums, say at point A, no additional number of tulips will add any utility to Frank unless they are accompanied in exact proportion by more mums. Recall that Frank starts out with \$150, which corresponds to the purchase of 75 tulips and 75 mums in the example (denoted by point A).

> *Zero substitution:* Two goods have zero substitution when, in a compensated sense, the consumer always chooses the same bundle of these two goods regardless of price.

In the Mums and Tulips problem, Uncle Dick promises Frank an additional \$100, thereby inducing Frank to purchase 125 mums. So, Frank anticipates attaining utility U_3 at point D. After Dick reneges, Frank finds himself at point B in the figure, which describes the purchase of 25 tulips and 125 mums. Since he has only 25 tulips, then only 25 mums have any value to Frank; the remaining 100 might just as well be thrown in the trash. Frank is on indifference curve U_1.

---

[10]It does not matter whether Dick gives Frank \$20 in cash or 20 tulips. In the former case, Frank's budget shifts outward, but he cannot follow the new budget to find the optimal combination of flowers because he is stuck at 125 mums, and the best he can do is stop at this point E, which allows him to enjoy his original level of utility.

[11]This utility function is given by $U = a \min (T, M)$, where a is some arbitrary constant. Frank only attaches value to the minimum number of tulips or mums in his garden. If he has 50 tulips and 30 mums, then any tulips beyond 30 are worthless to him.

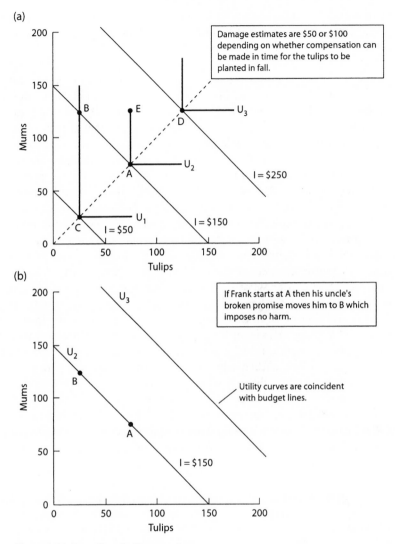

Figure 1-11. Bounding the Damage Amount

It is apparent that Uncle Dick's untrustworthy behavior has done the equivalent of reducing Frank's income to $50. At this income level, Frank could have purchased 25 tulips and 25 mums, which would have put him at point C in the figure, which has the same utility as point B. In this case, Dick owes Frank $100: this is the difference between his original budget curve ($150) and the budget line labeled I = $50 in panel (a).

Note that it is coincidental that the $100 that Dick owes Frank when the indifference curves are right angles is the same as the amount of the gift that Dick promised Frank in the first place. If the price of tulips and mums were different, then the amount that Dick owes Frank would be different from the amount promised.[12]

If Uncle Dick compensates Frank by buying more tulips before the ensuing fall, then he could get Frank back onto his original indifference curve by giving him 50 tulips. This compensation moves Frank from B to E in the figure. In this scenario, Uncle Dick salvages 50 of the 125 mums to which Frank currently attaches no value, by matching them with 50 tulips. This solution costs Uncle Dick $50.

Even though we do not know Frank's indifference curves, we know that if Frank attaches a *zero value* to mums without matching tulips, the short-run cost is bounded by $50 if Uncle Dick acts before tulip-planting season and by $100 if he waits until after the fall season to compensate Frank. This is the upper bound cost of the harm imposed upon Frank.[13]

The prior analysis gives us the upper bounds on damages. How can we find the lower bound cost of the harm? We do this by assuming that tulips and mums are perfect substitutes, that is, that Frank enjoys the same utility no matter what combination of tulips and mums he buys. He is just as happy to have 150 mums and no tulips as he is to have 75 tulips and 75 mums. In this case, his indifference curves are 45-degree downward-sloping lines from left to right, as shown by the downward-sloping lines in figure 1-11, panel (*b*). In this case, one of his utility curves is coincident with his budget line. Any point along this curve gives Frank the same utility. Suppose he chooses point A arbitrarily.

The fact that his uncle's promise induces him to purchase 125 mums is of no consequence, because having 25 tulips and 125 mums is the same as having 75 of each kind. This solution is depicted by point B in panel (*b*), figure 1-11. He has suffered zero utility loss from his uncle's untrustworthiness. Thus, the lower bound harm is zero.

---

[12]For example, if the price of tulips is $2 and the price of mums is $1, then if Frank's indifference curves are right angles his optimal allocation is 50 tulips and 50 mums based on his $150 flower budget. Let Dick promise Frank $75 and then renege. In this case, you should be able to show that Frank ends up with 37.5 tulips and 75 mums. He only attaches value to the first 37.5 mums. He could have purchased 37.5 of each flower for $112.50, and so the harm imposed by Dick on Frank is $37.50 (= $150 − $112.50). In this case, the harm is only half of the amount Dick promised Frank.

[13]There is one other possibility that I have not considered. What if Frank not only attaches zero utility to each mum that comes up without a matching tulip, but also experiences disutility from it? One utility function that corresponds with this idea is as follows: $U = a \min(T, M) - b|T - M|$, which says that Frank obtains utility from the minimum number of tulips or mums in his garden and attaches a negative utility to the absolute difference in their numbers. The values of a and b measure the intensity of Frank's utility and disutility. In this case, the indifference curves are no longer right angles but evince an angle of less than 45 degrees, forming a kind of "arrow" look, where the arrows are pointed toward the origin.

By bounding the damages, Uncle Dick is in a better position to strike a deal with Frank to make him whole. If the argument takes place while there is still time for Frank to buy more tulips, then if Frank is asking for damages in excess of $50, Dick knows that his nephew is trying to pull a fast one. If the argument takes place after the tulip-planting season, then Dick knows that any claim for damages by Frank beyond $100 is a fabrication. Dick might split the difference between the upper and lower bound and offer Frank either $25 before or $50 after the tulip-planting season, depending on when he decides to settle the issue.

THE CASE FOR A $50 UPPER LIMIT ON THE DAMAGE AMOUNT, REGARDLESS OF SETTLEMENT TIME

In the context of the L-shaped indifference curves, I made the argument that if Dick settles up with Frank after the tulip-planting season, he owes Frank $100. But in fact as tulip-planting season approaches, Frank could have purchased an extra $50 of tulips on his own, and in so doing, reattain his old level of utility for a total cost of $50. His failure to do so increases the value of his losses to $100. Hence, an argument can be made that Dick owes Frank the lesser amount and that Frank himself is responsible for the remainder of his losses.

Alternatively, suppose that Frank's wife will not give him $50, but just prior to the tulip-planting season, Frank calls Dick to explain that an immediate payment of $50 will settle the dispute. Dick ignores Frank until after the tulip-planting season. In this case, Dick is responsible for the $100 losses that develop after the tulip-planting season.

We will revisit this issue in chapter 8 when the notions of contributory negligence and comparative negligence are introduced.

Question 1: Forget about Uncle Dick and suppose that next season, the price of mums is $2 and the price of tulips is $1. Frank has $150 to spend. If his preferences are described in panel (*a*), figure 1-11, how many tulips does he buy? How many mums?[14]

Question 2: Same problem except now assume that Frank's indifference curves are described by those in panel (*b*), figure 1-11.[15]

---

[14]With L-shaped indifference curves, Frank always chooses the same number of tulips, T, and mums, M. His budget constraint is $2M + 1T = 150$. Since $M = T$, then Frank buys 50 mums and 50 tulips.

[15]Since Frank is indifferent between tulips and mums, then he will purchase 150 tulips and zero mums. That is, if both are interchangeable to Frank, he simply spends all his flower money on the cheaper alternative.

4. The Second-Round Cost of Untrustworthiness

Assume that Frank and his uncle settle up for last year's unfortunate events. And suppose that next winter, Uncle Dick again promises Frank a $100 gift; in fact, he promises to show up with 100 mums for spring planting. He says, "Don't worry, Frank: this time, I am good for the $100 because I know I am getting a big tax refund." Figure 1-12 depicts the emerging problem.

If Frank believes his uncle, then he anticipates a total flower budget of $250, comprising his regular allocation of $150 plus Dick's contribution. Frank plans on locating at point D in figure 1-12 next season, which corresponds to 125 tulips and mums and utility level U_3. But Frank no longer trusts his uncle, and so he attaches zero merit to the promise. So Frank buys 75 mums for spring planting, leaving him with sufficient funds to plant 75 tulips in the fall. He figures on locating at point A in the figure.

When spring arrives, however, Uncle Dick comes through with the $100, and in fact, he brings 100 mums for Frank. Now Frank has 175 mums and 75 tulips for planting in the fall, which is depicted by point C in figure 1-12. Surely, Frank is better off than if his uncle did not bring more flowers, but he is not as well off as he would have been had he

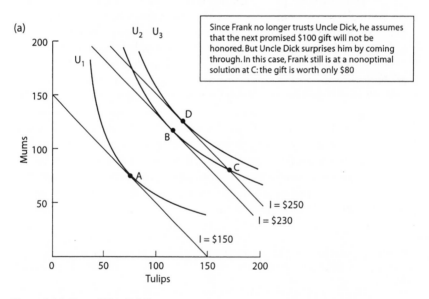

Figure 1-12. Cost of Unreliability

trusted his uncle. Indeed, at point C, Frank is on indifference curve U_2, which is lower than U_3.

Recall my assumption that because I know Frank's utility function, I can figure out the cost of Dick's unreliability. It is obvious from the figure that Frank could have attained utility level U_2 by purchasing an equal number of tulips and mums, which would put him at point B in the figure. Using Frank's utility function, I determined that he could obtain this allocation with only $230. Note that his money budget amounts to $250. Thus, Uncle Dick's $100 gift is worth only $80.[16] This explains why, when he sees his uncle coming up the driveway with the additional mums, Frank does not flash a $100 smile, but rather shows what his uncle perceives to be four-fifths of a $100 smile.

The wedge between the money Dick spent on mums for Frank and the value that Frank attached to them is a measure of the cost of untrustworthiness.

First lesson about reputation value: There is a cost to reneging on a contract because it builds a reputation for unreliability. The benefits of dealing with an unreliable person are lower than those of dealing with someone with a reputation for honesty and trustworthiness. Put differently, the gains from trade between parties are higher if both have a reputation for trustworthiness than if one has a reputation for untrustworthiness. Hence, we should expect the asset value of reputation to be positive. I will return to this theme later in the book.

B. DOMINIC'S REPORT CARD AND COMPUTER GAMES

Consider the following problem. Dominic is a pretty good student but is a better student when he gets paid to do well in school. In particular, if paid nothing for good grades, he turns in a 3.0 grade point average (GPA). For $300, he works sufficiently hard to earn a 3.5 GPA. For $400, he turns in a 4.0 GPA. He reacts the same way every quarter. His economist father decides that the $400 is worth the extra GPA and decides to pay this amount. Sure enough, the next quarter, Dominic brings home the desired 4.0.

---

[16]Using the utility function I have assumed for Frank as shown in note 7, utility at point D is $U_3 = 125^{1/2}125^{1/2} = 125$. Utility level at point C is $U_2 = 75^{1/2}175^{1/2} = 115$. Thus, if Frank has x number of tulips and mums, he could attain U_2 with the value of x that satisfies: $U_2 = x^{1/2}x^{1/2} = 115 => x = 115$. Since tulips and mums cost $1 apiece, then Frank can attain this utility with $230 in income.

1. The Solution at First

Dominic decides to allocate the money in the following way: six computer games at $50 each, with the remaining money spent on everything else. Suppose that we create a *composite good* to represent "everything else" and arbitrarily attach a price of $1 per unit. Thus, with $400, Dominic buys six computer games and 100 units of "everything else." Assume that Dominic will repeat this allocation every time he gets his pay-for-performance money.

This allocation is depicted in figure 1-13, panel (*a*). Note that Dominic's budget line is labeled $400 and that his optimal consumption is denoted by point *A*, which reflects six computer games. So far, everything is working out to the satisfaction of Dominic and Dad. It looks like a Pareto optimum solution.

2. The Problem That Arises

A problem arises, however, when Mom discovers how Dominic is spending his money. She feels strongly that he should be limited to three computer games per quarter and that he is better off purchasing 250 units of other things, like shirts and books. Dad tries to change her mind, explaining that this could turn out to be an expensive restriction, but to no avail. The restriction stands.

When he learns of the newfound restriction, Dominic retorts that effectively Dad is reducing his money payment to $300, even though Dad forks over $400. Accordingly, Dominic delivers a 3.5 GPA next time.

The three-game restriction effectively moves Dominic from point *A* to point *B*. That is, he still is on his $400 budget line, but he is restricted to only three computer games, leaving him with 250 units of "everything else." Notice that at this point, he no longer is on utility curve U_2 but instead attains utility level U_1. To put a dollar value on this lower utility, Dominic can ask: what level of income would allow me to attain this

---

Question: What value did Dominic attach to the restriction of three computer games per quarter? Put differently, how much more cash is Dad paying Dominic to obtain a 3.5 GPA compared to a world in which no restrictions are imposed on his spending?

Answer: Given the previous information, it is apparent that Dominic attaches a value of $100 to the three-game restriction. Put differently, to obtain a 3.5 GPA from Dominic, Dad must pay him an extra $100 above the amount that he would have paid for a 3.5 had Mom not imposed a restriction.

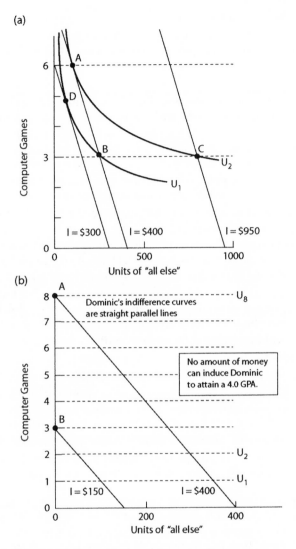

Figure 1-13. Report Cards and Computer Games

utility curve without any restrictions on my spending? The answer is found by dragging his budget line to the left in a parallel way until it is just tangent to utility curve U_1, which is denoted by point D. Since this budget line intersects the vertical axis at six games (which cost $50 each), we can infer that this new budget line must be $300, which squares with Dominic's response.

3. The Second-round Solution

Dad really wants that 4.0, and so he tries to figure out how to strike a deal with Dominic that respects Mom's wishes but still results in the desired GPA.

> *Question*: How much cash does Dad have to pay Dominic to induce him to produce the 4.0 GPA without violating the three-game restriction? While you do not have Dominic's utility function, you can read the answer from the information given in panel (*a*), figure 1-13.

We need to find a point where Dominic is on utility curve U_2 *and* on his budget line *and* satisfies the three-game restriction. Clearly, we are not looking for a tangency solution, because the restriction inhibits us from finding an optimum solution.

To find the answer, we need to shift Dominic's budget line to the right along the three-game line until the intersection of the budget line and the three-game limit touches his original indifference curve U_2. In panel (*a*), figure 1-13, this outcome is denoted by point C. Note that at this outcome, Dominic has only three games, so he is not in violation of the restriction, but he now has a sufficiently high income to regain utility level U_2. Dad knows that if Dominic attains U_2, he gets the 4.0 GPA on the next report card.

> *Answer*: The answer requires knowledge of Dominic's utility function. It turns out, given the function I have assumed for him, that Dad must give Dominic $950 in cash to push Dominic back to the utility curve that was attainable with only $400 in cash with no restrictions. We know that this is the budget line because it intersects the horizontal axis at 950 units of the composite good that costs $1 per unit.

> Dominic views "other things" as poor substitutes for computer games, and so requires a large number of additional units of other things to make him just as happy as he would be with six computer games and only 100 units of everything else. Thus, it turns out that Mom's restriction cost Dad $550. Dominic is just as well off as he was when the first contract was made, but now Dad is $550 worse off without making Dominic any better off, a clearly inefficient solution from their perspective.

4. The Extreme Case: A Corner Solution

I can expand on this example to illustrate the extreme case of preference. Suppose that Dominic's preference for computer games is absolute in the sense that no matter what the price of games is relative to "all else," Dominic always prefers spending all his money on games. This is an even more extreme case than the one depicted in figure 1-11, panel (*a*), for Frank's L-shaped utility curves, because the only combination that gives Dominic utility is zero units of "other things" and as many games as his budget permits him to purchase. These utility "curves" are portrayed in panel (*b*) of figure 1-13 by straight dashed horizontal lines, only some of which I have labeled.

In this utility mapping, more games yield more utility, but no amount of additional units of "all else" confers any utility. Thus, when confronted with his $400 budget line, Dominic chooses eight games and zero of everything else. He has a **corner solution** depicted by point *A*.

Corner solution: When considering two goods, a corner solution occurs when the highest level of utility is found by setting consumption of one of the goods to zero. These solutions tend to occur when the consumer views a competing good as a poor substitute for a favored good. In figure 1-13, panel (*b*), we have both a corner solution and zero substitution, meaning that the optimal solution is zero for everything else.

It is interesting to reconsider his economist dad's scheme together with his mom's restriction. If the restriction is three games, then this puts Dominic at point *B* in the figure. Dominic values this as the equivalent of $150, because he has no use for the additional $250 in cash. In this case, he will not deliver even the 3.5 GPA, let alone the 4.0. Moreover, as long as Mom's restriction holds, no amount of money will induce Dominic to budge from his 3.0 GPA. The marginal dollars of cash beyond the $150 he is allowed to spend on games has no value to him. This is an extreme case of the general lesson that income has more value to individuals if they have no restrictions on how to spend it.

EXERCISE:
Consider the real-life case reported in the *Washington Post* in August 2001. A mentally ill person who could neither hear nor talk was imprisoned pending a hearing on a trespass case. Let me call this person Mr. Smith. The judge dismissed the case, but owing to a paperwork mishap, the D.C. prison never released Mr. Smith. They kept him in the mentally ill section of the D.C. prison for two years until they realized their error, whereupon he was released. You are his

continued . . .

EXERCISE: *Continued*

lawyer. Assume that the court agrees that the District of Columbia was grossly negligent in this case. How much does the District of Columbia owe Mr. Smith? What principle will you invoke to try to convince a jury that Mr. Smith is owed some amount, X? Keep in mind that Mr. Smith does not work and has never worked. Moreover, no one was dependent on him; indeed, no one ever missed him for two years. Mr. Smith had a private cell, and so you can assume that he was free of the possibility of attack or personal injury while in jail.[17]

ECONOMICS IN A SHORT STORY: A PARETO OPTIMUM TRADE

To appreciate economics, and the gains from trade that lie at its core, it is not important to understand complex mathematics and graphical analysis, nor is it important to understand the business transactions involving major corporations or world trade treaties.

continued . . .

[17]One obvious approach is to invoke the compensation principle. Ask the following question to the jury: "Ex ante, how much would *you* have required in compensation to have the opportunity to be locked up in a prison for fully two years, without contact with the outside world?" This is not a silly question. It goes to the amount of money that makes two options equally valuable: (1) freedom with all its attendant benefits (and costs) and (2) going to prison for two years and receiving some amount of compensation in the amount X.

Presumably, there is some value of X that Mr. Smith would have agreed to accept in order to take prison over freedom. Ask yourself the question: would $200,000 make *you* willing to accept the jail option? If not, would $500,000 do the trick? Sooner or later, I will come to a number that will make the jail option appealing. Ideally, we want the honest number that Mr. Smith would have chosen. But he is not capable of telling us. But perhaps we can ask the jury to come up with their own estimates based on the mental exercise that you ask them to undertake. Will we obtain a perfect number? No. Consider the alternative: the District of Columbia owes Mr. Smith nothing because he does not work and no one depends on him. If you know that the latter answer cannot be correct, then you are beginning to understand the compensation principle.

A case that invokes this approach is *United States v. McNulty* (446 F.Supp. 90). In 1973, Mr. McNulty won about $530,000 (valued in 2001 dollars) in the Irish Sweepstakes, whereupon he deposited his winnings on the Isle of Jersey where secrecy laws put the monies beyond the reach of the Internal Revenue Service. He deliberately did not pay taxes. He apparently had no other assets and no significant income. The IRS brought him to court, whereupon he received a jail sentence for tax evasion. It is unclear when his sentence began, but it ended on January 23, 1978. At this point, the IRS brought him to civil court to obtain an order for Mr. McNulty to repatriate the taxes owed (about $250,000 in 2001 dollars, including interest and penalties). McNulty refused and was imprisoned for contempt of court for five months, whereupon he was released, free from further legal action owing to double jeopardy. In exchange for these five months, plus the perhaps three or so years he served for tax evasion, McNulty won the rights to the $250,000 he otherwise would have paid the IRS.

A *Christmas Memory*, an autobiographical essay by Truman Capote, conveys its essence. The story is about poor folk who live in Alabama in the midst of the Depression.

In the story, Buddy, who portrays Capote as a boy, lives with his underprivileged adult cousin, Miss Sook Falk. She has been endowed with neither wealth, education, nor ability, but she has lots of love to give Buddy. Upon entering the holiday season, Buddy and his cousin decide to make pecan fruitcakes for about two dozen Americans they admire, most of whom they do not know. These people not only include great Americans like the president of the United States, but also include people who crossed their lives, like the family whose car broke down in front of their house last year and with whom Miss Falk had a very interesting conversation. After collecting their spare dimes, nickels, and pennies, they set out to collect their supplies— some at the store, where real money is required, and some that require climbing over fences to collect pecans that have fallen from trees in a local orchard. But the critical input to the fruitcakes is more difficult to come by—legally anyhow.

So, they set out for a strange place in the middle of the woods, owned by one Mr. Haha Jones, who has some clear stuff in used-over bottles. Upon coming to the door, a giant man howls, "What you want?" Buddy hides behind his cousin, who says, "Uh, Mr. Haha Jones, we need some of your best, uh, stuff." "What fer?" says Mr. Haha Jones. "Well, we are making fruitcakes, and we need the finest ingredients to make them taste just right." Mr. Jones returns with a bottle. Holding it in one hand and holding out the other, he demands, "That'll be two dollars."[18]

"Count it out, Buddy," says Miss Falk, whereupon Buddy starts counting out the amount, one dime, nickel, and penny at a time. Finally, Mr. Haha Jones, who looks like he's eaten nothing homemade in years, at least not anything made by a competent cook, says, "Tell ya what, ma'am, you take this here bottle [and just as she was about to refuse on account of she doesn't take charity, he continues] . . . you just give me one of those pecan fruitcakes when you make 'em." Whereupon, Ms. Falk's eyes light up. A great smile comes upon her face as she says, "You mean like a *Trade*?" "Yes 'um, ma'am, I reckon so," says Mr. Jones with a slightly less hardened look on his face.

continued . . .

---

[18]Quoted remarks are my memory of the exchange. Actual language in the book may differ. See Truman Capote, *A Christmas Memory* (New York: Scholastic, 1997).

Economics in a Short Story: *Continued*

And so, the bottle passes hands. Buddy and Sook, who have so little cash but are about to be so rich in fruitcakes, have made a deal with Mr. Haha Jones, who has plenty of two-dollar bills and clear liquid, but so little good food. The trade has made both better off.

As the scene closes, we see Mr. Haha Jones cracking a small smile in the background as Buddy and his cousin laugh, dance, and sing their way off his property with their prize, thankful that they still have enough change to pay the postage that will be due on all the fruitcakes they need to send, except of course the one for Mr. Jones, which she tells Buddy will have "an extra cup of raisons" and no doubt will be delivered in person.

Most everyone tries to make economics too complicated. The essence of all economics is contained in the trade between Miss Sook Falk and Mr. Haha Jones. It's all about creating surplus through trades. If you keep this in mind, economics will never be hard.

Chapter 2

Demand Curves and Consumer Surplus

Main Economic Concepts	1. Consumers usually are willing to pay more for a product than the market price.
	2. We can have a net gain to society even if some participants are worse off.
	3. Market demand for any product is merely the sum of individual demands.
New Terms	1. Compensated demand curve
	2. Value of a marginal unit of consumption
	3. Consumer surplus
	4. Complements and substitutes
	5. Deadweight loss
	6. Kaldor-Hicks concept of efficiency
	7. Tax distortion
	8. "On the margin"
	9. Demand elasticity
	10. Ramsey Pricing
	11. Transfer
	12. Tax distortion
	13. Delta-Q rule

In chapter 1, I described how a consumer went about the task of allocating scarce income among competing demands. While the indifference curve model is useful for assessing some economic problems, notably those involving the restriction of free choice on the allocation of income, in general, most economic problems that we care about occur at the market level. In this chapter, I derive the demand curve for some commodity, like clothing, at the market level and begin the analysis of "efficient" market transactions at the more aggregate level.

I. From Indifference Curves to Demand Curve

I start by deriving the demand curve for clothing for a single consumer. In particular, I will illustrate the problem for Ken. I assume that, like Jane, Ken also has an income of $100 but has a different utility function.

> Ken's utility function:
> $$U = \sqrt{C} + \sqrt{H}$$

That is, whereas Jane's utility was the *product* of the squares roots of clothing and housing, Ken's utility is the *sum* of these square roots. Both functions evince diminishing marginal utility and are well behaved. Both have convex indifference curves, but Ken trades off clothes and housing a bit differently than Jane.

I portray a two-part chart in figure 2-1. The top part of the figure depicts Ken's indifference curves.[19] The budget line reflects income of $100 and prices for housing and clothing of $1 and $2, respectively. Point A depicts his optimal level of consumption.[20]

> EXERCISE:
> *Step 1:* Start by creating a two-part figure, one showing indifference curves and one below with the same horizontal axis (units of clothing). The difference in the two charts is that the vertical axis on the bottom chart is not units of housing, but price of clothing.

The bottom part shares the same horizontal axis; that is, it measures units of clothing. The vertical axis, however, does not portray units of other goods but instead depicts the price of clothing.

---

[19] For some fixed utility, I solve H in terms of C and plot the results.

[20] This solution is found in the same way as for Jane in note 3. That is, I maximize utility $U = C^{1/2} + H^{1/2}$, subject to the income constraint, $I = P_H H + P_C C$. The first-order condition is $H = (P_C/P_H)^2 C$. Substituting this solution into the budget constraint, I have $C^* = I P_H / [P_C (P_C + P_H)]$, which describes Ken's optimal choice of clothing, given the price of housing, P_H, and income level, I. Using the first-order condition, you can verify that H^* is the same as C^* except that the prices of clothes and housing are interchanged. Note that the solution for C^* is the uncompensated demand curve for clothing; it describes the units of clothing demanded when the price of clothing changes, all else constant. Note that when P_C and P_H are equal, then Ken's optimal choice of housing and clothes is the same as Jane's (see note 3). But as prices change, Ken reacts differently than Jane. Thus, if $P_H = 1$ and $P_C = 2$ and $I = 100$, then $C^* = 16.67$ and $H^* = 66.67$, and hence, $U^* = 16.67^{1/2} + 66.67^{1/2} = 12.25$. To obtain the compensated demand curve for Ken, substitute the optimal choices of clothes and housing, C^* and H^*, expressed in terms of income and prices, described previously into Ken's utility function; this gives us U^* as a function of prices and income. Solve this equation for income, I: this gives the income level required to maintain U^* when relative prices change. $I^* = U^{*2} P_C P_H/(P_C + P_H)$. Now substitute I^* back into the uncompensated demand curve, which yields the compensated demand curve $C = [U^* P_H / (P_C + P_H)]^2$.

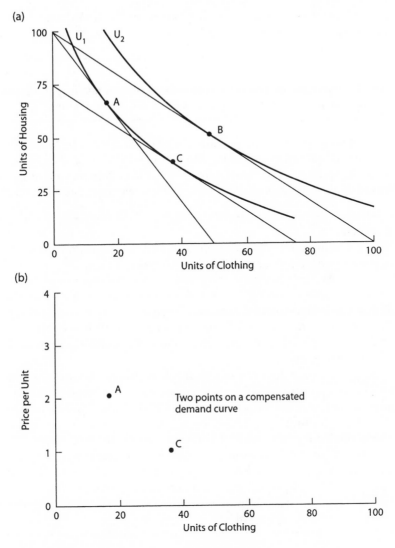

(a)

(b)

Figure 2-1. Derivation of a Compensated Demand Curve

A demand curve depicts the relationship between price and quantity consumed, holding constant utility and other prices. To derive Ken's demand curve for clothing, I suppose that we start with the price of clothing as $2, as shown in the top portion of the figure at point A. At this point, Ken consumes 17 units of clothing. Carry the 17 units downward to the bottom portion of the graph, and make a point where this amount intersects with the $2 price. This gives one point on Ken's demand curve for clothing which I label *A* in panel (*b*).

EXERCISE:
Step 2: Depict the quantity and price that corresponds to point *A* in the top portion of the figure, and plot it on the bottom figure.

To obtain a second point, I reduce the price of clothing to $1 and find Ken's optimal allocation of clothing and housing, which is denoted by point *B* in the top portion of the figure. However, it will be convenient to derive a demand curve with the price effect only, and so I net out the income effect.

EXERCISE:
Step 3: Change the price of clothing and find the *compensated* change in clothing consumption as a result of this price change.

Why I Use a Compensated Demand Curve
The most important reason to use it is pedagogical. It is convenient to use this approach to describe the notion of consumer surplus later on, as I shall show.

In any event, it does not matter much in practice because income effects normally are trivially small. For example, if I spend $1,000 on gasoline per year out of an income of $50,000, then a reduction in price from $2 to $1 per gallon increases my income by 1 percent, only a small amount of which I will use to purchase more gas.

Often income effects from price changes are netted out in aggregate. For example, if gasoline dealers conspire to increase the price of gas from $2 to $3 per gallon, consumers suffer a negative income effect, but gasoline dealers enjoy a positive income effect. The income effects offset in the aggregate.[21]

As before, I derive the compensated change in clothing consumption by dragging the new budget line to the left in a parallel way until it is just

---

[21]More experienced students might recognize a less intuitive approach. It is conventional to describe substitute and complementary products on the basis of substitution effects only; inclusion of income effects introduces odd results. For example, when there are only two products, they must by definition be substitutes: we can maintain a given level of utility only by switching one for the other. Yet, when we include income effects from price changes, we can have the odd result that the quantity of clothing *and* housing increases, suggesting that housing and clothing are complements even though there are only two goods.

tangent to Ken's original indifference curve. At the lower price, given the particular utility curve I have assumed for Ken, his optimal consumption choice is depicted by point C, which corresponds to 37 units of clothing. Tracking this quantity to the bottom portion of the chart, and plotting a point where this quantity intersects with the $1 price (Point C), I now have a second point on Ken's demand curve. If I connect these points, I have a small segment on Ken's demand curve for clothing.

EXERCISE:
Step 4: Continue the exercise by choosing other prices, finding the optimal number of units of clothing, and plotting the resulting combinations of price and quantity.

If I continue plotting points, I eventually have a continuous line describing Ken's compensated demand for clothing for every price along the vertical axis. The dark bold line in figure 2-2 shows the result. By construction, every point on this demand curve hold's Ken's utility at the same level U_1 as depicted in figure 2-1(*a*), and thus I label this demand curve $D(U_1)$. We now have Ken's compensated demand for clothing, given that he has $100 in income. Demand curves are downsloping. Quantity demanded increases as price declines.

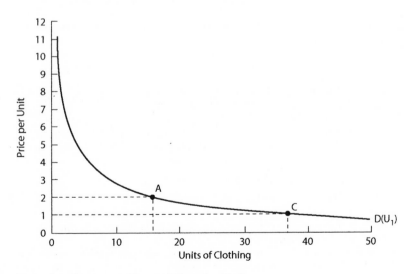

Figure 2-2. Compensated Demand Curve for Clothes

Compensated demand curve: The relationship between price and the optimal quantity consumed for some good, holding constant the consumer's income (really, level of utility) and other prices.

Uncompensated demand curve: The price-quantity relationship not subtracting out the income effect. Utility levels increase along the uncompensated demand curve.

If you are more comfortable deriving an uncompensated demand curve, then take point B from panel (a) in figure 2-1 and plot it at the $1 price in panel (b). Erase plot point C. Connect points A and B. Repeating this exercise for a few prices gives you the uncompensated demand curve. It turns out that consumer surplus using the uncompensated demand curve works out to be pretty close to surplus using a compensated demand curve.

For advanced students, or the really curious, this chapter's appendix explains how surplus is measured using either demand curve concept, but postpone this exercise until you have absorbed the materials presented in the chapter.

EXERCISE:

1. Using the information from figure 1-9, derive two points on Jane's compensated demand curve for clothing.[22]

2. Using the information from figure 1-11, panel (a), derive Frank's compensated demand curve for tulips, assuming his flower budget is $150. Redo the exercise assuming that his budget is $250.[23]

II. Consumer Surplus

Viewed along the horizontal axis, a demand curve represents the quantity of some good, X, that a consumer is willing and able to purchase at every possible price, P_x, holding constant income and other prices. Viewed along the vertical axis, however, a demand curve represents the maximum amount that an individual is willing to pay for each marginal unit of consumption. Owing to diminishing returns, the value that an individual attaches to each unit of some good on the margin is lower the more of the good that he already consumes. This is why demand curves are downsloping.

[22]At price $2, Jane consumes 25 units of clothing. At price 50 cents, she consumes 50 units after netting out the income effect.
[23]Regardless of the price change, after netting out the income effect, Frank always chooses 75 tulips. Thus, his compensated demand curve is a vertical line at 75 tulips. At income level $250, his demand curve is a vertical segment at 125 tulips.

A Demand Curve: Two Perspectives
Viewed along the horizontal axis, a demand curve is the quantity that a consumer is willing and able to purchase at any given price, holding constant income (really utility) and other prices.

Viewed along the vertical axis, the demand curve represents the maximum price that a consumer is willing to pay for each additional unit of consumption. This perspective is sometimes referred to as the "inverse demand curve."

To study the demand concept more carefully, I replicate Ken's demand curve in figure 2-3. This figure is similar to figure 2-2 except that I assume that the market price is $2 and magnify that portion of the demand curve over the relevant range. At the $2 price, Ken consumes 17 units of clothing.

A. AN INTUITIVE WAY TO UNDERSTAND CONSUMER SURPLUS

I want to quantify the value to Ken of being able to obtain 17 units of clothing for $34. Note that he is willing to pay more than $2 for every unit, except the marginal (17th) unit, where the value he attaches to this marginal unit of consumption is very close to the market price. The downward-sloping nature of the demand curve is the key to consumer surplus because it conveys the marginal valuation that Ken attaches to each unit of clothing that he consumes.

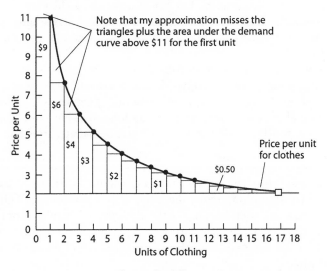

Figure 2-3. Comparing Slopes of Indifference Curves vs. Budget Lines

The demand curve is downsloping because of the diminishing marginal utility of further consumption.

On the margin: Ken is willing to pay more for the 1st unit of clothing than he is for the 2nd or 3rd, and thus, it is important to distinguish that we are referring to value for the marginal unit. When we talk about the "value Ken attaches to clothing consumption on the margin," it means the value he attaches to his last (or marginal) unit of consumption.

The difference between the price that a consumer is willing to pay and the price he has to pay is called **consumer surplus**. For example, Ken is willing to pay $11 for the 1st unit of clothing that he consumes. He has to pay $2. This means that he enjoys a $9 surplus from purchasing this unit, which I label in the long column in figure 2-3.

Put differently, when Ken consumes 1 unit of clothing, his indifference curve slopes sharply downward, conveying his willingness to give up lots of housing to obtain another unit of clothing. But the slope of the budget line is much flatter, reflecting the fact that Ken can obtain more clothing without giving up as much housing as he would if he had to. Thus, Ken sees this "exchange rate" as a good deal, and so he is happy to give up such a small amount of housing for additional clothes. This concept is shown in the demand curve by the vertical distance between Ken's demand curve and the market price.

The way I have depicted Ken's demand curve, I implicitly assume that he can consume partial units, but for illustration, I calculate consumer surplus using the value that Ken attaches at each discrete unit. Though this method understates the final result, it illustrates how consumer surplus is derived.

Ken is willing to pay $7.65 for the 2nd unit. In this case, since he can buy the 2nd unit at $2, he enjoys $5.65 in consumer surplus, which I round to $6 in the figure. I label this amount in figure 2-3, as well as a few additional consumer surplus amounts for some, but not all, units of consumption for illustration. If I add 17 numbers that correspond to the

Consumer surplus: The amount that a consumer is willing to pay for a unit of consumption, minus the price. If Ken consumes C_t units of clothes, then the total surplus is the addition of surplus from each unit from his 1st to the tth unit. It is represented on a graph as the area under the demand curve through C_t units of clothing above the market price.

consumer surplus for each unit from the 1st to the 17th unit consumed, I arrive at an approximation of Ken's total consumer surplus. This number turns out to be $33.50.

B. USING THE COMPENSATION PRINCIPLE

A second way to think about consumer surplus is to apply the compensation principle. That is, when the price of clothing increases, Ken's budget line swings toward the zero origin, and so Ken is forced to a lower level of utility. But in calculating Ken's demand curve, we compensated Ken with enough additional income to return him to his original level of utility. It turns out that for very small price changes, the amount of compensation we had to give Ken is equal to the change in price times the number of units he was consuming before the price changed.

This equivalence does not work for large price changes, but we can think of a large change in price as a sequence of smaller changes, say in increments of 10¢. If we calculate each compensation amount required to keep Ken on his indifference curve each time we change price by 10¢, then we can add each of these amounts to arrive at an estimate of the dollar value that Ken attaches to the loss in utility from a price increase. In Ken's case, if we start at the $2 price and gradually increase the price to $11 and then sum these amounts, we arrive at the total amount of compensation that we would have to give Ken to maintain him on his original indifference curve if the price increased from $2 to $11. Put differently, this is the dollar value to Ken of moving him from the utility he attains at the $11 price to the utility he obtains at the $2 price. We have converted utility into a dollar value, which gives us an equivalent way of calculating consumer surplus.

I show this process visually in figure 2-4, which is a reproduction of figure 2-3, except the boxes are horizontal instead of vertical. To keep the figure uncluttered, I use $1 increments in price instead of 10-cent increments, and so I can obtain only a rough approximation of consumer surplus. I have labeled the compensation amounts based on this approach at each point along the demand curve. At the lower prices, the change in price by $1 is multiplied by larger quantities of clothes, and so the length of the boxes is greater. But as the price increases, Ken chooses to consume fewer units of clothes relative to housing on the same indifference curve, and so the compensation he needs from subsequent price increases of $1 each is multiplied by smaller numbers, and thus the length of the boxes becomes smaller.

After making nine calculations, I sum them to arrive at an approximation of the compensation I can give Ken to make him indifferent between the $2 and $11 prices of clothes. This approximation turns out to be $30.54, which is pretty close to the answer I estimated from my first approximation of $33.50.

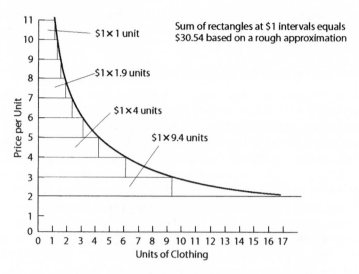

Figure 2-4. Consumer Surplus by Using the Compensation Principle

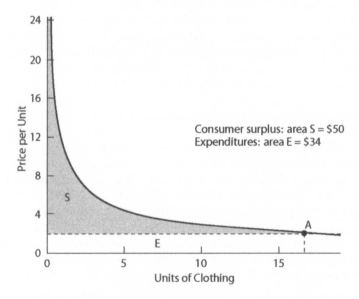

Figure 2-5. Consumer Surplus

Now that we know how to calculate consumer surplus, we do not need to show the rectangles in figures 2-3 and 2-4. Thus, I reproduce a clean version of Ken's demand curve in figure 2-5. Area S depicts consumer surplus from the consumption of 17 units of clothing at the $2 market price. It turns out, however, that area S amounts to much more than $33.50. This is because the discrete measures I used in both figures 2-3 and 2-4 are poor approximations for this total area. If I use smaller intervals, I can obtain a much closer approximation to the true value of area S. More specifically, if I use tiny price changes and assume that units of clothing can be consumed in small fractions of units, then it turns out that consumer surplus is exactly $50. The biggest reason for the underestimates of this surplus in the prior two figures is that they dramatically understate the value Ken attaches to the fractional units of clothing that he consumes between zero and 1 whole unit.[24]

C. CHECKING BACK WITH THE INDIFFERENCE CURVE MAP

I can verify that the $50 calculation for consumer surplus is correct by returning to Ken's indifference curves. Figure 2-6 reproduces the indifference curve that Ken attains when he chooses bundle A in panel (a) of figure 2-1. Notice, however, that in comparison with the earlier illustration, I now expand the vertical and horizontal axes to accommodate more units of clothing and housing consumption. It turns out that the indifference curve U_1 touches each axis at 150 units of housing or clothing. In other words, when his income is $100 and the prices of clothing and housing are $2 and $1, Ken's optimal choice is to consume 17 units of clothing and 66 units of housing. To attain the same level of utility on the assumption that he consumes zero clothing and all housing, then he would require 150 units of housing.[25]

---

[24]To obtain the correct answer, I integrate under Ken's demand curve above the $2 price. This effectively sums up the surplus from each tiny increment of clothing that he consumes. Since I have assigned Ken a specific demand curve, I can calculate consumer surplus exactly. I recognize the expression for Ken's demand curve from note 20, and solve for P_C in terms of C. Setting the price of housing to $1, I obtain: $P_C = U*C_2^{-1/2} - 1$, where C_2 denotes optimal consumption of clothing at price $2. Consumer surplus is the area under this curve minus price times quantity: $CS = [_0\int^{C_2} U*C^{-1/2} - 1]dC - P_C C = \{_0\int^{C_2} 2 U*C^{1/2} - C]dC - P_c C$. Note that when $P_C = 2$ and $P_H = 1$ and I = 100, then $C_2 \sim 17$ units and $U* \sim 12.25$ (see note 20 to see how $U*$ falls out of the optimal solution). If I integrate from C = 0 to 17 then CS turns out to be approximately $50. It is easy to check if this answer is correct by using the compensation principle. If Ken consumes 17 units of clothing at price $2, how much would we have to compensate him to consume zero clothing (and hence consume only housing)? The answer is given by the value of H that solves the formula: $U* = 0 + H^{1/2}$, where $U*$ is the level of utility Ken currently enjoys (namely, $U* = 12.25$). Hence, the quantity of housing required is $H = 150$ units. Since housing is priced at $1 per unit, Ken needs $150 to attain utility $U*$ consuming only housing and no clothing. Since his current budget is $100, we need to compensate him in the amount, $50, which is the answer we arrived at earlier by integrating under the demand curve above the $2 price.

[25]Recall that Ken's utility function is $U = C^{1/2} + H^{1/2}$, and thus, when C = 17 and H = 66, then $U = 12.25$. For Ken to attain this level of utility when C is set to zero, the H must equal H_0, where: $H_0^{1/2} = 12.25$, which means that $H_0 = 150$.

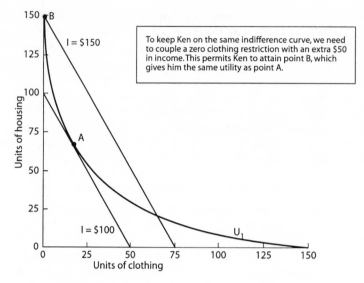

To keep Ken on the same indifference curve, we need to couple a zero clothing restriction with an extra $50 in income. This permits Ken to attain point B, which gives him the same utility as point A.

Figure 2-6. Verifying Surplus from Indifference Curve Map

This "corner" solution is the key to calculating consumer surplus. If we evaluate Ken at point A, we can ask: how much would we have to compensate Ken in order to make him indifferent between consumption bundle A and one that included only housing, that is, zero clothing? To obtain the answer, we expand his budget line outward until it intersects the vertical axis at the same spot that his indifference curve just touches the vertical axis, as shown by point B in the figure. He requires $150 to attain this point (that is, 150 units of housing times $1 per unit).

The incremental income required to move Ken from point A to point B in figure 2-6 is $50. This is the same number that I obtain by carefully calculating the area under his compensated demand curve above the $2 price (area S in figure 2-5). This verifies that the surplus we calculate on the demand curve is equivalent to applying the compensation principle on the indifference curve map from which we derived Ken's demand curve. In terms of figure 2-5, if we want to move Ken away from point A to the zero value of clothing and still keep him at the same level of utility, then we need to compensate him by giving him an additional $50 to spend on other things (notably housing).

III. Market Demand Curve

Thus far, we have been dealing with concepts that are not observable. We do not observe individuals' indifference curve maps, nor do we typically see the demand curve for some product for a single individual. We can, however, observe the demand for a good for all consumers together, which is the market demand. That is, at any given time, we observe a market price for any good and the total quantity consumed at that price, and we observe changes in quantity demanded in response to a price change. Indeed, after observing many different price-quantity combinations, we can, and often do, estimate market demand curves for some good or service.

Assume that there are only two consumers. Figure 2-7, panels (a) and (b), shows, Kathy's demand curve, D_1, and Jim's demand curve, D_2. Kathy's demand curve intersects the vertical axis at a higher price. Compared to Jim, she attaches a relatively high value to the first units of consumption, but diminishing returns also set in sooner, so that at low prices, Jim demands greater quantities than Kathy.

Linear Demand Curves
While I do not explicitly derive these demand curves, each nevertheless is derivable in principle from different sets of utility curves and income levels. Importantly, now that we know how demand curves are derived from utility and how to measure surplus under the demand curve, we no longer need the benefit of this derivation. In truth, it takes a pretty special indifference curve mapping to derive an exactly linear demand curve, but for convenience, we often use this form because it lends itself to simple solutions with a minimum of mathematics. Another way to think about it is that most analyses that we do using demand curves involve fairly small changes in price and quantity, and thus, even if demand curves are not linear, we can approximate any demand curve over the relevant range with a linear segment. This is the approach that I take in this book.

To obtain a market demand curve, simply add the individual demand curves *horizontally*; that is, add the quantities demanded by each consumer at every price and plot the result on a separate chart. I show the result in panel (c). Jim is not in the market when price exceeds $10. Hence, over the range of prices, $10 to $15, the market demand curve is coincident with Kathy's demand curve. Below the $10 price, Jim enters the market, and so market demand for this product begins to diverge from D_1. Note, for example, that at $5 both consumers (coincidentally) demand 10 units of the good; hence, total demand is 20 units at this price. At price zero, Kathy demands 15 units while Jim demands 20 units; hence, market demand at this price is 35 units.[26]

---

[26]Note that the market demand has a kink at the $10 price where Jim enters the market. But if we had drawn individual demand curves for hundreds or thousands of different consumers, these kinks would hardly be noticeable, and so it is reasonable to assume linear aggregate demand curves.

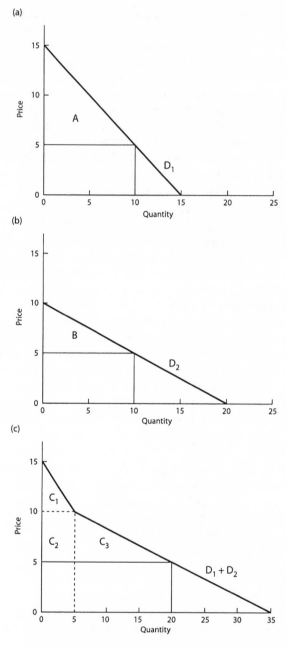

Figure 2-7. Deriving a Market Demand Curve

The *market demand curve* for a product shows the total quantity demanded by all consumers at each price.

Derivation of market demand: Plot the demand curve for the first consumer. Array the second consumer's demand curve along a horizontal segment, and then draw a third, and so on. For each price, add the quantities demanded for every consumer horizontally, and depict the final result in a separate graph.

Consumer surplus for market demand curves is derived in the same way as for individual demand curves. Suppose that the market price for this product is $5 per unit. (Chapter 3 addresses the question, how is market price determined?) Consumer surplus for Kathy is denoted by area A and for Jim by area B in panels (a) and (b) in figure 2-7. Total consumer surplus is the sum of areas C_1, C_2 and C_3, in panel (c) which is equivalent to the sum of areas $A + B$.

EXERCISE:

Show that consumer surplus in panel (c) of figure 2-7 denoted by areas $C_1 + C_2 + C_3$ add to the same number as the two consumer surplus calculations in panels (a) and (b) (that is, area A plus B).[27]

A. CONSUMER SURPLUS WHEN DEMAND CURVES ARE LINEAR

If demand curves are linear, it is easy to calculate consumer surplus if we know the price and output in current equilibrium and one other point

A LINEAR DEMAND CURVE

$$Q = a - bP.$$

To draw the curve, set Q equal to zero to find the price at which quantity equals zero. Then set P equal to zero to find the quantity demanded when price is zero. Connect these points by a straight line. The parameter, a, gives quantity demanded when price is zero.

continued . . .

---

[27]Note that areas A and B in panels (a) and (b) are triangles, and thus, you can obtain these dollar values using the formula for the area of a triangle. In panel (c), areas C_1 and C_3 are triangles, and thus, can be separately calculated; area C_2 is a rectangle. Area $A = \$10 \times 10 \times \frac{1}{2} = \$50$; area $B = \$5 \times 10 \times \frac{1}{2} = \$25$; thus, the two consumer surpluses add to $75. Now consider panel (c). Area $C_1 = \$5 \times 5 \times \frac{1}{2} = \$12.50$; area $C_2 = \$5 \times 5 = \$25$; area $C_3 = \$5 \times 15 \times \frac{1}{2} = \$37.50$; hence, $C_1 + C_2 + C_3 = \$75$. The consumer

A LINEAR DEMAND CURVE *Continued*

The slope parameter, $-b$, gives the change in quantity in response to a change in price. The slope parameter describes the change in quantity ΔQ that results from a change in price ΔP:

$$-b = \frac{\Delta Q}{\Delta P}$$

Note that the slope of the demand curve, often described by the parameter $-b$, is not the familiar "rise over run" slope that everyone learns in grammar school. There is nothing wrong with what you learned. It is just that economics adopts the unusual convention of graphing demand with the dependent variable Q along the horizontal instead of the vertical axis. Thus, the linear demand curve is written backwards so that the slope is the inverse of "rise over run." To keep matters straight, I refer to $-b$ as the "slope parameter" as a subtle reminder that it measures "run over rise."

on the demand curve, for example, the price at which quantity demanded is zero. Figure 2-8, panel (*a*), depicts a linear demand curve for some product. To plot the demand curve, solve quantity when price is zero, then solve the price at which quantity is zero. Draw a straight line connecting these points.

Panel (*b*) of figure 2-8 gives the calculation of consumer surplus for a specific linear demand curve. At price $5 a total of 1,000 units are consumed. At price $15, quantity demanded is zero. Rectangle *B* denotes the total amount spent on this product ($5,000). In addition, we know that the value of consumer surplus is denoted by the triangle, labeled *A*. To derive this amount, I simply use the formula for a triangle.

The area of a triangle is one-half the area of a rectangle, or one-half times height times the base:

$$A = \frac{1}{2} hb.$$

In figure 2-8, the height of the triangle is $10 and the base is 1,000 units. Thus, consumer surplus is $10 times 1,000 times 1/2, or $5,000.[28]

---

surplus in the aggregate market is the sum of the surpluses for each individual represented in the market.

[28]When demand curves are not linear, then we need to integrate under the demand function and subtract the amount spent on purchasing the good. See note 24.

$$Q = a - bP$$

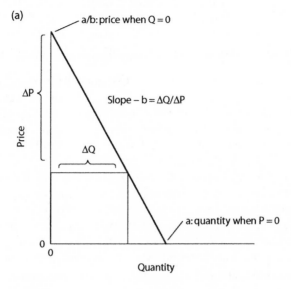

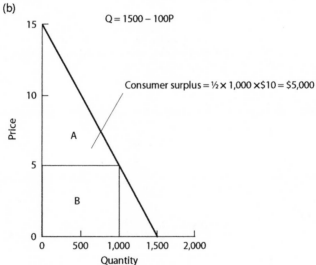

Figure 2-8. Consumer Surplus when Demand Curve Is Linear

B. COMPLEMENTS AND SUBSTITUTES

Complements and substitutes are easy to define using compensated demand curves. That is, since we do not incorporate income effects in these demand concepts, all substitutes and complements are defined purely on the basis of the price effect (also known as the substitution effect). When there are only two goods then it is apparent that they must be substitutes. That is, with two goods, we can remain on the same indifference curve *only* if we trade one for the other. When there are more than two goods, however, some goods (though not all) can be complements to others.

A simple example illustrates the point. Consider three goods, tickets to a Baltimore Orioles baseball game at Camden Yards, tickets to the opera at the Kennedy Center, and hot dog sales in the vicinity of Camden Yards. Oriole games and Kennedy Center operas both compete for consumers' entertainment dollars. Hot dog vendors around the stadium depend on Oriole attendance to sell their product.

Suppose that the Orioles' management decides to double the price of admission to their games. At the higher price, consumers are expected to attend fewer games and to instead consume other products in their leisure time, like events at the Kennedy Center. If Oriole ticket prices increase, demand for Kennedy Center tickets increases; Kennedy Center tickets are said to be substitutes for Orioles baseball games, as illustrated in panel (*a*) of figure 2-9.

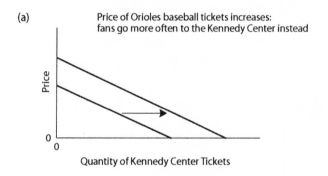

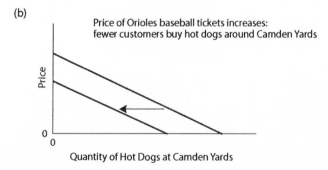

Figure 2-9. Substitutes and Complements

In contrast, since fewer fans attend Orioles games, hot dog vendors around the stadium suffer a reduction in sales. That is, fans not only attend games but also buy hot dogs around the stadium. The demand for hot dogs around the stadium falls when the price of Orioles' tickets increases. Hot dog sales around Camden Yards are said to be complements to Orioles baseball games, as illustrated in panel (*b*) of figure 2-9.

> Product Y is a *substitute* for X if the demand for Y increases when the price of X increases; product Z is a *complement* of X if the demand for Z falls as the price of X increases.
>
> When there are only two goods, they *must* be substitutes. When there are many goods, every good has to have at least one substitute.[29]

C. CHANGES IN INCOME

If consumers of product x enjoy an increase of income or more people enter the market, the demand curve for the product shifts to the right, and vice versa for reductions in income.

> ### INCREASE IN QUANTITY DEMANDED VERSUS INCREASE IN DEMAND
>
> An increase in quantity demanded is a movement along a demand curve. An increase in demand is an outward shift of the demand schedule.

IV. Demand Elasticity

We can construct many demand curves for hundreds of products and services. We need some common denominator to help us characterize the general features of these schedules. One such concept is **demand elasticity**, which describes the sensitivity of quantity demanded to a small change in price. It is defined in percentage terms, which means that it is independent of units and thus comparable across markets.

> *Demand elasticity* equals the percentage change in quantity demanded, divided by the percentage change in price:
>
> $$\eta = \frac{\%\ Change\ in\ Quantity}{\%\ Change\ in\ Price}$$
>
> *continued* . . .

[29]Suppose there are three goods: x_1, x_2 and x_3. If x_1 and x_2 are complements, then when the price of x_1 falls, consumption of x_1 and x_2 both increase. To maintain utility at the starting level and it follows that x_3 must decrease (meaning that it must be a subsititute).

Continued

Demand elasticity is always negative but often is referred to an absolute number.

Suppose that quantity and price are Q_0 and P_0. Price increases to P_1, thereby reducing quantity demanded to Q_1. If the percentage change in price is not too large, the demand elasticity exactly at quantity Q_0 is calculated as follows:

$$\eta_0 \approx \frac{Q_1 - Q_0}{Q_0} \bigg/ \frac{P_1 - P_0}{P_0}$$

Thus, suppose that a price change from \$10 to \$10.25 reduces quantity demanded from 1,000 to 950. In response to a 2.5 percent price change, quantity demanded falls by 5 percent. The demand elasticity is −2. This says that in this vicinity of the demand curve, a price change of 1 percent results in a quantity reaction of 2 percent.

If the elasticity is less than unity in absolute terms, then the demand curve is "inelastic" in this range. If it exceeds unity, then it is "elastic."

A. CALCULATING THE ELASTICITY FOR A LINEAR DEMAND CURVE

The elasticity formula for a linear demand curve is easy. At any price-quantity combination, it equals the slope parameter, $-b$, times the ratio of price to quantity:

CALCULATING A DEMAND ELASTICITY FOR A LINEAR DEMAND CURVE
$Q = a - bP$

Elasticity at Price P: Apply the elasticity formula to this demand curve to obtain the following expression:[30]

$$\eta = -b\frac{P}{Q},$$

where $-b$ is the slope parameter in the demand curve, and P and Q denote the particular point on the demand curve at which the elasticity

continued . . .

---

[30]Consider the linear demand curve $Q = a - bP$. Take the first derivative with respect to price P and multiply both sides by P/Q. This gives the exact elasticity at quantity Q_0: $\eta_0 = -bP/Q$. Now consider a large change in price ΔP. The elasticity equals $(\Delta Q / Q_0) / (\Delta P / P_0)$. But $\Delta Q = -b\Delta P$. Making this substitution gives $\eta_0 = -bP_0/Q_0$. So, we get the exact elasticity at Q_0 even for a large change in price.

CALCULATING A DEMAND ELASTICITY FOR A LINEAR DEMAND CURVE
$Q = a - bP$ *Continued*

is calculated. Thus, if the demand curve is $Q = 10 - 2P$, the elasticity of demand at price \$4 is -4.0.[31]

The elasticity changes at every point along the linear demand curve. It falls toward zero as price falls toward zero and rises toward infinity as quantity falls toward zero. The elasticity equals unity at the midpoint.

Elasticity over a Range of Prices, P_0 to P_1: For a large price change from P_0 to P_1, there are three elasticities that can be calculated: the one at the original price, P_0, the one at the ending price, P_1, and the average over the range of the price change. The latter calculation, sometimes called an "arc" elasticity, is defined as follows:[32]

$$\bar{\eta} = -b\left[\frac{P_0 + P_1}{Q_0 + Q_1}\right]$$

Consider the two linear demand curves in figure 2-10. In both cases, quantity demanded at price \$5 is 1,000 units. In panel (*a*), this price bisects the demand curve, and thus the demand elasticity is -1. Using the formula in the box tells us that the elasticity of demand at the same price in panel (*b*) is $-.5$.[33] A 1 percent reduction in price reduces quantity demanded by 1 percent in panel (*a*), but only one-half of 1 percent in panel (*b*).

Panel (*b*) also shows an arc elasticity calculation over the price range \$3 to \$5. The elasticity at \$5 is .5. The elasticity at price \$3 is $-.25$. But the elasticity over this range of prices \$3 to \$5 is not the simple average of $-.25$ and $-.50$. Instead, use the formula for the average elasticity over the range. This gives the result that the arc elasticity is $-.364$ (which admittedly is pretty close to the simple average of the two point elasticities).

Columns 1 and 2 in table 2-1 show the prices and quantities for the demand curve in panel (*b*). Column 3 shows total revenues collected at

[31]At price \$4, quantity demanded is $Q = 10 - 2 \times 4 = 2$. The value of b is 2. Thus, demand elasticity at this price is the slope parameter $(-b)$ times the ratio of price to quantity, or $\eta = -2 \times 4/2 = -4.0$.

[32]The elasticity over the range of prices is the same as the general formula for the elasticity: $\Delta Q/Q \div \Delta P/P$, where the quantity and price in the denominators are the averages over the relevant range. Manipulating this expression gives the alternative in the text box.

[33]Multiply the slope parameter, -100, by the price-to-quantity ratio, $5 \div 1,000$, to obtain $-.5$.

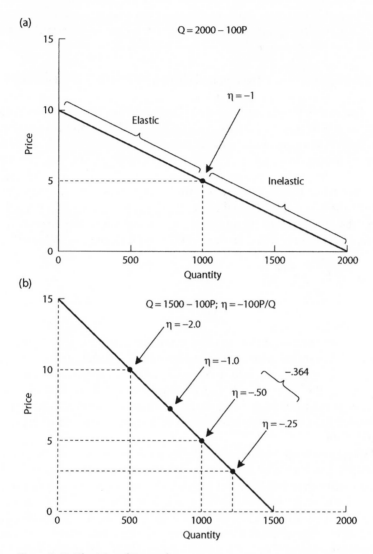

Figure 2-10. Elasticity of Demand

each price (revenue equals price times quantity). Column 4 gives the demand elasticity at each price.

Demand elasticity predicts the effect of a tax. For example, suppose that the price in the markets in both panels in figure 2-10 is $5. A 100 percent tax is proposed in both markets to increase price to $10. In one case (panel [*a*]), quantity demanded falls by 100 percent. In the other

TABLE 2-1. DEMAND ELASTICITY, ONE DEMAND CURVE

Price (1)	Quantity (2)	Revenue (3)	Elasticity (4)
15	0	0	
14	100	1,400	−14.00
13	200	2,600	−6.50
12	300	3,600	−4.00
11	400	4,400	−2.75
10	500	5,000	−2.00
9	600	5,400	−1.50
8	700	5,600	−1.14
7.5	750	5,625	−1.00
7	800	5,600	−0.88
6	900	5,400	−0.67
5	1,000	5,000	−0.50
4	1,100	4,400	−0.36
3	1,200	3,600	−0.25
2	1,300	2,600	−0.15
1	1,400	1,400	−0.07
0	1,500	0	0.00

Note: $Q = 1,500 - 100 \, P$.

(panel [*b*]), quantity demanded falls by 50 percent from 1,000 to 500 units. In the first case, the tax produces no revenue. In the second, revenue is $2,500. If a tax is enacted to raise revenue, it is pretty important to know demand elasticity!

Similarly, in a public policy discussion, someone might say, "A 100 percent tax on cigarettes will have almost no effect on number of cigarettes smoked." This means that consumer demand for cigarettes is quite inelastic over this range in prices. In contrast, a statement that "a 100 percent tax on unfiltered cigarettes will eliminate all firms that produce these kinds of cigarettes" means that the elasticity for unfiltered cigarettes is quite high, partly because they are close substitutes with filtered cigarettes. Figure 2-11 shows how these demand curves might look in the relevant range. They suppose that the pretax price on a pack of cigarettes is $3.

B. RELATION OF ELASTICITY TO TOTAL REVENUE

Demand elasticity instantly conveys whether total revenues increase or decrease when the product price changes. This becomes an important notion in chapter 5 when we talk about prices in noncompetitive markets.

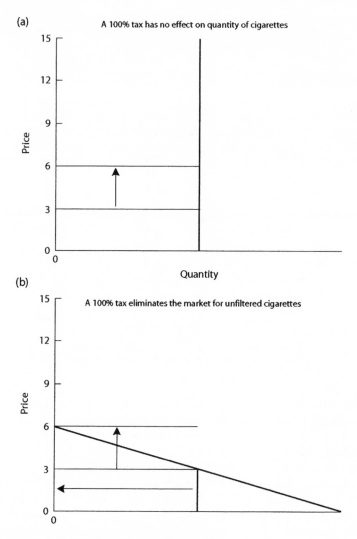

Figure 2-11. Two Reactions to a Cigarette Tax

Notice in table 2-1, column 3, that starting at high prices, a price reduction increases revenues. This is easy to see starting from zero quantity. No matter how high the price, if quantity is zero, so is total revenue. Thus, reducing price from $15 to $14 increases revenue from zero to $1,400. A high price alone does not generate the highest revenue. The maximum revenue depends on price *and* quantity demanded.

As price is further reduced, total revenues continue to increase, until around the midpoint in the demand curve. Note that at both $7 and $8, revenue is $5,600. Price $7.50 delivers $5,625 in revenue, which is the maximum possible. Revenues fall with further reductions in price. In the limit, if price is set to zero, even though 1,500 units are sold, revenue is zero.

It is not an accident that revenues increase from price reductions when the demand elasticity exceeds unity in an absolute sense, and fall when elasticity is less than unity. In our linear demand curve, total revenues are always maximized exactly where the elasticity of demand is unity, which always occurs at the midpoint on the demand curve.[34] Statements like "The demand curve is elastic" or "That demand curve is inelastic" are shorthand ways to refer to the idea that *over the relevant range of prices*, revenues will either decrease or increase with an increase in price.

Demand elasticity and total revenues: If demand is elastic, then price reductions increase revenue. If inelastic, then price reductions decrease revenue.

Figure 2-12 shows the information from table 2-1. Panel (a) shows the demand curve. Panel (*b*) shows the corresponding total revenue over the same quantities. Revenues are maximized when quantity equals 750 units, at the midpoint of the demand curve where demand elasticity is unity.

---

[34]A linear demand curve can be described as follows: $P = a + bQ$, where b is negative. I have deliberately written the demand with price on the left-hand side. Total revenue equals price times quantity; thus, multiply the prior expression by Q on both sides: $PQ = aQ + bQ^2$. Take the first derivative with respect to Q and set the results to zero. This gives the quantity at which total revenue is at a maximum. This quantity is $Q^* = -a/2b$.

This is the same quantity at which the elasticity of demand is -1. To show this, we need to bring Q on the left-hand side of the demand curve, because we need to determine the sensitivity of quantity to price. We have $Q = P/b - a/b$. Take the first derivative of Q with respect to P and multiply both sides by P/Q to obtain the percentage change in quantity with respect to the percentage change in price, which gives us the elasticity of demand: $\eta = (\partial Q/\partial P)(P/Q) = P/bQ$. Substitute for P in terms of Q using the demand curve ($P = a + bQ$), set the expression equal to -1, and solve for Q, which yields $Q^0 = -a/2b$, which is the same as the quantity Q^* that gave us the maximum revenue, and so $Q^0 = Q^*$.

Substituting Q^* back into the demand curve yields $P^* = \frac{1}{2}a$, which is the price midway between zero at which point quantity demanded is at a maximum and the price ($P = a$) at which quantity is zero. Hence, total revenue is at a maximum at the midpoint of the demand curve, where the elasticity equals -1.

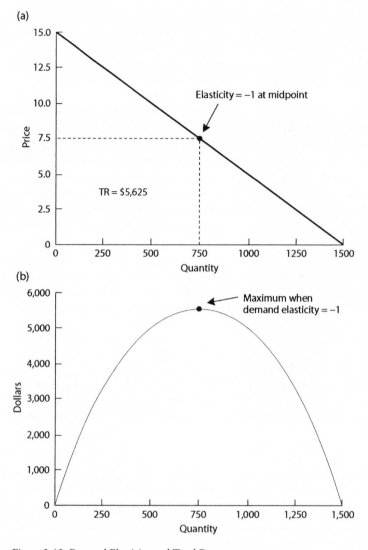

Figure 2-12. Demand Elasticity and Total Revenue

Suggested exercise: Suppose that the demand curve is $Q = 10 - 1P$, where Q is quantity and P is price. Create a table with eleven rows, one for each price from $0 to $10. Create columns showing quantity demanded at each price, total revenues, and demand elasticity.

continued . . .

> *Continued*
>
> Prove to yourself that the elasticity is high at first, then declines, passing by unity roughly at the midpoint of demand.[35]

C. LONG-RUN VERSUS SHORT-RUN ELASTICITY

Often a distinction is made between long- and short-term elasticity of demand, and so it is useful to review the meaning of these terms. Consider the market for cigarettes. Suppose that a tax is imposed that causes price to increase by 100 percent. In the short run, demand may be quite inelastic. That is to say, some smokers might quit. Others might reduce the number of cigarettes they smoke per day but smoke each cigarette to the last centimeter to squeeze out as much nicotine from each cigarette. In the short run, the number of cigarettes sold would not necessarily change very much, and the consumption of nicotine might fall even less.

In the longer run, however, owing to the high price of cigarettes, perhaps fewer young adults would adopt the smoking habit. In addition, perhaps some smokers will be encouraged to try various approaches to quit smoking, and some will kick the habit, and so on. Thus, in the long run, we might expect a stronger reaction to the tax than in the short run. Put differently, the long-run demand elasticity for cigarettes likely exceeds the short-run elasticity.

Similarly, if the tax on gasoline in the United States were increased by $3 per gallon, reflecting policies in most European countries, most consumers might not react much in the short run. They may need to commute a long distance to work, may own a car with poor gas mileage, and so on. In the short run, they might try to carpool or cut down on unnecessary trips.

In the longer run, the reaction may be larger. For example, the next time a consumer purchases a car, she might opt for one with better gas mileage. Similarly, some individuals might either move their residence or change their jobs to reduce their commuting distance, and so on. Thus,

---

[35]The first few entries are as follows. Note that total revenue TR equals P times Q, and demand elasticity equals the slope parameter, $-b$, times the ratio of price to quantity.

P	Q	TR	η
10	0	0	
9	1	9	-9
8	2	16	-4
7	3	21	-2.33
6	4	24	-1.5
5	5	25	-1
4	6	24	$-.67$

the long-run demand elasticity for gasoline likely is higher than short-run elasticity of demand.

V. Application: Imposition of a Tax

It is time to do our first application of the principles we have learned. We know from chapter 1 that any given level of income yields less utility if there is a binding constraint on how it is spent. Suppose that the price of housing and clothing each are $1 per unit. A tax is imposed on clothing, meaning that price increases to $2. I want to show the implications of the tax for Ken's welfare. Ken's income is $100.

A. SHOWING THE DISTORTION ON INDIFFERENCE CURVES

Figure 2-13 shows Ken's utility curves. Prior to the tax, Ken's optimal consumption is depicted by point A, which corresponds to 50 units of clothing and 50 units of housing.[36] The government attaches a $1 tax per unit of clothing. Ken's reaction to the tax is shown by point B.

You cannot know from inspection the quantities of housing and clothing that correspond to this point. But since I have assigned Ken a particular utility function, I can calculate that at point B, Ken consumes 17 units of clothing and 66 units of housing. At the higher price, Ken consumes fewer units of clothing. Government tax revenue is $17 (the tax per unit, $1, times 17 units). Ken's after-tax income is $83.

The problem that arises is not necessarily from the transfer of income from Ken to the government. We can suppose that the government simply gives this revenue to Jane. I make a fundamental assumption that Jane values $1 equally to Ken, and hence, Ken has effectively given some money to Jane. Jane has a positive income effect, and Ken has a negative income effect. Unfortunately, this is not the end of the story. Herein lies the rub: Ken's dollar value loss in utility exceeds the amount he gives to Jane.

To illustrate, suppose that instead of taxing clothing, the government enacts a 17 percent income tax. This tax raises the same $17 as the excise tax on clothing. Relative prices do not change, and thus, the slope of Ken's budget line is the same as the slope of his original budget line. Moreover, Ken's after-tax income must still pass through point B, as depicted by the dashed budget line. How do we know this?

---

[36]You can verify this allocation using the calculations in note 20, which describes Ken's utility function and the optimal allocation of income to clothes and housing at any given set of prices. Note that I slightly round the answer to retain whole units. You can do the problem exactly if you want. It does not change the problem to think of clothing and housing units as divisible into fractions of units.

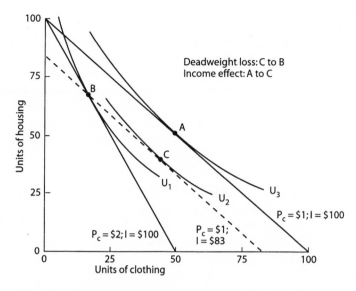

Figure 2-13. Deadweight Cost of a Tax on One Good

Since the clothing tax raises $17, then Ken's after-tax income is $83. Hence, if his income *is* $83 and the price of clothing and housing are $1, then we know that Ken can purchase 66 units of housing and 17 units of housing, which corresponds to point *B*.

The problem, of course, is that if Ken faced this budget constraint, he would not choose bundle *B*. He attains a higher utility from bundle *C*; compare utility level U_2 to utility level U_1. The difference in utility between points *B* and *C* represents the **deadweight loss** from a tax on clothing alone. That is, by distorting prices, the government induces Ken to choose bundle *B* instead of bundle *C*. Ken is worse off, but the recipient of the government transfer, namely, Jane, is no better off.

Put in the language used in the Edgeworth box, taxing Ken to subsidize Jane is not Pareto superior because Jane gains and Ken loses. If, however, we make the assumption that a dollar is a dollar no matter who holds it, the amount that Ken gives Jane (through the government) is just a transfer. Jane is better off in the same amount that Ken is worse off, and so the two effects cancel.

A dollar is a dollar (no matter who holds it): This assumption means that when some interference in a market occurs, causing income to pass from person *A* to person *B*, we assume that the dollar is worth

continued . . .

Continued

just as much to B as to A. This keeps us away from making judgments about a redistribution of income across individuals.[37]

Transfer: In economic parlance, a transfer occurs when a dollar loss to one person is exactly offset by a dollar gain by some other person. Using the assumption that a dollar is a dollar no matter who holds it, no net utility losses are inferred from this move.

Using the dollar-is-a-dollar assumption, the move from A to C in figure 2-13 does not imply a loss of net utility to society. However, the move from C to B imparts a loss on Ken without any gain conferred to another person, which is why it is called a deadweight loss. The latter move is clearly Pareto inferior.

Deadweight loss: A loss to one person not offset by a gain to others. When one person loses utility from some market interference, such as a tax, and no one gains any utility, then a deadweight loss is said to arise.

B. EFFICIENCY IN A KALDOR-HICKS SENSE

One could legitimately ask, "If I do not like the dollar-is-a-dollar assumption, can I still characterize the tax distortion as an inefficiency in a societal sense?" Yes, by utilizing the notion of **Kaldor-Hicks efficiency**. In a Kaldor-Hicks sense, starting from zero tax, the imposition of the $1 clothing tax results in a clear loss in efficiency, because *in principle*, Ken and Jane could strike a deal, which would make both better off. In principle, Ken would be willing to pay Jane some amount of money, say $x, in exchange for substituting an income tax that raised the same amount of money as the clothes tax. How much?

We can figure this amount using the compensation principle. To show this, I reproduce and enlarge figure 2-13 as shown in figure 2-14. Imagine dragging the budget constraint touching point C to the left until it is tangent to utility curve U_1. The difference in these two budget lines

---

[37]Some individuals believe that if we take $100 from someone who earns $80,000 and give it to someone earning $20,000 (an income redistribution), somehow these dollars are worth more to the lower-income individual, and thus we should weight dollars that transferred depending on whether they go toward lower earners versus higher earners. Economics does not add insight to address this question, and so I ignore the issue throughout the book.

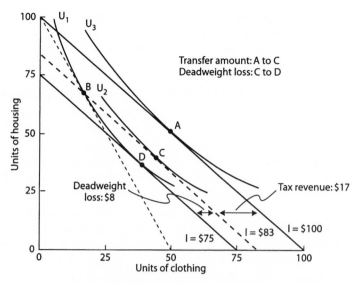

Figure 2-14. Value of Deadweight Loss on Indifference Curve Mapping

represents the dollar equivalent of Ken's loss in utility measured by the difference between U_2 and U_1. Since I know Ken's utility function, I can make this calculation. It turns out to be $8.[38] The tax revenue amount is measured by comparing the budget lines that pass through points A and C in the figure. The deadweight loss is measured by comparing the budget lines that are tangent to points C and D.

Recalling the Edgeworth box diagram, Ken would be willing to pay Jane the $17 transfer *plus* some portion of $8 if she would agree to support the elimination of the clothing tax in favor of an income tax. Both would be better off. As long as it is *possible* to think that Ken can make it worthwhile to Jane not to pursue the tax policy, then the imposition of the clothing tax is Kaldor-Hicks inefficient.

---

[38]Ken's utility function is $U = C^{1/2} + H^{1/2}$. At point B, we know that $C = 17$ units and $H = 66$ units, and so $U_1 = 12.25$ (see note 20). At point C, we know that prices of both items are $1 and income is $83; hence, Ken consumes 41.5 units of each at this point. Hence, $U_2 = 41.5^{1/2} + 41.5^{1/2} = 12.88$. Because the utility function is perfectly symmetrical, I know that Ken always chooses an equal amount of clothes and housing if prices are the same. Hence, I know that I can reach U_1 when prices both are $1 if I have x units of clothes and housing. These need to satisfy: $x^{1/2} + x^{1/2} = U_1 = 12.25 \Rightarrow x = 37.5$; that is, Ken attains U_1 if he has 37.5 units of housing and an equal number of units of clothes. Since the prices of both goods are $1, I can attain this level with income equal to $75. So, the move from C to B is the equivalent of reducing Ken's income from $83 to $75, or a reduction of $8.

At the risk of redundancy, I can restate this principle four different ways: (1) Any move is Kaldor-Hicks efficient if Pareto efficiency *could* be attained by some side payment. (2) If the party who gains from the move can in principle compensate the one who loses and still be better off, it is at least Pareto efficient in some *potential* sense, and hence, Kaldor-Hicks efficient. (3) If the party who loses from the move can in principle compensate the winner not to pursue the move and still be better off then the move is Pareto inefficient in a *potential* sense, and hence Kaldor-Hicks inefficient. (4) The dollar-is-a-dollar assumption is a shorthand way of applying the Kaldor-Hicks principle. If one party loses more dollars than the winner gains, then in principle a deal can be made to prevent the move and make everyone better off.

Kaldor-Hicks efficiency: A move is said to be Kaldor-Hicks efficient if, *in principle*, the party who gains can compensate the party that loses and still be better off from the move. Kaldor-Hicks is a hypothetical check to see if a Pareto efficient move *could* be found if a side payment were made as a part of the transaction. It does not matter whether the transaction is made or not.

The dollar-is-a-dollar assumption: A shorthand way of invoking Kaldor-Hicks in analyzing the welfare loss of some policy. As long as gains from a move exceed losses, then it is possible for a side payment to make all parties better off.

Note that government imposition of a $1 tax on clothing is equivalent to the following two-step process. First, assess a $17 income tax on Ken, thereby moving him from point A to point C in figure 2-14. Second, impose a 17-unit limit on the amount of clothing he can purchase, which moves him from point C to point B. The result is similar to one we observed when Mom put a restriction on the number of computer games that Dominic could purchase with his report card payoff in chapter 1. It also is reminiscent of the effect of Frank's uncle duping him into a misallocation of his income across tulips and mums. In this sense, tax distortions can be thought of in the same family as restrictions on free choice.

EXERCISE:
Refer to figure 2-13. Characterize the following moves using both the Pareto and Kaldor-Hicks concepts: (1) A to C, (2) C to B, and (3) A to B.[39]

---

[39]The move from A to C is neither Pareto superior nor inferior because one person gains and the other loses, and is Kaldor-Hicks neutral because one does not gain more than the

Tax distortion: A tax distortion occurs when it artificially alters a price. It "distorts" or alters the optimal allocation of income. The tax makes consumers act as though some activity or product or service is more costly to supply to society than it really is. Distortions almost always confer deadweight losses.

A tax on a good imposes no distortion when the demand elasticity is zero.

An example is Frank's right-angle indifference curves depicted in figure 1-11, panel (*a*). In this case, a tax on tulips reduces Frank's income, but he continues to purchase mums and tulips in exactly 50-50 proportions. In the context of figure 1-11, panel (*a*), points *B* and *C* in figure 2-13 would be coincident.

C. SHOWING THE DISTORTION ON THE DEMAND CURVE

Tax distortions are more conventionally shown on demand curves. Figure 2-15 depicts Ken's compensated demand curve for clothes, which I reproduce from figure 2-2. At the $2 clothing price (which includes the $1 tax on clothing), Ken consumes 17 units of clothing (corresponding to point *B* in figure 2-14). If the price falls to $1, holding constant his utility level at U_1, he chooses 37 units of clothing (corresponding to point *D* in figure 2-14).

Tax revenue amount is depicted by area *E*, which equals $17 (which you can confirm by inspection). This area corresponds to the difference in the budget lines that pass through points *A* and *C* in figure 2-14.

The deadweight loss on the demand curve is depicted by area *F* in figure 2-15. Unlike the tax revenue effect, the dollar value of area *F* is not apparent from inspection. Since I know Ken's utility function, however, and since I derived his compensated demand curve from this function, I can calculate area *F* exactly. It turns out to be $8, which is the same amount represented by the difference in the budget lines that pass through points *C* and *D* in figure 2-14.[40] Thus, the revenue and the

---

other loses, and thus there is no potential for a deal not to move. The move from C to B is Pareto inferior because one person loses without the other gaining (it always is Kaldor-Hicks inefficient if it is Pareto inefficient). The move from A to B is neither Pareto superior nor inferior because one person gains and the other loses, but it is Kaldor-Hicks inefficient because one person loses by more than the other gains, meaning that a deal could be made in principle to prevent the move that could make both parties better off.

[40]Ken's compensated demand curve solved for price on the left-hand side is given in note 24. When the price of housing is $1, this function is described as follows: $P_C = U^* C_2^{-1/2} - 1$, where C_2 denotes optimal consumption of clothing at price $2. Note that U^* is the utility on

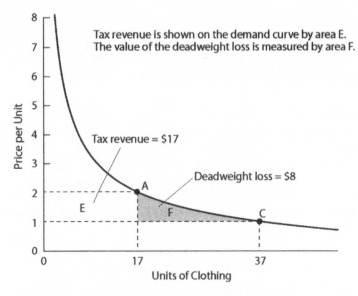

Tax revenue is shown on the demand curve by area E.
The value of the deadweight loss is measured by area F.

Figure 2-15. Transfer Amount and Deadweight Loss

deadweight loss effects of the tax can be calculated by using either the indifference curves or the demand curves.[41]

This is an important connection. There are three steps to the logic. First, consumer surplus can be evaluated using an individual's demand curve. Second, the market demand curve merely reflects the surplus of each individual demand curve. Third, this is a fortunate outcome because we never observe indifference curves and seldom observe individual demand curves but often have estimates of market demand curves. Ergo, we can measure surplus from observable demand curves, and we can put these estimates in dollar terms. We can now abandon the notion of utils!

---

the indifference curve where Ken consumes C_2 units of clothing (see note 20). Let the quantity of clothing demanded at price $1 be C_1. Finally, denote the corresponding prices as P_1 and P_2. Consumer surplus is the area under this curve over the range C_1 to C_2: $CS = \int_{C_2}^{C_1} U^* C^{1/2} - 1] dC - P_1(C_2 - C_1) = \{_{C_1}|^{C_2} 2U^* C^{1/2} - C] dC - P_1(C_2 - C_1)$. Substituting $P_1 = \$1$, $P_2 = \$2$, $C_1 = 37$, and $C_2 = 17$, then $CS = \$7.90$. Note that I have rounded C_1 and C_2 so that the correspondence between the deadweight loss on the indifference curves is slightly different from using the demand curves. But if I use the fractions that come out of the optimal solutions, the numbers would correspond exactly. This is essentially the same method that we used to calculate Ken's consumer surplus when the price was $2 (see note 24).

[41]For this purpose, I am using the compensated demand curve, but as I show in the appendix, consumer surplus can be calculated from the uncompensated demand curve. So it is not very important for you to qualify the differences in these concepts.

Surplus is the dollar value of "utils." We can use the compensation principle to attach a dollar value to changes in utility.

Figure 2-16 shows the market demand curve for some commodity. Price is P_0 per unit. Total quantity demanded at this price is Q_0. In this equilibrium, total consumer surplus is measured by the sum of areas A, B, and C. The imposition of a tax t on each unit of clothes increases price to $P_0 + t$, which in turn induces consumers to reallocate their incomes away from clothing from quantity Q_0 to Q_t.

Tax revenue equals the tax rate, t, times the quantity of clothes demanded after the tax, Q_t, which is shown as area B in the figure. We suppose that those dollars are valued just as highly in some other use, and so they are a transfer.

Notice however that consumers also lose the area C, which represents deadweight loss from the imposition of the tax. Using the formula for a triangle, this loss is measured by the tax rate, t, times $Q_0 - Q_t$, times $\frac{1}{2}$. In principle, consumers would rather pay the amount B in tax *and* pay some additional amount up to the dollar value denoted by area C to eliminate the tax distortion. *Area C is referred to as a deadweight loss, a welfare loss, or a "triangle" loss.*[42] Area A denotes the consumer surplus that Ken retains after the tax.

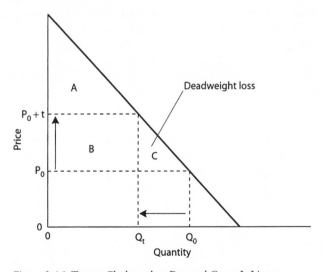

Figure 2-16. Tax on Clothes when Demand Curve Is Linear

[42]In the two-goods model, resources must have shifted from the production of clothes to housing. Note, however, that the change in consumer surplus is measured completely by

> *A delta-Q Rule*: Deadweight losses come about because market output is different from the efficient solution. Call this change in output ΔQ. The deadweight loss is a triangle located directly above ΔQ.

Another way to think about area C is that for every unit of clothes beyond Q_t until Q_0, consumers would willingly pay clothing suppliers a price in excess of the cost of making it available. This voluntary trade between consumers and producers is inhibited because the government encourages consumers to act *as though* the resource cost is $P_0 + t$, which is the cause of the distortion.

The tax has the same effect as putting a quota on clothes supplied equal to Q_t. In this case, market price would be forced up to $P_0 + t$ to reflect the artificial scarcity caused by the reduction in supply. Either way, the interference has the effect of preventing trade opportunities to happen that confer surplus on market participants. It is as though Ken and Jane in chapter 1 are artificially induced to find a solution off their contract curve.

EXERCISE:

Suppose that the demand curve is described by $Q = 10 - P$ and that the competitive price is \$1. What is the quantity demanded at this price? What is consumer surplus? Suppose that a \$2 tax is added to the price. What is the tax revenue? What is the dollar value of the deadweight loss? Is the demand curve elastic or inelastic in the relevant range of the tax? What is consumer surplus after the tax is imposed? You can solve this problem by plotting this demand curve on graph paper.[43]

D. TAX BURDEN: APPLICATION OF DEMAND ELASTICITY

How can we show that a tax on x is more efficient than a tax on y? One consideration is the administrative cost of collecting the tax. But if these costs are similar, then one needs to consider the deadweight loss in relation to the revenue raised. If we can raise lots of revenue by imposing a

---

area C. The market for housing conveys no additional information. Think of the imposition of the tax as a series of tiny increments. At each increase in price, the switch from clothing to housing is done on the assumption that consumers remain on their indifference curves; thus, each substitution out of clothes toward housing does not change utility.

[43] Answers: $Q = 9$; CS before the tax = \$40.50; tax revenue = \$14; deadweight loss = \$2; inelastic; CS after the tax = \$24.50.

small triangle loss, then this alternative is more appealing than one that delivers large deadweight costs and little revenue.

In terms of figure 2-16, the deadweight cost of raising the tax is denoted by area C. Tax revenue is denoted by area B. A simple way to characterize the cost of raising the amount B is to express the deadweight cost, C, as a percentage of tax revenue, B. To do this, I can use the formulas for a rectangle and triangle and invoke the definition of demand elasticity.

Efficiency of an excise tax: The cost of an excise tax equals the ratio of deadweight losses to tax revenues. It is easy to show that this ratio can be expressed by a simple formula:[44]

$$\xi = \frac{DW}{TAXREV} = \tfrac{1}{2}\left|\eta_\tau\right|\tau$$

where $\left|\eta_\tau\right|$ is the absolute elasticity of demand at the price inclusive of the tax, and τ is the tax expressed as a percentage of price inclusive of the tax.

Suppose that for some linear demand curve, $Q = 1{,}500 - 100\,P$, 20 percent of the existing price includes a tax. Price equals $10. The demand elasticity is $\eta = -bP\,/\,Q$. But $-b$ is -100, P is $10, $Q\,(= 1{,}500 - 100 \times \$10)$ is 500, and so $\eta = -2$. So the ratio of deadweight costs to tax revenues is $\tfrac{1}{2}\,|{-}2|\,.20$, or .20. This says that 20¢ out of each dollar of tax revenue is burned up in deadweight losses.

Obviously, if demand elasticity is zero, there is no deadweight cost to raising the tax. In general, the burden imposed by the assessment of a tax is proportional to its elasticity. If the tax represents 20 percent of price and the absolute value of the elasticity of demand at this price is 1, then the cost-to-revenue ratio is 10 percent. If the elasticity of demand is 5, then the cost-to-revenue ratio is 50 percent. In short, the efficiency of a tax is inversely related to the elasticity of demand.

---

[44]To calculate a positive deadweight loss, define the change in quantity demanded from the tax as a positive number $|\Delta Q| = |Q_t - Q_0|$. The change in price ΔP equals the per-unit tax T. $DW = \tfrac{1}{2}\,T|\Delta Q|$. Tax revenue equals the tax per unit, T, times the equilibrium output in the new equilibrium, Q_t: $TAXREV = T\,Q_t$. Calculate the ratio $DW\,/\,TAXREV = \tfrac{1}{2}\,|\Delta Q|\,/\,Q_t$. For a linear demand curve we know that $|\Delta Q| = b\,\Delta P$. Make this substitution and multiply and divide by P_t to obtain $DW\,/\,TAXREV = \tfrac{1}{2}\,b\,\Delta P\,P_t\,/\,P_t\,Q_t$. But $b\,P_t\,/\,Q_t = |\eta_t|$ and $\Delta P = T$. Make these substitutions to obtain: $DW\,/\,TAXREV = \tfrac{1}{2}|\eta_t|\,\tau$, where $\tau = T\,/\,P_t$ is the tax as a percentage of the posttax price.

Two Extreme Cases
A *confiscatory tax* is one designed to affect behavior, not raise revenue. In the limit, the tax is so high that it generates zero tax revenue, which means that the value of ξ above approaches infinity; that is, the entire amount of consumer surplus is eliminated and tax revenue is zero because consumption falls to zero. Panel (*b*) in figure 2-11 is an example of this outcome.

A *nondistortionary tax* is one that generates revenue but induces no change in behavior. The ratio ξ above is zero. This result occurs if the demand curve is perfectly vertical over the relevant range. Vertical demand curve segments are more likely to occur in the short run than the long run. Panel (*a*) in figure 2-11 is an example of this outcome.

This constraint explains why, other things being equal, tax authorities try to tax products that do not cause a large reaction from consumers. Large taxes in most European countries on gasoline and cigarettes, for example (sometimes more than 100 percent), might be explained by the inelastic nature of demand for these goods rather than some other cited reason having to do with health or national energy policy. Attaching taxes in inverse proportion to demand elasticity as a way to minimize the deadweight costs of collecting a given amount of revenue is called *Ramsey pricing*.[45]

EXERCISE:
Calculate the efficiency of a 100 percent tax in the two markets described in figure 2-10. Assume that the price before the tax is $5.[46]

---

[45]In a famous paper, Frank Ramsey showed that the overall societal cost of collecting a tax is smallest if taxes are assessed in inverse proportion to demand elasticity across goods. See Frank Ramsey, "A Contribution to the Theory of Taxation," *Economic Journal* 37 (March 1927): 47–61.

[46]The analysis of panel (*a*) is pretty easy because it is a confiscatory tax. There is a large triangle loss and no tax revenues, and thus the ratio ξ is infinitely large. In panel (*b*), tax revenues are $2,500. The triangle loss is $1,250, and so the value of ξ is 50 percent, still pretty high. In the latter case, you can check the formula. The panel shows that the elasticity is -2 at the posttax price of $10. The tax is 50 percent of this price ($\tau = \frac{1}{2}$). So the formula is $\xi = \frac{1}{2} |\eta_t| \tau = \frac{1}{2} \times 2 \times \frac{1}{2} = .5$, which gives the right answer.

MAJOR LESSONS SO FAR

Thus far, while we have covered a lot of ground, the critically important lessons that have been conveyed boil down to a precious few.

Free choice. Free choice is an important feature of economics. The value of $100 in income is not as high if consumers are restricted from allocating these monies to maximize their utility. It matters whether mums and tulips are planted in a particular proportion.

Gains from trade. Left to their own devices, if the net surplus from doing so is positive, then market participants will find ways to trade with each other. Think of Ken and Jane in the Edgewood box or consumers trading dollars for goods as long as surplus from marginal units is positive. This principle is general and shows up under various guises throughout economics.

The compensation principle. Changes in utility can be approximated by dollar values. In principle, we can ask participants, "How much would it take to make you whole?" which teases out a dollar value of changes in utility. Remember Frank and Uncle Dick and Dominic and Mom. In both those cases, we discovered the price that made things right after a distortion was imposed.

Distortions are costly. Anytime that free-market outcomes are distorted by either taxation, regulation, or, as we shall see later, monopoly pricing, a deadweight loss is imposed. Even though resources flow elsewhere to produce something else, we do not end up with the same utility from the production and income that are generated. The efficiency of those dollars has been reduced because we have imposed artificial distortions in consumer choice. This principle is a natural outgrowth of the first three points.

Demand curves are downsloping. Consumers demand more of the product the lower its price. This fundamental reality, which stems naturally from the principle of diminishing marginal utility, limits revenues obtainable from artificial increases in price and is the underlying reason why "distortions" characterize most price changes that are unrelated to the cost of production. A shorthand description of demand conditions is given by demand elasticity.

Appendix: Consumer Surplus and Uncompensated Demand Curves

This appendix looks closer at Ken's indifference curves and his derived demand curve for clothing presented in figure 2-1. It shows why the area under an uncompensated demand curve gives a pretty good estimate of consumer surplus.

When drawing parallels between demand curves and indifference curves, it is useful to use compensated demand curves because the areas under the demand curve exactly match the counterpart measures on the indifference curve map. But it is natural to ask two questions. First, since market demand curves include income effects, do the surplus calculations still work? And second, Ken was on utility level U_1 prior to the price reduction from \$2 to \$1. What if price is \$1 to start with, so that Ken is on utility curve U_2; then price increases to \$2, reducing Ken's utility to U_1. Would the new compensated demand curve be different going in this direction? The answer is yes, which of course adds greatly to the confusion in some people's minds about what is going on.

To illustrate these concepts, I redid the problem in the text so that indeed the original price was \$1, which means that Ken starts at point B in figure 2-1, panel (a), which puts his starting utility level at U_2. I increase price to \$2 and then find the compensated demand curve that maintains Ken at the higher level of utility. I do not show this derivation here, but figure 2-17 shows both the original compensated demand curve taken from figure 2-2, which passes through points A and C, and the new compensated demand curve, the dashed-line schedule to the right of the original, which passes through points E and B. How can there be *two* compensated demand curves? Actually, there are more than two. There's a different compensated demand curve for every starting price. Why? Because, at every price, Ken starts on a different utility curve, and a compensated demand curve by construct holds constant utility. Ergo, there must be one for every indifference curve!

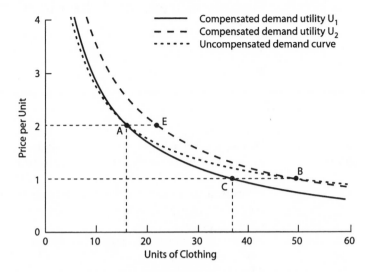

Figure 2-17. Reconciling Compensated and Uncompensated Demand Curves

While this explanation is fine as far as it goes, it seems in the short run to make the matter even more confusing. It turns out, though, that if we pursue the matter further, everything clears up.

Start by stating the obvious problem. If we start at $2 and reduce price to $1, we already figured out that the dollar value of this utility change is measured by the areas bounded by the vertical axis between these prices and points A and C on his compensated demand curve (that keeps him at utility U_1). Going the other way, we start at B at the $1 price and increase price to $2. The dollar cost of the utility change increases by the area bounded by ACBE. This is the extra amount it costs to keep Ken at the higher level of utility. Which one is right? Well, both are right. If both are right, which one do we use? The answer is neither one. In fact, it turns out that we will use a demand curve that sort of splits the difference.

The good news is that the demand curve that gives us this average estimate is the one that most students want to use in the first place, namely, the uncompensated demand curve! In terms of figure 2-1, the uncompensated demand curve in panel (b) would plot points A and B from panel (a), not points A and C. The dashed-line schedule in figure 2-17 shows this demand curve. It is apparent that using the uncompensated demand curve to measure consumer surplus between two prices splits the difference between the two measures using compensated demand curves, and as a bonus, it is the same regardless of whether we start at price $1 or $2. So, in the end, it is OK to use the uncompensated demand curve to measure consumer surplus.

Chapter 3

Supply Curves and the Flow of Resources
Also Sunk Cost, Opportunity Cost, and Transactions Cost

Main Economic Concepts	1. Short-run supply depends only on marginal cost; competitive firms always set quantity at the point where marginal cost equals price.
	2. Long-run supply also depends on the number of firms in the industry, minimum average total cost of the marginal firm, and industry effects on input prices.
	3. Profitability governs the flow of resources in the economy.
	4. The act of producers pursuing their own self-interest moves price toward the point that ensures zero excess profits.
	5. In the long run, firms do not expect to earn any surplus; that is, they expect revenues to equal their costs, inclusive of a competitive rate of return.
	6. Some inputs to the industry can earn surplus in equilibrium, a concept called rent in input markets.
New Terms	1. Marginal cost curve
	2. Average total cost curve
	3. Sustainable price
	4. Economic profits
	5. Excess returns
	6. Producer surplus, long and short run
	7. Economic rent
	8. Sunk or past cost
	9. Opportunity cost
	10. Tax burden
	11. Supply Curve
	12. Equilibrium price
	13. Market-clearing price
	14. Ex ante and ex post
	15. Long-run supply

We now have derived the demand side of the market. The market demand curve is the summation of many individual demand curves, each of which reflects optimal consumption choices based on income and tastes. Price was simply given. In this chapter, I show how supply conditions are developed in the market. I then combine demand and supply concepts to develop the notions of equilibrium output and long-run sustainable price in a market.

I. The World Market for Nickel

A. THE SUPPLY OF NICKEL WITH NO FIXED COSTS

The easiest place to begin is to think of some ore like nickel. Suppose that there are two countries in the world that have nickel deposits, country A and country B. I suppose that the government owns these resources and that there are no fixed cost to production. To mine ten tons of ore, a producer needs to send in x workers with picks and shovels. To supply more nickel, the producer sends more workers with more picks and shovels. Ignore the cost of transporting the ore from suppliers to users. Suppose that our problem is only one period long, so that we do not have to introduce the complexities of determining the optimal rate of extraction over time.

Suppose country A has some deposits of nickel that are close to the surface. Other sources are deeper, requiring more workers to extract. Think of lining up these sources from the easiest to mine to the hardest. The first few tons can be mined for say $100 per ton, the next few for $125, and then those that cost $150 and so on. The upsloping line in figure 3-1 panel (*a*) depicts this relationship. It describes country A's marginal cost of producing each ton of nickel. It also is the schedule of tons available from country A as a function of price of nickel, which is its supply schedule. The higher the price, the more tons that country A can profitably mine.

Country B also has nickel deposits. This country has no deposits that it can mine for $100 per ton. Its cheapest source costs $200 per ton. The next best sources require increasing numbers of workers to obtain each

---

Marginal cost curve: The schedule that denotes the cost of producing each unit on the margin. It is to be distinguished from the average cost of producing all units, because the latter concept is the average of marginal costs incurred in the production of each unit.

Individual supply curve: A schedule of quantities offered as a function of price. It is the marginal cost curve.

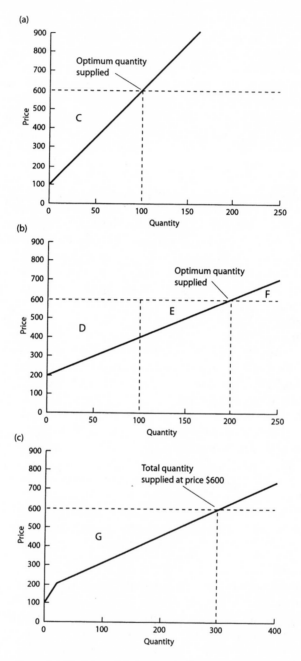

Figure 3-1. Deriving a Market Supply Curve

additional ton of nickel. Arraying its mines from the cheapest to most expensive, its supply schedule is shown in panel (*b*). Notice that its supply schedule starts at a higher price than country *A*'s schedule, but it has lots of mines in the middling deep range, and so its supply curve does not rise as sharply.

To determine world supply, I follow the same procedure that I did for demand. Simply sum the quantities made available from each country at each price. I show market supply in panel (*c*) of figure 3-1. At any price less than $100, no nickel is forthcoming. At $100, country *A* can mine its first units of nickel economically. Thus, I plot the first point on the market supply curve at the $100 price. Between prices $100 and $200, country *A* is willing to supply more nickel, but country *B* still has not entered the market because it cannot economically mine any nickel for less than $200 per ton. Until this price is reached, the world supply is coincident with country *A*'s supply curve.

Once the price reaches $200, country *B* makes some nickel available to the market. As price increases above $200, both country *A* and country *B* expand output, and so, total quantity of nickel offered is the horizontal sum of these two countries' outputs. The market supply curve is flatter than each individual supply curve, because more incremental output is mined in total for any change in price, compared to each country individually.

Market supply: The horizontal summation of marginal cost curves offered by each individual supplier at each price.

B. PRODUCER SURPLUS

Suppose that the market price of nickel is $600. Each country determines its output by setting its marginal cost equal to market price. For example, country *B* chooses output of 200 units. If country *B* offers less output at the $600 price, say 100 tons, then for every unit of output between 100 and 200 tons, it forgoes profitable opportunities because it can produce every ton over this range at a cost of less than $600. By expanding output from 100 to 200 tons, it earns an incremental surplus measured by area *E*.

Nor does it pay for country *B* to expand beyond 200 tons. Suppose it produces an extra 50 tons for a total of 250 tons at the $600 price. In this case, for the marginal 50 tons, it costs more to produce each ton than the price it fetches in the market. In this case, the country would incur losses measured by area *F*. *Like all producers, country B maximizes its surplus by producing where marginal cost equals market price.*

At this output level, for every ton that country B supplies to the market, it earns some surplus. On its first ton supplied, it incurs cost $200, and collects $600, thereby earning $400 in surplus. Its 100th ton cost $400, which yields $200 in surplus. Areas $D + E$ measure the total surplus earned by country B. Using the same rationale, country A sets output at 100 tons. It earns surplus measured by area C in panel (a).

Market supply at the $600 price (300 tons) is the sum of the output chosen by country A (100 tons) and country B (200 tons). Producer surplus in the market, measured by area G, is the sum of surplus measured for each country.[47]

Optimal output for each supplier: Each supplier determines output by setting price equal to its marginal cost of production. Any other output reduces its surplus.

Producer surplus: The difference between market price and the marginal cost of production. Hence, total producer surplus is the area above the supply curve but below market price over the range of output supplied.

C. THE WORLD PRICE FOR NICKEL

I have thus far assumed that the price of nickel is given. In fact, price is determined by the interplay between demand and supply factors. To obtain a description of world price, I need to depict world demand. World demand for nickel is the amalgamation of thousands of individual demand curves, some from individual consumers and others for various industrial users.

Figure 3-2 depicts the world demand for nickel as the downsloping schedule and world supply as the upsloping schedule. Combining nickel supply from many countries using the same process depicted in figure 3-1

---

[47]I need to provide one more piece of information to prove this. The "kink" in panel (c) occurs at 20 tons. You can obtain the area G by breaking the area into two pieces. Draw a vertical line at 20 units and a horizontal line at $200 over these 20 units. This gives us a tiny triangle plus a rectangle over these 20 units. The rectangle has height $400 and base 20 units, for a total surplus of $8,000. The tiny triangle has a height of $100 and base of 20 units and so has the value $\frac{1}{2} \times \$100 \times 20 = \$1,000$. This leaves a big triangle (the remainder of area G) with height $400 and base 280, which has a value of $\frac{1}{2} \times \$400 \times 280 = \$56,000$. Hence, area G equals $65,000. Now consider the surplus in country A, which is measured by the triangle denoted by area C in panel (a). The height of this triangle is $500 and the base is 100; hence, its area is $\frac{1}{2} \times \$500 \times 100 = \$25,000$. The surplus for country B is the large triangle denoted by the areas $D + E$ in panel (b). The height is $400 and the base is 200; hence, surplus equals $\frac{1}{2} \times \$400 \times 200 = \$40,000$. Adding the amounts for both countries equals $65,000, which is the same surplus found in panel (c).

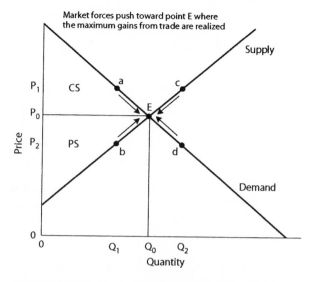

Figure 3-2. Equilibrium Price and Quantity

derives the latter schedule. Note that there is only one price that is a candidate for equilibrium, namely, P_0, which corresponds to quantity Q_0. This solution occurs where the demand and supply curves intersect, which I label point E.

We can convince ourselves that this output is equilibrium by supposing that quantity is something other than Q_0, say Q_1. At the latter quantity, consumers are willing to pay price denoted by point a for the next unit. Suppliers are willing to sell this unit for a lower price denoted by point b. Producers have an incentive to produce more output and make it available to consumers who, in turn, are willing to pay more than the marginal cost of production for these units. It is analogous to Jane and Ken working their way from the tip of a "cigar" to the contract curve in the Edgeworth box (see chapter 1).

Any point past quantity Q_0 also is unsustainable. Suppose that output is Q_2. In this case, producers can make another unit available for an amount denoted by point c. But consumers are willing to pay a lower price denoted by point d for marginal units. Hence, producers have an incentive to reduce output. At any output level besides Q_0, the market exerts forces in the direction of quantity Q_0. This quantity is "cleared" from the market at price P_0.

Viewed from the perspective of price, suppose that price is P_1. There are Q_2 units supplied but only Q_1 units demanded. The only way suppliers can sell their excess output is to reduce price. Similarly, if price is P_2, then there are Q_2 units demanded and only Q_1 supplied. The excess demand exerts an upward pressure on price. At price P_0, these forces are equalized. We have a stable equilibrium. All consumers are satisfied who are willing to pay the marginal cost of the last unit willingly supplied by producers.

Equilibrium price: Equilibrium price is found where the supply schedule intersects with the demand schedule. At any output lower than this, there are net gains to trade that can benefit both producers and consumers. At any output higher than this, consumers are unwilling to pay the marginal cost of bringing the marginal units to market.

In equilibrium, all consumers are satisfied who are willing to pay the marginal cost of the last unit willingly supplied by producers.

D. SURPLUSES IN MARKET EQUILIBRIUM

Consider the surplus that characterizes equilibrium. In chapter 2, I showed the surplus enjoyed by consumers. In terms of figure 3-2, for each unit of output purchased up to Q_0, consumers are willing to pay more than price P_0. Since they can purchase units at price P_0, they gain surplus measured by the area labeled CS in the figure.

THE MAGIC OF THE MARKET

Consider the magic of market equilibrium. None of the producers necessarily know any of the consumers of nickel, and the only reason that they supply the product is because it is in their interest to do so. Similarly, consumers choose to purchase nickel because it represents the best allocation of their limited resources. They could care less whether producers are earning a profit or loss on these units. Yet, by each pursuing their own interests, consumers and producers have in the aggregate conferred great value to each other, measured by the consumer and producer surplus in figure 3-2.

Put differently, for the market to work, we do not need to believe that market participants are nice people or care about helping producers earn a living and so on. It relies solely upon participants pursuing their self-interests. In so doing, they confer surplus on each other. In other words, as though guided by an "invisible hand,"[48] anonymous forces replicate the principle of gains from trade that characterized the Pareto superior trades in the Edgeworth box.

---

[48]The famous phrase "like an invisible hand" is from Adam Smith's *The Wealth of Nations: An Inquiry into the Nature and Causes* (New York: Modern Library, 1994).

THE MILTON FRIEDMAN PENCIL STORY

Milton Friedman would tell a pencil story to convey this idea.[49] Pencils were invented by the English and perfected in early America. Rubber comes from Brazil, the graphite from some faraway mine. Some lumber company provides the wood, someone else the paint. The product might be assembled in China, then shipped across the oceans, and then across the interstate highways to warehouses until finally they arrive at Office Depot, where you shop. The process occurs as if by magic, with no guidance from any central authority or government intervention, but instead by market participants, who usually do not know each other, each trying to make a buck. Consumers buy a pack of pencils for 60¢. They think: "What a deal! These pencils are so valuable to me, and yet I can buy them for a fraction of the value I attach to them." Meanwhile, all the producers who combined their talents to make the pencils might be heard collectively saying, "Can you believe that consumers pay us 60¢ for pencils that hardly cost us anything to produce?" Both are better off, and yet both conferred a gift on strangers in the form of either consumer or producer surplus.

Producers also earn a surplus. For all units of nickel sent to market until quantity Q_0, producers are paid a price for their output in excess of the marginal cost of production. This surplus is measured by area PS in the figure.

II. The Solution with Fixed Costs and Many Firms

The previous illustration abstracts from the existence of fixed costs, which makes the problem simpler but denies us the opportunity to evaluate the conditions under which firms enter and exit industries. The introduction of fixed costs does not affect the main concepts reflected in figure 3-2, but it introduces an additional condition. In particular, we need to ensure that the price we observe is sustainable.

To learn more about a "sustainable price," I need to consider two kinds of costs: variable costs, which vary with the amount of output, and fixed costs, which are independent of output. A firm's revenues must be sufficient to pay for both variable and fixed costs. Since marginal cost curves reflect only variable costs, we need to find a way to

[49]The story is repeated from the essay "I, Pencil: A Family Tree as Told to Leonard Read," which can be found in its entirety at www.fee.org.

demonstrate that all costs are covered at that price, not just marginal costs. Since product price is already expressed on a per-unit basis, it makes sense to derive a comparable measure for costs. Toward this end, I calculate the average total cost of producing the product at every level of output.

A. CONSTRUCTING THE COST CURVES

Consider the production of any product. Suppose that the marginal cost of producing further units is increasing, as depicted in figure 3-3.[50] For concreteness, I suppose that this cost is described by a particular schedule.

Marginal cost assumption:

$$MC = \$150 + \$5q$$

where q is the quantity of output. This schedule says that the marginal cost of production starts out at \$150 and increases by \$5 for each succeeding unit.

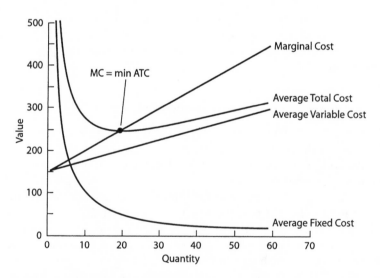

Figure 3-3. Cost Curves for One Firm

---

[50]I could portray the marginal cost curve as decreasing at first, but as long as it slopes upward eventually, the same analysis pertains.

The supply schedule for this firm is its marginal cost curve. Just as for countries *A* and *B*, every producer maximizes surplus by choosing an output where the marginal cost of production equals market price. If there are ten such firms, all with the same marginal cost curve, then market supply is the horizontal summation of ten of these marginal cost curves. This schedule, together with the demand curve, is sufficient to determine market price. The question remains: is this price sustainable? To make this determination, we need information about average cost per unit of output. There are two components to this cost: average marginal cost and average fixed cost.

Average variable costs. Average variable costs are the sum of the marginal costs of producing *x* units, divided by *x*. If the marginal cost of producing the first unit of output is $155, and the marginal cost of producing the second unit is $160, then the average variable cost of producing these two units is $157.50 (= ($155 + $160)/2). If the marginal cost of producing the third unit is $165, then the average cost of producing three units is $160 (= ($155 + $160 + $165)/3), and so on. Note that the average variable cost at any given output is always less than the marginal cost at that point, because cheaper units that were produced prior to the marginal unit influence the average (for example, when $q = 2$, average cost is $157.50, which is less than marginal cost, $160). This curve is shown below the marginal cost curve in figure 3-3.

Average variable cost (AVC): The average of all the marginal costs incurred in producing quantity *q*.

$$AVC_q = \frac{MC_1 + MC_2 + \cdots + MC_q}{q}$$

If the marginal cost increases with output, then *AVC* is less than *MC* at every unit of output.

Average fixed costs. Next, consider fixed costs. Suppose that regardless of actual output attained during the next period, office and equipment must be rented, an office manager hired, and so on. Regardless of output level, these overhead items need to be covered. Otherwise, it is not profitable to enter this business. Suppose that these costs are $1,000. Expressing these costs on a per-unit basis is simple. Divide the $1,000 by units of output. At the first unit of output, average fixed costs are $1,000; at two units of production, they are $500 because they are spread over two units, and so on. When output reaches 10 units, average fixed costs are only $100. Eventually, average fixed costs approach zero. This schedule is shown by the downsloping nonlinear schedule in figure 3-3.

Fixed costs: Those that do not change with output level.

Average fixed cost (AFC): Fixed cost, *F*, divided by quantity produced, *q*.

$$AFC_q = \frac{F}{q}$$

As output levels become high, *AFC* falls toward zero.

Economic costs. It is important to note that an economic definition of costs includes *all* expenses, including the salaries of overhead employees, interest payments due the bank for loans, a competitive wage for the principal officers, and a competitive rate of return to investors in the company. When revenues just equal the sum of these expenses, then economic profits are zero. When revenues exceed total costs, then economic profits are positive, which means that extraordinary returns beyond competitive returns are earned; when they are negative, it means that investment returns are lower than available in the capital market.

Economic cost and economic profit: Economic costs include competitive rates of return on investments made in the firm. Hence, a zero-profits equilibrium condition means that the firm earns a competitive return on its investment.

Economic profits, also referred to as *excess returns, excess profits*, or *abnormal profits*, are those that exceed the competitive rate of return on investments.

Average total costs. Average total cost is the *vertical* summation of average variable cost and average fixed cost. This sum is given by the U-shaped curve in figure 3-3. It is downsloping at first, reflecting the pull of falling fixed cost per unit, but eventually the rising marginal costs dominate, creating an upward slope. Minimum average total cost occurs at output level Q_0, which corresponds to 20 units of output in figure 3-3.

Average total cost (ATC) equals variable plus fixed cost, divided by quantity supplied. To derive the *ATC*, add the average variable and average fixed costs vertically at each output level. To obtain total costs, *TC*, multiply average total cost times quantity.

$$ATC = AFC + AVC$$
$$TC = ATC \bullet q$$

The U-shaped average cost curve conveys the intuition that as firms grow, they take advantage of economies of scale, which gives them some cost advantage. But size also means more expense to maintain quality control over the product. For example, as a law firm increases in size, the managing partner's salary and other overhead expenses are spread over more cases, but the firm also must expend more resources to ensure that cases are pursued to the satisfaction of the firm's standards. The firm needs to know if two of its lawyers are bringing separate cases on theories that contradict one another, or if one of its lawyers is pursuing a position in a regulatory proceeding for one client that is detrimental to the position of another client. The bigger the firm, the more likely it is that the costs of coordination outstrip the advantages of economies of scale.

Marginal cost intersects the average costs curve exactly at the minimum. This is not an accident. If, in comparison to all prior units produced, the marginal cost of adding one more unit of output is lower, then it must exert a downward pull on the average cost curve. Once the marginal cost exceeds the average of all prior units, then an additional unit of output must increase average cost.[51] In my example, this intersection occurs at output level 20 units, which is labeled MC = min ATC in figure 3-3.

A key characteristic of cost curves: The marginal cost curve (MC) intersects the average total cost (ATC) curve exactly at the minimum of ATC.

A SUGGESTED EXERCISE

Reproduce figure 3-3 using the marginal cost curve MC = \$150 + \$5q$ and fixed costs equal \$1,000.[52]

---

[51]There are two other ways to think of this idea. Average cost for the nth unit is a_n. I can write the following identity: $a_n = a_n n / n$. Thus, the average cost for $n + 1$ units must be $a_{n+1} = (a_n n + MC_{n+1}) / (n + 1)$. Suppose $MC_{n+1} = a_n$; then $a_{n+1} = a_n$. It follows that if $MC_{n+1} > a_n$, then $a_{n+1} > a_n$. Similarly if $MC_{n+1} < a_n$, then $a_{n+1} < a_n$. Alternatively, consider the marginal cost in my example, $MC = 150 + 5Q$. To obtain total variable costs, integrate the MC function over Q units of output, which gives $TVC = 150Q + (5/2) Q^2$. Thus, average variable cost are $AVC = 150 + (5/2)Q$. Average fixed cost are $1000/Q$. Thus, average total costs are $ATC = 150 + (5/2)Q + 1000/Q$. Setting the first derivative of ATC with respect to Q to zero gives us the minimum point on the average total cost curve: $(5/2)Q_0^2 = 1000$, or $Q_0 = 20$. Now find the solution where the marginal costs equal average total costs $MC = ATC$. Thus, $150 + 5Q = 150 + (5/2)Q + 1000/Q$, which is satisfied when $Q_0 = 20$.

[52]The solution using algebra and a little calculus is given in the prior note. If you solve the problem by hand or by using a spreadsheet, your answer will differ slightly because you are using discrete whole units, whereas I treat units as infinitely divisible. Notably, at

B. SUSTAINABLE PRICE: EQUILIBRIUM IN A LONG-RUN SENSE

Now that I have derived the average total cost curve, I no longer need its components. Thus, I reproduce figure 3-3 in figure 3-4, retaining only the marginal cost schedule, now labeled MC for shorthand, and the average total cost curve, now labeled ATC. It is useful to pay attention to the point where marginal cost equals minimum average total cost, at point e.

Since I am assuming a specific marginal cost function ($MC = \$150 + \$5q$) and a specific fixed cost ($1000), I know that the point e corresponds to 20 units of output.[53] At this level of output, average total cost is $250. In addition, the marginal cost at this output level also is $250. Total costs

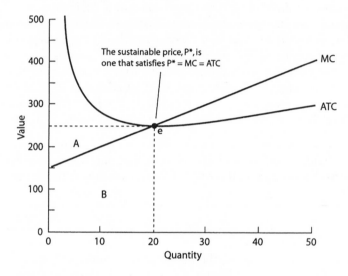

Figure 3-4. Implications of Price for Exit and Entry

output 20, ATC is a bit higher than MC. Don't worry about this approximation. Here are selected entries:

Quantity	MC	TVC	AVC	AFC	ATC
1	155	155	155.0	1,000.0	1,155.0
2	160	315	157.5	500.0	657.5
3	165	480	160.0	333.3	493.3
16	230	3,080	192.5	62.5	255.0
19	245	3,800	200.0	52.6	252.6
20	250	4,050	202.5	50.0	252.5
21	255	4,305	205.0	47.6	252.6
22	260	4,565	207.5	45.5	253.0

[53]This derivation is found in note 51.

equal the product of average total costs ($250) and output (20). Thus, total costs are $5,000, which is represented by areas *A* plus *B* in the figure.

Since we know that the area under the marginal cost curve must be the sum of all marginal costs, then the difference between total costs (areas *A* + *B*) and total variable cost (area *B*) must be fixed cost. We can check this using our triangle formula. The height of the triangle that outlines area *A* is $100 (that is, $250 minus the intercept of the marginal cost schedule, $150). The base is 20. Thus, the area of triangle *A* is $100 times 20 times ½, which equals $1,000, which indeed equals fixed costs.

We have not yet determined how price in this market is determined, but suppose that market price is $250. This price covers all costs, both marginal and fixed, and thus, invites neither exit from nor entry to this market. Since economic cost includes a competitive return on investments, there is neither an incentive to withdraw resources from this industry nor one to attract further investments. If the market price is at any other level, forces are created to reestablish $250 as the market-clearing price. Thus, we would say that $250 is the only *sustainable price* in this market.

Sustainable price, P*: That price at which there are forces neither attracting entry into the market nor encouraging exit. A sustainable price is one that generates a competitive return on investments in this industry. It corresponds to the output level where average total cost equals marginal cost.

III. Market Equilibrium: Entry, Exit, and Competitive Returns

To understand equilibrium, it is useful to recall three rules we already know. First, the supply curve for any firm is its marginal cost curve. Second, industry supply is the horizontal summation of all the individual supply curves in the market. Third, each firm determines its output by setting marginal cost equal to price. These market characteristics of the solution are not affected by the discussion of a sustainable price.

A. HOW TO EVALUATE THE SUSTAINABILITY OF A MARKET PRICE

It is useful first to reconsider figure 3-4 when price is something other than $250. Figure 3-5 reproduces this figure and portrays three different prices: $250, which is the sustainable price; $300, which confers excess profits; and $200, which generates losses in a long-term sense.

Consider a price of $300. The firm chooses output level 30 because at this output, marginal cost equals price, which is denoted by point *c* in the figure. The firm is earning excess profits because price exceeds average total costs (reflected by the vertical distance between points *c* and *d*).

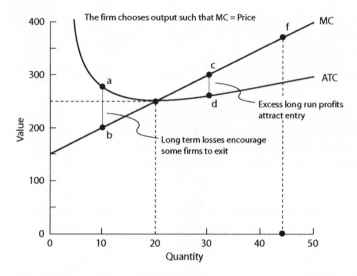

Figure 3-5. The Firm's Reaction to Market Prices

The excess return earned by these producers beckons entrants, each of whom wants to earn excess profits. But the process of entry works to expand industry output, which exerts a downward pressure on price.

Suppose alternatively that price is $200. In this case, the firm chooses output level 10 because this output corresponds to the point where price equal marginal cost (denoted by point b). At this solution, however, each firm is earning negative economic profits because price is less than average total costs (measured by the vertical distance between a and b in the figure). Under these conditions, reinvestments in this industry will diminish, and some firms will depart. This exit process works to reduce supply in the industry, which puts an upward pressure on price.

B. THE DYNAMICS OF ENTRY

Suppose that there are 75 firms in this industry, all of whom have exactly the same cost curves. In this case, at every price, the market supply of output is 75 times the output of one firm. To show this, recall that the marginal cost curve for the firm is described by $MC = 150 + 5q$. Thus, if output q is always chosen so that MC equals price, P, then we can find the quantity that the firm would supply at each price. Market supply is 75 times this number. I depict individual quantity supplied as q and market supply as Q. The following steps show how the market supply is calculated.

Figure 3-6 depicts the market supply curve as the upsloping schedule labeled S_1. Suppose that the demand curve is D_1, and hence, the

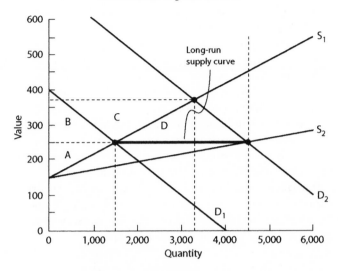

Figure 3-6. Dynamics of Price Adjustments

Market Supply Derived

Steps to derive market supply (assuming n identical firms):

Step 1: Set marginal cost equal to price
for one firm: $MC = P$

Step 2: Substitute the expression for
marginal cost: $150 + 5q = P$

Step 3: Solve for quantity in terms of
price $q = .2P - 30$

Step 4: Multiply individual quantities
supplied by n: $Q = nq = n(.2P - 30)$.

For example, suppose that there are 75 firms. Then at price $250, market supply is 1,500 units, which is exactly 75 times the 20 units for our individual firm. Note that for price less than $150, quantity supplied is zero.

---

market-clearing price is $250. Area A in this figure is comparable to area A in figure 3-4, except that it represents the fixed costs for all 75 firms in the market.[54]

---

[54]Area A in figure 3-6 is $75,000; area A in figure 3-4 is $1,000.

Suppose now that demand increases to D_2. Market price increases to $370 and output increases to 3,300 units.[55] Consider the impact of this effect for a single firm. Its marginal cost curve is $MC = 150 + 5q$. Since the firm sets MC equal to price, then at price $370, the firm chooses output, q, equal to 44 units (where 44 units times 75 firms equals 3,300). I depict this output by point f in figure 3-5. At this price and output, price exceeds average total costs, and thus, each firm in this industry earns excess profits.[56] Areas $B + C$ in figure 3-6 denote excess profits for the industry.[57]

What do you think will happen when the market learns that there are excess profits in an industry? In a word: *entry*. New firms enter in an attempt also to earn excess profits. Think what happens to industry supply as more firms enter. Recall that the market supply curve is equal to the horizontal summation of marginal cost curves for all firms in the market. Suppose 25 firms enter. At each price, I multiply the quantity supplied by one firm by 100 instead of 75.[58] Thus, as more firms enter, the market supply curve shifts farther to the right.

This process stops when a sufficient number of firms enter so that market supply and demand forces are equated at price $250. In this case, the solution is found when 150 additional firms enter. Once the market clearing price returns to $250, each firm is earning the competitive return on investment, and thus, there is an incentive for neither entry nor exit. In terms of figure 3-6, the final supply curve is depicted by the schedule labeled S_2. In the new equilibrium, 4,500 units are produced, comprising 225 firms each operating at output level 20 units. I could evaluate the problem if demand falls and show how the exit of some firms creates forces to reduce supply to reestablish the $250 sustainable price.

> *Profits as a signal*: An excess profits condition in an industry attracts entry, creating a force to reduce price and reestablish a competitive return on investment. Negative excess profits create the opposite force. The market price is sustainable when excess profits are zero.

[55]The total supply curve derived earlier is $Q = 15P - 2,250$. The demand curve, D_1, is defined as $Q = 4,000 - 10P$; thus, in original equilibrium, we have $P = 250 and $Q = 1,500$. Demand curve, D_2, is defined as $Q = 7,000 - 10P$, and hence the new price and output are $P = 370 and $Q = 3,300$.

[56]Since $ATC = 150 + (5/2)Q + 1000/Q$, then when $Q = 44$, $ATC = 282, which is less than the $370 price.

[57]Excess profits in figure 3-6 equal additional revenue at the higher price, denoted by rectangle $B + C + D$, minus additional costs incurred in producing the higher output, denoted by area D. Thus, excess profits are denoted by areas $B + C$.

[58]If each firm has slightly different marginal cost curves, then I cannot multiply any one of them by the number of firms. Instead, I have to sum each marginal cost curve horizontally to obtain market supply. In this case, the sustainable price is determined when the marginal firm earns zero profits.

C. THE CONCEPT OF LONG-RUN SUPPLY

By working through the dynamics of disequilbrium price, we have segued into the notion of **long-run supply**. In the short run, supply is the horizontal summation of all marginal cost curves in the industry. The idea of a sustainable price, say P^*, tells us that if demand increases or decreases so that price wanders from P^*, entry or exit will reestablish the zero-profits condition. Hence, as long as the expansion or contraction of the industry does not affect any input prices (an assumption that I relax in the next section), the long-run supply curve is a horizontal line at the sustainable price. Sometimes this condition is referred to as a "constant cost industry." I show the long-run supply schedule as the bold line segment in figure 3-6.

> *Long-run supply*: As long as the expansion or contraction of the industry does not affect input prices, the long-run supply curve is a horizontal line at the sustainable price. Sometimes this condition is referred to as a "constant cost industry."

> SUGGESTED EXERCISE 1:
> Assume that the problem stays the same, but suppose that market demand falls instead of increases. Work through the dynamics to show how a sustainable price will be re-created in this market.[59]
>
> SUGGESTED EXERCISE 2:
> Suppose that marginal cost is described by $MC = \$50 + \$10q$ and fixed costs by $FC = \$1,000$. Use graph paper to find the sustainable price in this market.[60]

[59]Price is less than ATC, and therefore a force is created for some firms to exit the industry. As they exit, the market supply curve shifts to the left, which works in the direction of increasing price. In equilibrium, price is $250, fewer firms operate, and each operates at output level 20 units.

[60]Using algebra, set $ATC = MC$. To get ATC, integrate MC to obtain total variable costs and add fixed costs. To obtain ATC, divide by q, set equal to MC and solve for q. The answer is $q \sim 14$ units and price $\sim \$190$. On graph paper, the first couple of entries are as follows (the answer will be slightly different because of the use of discrete units):

Units	MC	AVC	AFC	ATC
1	60	60	1,000	1,060
2	70	65	500	565

IV. Producer Surplus, Long and Short Run, and Economic Rent

I have now introduced a sufficient number of concepts to sow the seeds for some confusion. My discussion of sustainable price invoked the intuitive idea that entry and exit occur until the sustainable price is reestablished. In my example, this price was $250. Ponder this question: if the price continues to move toward $250, how does this square with the idea of producer surplus? If $250 is the required price to ensure zero profits, and we always drift toward that price, how can there be any producer surplus? This section addresses this puzzle and hopefully will clear up the confusion.

A. PRODUCER SURPLUS IN A SHORT-RUN SENSE

Suppose that we are in equilibrium at the $250 sustainable price. I said before that the area below price but above the industry supply curve is producer surplus, *but now I qualify myself by saying that this claim is true only in a short-run sense*. More particularly, in equilibrium, I have already demonstrated in figure 3-4 that the entirety of the producer surplus is equal to area *A*. But this amount is required to cover fixed costs. Thus, in an entry sense, there is no surplus.

Look at it this way: once the firm has committed to a three-year lease for office space (the fixed costs), it wants to reap as much excess over marginal cost as possible. Even if it becomes apparent that it will not collect an amount sufficient to pay for all the rent, the firm still is better off if it can collect some surplus above marginal cost to reduce the size of its losses. In this sense, area *A* in figure 3-4 is surplus, because once the lease is paid, the firm would indeed continue to operate for three years even if could only collect marginal costs plus some small increment that covers only a fraction of fixed costs.

In a longer-term sense, however, area *A* is not surplus but rather revenues required to pay for fixed costs. In the context of my example, once the three-year lease is up, the firm will not opt for another lease unless it thinks it can collect sufficient revenues in excess of marginal cost to cover the full amount of the lease.

Producer surplus in the short-run sense: Even at the sustainable price, the accumulation of price over marginal costs for any level of output is surplus in the short-run sense. This means that since fixed costs already have been incurred, the firm is willing to supply the product according to its marginal cost curve; hence, any excess is surplus in this limited sense.

Can true producer surplus arise in a longer-run sense? The answer is yes *if* underlying input prices increase with the level of market demand. In my previous discussions of equilibrium, I implicitly assumed that underlying input prices are invariant to the level of demand. But what if the condition is not satisfied? For example, suppose that one of the inputs in some product is nickel. Then as demand for the product increases, the demand for nickel also increases, causing its price to rise. *If the supply of inputs to an industry is increasing in price, then there is a separate sustainable price for every level of demand.* This condition provides the basis for having both a zero-profits condition *and* long-run surplus.

B. THE CONCEPT OF "RENT"

Consider the market for litigation services. Law firms want to maximize the return on their investments. Lawyers are an important input into the production of these services. It is likely that the supply of lawyers to this market is upsloping.

Some individuals thrive on the aggravation, long hours, deadlines, travel, arguing, and the overall anxiety that is part of the litigation market. These lawyers are willing to provide such services for a relatively low salary. They love this job. Indeed, there may be a few lawyers willing to do litigation work for free.

Presumably, this kind of person is not typical. More lawyers are willing to tolerate the rigors of the job vis-à-vis other alternatives availed to lawyers. Some might demand $100 to provide these services, others $200 and so on. Thus, a rising supply schedule reflects the underlying differences in lawyers' willingness to tolerate the requirements of litigation work. To provide a concrete example, I assume a particular supply curve of lawyers.

Assumption about the supply of lawyers:

$$L^s = 10W$$

For every $10 increase in wage, the supply of litigation lawyers increases by 100.

Figure 3-7 depicts this supply curve. To attract 1,000 lawyers to litigation work requires a wage of $100 per period. To attract 2,000 lawyers requires a $200 wage.

The demand for litigation lawyers derives from the market for litigation services. Suppose that the law firm needs to use 1 lawyer to produce 1 unit of litigation service. Then I can rewrite the marginal cost curve as a function of the wage.

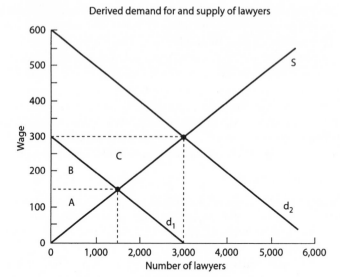

Figure 3-7. Market for Litigation Lawyers

The assumed marginal cost curve as a function of wage:

$$MC = W + 5q$$

This function says that the marginal cost curve for litigation services rises vertically with increases in the wage rate for litigation lawyers.

Assumption: 1 unit of legal time produces 1 unit of litigation services.

Notice that if the wage is $150, then the marginal cost to the law firm that produces 20 units of litigation services is $250, which is exactly the price I depicted in figure 3-6. Since we now need to worry about the wage changing at different output levels, however, it is useful to show how the equilibrium wage for lawyers is determined.

It turns out naturally enough that the demand for litigation lawyers is tied directly to the demand for litigation services. To derive the law firm's demand for lawyers, suppose that consumers are willing to pay some price P per unit of litigation services. We know that if the law firm operates at minimum total average cost (which it will do in equilibrium), it faces a marginal cost from nonlawyer inputs of $100 (that is, optimum output is 20 units; hence $5q = \$5 \times 20 = \$100$). This means that the maximum wage that the law firm is willing to pay for a lawyer's time to perform the marginal unit is $P - \$100$.

For example, if consumers are willing to pay $400 for the next unit of service, then the firm is willing to pay as much as $300 for the lawyer's time required to perform this service. If consumers are willing to pay $250 for the next unit of service, then the law firm is willing to pay up to $150 to the lawyer for her time, and so on. *That is, to derive the demand curve for lawyers in our problem, simply subtract $100 vertically from the demand curve for litigation services.*

I show the derived demand as d_1 in figure 3-7 (which is the demand curve for litigation services D_1 in figure 3-6, reduced vertically by $100

Economic rent: The excess of price paid to some input over the price at which it is willingly supplied. In the case of litigation lawyers, area A measures the excess of the market-clearing wage, W_0, over the wage at which these lawyers are willing to work.

Normally, the term *rent* is used to describe surplus in an input market, and *producer surplus* is used to describe surplus in a final market. But often, the terms are used interchangeably. The concept of rent has a permanence to it, in the sense that it is consistent with long-run equilibrium.

---

at every quantity level). Note that the market is in equilibrium when 1,500 lawyers do litigation work earning a wage of $150. The last lawyer hired in equilibrium requires wage $150, but this wage seems high from the perspective of a lawyer farther down on the supply curve. What the marginal lawyer views as barely a sufficient salary to do the job, the *inframarginal* lawyers view a significant portion of the salary as "gravy." Economists call this surplus "rent" in the context of input markets. Rent at wage $150 is shown as area A in figure 3-7.

I have drawn d_1 in such a way that $150 is the market-clearing wage, which is consistent with the $150 intercept on the marginal cost curve I used earlier; that is, when the wage is $150 then the marginal cost of producing litigation services is described by the marginal cost curve in figure 3-6. *In that figure, I implicitly assumed that a horizontal line at $150 described the supply of lawyers over the relevant range.* If the supply is upsloping, however, an increase in the demand for litigation lawyers increases the wage. This means that the sustainable price in the litigation market is higher at the higher level of demand.

C. THE DYNAMICS OF AN INCREASE IN RENT

Suppose that a new law is passed repealing previously imposed damage limits in civil suits. This immediately increases the demand for litigation services (because claimants have a much bigger potential gain from favorable judgments). To be concrete, suppose that the increase in demand is such that at every quantity level, clients are willing to pay $300 more per unit of litigation service. This means that the demand for litigation lawyers also increases by $300, which I depict by schedule d_2 in figure 3-7. In the new equilibrium, more lawyers work in the litigation market at a higher wage.[61] The new market-clearing wage is $300, which is $150 higher than the wage in the old equilibrium.

Areas $B + C$ depict the increase in economic rent to lawyers in the new equilibrium. Lawyers who are attracted to the work on the margin view $300 as the lowest wage they are willing to accept. Meanwhile, the inframarginal lawyers view some portion of this wage as largesse, particularly those on the lowest portion of the supply curve.

Question: Why do firms pay *all* workers the marginal price? Why don't they just pay the *marginal* worker $300 and pay all the previously employed workers $150?[62]

D. PORTRAYING THE SOLUTION IN THE MARKET
FOR LITIGATION SERVICES

How does the increase in demand show itself in the market for litigation services? I portray this market in figure 3-8. The original demand for litigation services is depicted by D_1. The original supply curve is shown as S_1. The old equilibrium price is $250 per unit of service ($150 goes to the lawyer and $100 covers the other per-unit costs). This price is sus-

---

[61]To obtain the solution, write the marginal cost curve for each firm, $MC = W + 5q$. Next, recognize that the way I have set up the problem, the optimum output for each firm in equilibrium is independent of the wage (see note 51, where you can see that the quantity at which MC intersects ATC is independent of the intercept in the MC curve). We know that this output is 20 for each firm. In equilibrium, all firms operate at 20 units; the marginal cost of the 20th unit of output in each firm for nonlitigation lawyers is $100 (equal to $5 times 20). The derived demand for lawyers equals the demand price in the final market minus nonlitigation-lawyer expenses: $W^d = a - bQ - \$100$. The supply wage by assumption is $W_s = .1Q$. The demand curve D_2 in figure 3-8 is described by the following schedule $P^d = 700 - .1Q$, which means that $a = 700$ and $b = .1$; thus, the derived demand for lawyers is $W^d = 700 - .1Q - \$100$. To depict the new equilibrium wage for lawyers, set $W^s = W^d$ and make these substitutions to obtain $.1Q = 700 - .1Q - 100$, which yields the equilibrium quantity and wage for lawyers: $Q = 3,000$ and $W = \$300$.

[62]Because if new workers must be paid $300, existing workers will quit to become "new" workers that someone else is trying to hire. The promise of these quits means that firms must increase the wage for all their lawyers. This adjustment does not occur instantly but over some period as it becomes apparent that the market wage has increased. If there were only one law firm, then we might get a different answer. But I am dealing with a competitive market, and so no firm has any control on setting wages.

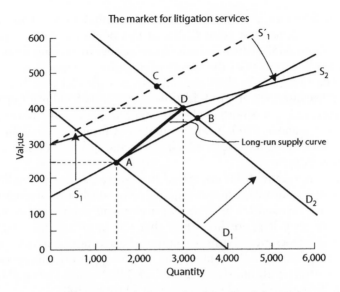

Figure 3-8. Long-run Supply Curve when Input Supply Increases

tainable at this level of demand, meaning that there is no incentive to either enter or exit the industry.

The schedule D_2 represents the new level of demand for these services. It is the same as the demand curve for lawyers' services except it is $100 higher at every level of quantity. It is a bit more difficult to derive the new supply curve, which I show as S_2 in the figure. Why does it not just "fan out" from $150 on the vertical axis as in figure 3-6? Why does it also increase vertically? The answer is that in addition to more law firms entering (which is what causes the supply curve to fan out), the wage paid to lawyers also increases.

From the perspective of law firms, the higher wage is viewed simply as an increase in an input price. As such, the marginal cost of providing litigation services is now higher. Indeed, at wage $300, the marginal cost curve shifts upward by $150 at every output level. Owing to this vertical shift, the market supply curve of litigation services also must shift vertically by this same amount. I show this as the supply curve labeled S'_1.

It might be easier to understand if I make believe that the new equilibrium is determined in a series of steps (even though the dynamics are not quite this simple). Point A denotes original equilibrium. Demand increases, which encourages all existing law firms to expand output along the old supply curve S_1, creating more output and a higher price, denoted by point B. But as firms try to move from A to B, their collective call for more lawyers increases wages, which in turn causes the supply curve of litigation services to increase (vertically) to S'_1. This supply curve equals demand at point C. But at this point, the market-clearing price is about $450, which awards excess profits to existing firms. This invites entry. Entry causes the supply of litigation services S'_1 to increase to S_2. The supply curve does not increase in a parallel way, but rather fans out because each unit of litigation service costs $300 just to pay for the lawyer, and so it is not possible to offer any services at a lower price. At any price above $300, a larger number of firms (including new entrants) react to higher prices, which swells the quantity of services offered at each price.

You cannot know from inspection that S_2 represents the equilibrium number of law firms because it requires some algebra to determine the point where demand for litigation services equals supply and economic profits are zero. It is not important that you work out the particular numbers that describe the new solution. I have done this for you. It turns out that in the new equilibrium, 150 law firms offer litigation services (each offers 20 units), for a total of 3,000 units. The equilibrium price for litigation services increases from $250 to $400.

The important point to grasp is simply put: An increase in demand for litigation services translates to more resources and more firms in the industry. But when the supply of inputs to the industry is upsloping (like nickel or litigation lawyers), an increase in demand results in an increase in equilibrium price.

THE MAGIC OF THE MARKET: PART 2

Think about the scenario I just described. As a result of a change in law, thousands of individuals now attach more value to litigation services. The amalgamation of these decisions increases market demand, which in turn increases price.

The price increase serves several functions. First, it rations the available services to those who attach most value to obtaining them. Second, it provides an incentive for existing firms to increase the quantity of services supplied (they can profitably ride farther up their marginal cost curve). Third, it signals a change in profitability to the industry, which ultimately leads to entry. The entry of new firms increases the supply of services, which works to reduce price until it reaches its new long-term equilibrium.

The reason that more law firms and more lawyers come to the litigation industry is not because someone directed them to offer more services. Consumers in the aggregate effectively "called" them via the

continued . . .

THE MAGIC OF THE MARKET: PART 2 *Continued*

price system. Each consumer is pursing his interests—the new law permits consumers to obtain more damage awards, which they pursue for selfish (but honorable!) motives. Each law firm enters not to help out consumers (though they will end up helping them out) but because they are greedy (with a small *g* of course). More lawyers enter litigation work not because they want to do charitable work (though they undoubtedly give monies to charities) but because litigation firms are offering them wages that promise to give them more rent than they receive in their current job.

Even though everyone acts in their own self-interest, the end result is that more resources have moved to an industry at the behest of consumers. In the new equilibrium, consumers obtain their desired services at the lowest possible price consistent with a competitive rate of return. It is as though a whole bunch of lawyers and resources came to help out consumers by providing them services at what seems like a bargain price, while as the same time consumers seemingly act as though they are helping out lawyers by paying them more rent. Is that cool or what?

E. THE LONG-RUN SUPPLY CURVE

The long-run supply price is a schedule that shows the combination of quantity supplied and sustainable prices at each quantity level. In figure 3-8, I show this schedule as the upward-sloping bold line connecting points *A* and *D*. Hence, in contrast to the "constant cost industry" described in figure 3-6, the market in figure 3-8 is an "increasing supply industry."

Figure 3-9 shows how the market equilibrium corresponds with the firm level outcome. Panel (*b*) is a reproduction of figure 3-8 except that I portray only the long-run supply curve over the relevant range. Area *I* depicts the higher rent collected by lawyers at the new level of demand. It is equivalent to areas *B* + *C* in figure 3-7.

Panel (*a*) reflects the new higher cost curves facing law firms, given the now-higher salary level for lawyers. The cost curves shift upward from MC_1 and ATC_1 to MC_2 and ATC_2. The sustainable price increases from $250 to $400.[63] It is evident that producer surplus is consistent with zero-profits equilibrium.

Figure 3-10 gives a comprehensive final look at the new equilibrium. Panel (*a*) shows the input market for lawyers, panel (*b*) shows equilibrium

---

[63]Note that the optimal output in each law firm is 20 units. This could change depending on how underlying input prices change in the industry, but this is not an important detail for our purposes.

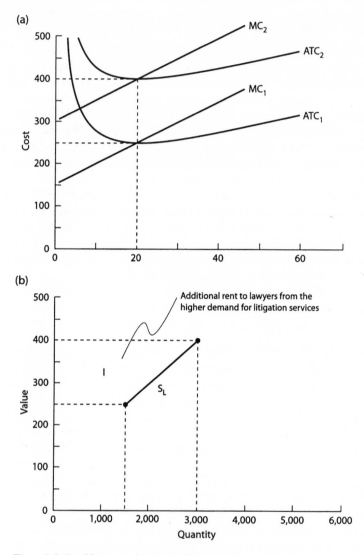

Figure 3-9. Equilibrium in the Market Following Increase in Demand

for one law firm, and panel (c) shows the market demand, long-run market supply, and short-run supply in the market for litigation services (the latter is the dashed line).

At the higher level of demand, the market-clearing price for litigation services is $400, which corresponds to 3,000 units of output. Each firm earns zero profits (panel [b]), but litigation lawyers collect rent denoted

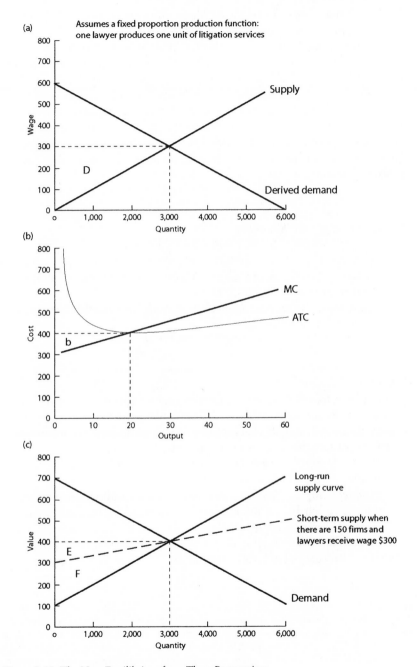

Figure 3-10. The New Equilibrium from Three Perspectives

by area D (panel [a]). In panel (c), these rents are shown by the sum of areas $E + F$, which we often call producer surplus.

The upsloping dashed line in this panel also shows the short-run supply curve for 150 firms assuming a $300 wage. It is the horizontal sum of the 150 identical marginal cost curves, like the one shown in panel (b). Area E in panel (c) denotes total fixed costs collected by 150 firms; that is, area E equals area b in panel (b), times 150. Be careful, however, not to double count these costs. Normally, the short-run supply curve is not superimposed on a chart with long-run supply. The area under the latter schedule includes all resource costs, including fixed costs, as the following accounting table shows.

Accounting for the Revenues

Lawyers' wages	$ 900,000	$450,000 is rent
Fixed costs	$ 150,000	$1,000 per firm times 150 firms
Nonlawyer costs	$ 150,000	$1,000 per firm times 150 firms[64]
Total revenues	**$1,200,000**	

Remember: Costs are defined to include the market return on investment with similar risks.

Review of Terms

Multiple sustainable prices in a long-run sense: Given a demand curve, there is a unique sustainable price that equates the forces for exit and entry in an industry. If the supply price of some input is upsloping, then the sustainable price is higher at a higher level of demand.

Long-run supply curve: Describes a schedule of sustainable prices consistent with every possible level of demand.

Producer surplus in a long-run sense: The area above the long-run supply curve but below price. It is rent collected by inputs that have an upward-sloping supply schedule.

Increasing cost industry: One for which the sustainable price increases with successive levels of demand.

continued . . .

---

[64]Remember that the *marginal* cost per unit of litigation services for nonlawyer time is described by $5q$. This means that the first unit of output costs $5, the second $10, and so on until the 20th, which costs $100. Adding up these numbers comes to $1,000 for 20 units. Each firm operates at 20 units in equilibrium. (Note: I integrated this function, which gives an exact number; if you add up the increments over 20 units, your answer will be slightly different.)

> *Continued*
> *Constant cost industry:* One for which the sustainable price is unique regardless of the level of demand. Sometimes you will hear the phrase "assume constant cost over the relevant range." This means that we want to abstract from the second-order consideration of a different sustainable price within some problem we are studying.

V. Bringing It All Together: Reconsidering a Tax on One Good

We can bring together many of the concepts we have learned by evaluating the implications of an excise tax on one good. We already solved this problem in chapter 2, but it turns out to be more interesting now because we know something about how supply curves are developed. To simplify the analysis, I assume that the long-run supply curve in this industry is constant over the relevant range.[65]

A. SHORT-RUN IMPACT OF THE TAX

Consider figure 3-11. Price and output P_0 and Q_0 depict equilibrium in this market prior to the imposition of a tax. I assume that at this price, there is an incentive for neither entry nor exit (it is the sustainable price).

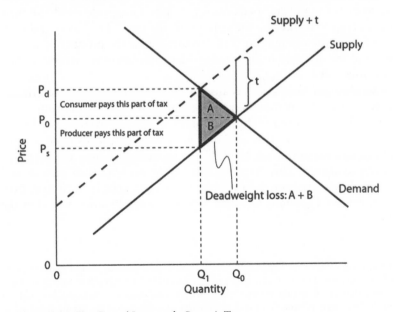

Figure 3-11. First Round Impact of a Per-unit Tax

[65]I also assume that the demand elasticity is the same in the short and long run.

The government decides to attach a tax in the amount t per unit of output, payable by the producer. (It does not matter whether the tax is assessed against the consumer or producer; the same outcome results.)

Each firm views its marginal cost curve as higher by the amount of the tax, t, and thus, its *gross-of-tax* supply schedule increases vertically by exactly the amount of the tax. The market supply schedule gross-of-tax also increases vertically by the amount t, as shown in the figure. If the demand curve were perfectly inelastic in the relevant range (that is, it was vertical), consumers would pay the tax and there would be no change in output. The analysis would be complete. As long as the demand curve is downsloping, however, quantity demanded is lower at the new price, which triggers a series of adjustments in the market.

It is apparent from inspection that the tax causes the price paid by consumers, say P_d, to increase from its previous equilibrium. Thus, quantity demanded decreases from Q_0 to Q_1. Also note that the price net of the tax, which is the only price that suppliers care about, falls from P_0 to P_s. The difference between the price that consumers pay for the product and the price collected by suppliers is the amount of the tax, t, which goes to the government.

In effect, even though producers try to pass along the tax, consumers are not willing to purchase the same quantity at the higher price. In effect, from the suppliers' perspective, it is as though demand for their product fell (vertically) by the amount of the tax.[66] Producers and consumers share the tax burden. Tax revenue equals the product of the tax rate t and the quantity of the product that consumers are willing to buy at the now-higher price, Q_1.

A deadweight loss arises because at the distorted price caused by the tax, consumers act as though it is more costly for society to produce the product than it really is. Thus, the units of output from Q_0 to Q_1 no longer are produced. This outcome is unfortunate because over this range, consumers attach a higher value to each unit than the marginal cost of production. This "triangle loss" is the area between the demand and supply curves over the range of the output that is no longer produced, namely Q_0 minus Q_1. This loss is denoted by area $A + B$ in the figure.

---

[66] This is what would have happened if the tax t had been assessed against consumers instead of producers. That is, if consumers were required to send a check to the government each time they purchased the product, then their demand curve for the product would fall vertically by exactly t. Note that the demand curve would intersect the supply curve at exactly price P_s because, by construction, the net and gross of tax supply schedules are separated (vertically) by the distance t. Either way, the price paid by consumers and the price received by suppliers are the same.

Short-run impact of a tax on good x: Quantity demanded falls, price paid by the consumer increases; price received by producers falls; the government collects tax revenue equal to the tax rate times the quantity demanded at the new price; consumer and producer surplus fall by more than the amount of tax revenue, thereby creating a deadweight loss.

B. LONG-RUN IMPACT OF THE TAX

The unresolved problem from figure 3-11 should be apparent. If price P_0 was the sustainable price for producers prior to the imposition of the tax, then on the assumption that this is a constant cost industry, price P_s collected by suppliers after the imposition of the tax must be less than the sustainable price. In terms of figure 3-5, the price no longer is coincident with the output level characterized by marginal cost equal to average total cost, but instead is akin to some price like $200, which is less than *ATC*. Thus, we know that exit will occur in this industry.

As exit occurs, you can envision the process as follows. Imagine that the two supply schedules, with and without the tax, are permanently tied together by vertical segments of length t. Thus, as one of these supply curves moves, they both must move together and always remain separated by the vertical distance t.

To determine the final equilibrium, slide these schedules as a unit to the left until the supply price inclusive of the tax (the upper supply curve) intersects the demand curve at price $P_0 + t$. At this point, since the vertical distance between the two supply curves always is t, then the supply price received by producers must be exactly P_0. We know that in the long run producers must receive this price because it is the unique sustainable price in this industry.

I show this equilibrium in figure 3-12. The figure shows the new short-run net-of-tax and gross-of-tax supply schedules in the new equilibrium (labeled S_1 and $S_1 + t$). The long-run supply curve is the dark black solid line that connects the old and new output levels in this industry at

Long-run impact of a tax on good x: If a unit tax is imposed on some product: price paid by the consumer increases by the full amount of the tax; quantity demanded falls by more than in the short run; price received by producers is the same as before the tax was imposed; government revenue is smaller in the long versus short run; and fewer firms exist (and fewer workers are employed).

Assumption: Constant cost industry.

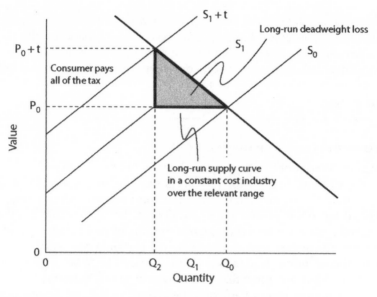

Figure 3-12. Second Round Impact of a Per-unit Tax

price P_0. The long-run deadweight loss is the shaded area under the demand curve but above the long-run supply curve. Consumers now pay the full tax. Producers absorb none of the burden. The output effect is

---

EXERCISE I:

Suppose that the demand curve for some product is described by $Q^d = 10 - P^d$ and that the short-term market supply curve is described by $P^s = Q^s$. Find the price and quantity that characterize this market. Now suppose the government attaches a tax of \$2 per unit. Describe the short- and long-run effects on quantity, prices; calculate tax revenue and deadweight losses in the short and long run. Solve using graph paper or by using algebra.[67]

continued . . .

---

[67]If you solve this problem using graph paper, you will discover the same answers as I give later. Using algebra, solve for price in terms of quantity for both supply and demand, set them equal, and obtain equilibrium price, then plug into the demand curve to find quantity ($P = \$5$, $Q = 5$). Repeat the exercise, except this time set supply price $P = Q + t$, where $t = 2$. The solution is $P^d = \$6$; $P^s = 4$; $Q = 4$; $TR = \$8$; $DW = \$1$. In the long run, you know that the supply price must be \$5 and thus demand price must be \$7. Thus, quantity demanded is 3 units. The solution is: $P^d = \$7$; $P^s = 5$; $Q = 3$; $TR = \$6$; $DW = \$2$.

EXERCISES *Continued*
EXERCISE 2:
Suppose that instead of assessing a tax to this product, the government pays a subsidy to producers in the amount T for each unit of product that they produce. Show how figures 3-11 and 3-12 would look in this case. Solve the problem using the demand and supply curves in exercise 1.[68]
For both exercises assume a constant cost industry.

larger in the long run than the short run because the long-run price to consumers is higher by the full amount of the tax.

VI. A Few Miscellaneous Cost Issues

We have covered lots of ground in this chapter, and I have introduced most of the cost concepts that you will encounter elsewhere in the book, but a few issues remain that should be clarified sooner rather than later. These issues include *sunk cost*, *opportunity cost*, and *transactions cost*.

A. SUNK COST

We have already had an introduction to the notion of sunk cost, also known as past cost. Once a firm makes a fixed investment, the only rele-

Ex ante: Refers to the period prior to a decision to commit to an action; ex post refers to the period after a commitment has been made. Ex post decisions usually are constrained by ex ante decisions that limit choice after the fact. Both kinds of decisions consider all the options still available, but ex post options are fewer than ex ante options.
Sunk costs: Used interchangeably with "past cost," sunk costs are those incurred regardless of a decision that must be made prospectively. Decisions prior to incurring any costs take into account all costs, including fixed costs. After an irrevocable commitment has been made to incur expenses, they are no longer relevant to future decisions.

[68]The answer is provided in the appendix to the chapter.

vant decision is to select a level of output where *marginal* cost equals price, independent of any cost incurred in the past. Ex ante, a firm would not have incurred a fixed cost of entry unless it expected to earn a competitive rate of return. Ex post, however, the only relevant decision is to do the best it can, given its current circumstances. Even if it is a foregone conclusion that, in hindsight, it made a poor decision ex ante, it still can salvage some gain by producing at a level where marginal cost equals price.

The key principle to remember is simply put: *once a commitment has been made to incur a fixed cost, it becomes an irrelevancy to any decision to move forward from that point.* A few illustrations will help illustrate this point, which sometimes can take a subtle form.

Everyday reminders to forget about past costs:
  Don't cry over spilled milk.
  You can't turn back the clock.
  We already crossed that bridge.
  We just passed the point of no return.
  Cut your losses.
  What's done is done.

---

1. A Trip to See the Empire State Building

Suppose that you live in Washington, D.C. Tomorrow you are moving to Paris and may never be on the East Coast again. Your flight tomorrow is sufficiently late in the day so that it does not factor into figuring out the problem that follows. You want to see the Empire State Building (ESB) in New York City. You think about going to New York today to accomplish that goal. It will take you four hours to make the drive. Assume that gas is free and that there are no other costs of driving. This limits the cost of the trip to the value of your time. You can sell your time for $50 per hour, and so the drive will cost you $400 both ways. The total value to you of seeing the ESB is $500, and so you anticipate $100 of surplus. Ex ante, the optimal decision is, "Go."

Once you get within sight of the city, however, you encounter a tremendous traffic jam; the radio station announces that normal rules have been suspended to allow drivers to take a U-turn on U.S. 95. If you do this, assume that there is no other way to get to New York. Otherwise, you can wait until the jam dissipates, which, according to the radio broadcast, will take exactly seven hours. What is your decision and how do you arrive at your answer?

Decision: Wait in Traffic to See the Empire State Building or Make a U-turn?

Choose one of the following options as your answer:

Option 1: Turn back because you already spent four hours getting here, and if you spend another seven hours, that means eleven hours up and four hours to return, and so surplus is negative (15 hours times $50 is $750, but you only valued seeing the ESB as $500). (Hint: This is not a good answer.)

Option 2: Turn back, not because you have to incorporate the four-hour return trip in your decision making, since you have to incur that expense regardless of whether or not you continue on to see the ESB. (Hint: This sounds like sound reasoning.) *But* since you already spent four hours to get here, once you add the seven additional hours to get to the ESB, you will have spent eleven hours getting here, which by itself swamps the $500 value you attached to seeing the ESB. (Hint: Everything said after the word *But* is wrong.)

Option 3: Wait the seven hours because you already incurred the four-hour drive to get here and so if you return now, you will have wasted those four hours. (Hint: Correct decision, wrong reason.)

Option 4: Wait the seven hours. The time you spent getting here has already been incurred. At this point, the only relevancy is the marginal cost of getting to your destination compared to the value of getting there. Since you attach a $50 cost to your time, then the cost of getting to the ESB is $350 as compared to the $500 value you attach to seeing it. The return trip of four hours will be incurred whether or not you see the ESB, and thus it is an irrelevancy to the decision to take the U-turn or wait. (Hint: 🔔 ☺ ☼.)

Put yourself back in the position before you hear the first radio announcement. You say to yourself, "If the radio announcer says the wait time is any more than x hours, I turn back." What is the value of x?[69]

Options:
(a) 7
(b) 8
(c) 9
(☺) 10
(e) 12

[69] You are willing to wait no more than ten hours because prospectively, it costs $\$50 \times 10 = \$500$ to see the ESB, which is worth only $500 to see.

OH NO! ANOTHER RADIO ANNOUNCEMENT!

Suppose after waiting four hours in the traffic jam, you hear another radio announcement. This time the announcer says she was wrong before: now it will take twelve hours to clear the jam, and she is positively sure that twelve hours is the exact wait time. Now you have invested a total of eight hours getting to where you are, plus you have the four-hour return trip. This is twelve hours. Surely you are not going to waste this investment by turning back now! Are you?

Answer: You will if you are rational. Cut your losses and make the U-turn. These twelve hours are now an irrelevancy. You incur these costs regardless of whether or not you see the ESB. You now know, however, that it will take twelve incremental hours to see the ESB, which, at a cost of $50 per hour, means that the marginal cost of seeing the ESB is $600. You attach a value of $500 to seeing the ESB. Turn back.

Another question: Suppose you make the U-turn and get back to Washington that night. On your recorder, you find a message from Air France saying that your flight to Paris has been postponed for twenty-four hours. You still value seeing the ESB at $500. Do you go see the ESB today? Assume that there is a zero chance of encountering any traffic jams today.

Option 1: No! You've already sunk twelve hours into this project ($600 of wasted time), and so you have a negative $100 surplus on this idea so far. To invest another $400 into this project sinks you further in the hole. (Hint: Wrong answer.)

Option 2: No, because if you had had all this information ahead of time, including all the time you wasted yesterday, you would never have gone to New York; hence, you can make the decision today that you should have made yesterday. (Hint: Does the phrase *You already crossed that bridge* mean anything to you? How about *Today is another day*? No? How about *You can't turn back the clock*?) (Extra hint: The decision and the reasoning are completely wrong!)

Option 3: Yes. What happened yesterday is an irrelevancy today. Prospectively, it pays to expend $400 in costs to obtain $500 in surplus. Don't cry over spilled milk.

Another twist: Put yourself back in the traffic jam yesterday, but suppose I change the problem to say that you are not leaving the East Coast tomorrow or anytime soon. So, you could decide to drive to New York on another day to see the ESB. How does this change your decision to make a U-turn? Put yourself back in the traffic jam, before you heard the first radio announcement. Assume that the traffic jam that you hit today is a once-in-a-lifetime happening. There is no chance of encountering another traffic jam on any other day. How does this change your calculus about turning back?

Answer: Instead of viewing the benefits of staying in line at $500, you attach a benefit of $400. Why? Because on another day, you can get to New York and back at a cost of $400. Hence, assuming that you can rely on the radio announcer's wait time estimate, it is irrational to remain in the traffic jam more than eight hours, even though you attach a value of $500 to seeing the ESB.

2. Accepting a Case

Suppose that as a partner in a law firm, you are presented with a case involving Ms. Jones. The standard remuneration for the law firm is one-third of any judgment that it wins for a client. The damage claim is $1 million of which your firm expects $333,333. You and your partners assess the likelihood of winning the case as 75 percent, and so your expected revenue is 75 percent times $333,333, or $250,000. You know that it will take a fixed investment of $100,000 to collect all the facts of the case, and then it will take $10,000 worth of time per month until resolution. Assume that the court date is set for ten months from now. A short trial is expected, after which you are assured of an immediate verdict and no further expenses.

Suppose that your estimate of expenses includes the competitive rate of return on all the investments in the firm, and thus, any case with a "profit" is one with extraordinary return for the firm. Suppose that currently your firm is accepting all cases with a positive "profit." Ex ante, it is a sound decision to take the case. After paying all salaries including your own and all other costs, you expect to earn a profit for the firm equal to $50,000 ($250,000 expected revenue minus $100,000 fixed costs minus $10,000 times 10 months). So you accept the case and incur the $100,000 up-front cost. Soon thereafter, a court in this jurisdiction decides a similar case in favor of the defendant, which is bad news since you are representing a plaintiff in a similar case. You now assess your chances of winning the Jones case at 40 percent.

Question: Do you continue the case?

Option 1: Abandon the case because the expected revenue to the firm now is only $133,333. In addition to the $100,000 fixed cost that you incurred, you need to incur another $100,000 in monthly bills prior to decision, which means that you expect to book a loss of $67,000 on the case. (Hint: The fact that you spent the $100,000 is not relevant to the decision. These monies are spent regardless of whether you continue the case.)

Option 2: Continue with the case because even though expected revenues are only $133,333, this exceeds the additional expenses of $100,000 that you need to incur in order to obtain a verdict. (Hint: this option is correct.)

Another reestimate: Suppose you decide to continue the case. After incurring monthly costs for six months plus the fixed costs, you hear about a verdict in yet another related case, and so now, you and your partners estimate the probability of success at only 10 percent. Should you continue with the case?

Answer: No, because four additional months of expenses until your court date amount to $40,000. Your expected revenues are only $33,333; hence, it pays to abandon the case, even though you already have spent $160,000. The reason is that these expenses are sunk—that is, they are incurred regardless of your decision. The question is whether you are engaged in an action where you expect to lose *another* $6,667.

A rational decision depends on future costs under your control against the expected gain from continuing. Past costs are irrelevant. Drop the case.

B. OPPORTUNITY COST

Sometimes there is a tendency to speak about "costs" as out-of-pocket expenditures. Thus, the cost of attending a baseball game is the ticket cost plus the costs of transportation and parking. But a broader way of thinking about the problem is to consider "opportunity cost." The cost of going to the ball game is that you did not spend your money and time engaging in the next best thing you could have done.

For example, suppose that you were thinking about going either to the Orioles versus Red Sox baseball game to see Roger Clantinio pitch, or to the Kennedy Center to see Luchenzo Vincenti perform in the opera *La Socia*. Both are in town only tonight. Suppose ticket prices are zero at the Kennedy Center and Orioles game, transportation is free, and your employer pays you your full hourly pay for the time spent at either of these two events. Is there a cost to going to either event? Or is it free? The answers are yes and no, in that order.

The opportunity cost of going to see Clantinio is that you did not see Vincenti. If you went to see Vincenti, then the opportunity cost is that you did not see Clantinio.

A *basic tenet of economics*: It is never free, even when it's free.

The cost of going out with John is that you do not go out with Tony. The opportunity cost of going out with Tony is that you did not go out with John. The cost of studying is that you do not have a good time at the party tonight; the cost of going to the party is that you do not study, and so on. Among competing alternatives, we choose our best alternative, which means that we maximize our surplus. But every time we make a choice, it comes at the expense of either not purchasing or not doing something else.

Opportunity cost: The value of the next best use of time and money used in the activity we choose or the product we purchase.

Suppose that we return to the Jones case considered earlier. Consider the situation after the law firm discovers that the probability of earning $333,333 in fees is 40 percent. Expected revenue is $133,333. Costs over the ensuing ten months will be $100,000, which comprises legal time employed in the firm. Hence, the firm expects a $33,000 net profit from continuing the case. But what if, at the time this case is being reconsidered, another partner announces that he is about to reject a new case involving Mr. Smith because there are no available lawyers in the firm right now. The alternative case generates expected revenues of $200,000. Total costs of pursuing that case are $100,000: in other words, by deploying the existing lawyers from the Jones case to the Smith case, the firm would expect a profit of $100,000, which is $67,000 more than they expect to earn by continuing the Jones case.

Under these circumstances the opportunity cost of legal time devoted to Jones is not only their $100,000 salary payments but also the $67,000 in additional expected profit that they forgo by not accepting the Smith case. That is, the cost of pursuing the Jones case is that they do not pursue the Smith case. If they pursue the Jones case, then the **opportunity cost** of the lawyers' time is really $167,000, which exceeds expected revenues. Thus, it pays for the firm to pursue Smith and drop Jones.

C. TRANSACTIONS COST

It is also worth introducing the concept of transactions cost. In truth, transactions costs are ill defined in the literature and often are clear only in context. I will offer a working definition of these costs in chapter 7 when they take on more significance. For now, a heuristic treatment will do. Think of transactions costs as those that are incidental to a good or service from which one derives utility. Bill lives in Washington, D.C. He likes baseball games. He is willing and able to pay $100 to see an Orioles game in Baltimore. The cost of the ticket is $40. The ticket cost embodies the cost of providing this service to whoever wants to attend. Think of this cost as *production cost*. It is the resource cost required to create a good or service that gives rise to utility.

Normally, production costs do not vary with the buyer's identity.[70] Transactions costs tend to be idiosyncratic to the buyer. Bill's brother, Dan, lives right near Camden Yards. He attaches the same value to the game as Bill. He realizes the full $60 surplus from attending the game. Bill will sit right near him and derives the same utility from the game but enjoys less surplus. The reason is that Bill needs to incur resources costs to put him in proximity to the game. Suppose that the value of his driving time, gas expense, parking, and so on amounts to $35. These are transactions costs. Unlike production costs, transactions costs do not increase the utility he enjoys from the game. They merely reduce his surplus, in this case from $60 to $25. Transactions costs explain the difference in surplus enjoyed by Bill and Dan.

In an informal sense, we can think of transactions costs as those that are ancillary to the exchange that gives rise to utility. They are real costs, just as real as the resource cost to produce any good or service. In the sense they are used in the economics literature, they almost always include transportation cost incurred by a consumer. Similarly, they almost always include the consumer's cost of acquiring information. Jane wants to purchase a black suit for interviews at the law school. She knows from prior experience that of the fifty clothing stores that carry suits and are within ten miles of her home, only ten have a suit in stock that provides a nice fit.

Jane is willing to pay $1,000 for a black suit that fits her well. The price of black suits is about $200 just about everywhere. This is the resource cost of acquiring the materials, cutting and assembling the suits, transporting them to Jane's proximity, and making them available in retail stores, where they await her inspection. Like most other shoppers, Jane sets out on her mission one Saturday (perhaps choosing a rainy one, so as to reduce the opportunity costs of the search).

---

[70]One exception is introduced in chapter 9 in the context of adverse selection. We can safely ignore this detail at this point in time.

If she knew which ten stores had the suits that fit her well, she would pick out the closest one, buy the suit, and be back home within the hour. Transactions costs would be minimal, say $25, and so she would realize $775 in surplus. Undoubtedly, most readers at this point are saying to themselves, "Yeah, right!" In reality, everyone knows from experience that it will likely take several stores, many locations, and a significant chunk of Jane's life before the right suit appears. These are all transactions costs. None increase the value to Jane of having the nice suit, once discovered; they merely erode consumer surplus. Suppose that the transactions cost in this case turn out to be as high as the production cost. She still gets $600 in surplus. In the absence of transactions cost, she would enjoy $800 in surplus.

Jane's quandary is rediscovered in every corner of every market. To find a suitable job in the labor market, job seekers engage in lots of search, and companies invest large amounts of resources to learn more about the attributes of applicants. In the absence of transactions costs, all job seekers know about all job opportunities without expending any time and effort. Employers know everything about candidates' skills and abilities without expending any resources.

Similarly, to buy a car we spend time searching for information, test-driving cars, evaluating trustworthy dealers, and so on. These costs are in addition to the cost of the car itself. When transactions costs are high, it is easy to imagine that we might end up with a different contractor, job, or car than we would in a world of zero transactions costs; yet, sometimes it is useful to make the simplifying assumption that these costs are zero to make it easier to understand some underlying market behavior.

Transactions costs: Those that are ancillary to a market transaction that gives rise to utility. Production costs give rise to a product or service that generates utility. Transactions costs do not increase utility but merely reduce consumer surplus.

These costs as they are commonly referred to include the time and out-of-pocket expenses incurred to accumulate and evaluate information and to effect the desired exchange. For simplicity, we often ignore these costs in many problems, but they can become important in some market settings. When an economist says, "I assume zero transactions costs," it can mean many things, but usually it conveys an attempt to abstract from many unspecified practical difficulties that substantially complicate the problem. As a practical matter, it means "I assume away any issues that make the problem more complicated than I intend for it to be." In chapter 7, we will need to give more thought to the meaning of this matter.

A Review of the Most Important Cost Concepts

Sustainable price. Given demand conditions in the industry, there is only one price that is free of forces to create entry or exit. At this price, firms earn a competitive return on investment, and consumers enjoy the maximum amount of surplus consistent with firms earning zero economic profits.

Long-run supply and producer surplus (rent). When demand increases in some industry, the new sustainable price may be different, and often will be higher, at higher levels of demand. In these "increasing cost industries" permanent surplus is created in a long-term sense (given some level of demand), which reflects underlying "economic rent" earned by inputs in the industry.

Mobility of capital and other inputs. Resources are directed toward or away from an industry according to whether it earns positive or negative economic profits.

The market reacts to interference to find a new equilibrium. The imposition of a tax has numerous short- and long-term impacts on an industry. As long as demand curves are downsloping, the imposition of a tax on a product causes quantity demanded to fall; and as long as (short-term) supply curves are upsloping, and we previously were at the sustainable price, the tax sets in motion a process of exit from the industry until a zero-profits condition once again is reestablished.

Past costs are an irrelevancy in a going forward sense. Decisions involving future choices depend only on factors still in your control. For example, once it incurs the obligation to pay its fixed costs, the firm's decision about what output level to produce depends only on the marginal cost of producing those units.

Appendix: Short- and Long-term Impact of a Subsidy

The impact of a subsidy operates just like a tax, except that it is a "negative tax." The short- and long-run impact of a subsidy in the amount *-t* is shown in panels (*a*) and (*b*) in figure 3-13.

Panel (*a*) shows the *short-run effect* of the subsidy. The subsidy vertically reduces the supply curve by the absolute amount *t*, but consumers experience only part of the subsidy in the short run. Part of the effect is felt in the form of higher prices to producers (consumers pay $4 and producers receive $6). Output expands by 1 unit. The deadweight loss now appears as the shaded triangle to the right of competitive equilibrium. Over this range of output, society is devoting resources valued above $5 to create output that consumers value by less than $5.

Panel (*b*) shows the *long-run effect*. The higher price to suppliers attracts entry, causing the supply curve to shift rightward. Since the problem assumes that this is a constant cost industry, then the long-run supply curve is horizontal at $5. The two short-term supply curves, connected by the vertical segments equal to the subsidy per unit, move to the right in tandem until the upper supply curve, which is the price received by suppliers, is $5. At this point, suppliers earn zero profits and output expands further by 2 units; consumers receive the entire benefit of the subsidy. The long-run deadweight loss is measured by the shaded triangle in figure 3-13 panel (*b*).

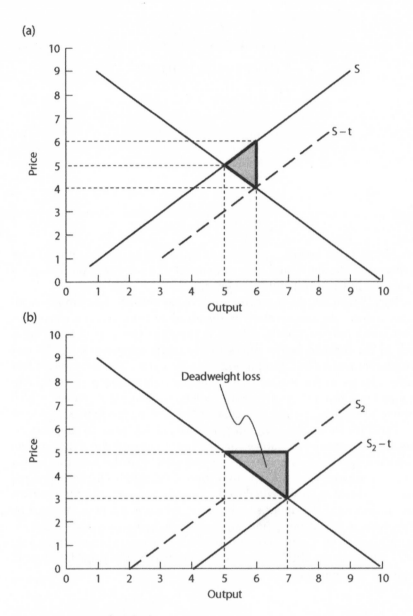

Figure 3-13. Impact of a Subsidy

Chapter 4

Using Demand and Supply Curves to Evaluate Policy

Main Economic Concepts	1. A simple model of supply and demand can help us evaluate many different economic questions.
	2. The imposition of maximum or minimum prices can impose large economic costs on society because they interfere with the ability of market participants to freely exchange with one another.
	3. When regulations prevent the market from attaining equilibrium price, then the highest-value users will find ways to squeeze low-value users from the market, usually resulting in larger social costs than first envisioned by "triangle" losses.
New Terms	1. Maximum price regulation
	2. Cost of queues
	3. Rent erosion
	4. Price supports
	5. Minimum wage
	6. Full price
	7. High-rent workers
	8. Low-rent workers
	9. Compensating differential

You now know how to derive market demand and supply, how to think about the idea of long-term sustainable price, and how to value the surplus that free trade confers. In this chapter, you will learn more about the "power of the market." Just like a river that wants to take the path of least resistance to the ocean, markets want to attain an equilibrium price and quantity. Rivers can be "trained" to attain different flows but only at great cost, and often unanticipated effects arise: building levees to block off all floodplains higher up on the Mississippi River, for example, increases the chances of flooding farther downstream and causes large amounts of fertile land to be dumped into the Gulf of Mexico. Similarly, in economics, attempts to interfere with the high-value users finding a way to squeeze low-value users from the market can be accomplished only at great expense and perhaps not at all in the long run.

I. Shifts in Demand and Supply Curves

It is useful as a first exercise to become more familiar with the price and quantity effects caused by shifts in demand and supply curves. When I refer to an "increase" in demand or supply, I refer to a horizontal or rightward shift, not a vertical or upward movement in these schedules, and similarly for decreases in demand or supply. The general question that I pose is: what happens to price and quantity in some market if we observe some combination of demand and supply increases or decreases? Figure 4-1 shows two possibilities.

Panel (a) shows a market in which demand decreases from D_1 to D_2 and, at the same time, the cost of production increases, causing a decrease in supply from S_1 to S_2. Consider for example the market for tax attorneys to answer everyday tax questions. The rise of specialized tax experts means that cheaper alternatives are now available to retail customers to obtain help on common tax problems. The new competition has resulted in a decrease in demand for tax lawyers in this market. At the same time, lawyer salaries have been increasing, owing to large increases in demand for litigation, regulatory, and other legal services. That is, the opportunity cost of tax attorneys has increased, meaning that the supply curve of tax attorneys has shifted to the left. These factors combine to unambiguously reduce the quantity of retail tax attorneys, but the effect on price is ambiguous: it depends on whether demand falls sufficiently in relation to supply.

Panel (b) shows a market in which the demand curve increases from D_1 to D_2 while the supply curve decreases from S_1 to S_2. This chart might depict developments in law schools over the past twenty years. Demand for a law school education has increased dramatically, but the cost of many inputs, notably law professors who have lucrative opportunities outside of law schools, has increased, which has the effect of reducing supply. This combination of factors exerts an unambiguous upward pressure on tuition. Whether the number of law students increases or decreases depends on whether demand increases sufficiently in relation to the decrease in supply. In the chart, I portray the realistic outcome that both the cost and number of law degrees has increased substantially.

Figure 4-2 provides a template that serves to organize your thinking about shifts in demand and supply curves. Starting equilibrium is given by point A. Every combination of demand and supply shifts results in a new equilibrium price and quantity in one of the four quadrants. When

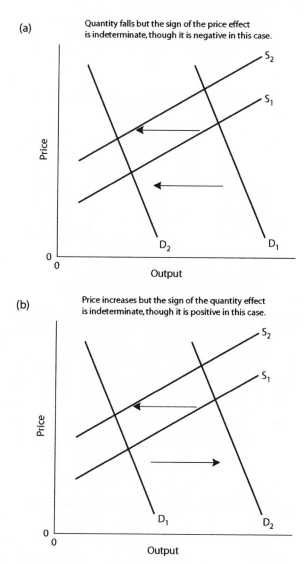

Figure 4-1. Effects of Shifts in Demand and Supply Schedules

only one curve shifts, the quadrant in which the new price-quantity combination lies is unambiguous. When both curves move, the new price-quantity combination in equilibrium could be in either of two quadrants. In these cases, the direction of change for either price or quantity is unambiguous, but the other effect is ambiguous.

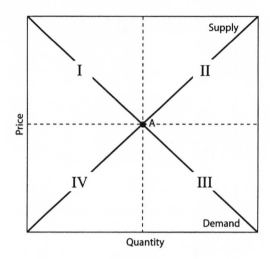

Figure 4-2. Quantity and Price Effects

TABLE 4-1(A). WHICH QUADRANT DO WE END UP IN?

	Supply		
Demand	Increase	Decrease	No Change
Increase	II or III	I or II	II
Decrease	III or IV	I or IV	IV
No Change	III	I	

TABLE 4-1(B). PRICE AND QUANTITY CHANGES FOR EACH QUADRANT

Quadrant	Price	Quantity
I	+	−
II	+	+
III	−	+
IV	−	−

Table 4-1, part (*a*), gives a matrix with all the possible combinations of demand and supply shifts, and which quadrants are possible outcomes. Part (*b*) provides a guide showing the price-quantity change that is affiliated with each quadrant.

EXERCISE 1:
Before studying the matrix in the table, create your own matrix and accompanying guide and see if you can properly fill in the cells.

EXERCISE 2:
What happens to price and quantity in the short run if (1) demand for cigarettes falls at the same time that the government attaches a per-unit tax paid by the suppliers? (2) demand for medical services increases at the same time that the government decides to subsidy units of medical care? (3) demand for housing in the District of Columbia increases at the same time that building costs increase?[71] Describe your answers in terms of the quadrants in figure 4-2.

II. Impact of a Maximum Price: The Case of Gasoline

The power of the market to allocate goods and services to the highest-value users is easy to take for granted. It is only when a governing authority interferes with these forces that their power is truly understood. Sometimes it is tempting for politicians to interfere when they think that price is "too high" and thus want to force the market to charge some lower price. There are no better examples than two instances in the 1970s, once under President Gerald Ford in 1974 and again under President Jimmy Carter in 1979, when each attempted to enforce a price of gasoline below the market-clearing level. For our purposes, it is not necessary to consider the underlying regulations in any detail.[72] Instead, I will concentrate on the salient features of these episodes and illustrate their main effects.

A. SETTING UP THE PROBLEM

Figure 4-3 shows the demand curve for gasoline in the United States, as well as the supply curve that prevails in the free market. The vertical axis represents price per gallon of gasoline; the horizontal axis represents millions of gallons of gasoline purchased each day. The supply schedule reflects the additional oil that can be pumped from existing oil wells in the

[71]The answers are (1) quadrant I or IV (2) II or III, and (3) I or II.
[72]In both cases, the genesis of the controls were actions in the international oil cartel to restrict world supply. Both presidents tried to control oil prices and, at the same time, tried to keep new supply prices unregulated for either "newly" discovered oil in the United States or imported oil. This led to all sorts of wasteful activity like exporting and then "importing" the same oil, labeling "old" oil, "new" oil, and so on. A full evaluation of the market distortions would take into account the wasteful activity that went into these activities. But I stick to the main impact of the regulations from the perspective of consumers.

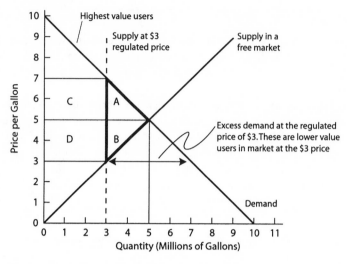

Figure 4-3. A Maximum Price: The Case of Gasoline

short run (it is the horizontal summation of the marginal cost curve of all existing oil suppliers). In a more complete analysis, we could also portray a long-term supply curve that lies flatter, reflecting the fact that at higher prices, oil companies will step up their efforts to drill more wells from existing sites or engage in more search activity. We could also portray a demand curve that showed more elasticity in the long run, as consumers reacted to higher prices by buying new cars that had better gasoline mileage, and so on. I can illustrate the main effects of a maximum price setting, however, without introducing these complications.

We can suppose that in some previous periods, supply was higher than portrayed, say intersecting at quantity demanded 7 million gallons at price $3. As a result of world restrictions on supply, the new supply curve facing the United States is the one depicted. Without interference, the new market-clearing price is $5 and the quantity of gasoline demanded is 5 million gallons. In their zeal to keep price low for consumers, both presidents decided to set a maximum amount that oil companies could charge for a gallon of oil, and they made it illegal to raise price beyond this level. For the sake of illustration, I suppose that the *maximum regulated price* is set at $3 per gallon at the pump.

The problem created by this regulation is readily apparent from the figure. At price $3, there is a demand for 7 million gallons of gasoline, but only 3 million gallons are supplied. I plot a vertical linear dashed-line schedule at 3 million gallons to show the quantity of gasoline available at $3 per gallon. Notice that at this level of supply, the market-clearing price is $7. In a free market, this price would attract additional oil from existing wells until price fell to $5. But since the price system is not working by virtue of public law, we know that this vertical supply curve represents the available gasoline for our problem.

Presumably, both presidents believed that their actions would benefit consumers. In terms of the figure, each is trying to reassign the property rights to the surplus measured by area D from producers to consumers. That is, absent any price controls, the consumer surplus denoted by area C was never in jeopardy because had they let market forces work, price would have been $5 and consumers would have captured the surplus measured by this area (plus they would have captured surplus measured by area A). The attempt to make this reassignment, however, set in motion competitive forces that dissipated surplus measured not only by area D but also by area C.

Notice that the individuals on the upper part of the demand curve— that is, above $7—are the highest-value consumers in the market. Perhaps most drivers are represented along this segment, conveying the idea that most individuals will attach lots of value to the first units of gasoline they can purchase; there may also be some individuals like salespeople who have a demand for lots of gasoline at these prices. But it is not obvious that these consumers will be able to secure the 3 million gallon supply, because at the $3 regulated price, there is a demand for an additional 4 million gallons by consumers who are represented by points lower down on the demand curve. How do the *high-value users* (those on the top part of the demand curve) squeeze out the *low-value users* (those users represented over the quantity range 3 to 7 million gallons) when price cannot move freely? In a word, **queues**.

B. THE QUEUE FOR GASOLINE

Suppose that each gas station owner has 1,000 gallons of gasoline to sell each day. To create some order, the owner erects a sign that says: "Open daily at 8:00 A.M. Limit 10 gallons per car. First 100 cars only." Each day, as the owner arrives, he counts 100 cars and puts a sign on the inside window of the 100th car that says "LAST CAR" and makes a record of its license plate. He might also put a pole in the ground to give customers an idea of where the 100th car usually is found in queue each day. For the sake of the argument, suppose that all consumers attach a price on their time equal to $20.

Consider a consumer who is willing to pay as much as $10 per gallon of gasoline. She faces a price of $3 at the pump, and hence, receives $7 of surplus for each gallon. Thus, for 10 gallons, she is willing to pay $70 above the pump price. Given a value of $20 per hour for her time, she is willing to stay in queue for three and a half hours. The consumer who values gas at $9 earns $6 surplus per gallon at the $3 pump price.

This surplus, times 10 gallons, is $60; hence, he is willing to wait three hours.

As we move down the demand curve, each successive consumer is willing to wait a shorter period of time to obtain the gasoline, until we reach the consumer at the $3 point on the demand curve. He is willing to pay only the $3 pump price, and hence, is not willing to spend any time in queue. The highest-value users demonstrate the intensity of their demand by staying in line longer, thereby squeezing the lower-value users from the queue. In the absence of a price mechanism, competition for the gasoline shows itself in the form of willingness to wait in queue.

> *Question*: What time does the queue form, and which consumers are in the queue?
>
> *Answer*: The daily queue begins to form by 6:00 A.M. At this time, there is a two-hour wait, meaning that the marginal queue participant is willing to pay $7 for gasoline, $3 at the pump, plus the equivalent of $4 in the form of wait time, or $40 per 10 gallons. Thus, the full price of gasoline is $7, which is consistent with the 3 million gallons supplied at the regulated price. There is not much point in coming much before 6:00 A.M. because lower-value users are already squeezed out with the 6:00 A.M. queue, and thus, why waste more time than necessary? The only consumers in queue are the highest-value users.[73]

We now have a new concept to introduce into our vocabulary, namely, **full price**. This term refers to the out-of-pocket cost of the gasoline in the figure ($3), *plus* the $4 queue expense; thus, the full price of gasoline is $7 per gallon.

> *Full price*: A term that normally arises when there is some cost that is borne beyond the out-of-pocket price of some item or service. For example, the full price of going to the Orioles' game on Thursday afternoon is the cost of the ticket, parking and transportation costs, plus the forgone wages that this person would have earned had he worked instead of taking the time off.

[73]I am ignoring the nuance that the queue of cars will take some time to obtain their gas once 8.00 A.M. arrives. If it takes one hour to service 100 cars, then we would expect the queue to start forming at 6.00 A.M. and the 100th car to arrive at 7.00 A.M. In this way, all cars in queue wait two hours. I also assume that no person wants to consume more than 10 gallons in a day, so I rule out the problem of waiting twice in queue during the same period.

The assumption that each consumer has the same value of time seems strong at first but not so upon reflection. Suppose that each driver solves his or her problem by finding some teenager who is willing to sit in queue to obtain gasoline, and suppose that "teenagers are all alike" in the sense that each is willing to sell his or her time at $10 per hour. Then, all the drivers in queue are either teenagers or other individuals who also have a relatively low value of time.

Oddly, the discovery of drivers with a lower cost of time does not reduce the social cost of the queue. It merely generates a longer time in queue. The same 100 high-value users still get the gasoline, and the social cost of the queue is the same. More particularly, each user still is willing to spend the same amount in queue costs as before. The existence of $10-per-hour teenagers, however, means that the high-value users compete by sending their stand-ins to queue ever earlier until only 100 cars are in queue for the available gasoline.

Question: What time does the daily queue start to form if all drivers find teenagers to obtain the gasoline for them at a price of $10 per hour? Who are their clients?[74]

C. THE SOCIAL COST OF THE QUEUE

The solution has one nice feature. The highest-value users get the gasoline. But at what cost? First, note that the maximum price restricts supply to 3 million gallons, fully 2 million gallons short of quantity that would be produced and consumed in an unregulated market. Thus, the social cost of the regulation is at least the deadweight costs denoted by areas A and B in figure 4-3.

Second, a queue cost is imposed. In our example, after the teenager market forms, 100 cars wait in line for four hours, where each hour has an opportunity cost of $10 per hour. Thus, the cost of the queue is $4 per gallon.[75] This cost is denoted by areas C plus D in figure 4-3. Thus, areas A + B + C + D denote the total cost of restricting the maximum price to $3. Notice that area D is the consumer surplus that presidents Ford and Carter were trying to preserve. The regulation squanders not only this surplus but also the surplus denoted by area C.

[74]If a market for teenagers is such that their market-clearing wage is $10 per hour, then the queue starts at 4.00 A.M. each day and their clients are the highest-value users. The total cost of the queue is the same, namely $4 per gallon.

[75]There are 100 cars in queue for four hours. Thus, the cost of the queue time is $10 × 4 hours × 100 cars = $4,000. Each car gets 10 gallons for a total of 1,000 gallons each day. Thus, the queue cost per gallon is $4.

One way to characterize the queue cost is to say that the regulation increased the transactions cost of obtaining gasoline. Prior to the interference, a consumer took perhaps five minutes to fill his tank. Now, it takes four hours. This is a correct characterization of the result. Not to want to complicate the terminology too much, but whenever surplus is replaced by competition for a "free resource" in the form of wasted expenditures, it is referred to as **rent erosion**. The price regulation seemingly offers a gallon of gasoline that has a market-clearing price of $7 for only

---

Rent erosion: The replacement of surplus by real resource costs caused by an ill-defined right to property. When property rights are unassigned ex ante but are attainable ex post after expending some resource costs, a kind of free-for-all solution arises that completely erodes the value of the asset. Later in the book, the problem resurfaces under the heading of a so-called common resource problem.

Question: How can you determine in principle how much value someone attaches to waiting in a queue?[76]

THREE EXAMPLES OF QUEUES

Queue for White House Tours. The federal government allows only a limited number of visitors to the White House tour. "Free" tickets are handed out at an office building located at Fourteenth Street and Pennsylvania Avenue each day. Queues begin forming prior to sunrise on summer mornings. The White House folks apparently are trying to do a favor to visitors by letting them in "free," but in reality, the visitors pay to enter in the form of queue time.

Queues for New Movies or Rock Concerts. Sometimes prices for some private events, like hit movies or rock concerts, are less than the market-clearing price. This maximum price causes large queues to form sometimes twenty-four hours prior to ticket windows opening. Thus, the patrons end up paying a high price for the tickets in the form of time in queue. The question often is asked why the owners of the movies and the rock concert groups do not charge higher

continued . . .

---

[76]Use the compensation principle: ask how much the driver is willing to pay to avoid having to wait X hours to obtain the gasoline.

THREE EXAMPLES OF QUEUES *Continued*

prices. One possibility is that sometimes they underestimate demand for their products. In other cases, perhaps the queues give free publicity to the event and send the signal that the movie or performance must be good to attract so many intense customers. This may encourage more people to either purchase tickets to subsequent performances or visit the record store to purchase the performer's video and CD recordings.

Double Queues for Roller-coaster Rides. Another example is the double lines for roller coasters at most large amusement parks—one for the regular seating and a much longer one for front-row seat assignments. Front-row riders indeed are paying a higher price in the form of time in queue. Why don't amusement parks simply charge a higher price for front-row seats to clear this market? One answer could be that the long line advertises the excitement of the ride and attracts more users to try the ride and spread the word about how exciting it is. Presumably, this benefit is worth more than the additional revenue that the park could collect from charging a higher price for the front-row seats.

$3. How does one gain the property rights to what amounts to a subsidy on gasoline? The answer is wasting time in queue. So, what at first seems as "rent" is eroded through waste.

D. A FIRST LESSON IN PROPERTY RIGHTS

It is easy to think of policy options that would have been more efficient ways to allocate 3 million gallons of gasoline.

1. Attach a $4 Tax to Each Gallon

Consumers pay the same price as in the queue system, but the property rights to areas C and D pass to the government, who could in turn use the monies to finance tax rebates. In this solution, deadweight loss is incurred as measured by areas A and B. Areas C and D, however, become pure transfers from consumers and producers of gasoline to taxpayers as a whole.

2. Randomly Assign the Property Rights to Gas Pumps

If the government does not want oil suppliers to collect the surplus measured by area D in figure 4-3, then it can award (to anyone) the right to operate a "toll booth" at the entry to each gas station. The toll collector has the right to collect the market-clearing excess price above the pump price. It does not matter whether this right is given to homeless people, charitable organizations, or randomly chosen citizens: all would quickly learn that $4 per gallon is the market-clearing entry fee. The market clears without dissipating the surplus measured by areas C and D in the form of social costs.

3. Mail Gasoline Coupons to Random Taxpayers
During World War II, ration coupons were handed out "equitably" to millions of motorists. The coupons did not have a name stamped on

---

Back to the White House Example
Incidentally, the White House could find the same solution by simply giving the tickets away to anyone at the start of the day; this approach arbitrarily awards the property rights to White House visits that day to random folks. By day's end, however, it is not likely that many of these people would actually see the White House. Instead, most would have cash in their pockets, and the highest-value sightseers would have seen the White House without having had to wait in line.[77]

A partial solution to the queue problem indeed has arisen. It is said that so-called street people and unemployed youths line up early in the morning and secure some of the tickets (limit four per person), then re-sell them on the Mall to higher-value users later in the day. If the White House cannot figure out how to allocate limited tickets, then apparently others will serve the "market maker" function for them!

The Market Makes Strange Bedfellows
In 1998, the Smithsonian Museum had a special three-month exhibit of Van Gogh paintings. Because it could handle a limited number of viewers, it handed out a fixed number of tickets each day on a first-come first-served basis. Large lines formed. An odd thing happened. People driving to work at 7:00 A.M. saw lines of sleeping street people still in their sleeping bags in front of the Smithsonian. Later in the day, one could observe blue-haired elderly women from Connecticut Avenue making deals with odd-looking folk on Constitution Avenue. The women got their tickets. The street people got the cash. Everyone had a smile on their faces (including the economists passing by). The market works!

---

[77]It is important in this solution that tickets be given randomly to anyone in town, not say to the first fifty people in line; otherwise the queue problem would redevelop.

them and thus were negotiable. A market in coupons soon developed, whereby lower-value users sold their coupons to higher-value users. In this solution, the property rights are assigned arbitrarily, but we still obtain the efficient outcome without wasting millions of hours every day doing what the price system does for us at almost no cost.

E. A CANDIDATE FOR AN EVEN MORE INEFFICIENT SOLUTION: REGULATION

There is one solution that might be even worse than queues. In Europe, they already have very high gasoline prices, but when world oil prices rise, they have a tendency to opt for a regulatory solution. For example, regulators might forbid driving on Sunday (except to church), make it illegal for fewer than two people to be in an automobile, outlaw cars that have gas mileage less than x per gallon, and so on. In the United States, Congress once enacted legislation that set speed limits to fifty-five miles per hour on all national highways to try to force consumers to conserve gasoline. And indeed the law was enforced for a while. Slowing motorists below safe speeds wastes millions of hours of time: it is kind of a "moving-queue" way to increase the full price of driving.

Regulatory solutions require armies of bureaucrats to write and enforce the regulations dictating what they think the highest-value uses must be (which are unlikely to be coincident with consumers' definitions except perhaps for some "median" citizen). In this system, it almost certainly is true that many high-value users will be squeezed out of the market in favor of low-value users, creating a large loss in total surplus.

VOCABULARY REVIEW

Upon reflection, in the *queue* solution, the *property rights* to the available gas were given to no one, and thus, to obtain them, participants had to waste time in queue. We can think of queue solutions as ones that impose a large *transactions cost* on consumers. By regulating gas prices, the government converts what was previously a five-minute stop at the gas station into a multihour ordeal. Indeed, the transactions cost of obtaining 10 gallons of gasoline became the dominant portion of its *full price*. Drivers have an *opportunity cost* of their time, which is why queues create social cost beyond *deadweight losses*. Whenever ill-defined property rights invite a kind of free-for-all solution, the inevitable loss of surplus is labeled *rent erosion*.

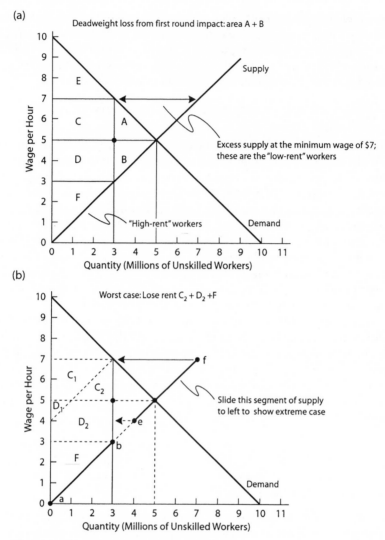

Figure 4-4. The Minimum Wage: Initial Effect

III. The Economics of the Minimum Wage

In some markets, the government imposes a maximum price. In others, it imposes a minimum price. A good example is the **minimum wage**. Figure 4-4, panel (*a*), portrays the market for unskilled labor. The supply schedule depicts the wage required by each successive unskilled person to make him- or herself available in this market. We might think of workers along the lower portion of this schedule acquiring labor skills, or retirees, teenagers, or homemakers from low-income homes trying to augment their income. At the higher points on the supply curve might be teenagers or homemakers from middle-class homes interested in augmenting their income if the wage is sufficiently high, but otherwise are not available to the market. We can think of those along the first portion of the supply curve as "high-rent" workers and those along the higher portion as "low-rent" workers.

High-rent workers: Those who obtain the highest amount of surplus from working in a job.

Low-rent workers: Those for whom the net benefits of the job are relatively low. Those not in the market earn negative surplus at the current wage, which is why they choose not to work.

The demand curve reflects the value that firms attach to each additional worker hired. Given some level of plant and equipment, the first workers employed add lots of value, but each marginal worker adds progressively less to the value of output. This law of diminishing returns is reflected by the downward-sloping demand curve. The interpretation of this demand is similar to product markets. Each point on the demand curve represents the marginal value of each employed worker and thus represents the maximum that firms are willing to pay for each worker on the margin.

If the market is allowed to work freely, then the equilibrium wage in my illustrative example is $5 per hour. At this wage, 5 million unskilled workers are employed. Firms earn a kind of "surplus" measured by areas $A + C + E$.[78] Workers earn rent in the amount denoted by areas B, D, and F. Total wages paid per period are denoted by the rectangle with height $5 and base 5 million. We can think of the impact of the minimum wage as a "three-round" affair.

A. UNSKILLED WORKERS STILL EMPLOYED GAIN RENT

Suppose that yesterday the going wage was $5. Today the government imposes a minimum wage of $7. The first-round effect is predictable. Firms demand a lower quantity of the now more expensive unskilled workers. Three million workers are employed compared to 5 million prior to the wage increase. Two million unskilled workers now are unemployed.

---

[78]In fact, area $A + C + E$ is the value of output earned by the owners of capital in the firm, and so in equilibrium, we expect that this amount is just sufficient to pay a competitive rate of return on capital. In a short-term sense, however, we can think of this amount as "surplus."

The 3 million workers still employed earn more rent, as denoted by area *C* in panel (*a*). Thus, workers as a whole give up rent in the amount *B* but gain the amount *C*. Areas *A* + *B* measure deadweight cost imposed by the wage regulation. The costs arise because firms willing and able to pay $6.80 are not permitted to hire workers willing and able to work for less than $6.80, and similarly for all other unemployed workers willing to work for $5. The first-round effect is similar to the imposition of a tax on unskilled labor, where the proceeds are paid directly to workers.

First-round effect of the minimum wage: Some workers become unemployed; those still employed earn higher rent; a deadweight cost arises.

B. SOME LOW-RENT WORKERS DISPLACE SOME HIGH-RENT WORKERS

The first round is a conventional but superficial evaluation of the impact of the minimum wage. Consider the next round. Note that the 2 million workers displaced by the minimum wage want a job at this wage level, and so we can imagine them in the applicant pool of any firm hiring un-skilled workers. In addition, in comparison to the $5 wage, more work-ers are willing to accept a job at the $7 wage. Fully 2 million workers not in the market at the $5 wage enter at the new minimum wage. There is a veritable "army of unemployed" workers: 7 million individuals are looking for, and willing to accept, a job at the minimum wage, but firms are willing to hire only 3 million.

Since workers do not have the "rent" they earn from these jobs posted on their foreheads, they all look alike from the perspective of ex-pected productivity to firms who hire workers out of the applicant pool. The additional social cost of the minimum wage should begin to become apparent: *some high-rent workers will lose their jobs to the low-rent workers*. The welfare loss from the minimum wage greatly exceeds the cost depicted in the first round.

To illustrate the potential magnitude of this loss, consider the extreme case, which occurs when, by coincidence, the 3 million workers who were hired into these jobs all come from that portion of the supply curve that earn the *lowest* rent. Panel (*b*) of figure 4-4 shows this case. Sup-pose that all the applicants hired for these jobs come from the supply curve segment, which I have labeled *e* and *f* at each endpoint. To calcu-late the social cost of the additional misallocation, I simply move the segment of the supply curve between points *e* and *f* horizontally in a leftward direction until the point *e* on the segment intersects the vertical axis, as shown by the upward-sloping dashed line. The segment on the supply curve below, which I label a and b at the endpoints, represents the workers who previously had these jobs.

The forgone rent from the misallocation of the now scarce minimum wage jobs to low-rent workers is measured by the trapezoid between these two supply segments areas $(C_2 + D_2 + F)$. The equivalent measure of this loss is the rectangle comprising areas $C_1 + C_2 + D_1 + D_2$ in panel (b), which is the same as areas $C + D$ in panel (G).[79]

Using my illustrative numbers, the dollar value of the traditional dead-weight loss (areas $A + B$) is \$4 million. The additional allocative inefficiency of hiring the low-rent workers is \$12 million.[80] At the other extreme, if firms by coincidence hire all the high-rent workers then the latter inefficiency is zero. In terms of panel (a), the total social cost of the minimum wage is the "triangle" loss (areas A plus B), plus some portion of the rectangle denoted by $C + D$. Assuming random hiring of applicants, the cost of the misallocation of jobs to some low-rent workers is somewhere in the middle, say \$6 million. The social cost is the sum of this misallocation plus the triangle loss valued at \$4 million, for a total of \$10 million.

Round 2: At least some low-rent workers along the supply curve displace the high-rent workers, creating a second source of welfare loss that may swamp the first-round measure of deadweight loss.

It is unlikely that this solution depicts equilibrium. The reason is that low-rent workers have displaced some high-rent workers. A bell should sound in your ears telling you that this solution is unstable. Somehow, the high-rent workers are going to displace the low-rent workers. Can you think how this might happen? How will this competition unfold?

C. HIGH-RENT WORKERS OUTHUSTLE LOW-RENT WORKERS

There is a strong force in this market that has yet not been tapped. At first, some high-rent workers may lose their jobs to low-rent workers. But the displaced high-rent workers want the jobs more than the low-rent workers. Lessons from the gasoline queue teach us that one way or another, the high-rent workers are going to end up with the jobs, but by what mechanism?

If minimum wage jobs are allocated arbitrarily to high- and low-rent workers, then it is predictable that the high-rent workers are willing to

---

[79]Triangles $(C_1 + D_1)$ and F have the same height and base and hence have equal area.

[80]Using Panel (a), note that the traditional triangle losses (areas $A + B$) has a height of \$4 and a base of 2, which gives an area equal to \$4 million. Rectangle $C + D$ has a height of \$4 and a base of 3; hence, it has area equal to \$12 million.

work harder to decrease the probability that they might be laid off or fired from a job that they really want to keep. Low-rent workers, on the other hand, are not getting that much surplus out of the $7 job, and hence, are unwilling to work much harder. In comparison to hardworking high-rent workers, low-rent workers look like loafers.

As firms realize that other hard workers are in the applicant pool, they are more willing to either fire or lay off loafers and retain hard workers. Alternatively, if supervisors push the loafers to produce as much as the hard workers, then loafers are likely to quit more often. As it keeps sampling the applicant pool and retaining hard workers and separating loafers, eventually the firm will have a concentration of hard workers in its minimum wage jobs. Indeed, to observers from the outside looking in, and even from the perspective of the employer, it may seem as though low-wage workers are working harder than the high-skilled workers.

This "effort competition" affects worker's supply prices. That is, a worker's supply price in part depends on how hard one must work on the job. The more work required, the higher the required wage. While the way in which harder work impacts supply price may differ across individuals, I assume that the supply price increases by an equal amount for all workers along the supply curve. The higher the level of energy required on the job, the higher the supply price facing employers of unskilled labor. Put differently, workers require a "compensating differential" to accommodate the harder work on the job.

Compensating differential: The additional compensation required to accept less desirable working conditions. As jobs require harder work, potential hires require a higher wage to accept these jobs. This concept is an application of the compensation principle. In this case, the disutility of the job requiring harder worker is translated into a higher asking wage.

For simplicity, I assume that the harder work does not affect the value of output in the firm (otherwise, I need to start moving the demand schedule, which complicates matters quite a bit). Suppose that a high-rent worker washes the windows on the boss's car. If a lower-rent worker steals this job tomorrow, then the higher-rent worker washes the entire car. If the other guy steals this job the day after, then the harder worker ups the ante: he *polishes* the car after work. Sooner or later, the other guy throws in the towel. Needless to say, the boss values the worker who is willing to make his car look best. In the end, the low-rent guys are out, the high-rent guys are in, and the boss has a very nice-looking car.

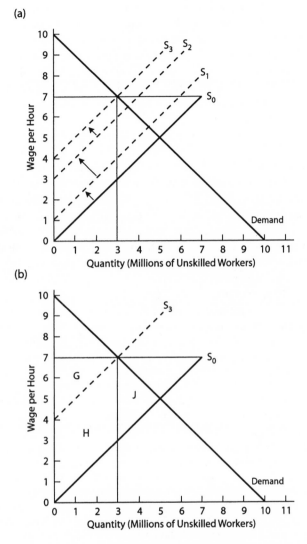

Figure 4-5. High-rent Workers Regain Jobs by Working Harder

Figure 4-5, panel (*a*), shows the effort effect visually. As workers compete over who is willing to work harder for the minimum wage, supply increases (vertically) from S_0 to S_1 to S_2, then S_3. Equilibrium is discovered when workers put sufficient energy into the job that the required compensating differential is the vertical difference between supply S_0 and supply S_3. At this point, only high-rent workers are employed. The excess supply of unskilled workers created by the minimum wage vanishes.

Panel (*b*) in figure 4-5 shows the net result. The social cost of the minimum wage has two components. First, we lose the gains from trade denoted by area *J*. This is the classic deadweight loss caused by the employment effect. Second, workers still employed work harder to keep their jobs. Area *H* denotes the dollar value of the additional disutility of harder work. There is some value added that offsets some of the cost of more energy expended. The boss has a nice-looking car. So, area *H* is not entirely wasted.

D. RENT TO UNSKILLED WORKERS

Area *G* denotes the rent collected by still-employed workers. Prior to the enactment of the minimum wage, these same 3 million workers earned rent denoted by areas *D* plus *F* in figure 4-4, panel (*a*). You can see by inspection that rent is lower in the new equilibrium. Area *G* in figure 4-5, panel (*b*), is the same as area *F* in figure 4-4, panel (*a*). Thus, rent falls by the amount denoted by area *D* in figure 4-4, panel (*a*). The 2 million unemployed workers also are worse off. They lose rent measured by area *B* shown in the same panel.

This gives us the interesting result that all unskilled workers are worse off from the minimum wage, including those still employed! Put differently, the minimum wage increases the money income of unskilled workers still employed but makes them worse off. Remember: the name of the game is surplus, not dollars!

> *Impact of the minimum wage on rent to workers*: While money income to workers increases from the minimum wage, rent falls because the utility of the additional wage is eroded by competition for these jobs in the form of harder work. Perhaps this is a good time to remind you that there is no such thing as a free lunch.

This result is general. We know this because everyone working at a lower-effort, low-wage job could have worked in a higher-effort, higher-wage job in the first place. The fact that they chose the job with more modest work requirements says that they attach a higher utility from this job than the higher-paying, harder-working one. Ergo, forcing them into a higher-paying, higher-effort job makes them worse off.

Think about the life of a law professor at George Mason University School of Law. Most faculty members have the option of practicing law at a much higher salary. But the work is more demanding and often less interesting. Faculty members made a decision that being a law professor at lower pay yields more rent than a position in a law firm at higher pay. If wage levels suddenly double at Mason, it is predictable that more would-be practicing lawyers will be interested in a law school job. Those who value the job most will demonstrate this intensity by working longer hours to produce more publications and prepare more interesting classes and the like. The dean will sit back, enjoy the competition, and ultimately choose the most productive faculty members. In the end, professors have a higher-paying job with much harder work. But these are the jobs that they rejected in the first place!

E. EFFORT ADDS VALUE, WHICH ATTENUATES JOB LOSSES

Finally, as the law school example demonstrates, if the effort effects occur within the job (not in the parking lot where the boss's car is parked), the effect of more effort produces a higher-quality product. The reputation of the school rises, owing to more publications. Students have higher bar passage rates and more productive law careers because they are better prepared by more motivated and better prepared teachers. As word gets out, the demand for education at Mason increases. Simply put, as a result of more effort, both supply and demand increase.

Figure 4-6 shows the end result. Demand increases from D_1 to D_2, reflecting the value added from additional effort. This means that equilibrium is discovered at a somewhat lower level of effort. Equilibrium occurs where supply S_2 intersects demand D_2. Compared to a world in which effort does not affect demand (figure 4-5, panel [b]), the value of output increases owing to higher effort. Area M denotes this value. Rent erosion is not as high because equilibrium is discovered at a somewhat

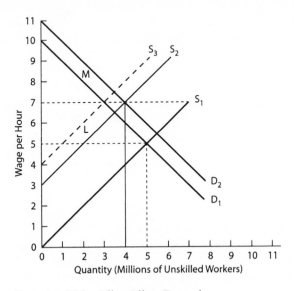

Figure 4-6. Higher Effort Affects Demand

lower effort level. Area L measures this improvement compared to figure 4-5, panel (b). Finally, employment loss is reduced (4 million employed compared to 3 million in figure 4-5, panel (b)).

Round 3: High-rent workers outhustle the low-rent workers and secure all the minimum wage jobs. The higher effort increases value added, which attenuates the employment effect. In the end, some unskilled workers are unemployed. The rest have more money income but less rent.

F. A NOTE ON UNIONS

Unions also prop up wages above competitive levels. In this case, it is not the government that sets the wage but a union that organizes workers in an industry across many competing firms. We can think of the union setting a tax on these firms in the form of a higher wage, where the surplus is measured by area C in figure 4-4, panel (a). Fewer workers are employed, but the additional rent earned by workers who still have a union job is significant. Would we expect this rent to be eroded? The answer is yes, and this is why unions enforce a strict contract that makes it difficult for some workers to work harder than others.

The contract does not permit some workers of a given class to earn a higher wage than anyone else in that class regardless of how hard they work. The union makes it difficult to fire workers unless they are in the extreme of worker performance. In the event of layoffs, the union requires a strict formula to be followed, usually based on seniority. The union does not allow its workers to start their job before the appointed time, nor stay later than anyone else (except for paid overtime requirements approved by the union), nor take shorter lunch hours than anyone else. In general, unions frown on workers doing anything beyond their job definition. One explanation for these featherbedding rules is to thwart the natural tendency of workers to compete for these jobs by working harder. Otherwise, it is apparent that the end solution could dissipate the rent conferred by the union wage premium.

IV. Price Supports

Price supports are natural cousins to the minimum wage, except that they refer to output markets. Agricultural sectors offer many examples. Supports can be operated in several ways. I consider two.

Figure 4-7, panel (a) depicts the market for wheat. Without outside interference, 5 million tons clear the market at $5,000 per ton. The

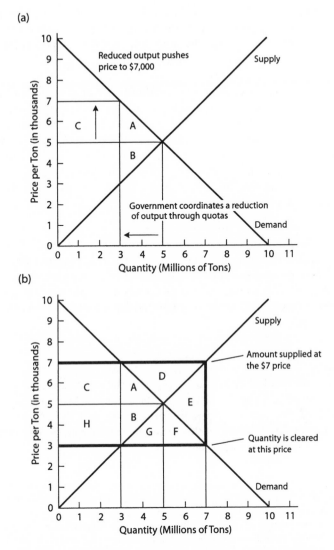

(a)

Reduced output pushes price to $7,000

Supply

C A

B

Government coordinates a reduction of output through quotas

Demand

(b)

Supply

Amount supplied at the $7 price

C A D

H B E

G F

Quantity is cleared at this price

Demand

Figure 4-7. Price Support: Two Programs to Raise Prices to Farmers

government sets the price to $7,000 per ton. At this price, consumers are willing to purchase only 3 million tons, whereas farmers are willing to supply 7 million.

A. RESTRICTION ON OUTPUT

Suppose that the government operates this system by coordinating the farmers, through their cooperatives. The co-ops assign quotas so that in combination, farmers will send only 3 million tons of wheat. The quotas are transferable so that farmer 1 can sell his allotment quota to farmer 2. This is an important detail because just like the coupon solution in the gasoline queue problem, it ensures that the most efficient farmers will produce the 3 million tons.[81]

In this case, there is nothing special about the solution. A deadweight loss measured by areas $A + B$ develops because quantity supplied to the market falls by 2 million tons. Price increases from $5,000 to $7,000. Farmers' rents increase by area C and fall by area B. In general area C must exceed area B in a support program; otherwise, why would farmers support it? Consumers are worse off not only because they lose consumer surplus measured by area A but also because they transfer their surplus measured by area C to producers.

Impact of a price support with efficient output allotments: Price increases, quantity falls, consumers transfer surplus to farmers; total rent to farmers increases; a deadweight loss is imposed. Note that this solution is the same as the government awarding farmers the property rights to tax revenue generated by attaching a $4,000 tax per ton of wheat.

EXERCISE:
Calculate the total of all surpluses prior to the price support. As a result of the price support, what are the dollar values of the deadweight loss, the increased rent to producers, and the reduction of consumer surplus? What is the difference in surpluses before and after the support is put in place?[82]

---

[81]Otherwise, some inefficient farmers displace output by efficient farmers. The social cost of the scheme will take on the same look as the minimum wage solution when low-rent workers displace high-rent workers. In the farm solution, however, we have no natural competition that will arise to ensure that the most efficient farmers will end up producing the output (putting aside a market to bribe officials to obtain the allotment tickets). I also could complicate the problem so that farmers are restricted in the acreage they use, not the output they send to market. In this case, we would need to take into account the incentive on the part of farmers to use an inefficient method of production (say more fertilizer or planting crops closer together) to try to increase their rents. This would change the supply curve and output.

[82]*Total* surplus prior to the support is denoted by the area below the demand curve but above the supply curve from output zero to output 5. This area is a triangle with height 10 and base 5 and hence is valued at $25 billion; deadweight loss = $A + B$ = $4 billion; change in rent = $C - B$ = $4 billion; reduction in consumer surplus = $A + C$ = $8 billion. The difference in surpluses is the deadweight loss.

B. NO RESTRICTION ON SUPPLY

An alternative is for the government to support price $7,000 but allow farmers to produce any amount they want and let market price be determined by demand conditions. In this solution, the government sends a check to each farmer equal to the difference between the market-clearing price and the price support. Panel (*b*) of figure 4-7 demonstrates the effects of this program.

At the support price, farmers produce 7 million tons. Consumers are willing to absorb this quantity only at price $3,000. In comparison to a free market, the market-clearing price falls by $2,000. Notice that in this solution, there is a deadweight loss, but it is not the usual and customary. That is, note that in this outcome, the distortion arises because farmers are encouraged to produce *too much* wheat. But isn't more output good? Yes, *if* the value consumers attach to it exceeds its marginal cost of production; otherwise, no. In the case illustrated in figure 4-7, the marginal cost of producing every unit in excess of 5 million tons exceeds $5,000, but consumers attach a value to these units that is less than $5,000. The difference represents a waste of resources.

The total amount of this waste is the vertical distance between the supply schedule and the demand curve for every unit of production between 5 and 7 million tons of output. This deadweight loss is measured by area *E*.

Another way to view this problem is to look at the gainers and losers from the price support. In comparison to competitive equilibrium, consumer surplus in this market is higher by the amounts *H* + *B* + *G* + *F*. Producer rents are higher by the amounts *C* + *A* + *D*. But if consumers and producers are better off, who is worse off?

The answer is the taxpayer. Notice that in this solution, the government sends a check to farmers equal to the difference between the price support of $7,000 and the $3,000 market-clearing price, times 7 million tons of output. I have denoted this amount by the rectangle outlined in bold. The difference between the subsidy amounts and the additional consumer and producer surplus in this market is measured by area *E*. Assuming that taxpayers value each of their dollars the same as the farmers (the dollar-is-a-dollar assumption), then the net loss is measured by area *E*. This is the amount by which market participants wasted taxpayers' income transfer.[83]

---

[83] I assume that taxes were raised to support the transfer without imposing deadweight costs.

Impact of a price support with no restriction on supply: Price falls, output increases, and consumer and producer surplus increases (offset by equivalent losses by taxpayers). A deadweight loss develops from an inefficient expansion of production. Note that this solution is the same as the government offering a subsidy of $4,000 per ton (see appendix to chapter 3).

EXERCISE:

What is the dollar value of the deadweight loss of the price support in Figure 4-7, panel (b)? How does this compare to the deadweight loss from the supply restriction depicted in panel (a)? In general, will the deadweight loss be higher or lower when there is no restriction on supply as compared to a support with output allotments? Why might politicians care about which solution they opt for? Which support system do farmers prefer?[84]

---

[84]The deadweight loss in panel (b), figure 4-7, is $4 billion, the same as in panel (a). In general, either loss could be larger depending on the elasticities of the demand and supply curves. Politicians prefer the output allotment scheme, since the tax on consumers is collected directly by farmers, thereby making it an off-budget transfer. Other things the same, farmers prefer the price support with no restrictions because they obtain more rent (measured by $A + B + D$).

Chapter 5

The Economics of Monopoly

Main Economic Concepts	1. A monopolist has the opportunity to choose a price-quantity combination. He chooses the one that maximizes his profits. Essentially, a monopolist wants to convert consumer surplus to producer surplus.
	2. Normally, a monopolist earns higher profits by charging different prices to different consumers.
	3. Monopolies do not simply appear. Actors have to incur resources to obtain market power. This process serves to erode prospective profits, which means that the social costs of monopoly exceed deadweight costs.
	4. Price discrimination can occur in competitive markets when fixed costs of production are important; this helps us understand when the market demand curve is found by *vertically* summing individual demand curves, a phenomenon that naturally segues into the topic of public goods considered in chapter 6.
New Terms	1. Marginal revenue
	2. Profit-maximizing price
	3. Perfect price discrimination
	4. Rent erosion (again)
	5. Patent monopoly
	6. Cheating
	7. Prisoner's dilemma
	8. Market for Monopoly
	9. Tie-in

Until this point, I have assumed that the market is competitive in the sense that there are a sufficient number of firms so that no one firm can influence price. The optimal behavior of each firm yields the market supply curve. The interaction of demand and supply conditions gives the equilibrium price. The relationship between this price and the sustainable price determines whether entry or exit occurs in the industry. In this chapter, I entertain the opposite assumption: there is only one firm in the industry, which means that it has the power to set price. I will argue later that these two models, perfect competitive and monopoly, are adequate to evaluate most markets that have some characteristics between these extremes.

> *Assumption about cost*: For simplicity, I make the assumption in this chapter that the firm's marginal cost curve is flat and fixed costs are zero. We can think of this schedule as the long-run marginal cost curve in an industry that is characterized by constant costs. This allows us to concentrate on the essential features introduced by monopoly pricing without undue complexity.

I. The Price Decision

Unlike a perfect competitor who accepts price as given by market forces, a monopolist recognizes that he can set price. Which one does he choose? The monopolist is limited in choices by the demand curve that exists for his product and by his cost structure. He needs to find the price along the demand curve that maximizes the difference between his revenues and costs, which defines excess profits.

A. THE RULE FOR FINDING THE PROFIT-MAXIMIZING PRICE

For concreteness, I assume a specific linear demand curve, namely, $P = 20 - Q$, where P is price and Q is quantity. I also assume that marginal cost, C, is \$4. I show these two schedules in panel (a) of figure 5-1.

> *Assumptions*
> Demand curve: $P = \$20 - Q$
> Marginal cost: $C = \$4$

Look for highest profits. Profits equal the difference between total revenue and total costs. I show total revenue in panel (b) of figure 5-1 as the solid hill-like function. Chapter 2 showed how to create this chart. Maximum revenues occur at the midpoint of the demand curve, where demand elasticity equals unity. This output corresponds to 10 units.

Beyond this level, total revenues fall with further units of output. Starting at zero, revenue increases with quantity until 10 units. Owing to the falling demand elasticity, the amount by which revenue increases becomes smaller for each incremental unit until it is zero at 10 units. Increasing quantity beyond this point reduces revenue. The change in revenue from each unit of output is called **marginal revenue**. I show this schedule as the downsloping line that intersects the quantity axis at 10 in panel (a).

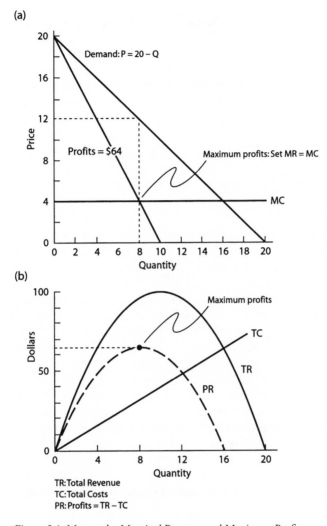

Figure 5-1. Monopoly: Marginal Revenue and Maximum Profits

The monopolist wishes to maximize profits, not revenues, and so must account for costs. Since there are only marginal costs in our problem, total costs are trivially calculated as the product of marginal cost ($4) times quantity. I show this schedule in panel (b) as the upward-sloping linear line. To obtain profits, at each quantity level, simply subtract the total costs from total revenues (vertically). This difference is excess profits at each quantity level, as shown by the dashed hill-like function in panel (b). Profits are highest when quantity is set equal to 8 units.

> *Marginal revenue*: The change in total revenue from a one-unit increase in output.[85]
>
> A firm in a competitive market cannot affect price, and so his marginal revenue from an additional unit of output is the market price. A monopolist is the only supplier and thus can control price. He takes into account that while a higher output alone works to increase revenue, it also causes price to fall, which works to reduce revenue.

To obtain price, simply read the price off the demand curve in panel (*a*). The demand price at quantity 8 units is $12. Profits per unit of output are the difference between this price and marginal cost, or $8 per unit. The monopolist's profits are $64.

Set marginal revenue equal to marginal cost. There is a second way to calculate the optimal choice of output that often is more convenient in application because it involves fewer calculations. This approach takes advantage of the marginal principle.

Indeed, if you think about it, it becomes obvious that a monopolist will choose an output level exactly where marginal revenue equals marginal cost, which corresponds to 8 units in figure 5-1, panel (*a*). Why? Suppose he chooses a lower level of output, say 7 units. In this case, he can charge a price of $13, which generates total revenue of $91. If he produces the next unit, he must reduce price to $12, but he sells 1 more unit, which in combination generates total revenue of $96. This means that the marginal revenue from producing the 8th unit is $5, but since his marginal cost is only $4, he can earn an extra dollar in excess profits by expanding output.

What if he chooses output 9? In this case, you can verify that his total revenue increases from $96 to $99, meaning that marginal revenue is $3. But the marginal cost of producing each unit is $4, which means that he loses a dollar of profit by expanding. Hence, the optimal output is 8 units.

> A monopolist maximizes profits by setting marginal revenue equal to marginal cost.

B. FINDING THE OPTIMAL PRICE

Now that you know the rule, what is the best approach to solve the problem? I demonstrate two ways: the long way, using a chart and a calculator, and the short way, using a little algebra.

---

[85]Using calculus, marginal revenue is the first derivative of the total revenue function with respect to output.

1. The Long Way

I have already described the long way. Simply search for the quantity that maximizes profits. Table 5-1 demonstrates this approach. I write a series of possible price-quantity combinations given by the demand curve (columns 1 and 2). I then calculate total revenues (column 3) and costs (column 4). Then calculate marginal revenue (column 5), which is the difference in revenue between two adjacent quantities. Marginal costs are $4 at every quantity in this problem (column 6). Column 7 shows profits, which are the difference between total revenues and total costs. The answer is found by looking for the quantity either where marginal revenue equals marginal costs, or equivalently, where total profits are highest. Either way, the solution is found at 8 units of output. As long as marginal

TABLE 5-1. SOLUTION TO THE MONOPOLY PRICE PROBLEM

Price (1)	Quantity (2)	Total Revenue (3)	Total Cost (4)	Marginal Revenue* (5)	Marginal Cost (6)	Profits (7)	Elasticity Demand (8)
20	0	0	0		4	0	
19	1	19	4	19	4	15	−19.00
18	2	36	8	17	4	28	−9.00
17	3	51	12	15	4	39	−5.67
16	4	64	16	13	4	48	−4.00
15	5	75	20	11	4	55	−3.00
14	6	84	24	9	4	60	−2.33
13	7	91	28	7	4	63	−1.86
12	8	96	32	5	4	64	−1.50
11	9	99	36	3	4	63	−1.22
10	10	100	40	1	4	60	−1.00
9	11	99	44	−1	4	55	−0.82
8	12	96	48	−3	4	48	−0.67
7	13	91	52	−5	4	39	−0.54
6	14	84	56	−7	4	28	−0.43
5	15	75	60	−9	4	15	−0.33
4	16	64	64	−11	4	0	−0.25
3	17	51	68	−13	4	−17	−0.18
2	18	36	72	−15	4	−36	−0.11
1	19	19	76	−17	4	−57	−0.05
0	20	0	80	−19	4	−80	1.00

*The marginal revenue is the change in total revenue from adding one more unit of output. This number is a bit different from the short way of calculating marginal revenue (discussed later); in the long way, the marginal revenue is lumpy because we are dealing with whole units. Don't worry about these small discrepancies.

costs are positive, the optimum monopoly output always occurs in the elastic portion of the demand curve (column 8).

When doing a discrete calculation, the optimal solution may not occur exactly where marginal revenue equals marginal cost because the condition might hold for a fraction of a unit (for example $Q = 8.5$). In this case, choose the last quantity for which marginal revenue exceeds marginal cost; that is, stop just short of the level at which marginal revenue is less than marginal cost.

2. The Short Way

The long way involves lots of calculations, which means that it takes a long time to solve the problem. Learning a rule for *linear* demand curves takes less time. The rule is simply put: the marginal revenue curve has twice the slope as the "inverse" demand curve (meaning that it is written so that price is on the left-hand side).[86] Notice that in writing the demand curve with price as the dependent variable, the slope that is doubled is the traditional rise-over-run calculation.

The Marginal Revenue Curve the Fast Way (for a Linear Demand Curve)

Write the demand curve with price on the left-hand side (sometimes called the inverse demand curve). The marginal revenue curve is the same as the (inverse) demand curve except that the slope is twice as great:

Demand curve: $$Q = a - bP$$

Inverse demand curve: $$P = \frac{a}{b} - \frac{1}{b}Q$$

Marginal revenue curve: $$MR = \frac{a}{b} - \frac{2}{b}Q$$

We can check if the marginal revenue expression is correct because we know that marginal revenue equals zero exactly at the midpoint of a linear demand curve. For the demand curve we are using in this chapter, $a = 20$ and $b = 1$, and thus, using the shortcut rule, $MR = 20 - 2Q$. The midpoint of the demand curve is $Q = 10$. Substituting this value

---

[86]Write a linear demand curve ($Q = a - bP$), except put price on the left-hand side: $P = \alpha - \beta Q$, where $\alpha = a/b$ and $\beta = 1/b$. To obtain total revenue, multiply both sides by quantity: $PQ = \alpha Q - \beta Q^2$. To obtain marginal revenue from very small changes in output, take the first derivative with respect to quantity, which yields $MR = \alpha - 2\beta Q$, which is the same as the inverse demand curve (the demand curve when the price is on the left-hand side), except the slope is 2β instead of β.

into this expression, we obtain $20 - 2 (10) = 0$, which confirms that marginal revenue is zero at the midpoint (see panel [a]).

Knowing this rule makes it easy to determine the optimal quantity for a monopolist. If marginal cost of production is C, then all we need to do is set marginal revenue equal to marginal cost, which yields the output level that maximizes profits.[87]

Optimal output choice in a monopoly when marginal cost, MC, is constant and demand is linear $Q = a - bP$:

Step 1: Set marginal revenue equal to marginal cost: $MR = MC$

Step 2: Substitute the expressions for MR and MC: $\frac{a}{b} - \frac{2}{b}Q = C$

Step 3: Solve for Q. This is the optimal quantity: $Q^* = \frac{1}{2}(a - bC)$

Step 4: Substitute parameter values: $a = 20$, $b = 1$, and $C = 4$: $Q^* = \frac{1}{2}(20 - 4) = 8$

Step 5: Substitute Q^* into the demand curve to find price: $P^* = 20 - 8 = \$12$

Note: When output has to be a whole unit, then round down to the nearest integer.

C. CHARACTERISTICS OF THE MONOPOLY SOLUTION

It is useful to consider a few more characteristics of the optimal monopoly price. First, the monopolist cannot choose *both* price and quantity. Once it chooses quantity, price is given by the demand curve and vice versa. Second, the monopolist does not charge the highest possible price; instead, he looks for the price that, in combination with the quantity demanded at this price, maximizes profits. If he chooses price $20 in our example, he earns zero profits. If he charges $15, he earns profits that are less than if he chooses $12.[88] Third, as long as a monopolist has a

---

[87]An alternative approach that yields the same answer is to find the output, Q^* that maximizes profits. Total costs are simply CQ, where C is marginal cost and Q is quantity. From note 86, we know that total revenue is $PQ = \alpha Q - \beta Q^2$. Profits are $\pi = PQ - CQ$. Substitute for PQ so that $\pi = \alpha Q - \beta Q^2 - CQ$. Take the first derivative with respect to Q and set the result equal to zero. This gives us the profit-maximizing output for a monopolist, which I denote as Q^*: $\alpha - 2\beta Q^* - C = 0$. Thus, when $\alpha = 20$, $\beta = 1$, and $C = 4$, $Q^* = 8$.

[88]At price $15, consumers purchase 5 units that cost $4 each to produce. Thus, excess profits per unit are $11. Since he sells 5 units, total profits are $55. At price $12, he earns only $8 in excess profits per unit but sells 8 units for a total profit of $64.

positive marginal cost of production, then it will choose a level of output where marginal revenue is positive (because in equilibrium, marginal cost equals marginal revenue). This means that absolute demand elasticity at the optimal price must be greater than unity.

A fourth characteristic is that, given that a monopolist produces only where the demand curve is elastic, its optimal markup above marginal cost is directly related to demand elasticity at the profit-maximizing output. This result is intuitive and easy to derive, but you only need to know the expression:[89]

Monopolist Percentage Markup and Demand Elasticity
The greater the (absolute) demand elasticity, the lower the monopoly percentage markup over competitive price. If M is the percentage markup, then we have:

$$M = \left[\frac{-1}{1+\eta} \right] \times 100, \text{ where } -\eta > 1$$

where η is the elasticity of demand at the monopolist's optimum quantity (remember that it is negative and greater than unity in absolute terms). If demand elasticity around the optimal price is -5, then the markup is 25 percent above competitive price, but if η is -2 then the markup is 100 percent.

For example, consider table 5-1. At the $12 price, demand elasticity is -1.5 and marginal cost is $4. Our formula tells us that the markup is 200 percent. That is, given this demand curve and marginal cost, the monopolist finds it optimal to set price ($12) equal to three times marginal cost ($4).

---

[89]Consider the linear demand curve, $P = \alpha - \beta Q$. Solve in terms of Q and take the first derivative with respect to price, then multiply by P/Q, which gives the demand elasticity $\eta = (-1/\beta)P/Q$. Now write the first-order condition for an output that maximizes profits from note 87: $a - 2\beta Q - C = 0$. Divide by price: $\alpha/P - 2\beta Q/P = C/P$; then write the second term as two separate but identical terms $(-2\beta Q/P = -\beta Q/P - \beta Q/P)$, and combine one with the first term: $(\alpha - \beta Q)/P - \beta Q/P = C/P$. Note that the first term is unity because the numerator is the demand curve in terms of price, P, and hence, cancels with the denominator. The second term is the inverse of the demand elasticity. So, we have $C/P = 1 + 1/\eta$, or $P/C = \eta/(1 + \eta)$. Subtract unity from both sides to obtain $(P - C)/C = -1/(1 + \eta)$. Note that as long as C is positive, the monopolist will choose an output in the elastic portion of the demand curve.

SOME RULES ABOUT MONOPOLY PRICE

A monopolist:
1. Chooses either price or quantity, not both.
2. Chooses the profit-maximizing price, not the highest price.
3. Chooses an output where absolute demand elasticity exceeds 1.
4. Sets a price that is closer to the competitive solution, the lower the absolute demand elasticity in the relevant range.

EXERCISE:
For the demand curve shown in figure 5-1 (a), find the optimal price when the marginal cost of production is $6. What is the price markup? Use the shortcut formula to determine marginal revenue. Then solve the problem again when the marginal cost is $9. Find three more solutions when marginal costs are alternatively $12, $15, and $18. This gives you five solutions, one for each assumed marginal cost. Do the results confirm your intuition that the optimum price for a monopolist is inversely related to absolute demand elasticity?[90]

II. The Social Cost of Monopoly

There are two sources of social costs attributable to monopoly pricing. First, a deadweight loss results from the restriction of output below the competitive level. Second, the creation of monopoly profits encourages other participants to replicate similar profits elsewhere, which sets off a "rent erosion" effect.

A. DEADWEIGHT LOSS

Figure 5-2 shows a clean version of the optimal monopoly solution. Of course, when I use the word *optimal*, I mean that it is *privately* optimal, meaning that it is optimal from the perspective of the *monopolist* to

---

[90]The answers are as follows. When doing a discrete solution, round down to the nearest integer, which means that that marginal revenue will exceed marginal cost by a small amount.

MC	Q^*	P^*	P^*/MC	η	M	Profits
4	8	12	3.00	−1.5	200	64
6	7	13	2.17	−1.9	117	49
9	5.5	14.5	1.61	−2.6	61	30.25
12	4	16	1.33	−4.0	33	16
15	2.5	17.5	1.17	−7.0	17	6.25
18	1	19	1.06	−19.0	6	1

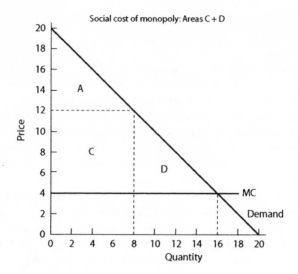

Figure 5-2. The Monopoly Solution

choose this price. It is not the *socially* optimal price. We already know that the socially optimal price is one where the marginal cost of producing an additional unit is just equal to the value attached by the marginal consumer to that unit. In terms of the demand curve that I use in the illustration, this output is 16 units. The monopolist restricts output to 8 units.

Owing to the restriction of output, the monopolist creates a deadweight loss measured by the triangle labeled D. While consumers are willing and able to pay prices in excess of the marginal cost of production over the range of output 9 through 16 units, they are deprived of the opportunity to make these trades.

In this sense, a monopoly price is similar to a tax on output. That is, we can think of a monopolist as someone who has been awarded a right to assess an excise tax that maximizes tax revenue and to pocket the proceeds. This private tax revenue of sorts is measured by area C. The deadweight loss is very similar to the tax solution. The difference is that unlike the government solution, the property rights to monopoly profits

---

The effects of monopoly pricing are akin to setting an excise tax that maximizes tax revenues from some market. The result in either case is lower output and a "triangle loss." There is, however, one further consideration: a private party (the monopolist) pockets the tax, which ultimately creates a **market for monopoly**.

are not typically awarded until after several would-be monopolists have expended monies trying to win the "monopoly prize."

B. MARKET FOR MONOPOLY

Society views the amount denoted by area C as a transfer from consumers to the producer. The monopolist views this amount as a gain. If monopoly pricing merely resulted in a transfer, then we could ignore this problem under the assumption that a dollar is a dollar no matter who holds it. The problem is that *potential* monopolists view the private gain worthy of expending resources to obtain; hence, the potential for excess profits invites wasteful activity.

Chapter 4 illustrates a case in which farm producers accomplish exactly this outcome. In one solution, wheat farmers convince Congress to help farmers act in concert by enforcing a quota system for deliveries to the cooperative silos. Output is set lower than competitive levels, which creates an upward pressure on price. This solution is similar to the one I show in figure 5-2, except that in the former case, the government helps farmers act *as though* they are a monopoly.

This discussion should stimulate a question: *how does a firm (or group of firms) obtain the property rights to a monopoly*? I already revealed one avenue to monopoly: the government has the authority to award one! In the case of wheat, it simply enacts legislation directing the United States Department of Agriculture (USDA) to coordinate a collective wheat output that is lower than the competitive solution. But is it plausible that Congress randomly decides one day, "Hey! Let's set up a complex system whereby the USDA helps wheat farmers obtain a higher price at the expense of consumers"?

Wheat farmers did not create something from nothing. Lobbyists for wheat farmers expended substantial resources trying to convince Congress that the government should engage in such a policy. Just as farmers expended resources to produce wheat, so too must they have incurred resource expense to create a defacto monopoly price. The latter resources could otherwise be used to create value for society (for example, by producing more wheat); hence, there is a real resource cost to industries lobbying Congress for special favors.

Market for monopoly: Refers to natural forces in the market to expend resources to obtain a monopoly, either by lobbying government, trying to effectively collude with other firms, or perhaps by finding a patent, a special case that I consider in the next chapter. In the market for monopoly, we expect the same competitive return on investments as in any other market.

C. RENT EROSION

To see where this process might lead, suppose that every industry can be characterized by the demand and cost conditions shown in figure 5-2. If an industry can get Congress to create a monopoly for them by enforcing a restricted output, then it would earn the collective profit in the amount $64.

1. The Game

Suppose that for fear of voter reaction Congress awards only one monopoly per period. If wheat farmers are the only ones to perceive this possibility, then surely they are willing to pay lobbyists to expend resources up to $64 writing letters, getting favorable editorials written, wining and dining members of congress and their staffs, inviting them to attend farm conferences at swanky resorts, and so on. Suppose that owing to ethics rules, Congress cannot take more than say $8 from any lobbying effort. Then it surely is a profitable activity for wheat farmers to hire lobbyists to obtain monopoly legislation. In exchange for expending $8, they receive a benefit worth $64.

What about the producers of other agricultural commodities? If wheat farmers can obtain such legislation, then why not tobacco farmers, corn growers, barley farmers, and so on? Consider tobacco farmers. Suppose that they see what the wheat farmers are up to. Suppose that they also spend $8 to obtain rights to restrict output. If the wheat and tobacco folks each expend the same effort, it is reasonable to assume that each has a 50:50 chance of winning the "monopoly lottery."

In this case, the tobacco farmers engage in the following logic: spend $8 and obtain a 50 percent chance to win $64. Is this a good deal? If you could play a game in Las Vegas that paid $64 with 50 percent probability and cost $8 to play, would you play? Hopefully, your answer is *yes*! You expect to make money in this activity. Hence, we can presume that the tobacco farmers play. What about barley farmers?

If wheat farmers and tobacco farmers already are "in the game," then barley farmers must figure: $8 to play with a 33 percent chance of winning $64. Play? *Yes.* What about cranberry growers? Pay $8 to play in exchange for a 25 percent chance to win $64. *Yes.*

Rent erosion: A term of art that refers to the process by which surplus is eroded by resource cost. The erosion occurs as a result of competition to secure the property rights to the rent.

2. The Number of Entrants

To see how many players enter the game, think of playing the same game in a casino. The game costs $8 to play. The payoff is $64, payable to the lucky player whose name is drawn from a hat. If only four people are playing, then they expect to make a fortune by repeatedly playing the game.[91] Expected profits from playing disappear only when eight players have their names in the hat.

Now return to our agriculture monopoly game. If the prize is $64 and the cost of playing is $8, how many industries play the game? The chance of winning is one out of N. Entry occurs until expected profits from this activity are zero. If N industries play, then each has the chance $1/N$ to win the amount $PRIZE$; hence, expected winnings are $1/N \times PRIZE$. The cost to play CP is $8. Since $PRIZE = \$64$, then the expected prize equals the cost to play when there are eight industries playing the game ($N = 8$). Thus, eight industries play the monopoly game, at a total resource cost of $64. In this case, each player views his chances of winning as one in eight. If each played the game many times, then each would expect to win one in every eight times he played.

With eight players, the expected return from playing the game is competitive; that is, there are no expected profits from investing in the monopoly game. As in any other market, we expect entry or exit in the market for monopoly until the excess return on investments in this market is zero.

Equilibrium Condition in the Market for Monopoly

The number of would-be monopolists, N, determines the chance that any one gains the rights to monopoly profits. Anticipated excess profits are the $PRIZE$. Assuming that each participant has an equal chance of winning, each has one chance in N to be the winner. Thus, the probability of winning is $1/N$. A competitive market for monopoly is in equilibrium when there are sufficient participants so that the chance of winning the prize, times the prize amount, equals the cost of playing, CP:

$$\frac{1}{N} PRIZE = CP$$

---

3. The Social Cost of Monopoly Reconsidered

Now reconsider the social cost of monopoly pricing. Whether one obtains a monopoly by lobbying Congress or consorting with other industry members to collude on price, or as I show in chapter 6, by obtaining a patent on a new idea, the expected social cost of monopoly equals

---

[91]Play the game 100 times. Total entry costs are $800. The player expects to win 25 times out of 100 for a total prize amount of $1,600 (25 × $64). This gives the gambler a profit of $800.

the usual triangle, *plus* the rectangle that denotes profits. In terms of figure 5-2, the social cost of monopoly equals the sum of areas *D plus C*.

In the example just used, the "winner" of the monopoly earns $64 in profits and expends only $8. But the seven losers in the game each also spend $8, for a total expenditure of $56. After accounting for all the resource cost of playing the game, it is apparent that the entirety of the prize is eroded by resource cost. That is unfortunate because before someone invented the monopoly game, area *C* was surplus.

To put some numbers on the problem, consider figure 5-2. In the competitive outcome, consumer surplus is the sum of areas *A plus C plus D*, which is worth $128. By allowing the market for monopoly to operate, we are left with a consumer surplus denoted by area *A*, which is worth only $32; the remaining $96 of surplus is lost, $32 of which is deadweight loss (area *D*), and $64 in rent erosion (area *C*).[92]

Rent erosion is one reason why antitrust laws exist. They deter wasteful activity. It also explains why society discourages property crime. After reading the remainder of the chapter, go back and read this section entitled "Why Is Auto Theft a Crime?" in the box on page 167.

The social cost of monopoly: Equals the deadweight loss from the restriction in output plus the total amount of excess profits. The erosion is incomplete if some inputs to the market for monopoly have a rising supply schedule, in which case some of the surplus will become economic rent.

EXERCISE:
For the demand curve, $P = 20 - 2Q$, and constant marginal cost, $MC = \$4$, determine the optimum monopoly price, profits, and deadweight loss.[93]

---

[92]The only way that rent erosion is not entirely wasteful is if some inputs in the market for monopoly are in scarce supply. For example, suppose that lobbyists' supply curve looks like the one I depicted for litigation lawyers in figure 3-7. In this case, rent to scarce resources accounts for a portion of area *C* in figure 5-2, and hence, is a pure transfer.

[93]Draw a diagram showing the demand curve and marginal cost curve, and show all your answers on that figure. When the demand curve is linear, the marginal revenue curve is the same as the demand curve with price on the left-hand side, except it has twice the slope. Thus, we have $MR = 20 - 4Q$. Since marginal cost, MC, is $4, then solve for the quantity, Q^*, for which $MR = MC$: $20 - 4Q^* = 4$. This gives us $Q^* = 4$. Since the demand curve is $P = 20 - 2Q$, then when Q is 4, it follows that price is $12. Thus, monopoly profits are equal to 4 units, times profit per unit of $8 ($12 - $4), or $32. To obtain deadweight loss, find the competitive level of output, which occurs at the quantity Q^0 where the marginal cost curve intersects the demand curve: $4 = 20 - 2Q^0$, which gives us

WHY IS AUTO THEFT A CRIME?

Rent erosion in the monopoly model helps explain why society enacts and enforces laws protecting private property. To illustrate, suppose that legislation is enacted making auto theft *legal*. Also, suppose that all drivers lease their cars and that the lease fees include theft insurance. Compared to a world in which auto theft is illegal and enforced, monthly lease fees are higher for two reasons. First, auto manufacturers spend more on sophisticated key systems and alarms. Second, notwithstanding the additional protections, more thefts are likely because thieves incur neither fines nor incarceration and cannot be thwarted completely by any economical antitheft devices. To keep the problem simple, assume that thefts, if successful, are done with zero chance that the owner herself will catch them in the act, thereby putting aside the cost of direct confrontations.

The Cost of Crime

Figure 5-2 can be recycled to portray the economic effects. Just change the horizontal axis to represent thousands of auto thefts and the vertical to represent monthly lease fees (in hundreds). When auto theft is illegal, the monthly lease fee is $400 and 16,000 autos are on the road (some of which are stolen from time to time). The $400 includes expenses on more modest auto protection devices and lower theft insurance. As a result of legalization, the monthly lease fee increases from $400 to $1,200, causing a reduction in the quantity of autos on the road from 16,000 to 8,000. The legalization of auto theft imposes two kinds of cost. First, a deadweight cost arises measured by area D (people give up driving that they otherwise valued more than $400 but less than $1,200). Second, a rent erosion cost arises, measured by area C.

Area C represents real resource expenditures of two kinds: more expensive theft-reduction devices and more stolen cars. At first, the latter component seems like a transfer. The property ownership of my car passes to a clever thief one night. But this is more than a transfer. Thieves spend real resources to steal autos. Instead of spending their work week producing something useful for society, they train for and execute auto thefts. Society loses the value of their otherwise productive output. As long as auto theft confers benefits in

continued . . .

$Q^0 = 8$. Deadweight loss equals the triangle with the base equal to the difference between monopoly output and competitive output, or 4 units (8 minus 4), and the height, which is the difference between the monopoly price and competitive price, or $8 ($12 minus $4). Using the formula for a triangle, this area is $16.

WHY IS AUTO THEFT A CRIME? *Continued*

excess of thieves' opportunity wages, entry into auto theft occurs. Entry stops when the value of the autos they steal give them a "weekly pay" equal in amount to what they could earn elsewhere.

For example, if a week's worth of work yields a 10 percent chance of a successful theft and the average auto is worth $10,000, then expected weekly salary from crime is $1,000. If the alternative wage is $200 per week, we expect entry. Equilibrium occurs when sufficient numbers of thieves work the market that the probability of a success per week falls to 2 percent. The *PRIZE* is $10,000. The cost to play is $200. The probability of "winning" is 2 percent. We have equilibrium, which ensures that all transfers of property rights are converted into social costs.

In the context of figure 5-2, legislation to make auto theft illegal confers the gains depicted by areas $C + D$. Against these gains are the resources costs expended in law enforcement (police salaries and such), court costs (judges, lawyers, and other staff diverted from productive work), and incarceration (correction guards, etc.). It makes sense to incur these costs if and only if they are less than the cost of crime (areas $C + D$).

Finally, it is interesting to note that the effect of legalizing auto theft is akin to an auto tax, with one important difference. State governments have a monopoly on tax collections, and thus, it is not possible for another entity to compete with the state to obtain these tax revenues. This is an important feature of state-mandated taxes. They stand a better chance of evading rent erosion problems.

The Optimum Level of Enforcement
It is reasonable to query: why, even when illegal, is there *any* auto theft? The answer is that zero auto theft is uneconomic. The key is the statement I made earlier alluding to the social cost of reducing crime, which we might generally refer to as enforcement costs. Figure 5-3 portrays the essence of the problem. The horizontal axis portrays the number of units of deterrence. Think of this as a quality-adjusted number of people devoted to the enforcement of auto theft laws.

The demand for enforcement comes from owners who gain from lower lease payments and less deadweight loss. It is the vertical summation of demands from all the auto owners in the city. I suppose that the schedule is downsloping, reflecting the fact that there may be diminishing returns to deterring theft (the first police officer on the street looking for auto thieves reduces the number of thefts more than adding the ninety-ninth officer). I suppose that the marginal cost

continued . . .

WHY IS AUTO THEFT A CRIME? *Continued*

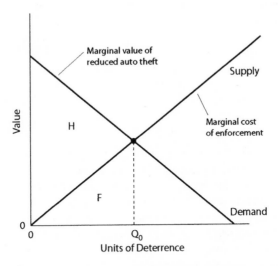

Figure 5-3. Optimum Quantity of Enforcement

of more deterrence units increases, perhaps reflecting the need for more (expensive) detectives versus uniformed police officers to reduce thefts on the margin, but the solution is similar if the marginal cost of more units of deterrence is constant.

The optimum number of deterrence units is Q_0. The marginal cost of more enforcement units exceeds the value of reduced crime. Since owners still express a demand for enforcement for units above Q_0, however, we know that some thefts still occur. This explains why in figure 5-2, the monthly lease cost includes a positive cost of theft insurance and some cost of theft deterrence. Deterrence is not free, and so we economize on it.

Why Does the Figure Not Have a Price?
Figure 5-3 represents a demand and supply for units of deterrence. The interpretation of these schedules is the same as before, and the solution satisfies the usual condition that demand price equals marginal cost (the supply price). Why do I not portray a horizontal line to the left axis to represent the price? One reason that jumps to mind is that there is only one seller (the city government), and so we do not have a competitive price outcome. But then why are we not talking about a monopoly solution? The reason is that the citizens also

continued . . .

WHY IS AUTO THEFT A CRIME? *Continued*

"own" the government, and so they are both buyer and seller. The citizens have no reason to pay more for each unit of deterrence than it costs to make available. Thus, they will pay a different price for each unit of deterrence along the marginal cost curve up to the optimum quantity. In terms of the figure, they pay taxes equal to area *F*, and they enjoy the entire amount of the surplus, *H*.

III. Monopoly Price Discrimination

I have assumed thus far that the monopolist can charge only one price. In general, however, a monopolist can generate substantially higher profits if he can set different prices to different consumers. To do this, of course, he needs to separate his market; that is, he must prevent consumers who pay a lower price from reselling it to someone paying a higher price. I explore a few ways in which this can be done and illustrate the potential for enhancing profits beyond those available by charging one price to all consumers.

Price discrimination: The term used when a firm sells the same product to different consumers at different prices, which is not explained by a difference in the cost of making it available to these markets.

A. TWO MARKETS: ICE CREAM MONOPOLY

Suppose that there is a town in which only one person sells ice cream. The city council awards the monopoly because it does not want its fine citizens to eat too much saturated fat, and so they reason that less is better. Assume that the marginal cost of an ice cream cone is $4.

You notice that you can separate the market. One is a nursing home where ten elderly widows are willing to pay upwards of $8 for an ice cream cone once per month out of their meager Social Security checks. The nursing home forbids food items from entering or leaving the building except by vendors; this constraint prevents the women from buying ice cream for one price at the front door and reselling it at a higher price out the back window to the general public. I depict this market in panel (*b*) of figure 5-4.

The rest of the market (the "outside world") is depicted in panel (*a*). The latter demand curve is the same one I used in figure 5-2, and so we already know that the optimal monopoly price in that market is $12, which generates $64 in excess profits.

(a)

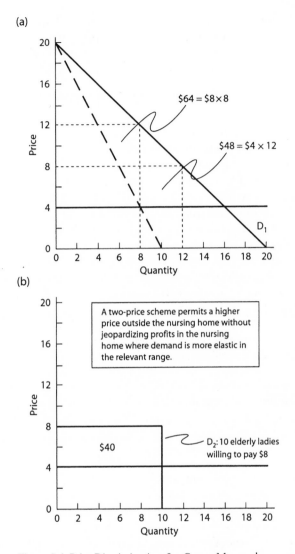

(b)

A two-price scheme permits a higher price outside the nursing home without jeopardizing profits in the nursing home where demand is more elastic in the relevant range.

Figure 5-4. Price Discrimination: Ice Cream Monopoly

A single price allowed. Suppose that the city council puts a restriction on the monopoly: the ice cream vendor can charge whatever price he wants, but he must charge the same price to everyone. The problem is that if the monopolist charges $12 for everyone, he forgoes the opportunity to sell any ice cream to the women in the nursing home, because at any price above $8, they are unwilling to purchase any ice cream cones. Given the one-price restriction, what is the best price to charge?

In this example, it turns out that the best price is $8.[94] In this way, the vendor earns only $48 in profits in his main market (he sells 12 cones, which yield $4 in excess profits each), but he earns another $40 in excess profits from his nursing home sales (10 units at $4 in excess profits each). Thus, total profits at the $8 price are $88. This outcome is better than charging $12, which yields only $64 in profits.

Two prices allowed. Suppose instead that the city council allows the vendor to charge different prices to different consumers. What is his optimal response? The answer is: charge $8 to the elderly women in the nursing home and $12 in the other market. In this way, the monopolist earns the maximum allowable profits in his main market ($64) and retains the $40 profit from the nursing home market. This gives a total profit of $104, which is superior to the $88 profit in the optimum one-price solution.

This result is general. Usually, a monopolist earns higher profits by charging different prices to different consumers. Separation of its markets is a prerequisite. In the previous solution, if the nursing home permits reselling, the elderly women purchase excess ice cream cones at $8, then turn around and sell them out the back window of the nursing home at a price less than $12, making it difficult for the ice cream vendor to maintain a two-price scheme.

> If a monopolist can separate markets based on different demand conditions, he almost always can earn higher profits by charging different prices.

While the ice cream model is illustrative, appendix A presents a real-world case of price discrimination organized by milk marketing orders with the help of the U.S. Department of Agriculture. This scheme props up prices of raw milk used for fluid milk purposes and has the unusual effect of also encouraging more output of raw milk than is socially optimum.

---

[94]You can figure out this solution easily. Since $12 is the optimum price to charge in the first market, then you know that profits must fall in that market as price falls below $12. This rules out charging a price less than $12 and greater than $8 because this reduces profits in the first market and does not attract any sales at the nursing home. This leaves $8 as a natural possibility. But first consider charging a price below $8. You continue to lower profits in market 1 and further, you clearly are losing money at the nursing home because their demand is fixed at 10 cones below $8. Hence, if $8 beats a $12 price, then $8 must be the optimal choice because you ruled out every other price.

EXERCISE:

Suppose that once the elderly women see these two prices, they are able to get the city council to require that ice cream sold in the nursing home must be sold at a 50 percent discount compared to the outside world. Since the price in the outside world is $12, they figure that they will get the ice cream for $6. Will they? What price would you set? Assume that you have to sell whole cones (no fractions), and assume that in case of a tie, you choose the higher price. What is your new profit? How much do the elderly women gain?[95]

B. PERFECT PRICE DISCRIMINATION

It is useful to think about the extreme case of price discrimination. What are the *maximum* profits that a monopolist could ever earn from price discrimination? To illustrate this case, consider figure 5-5, which merely reproduces figure 5-4 panel (a). It is the market for ice cream outside the nursing home. Suppose that the vendor knows how much Jane is willing to pay for her first cone, second cone, and so on. He also knows Ken's demand curve, as well as the demand curve for all other consumers. Assuming that he makes all the sales at the same time (which rules out customers reselling to each other), he can charge the maximum price (less one penny) that each consumer is willing to pay for each ice cream cone. In this case, the ice cream vendor would convert virtually *all* of consumer surplus into excess profits. This solution is known as **perfect price discrimination**. Total profits in this solution are illustrated by the shaded area in the figure.

---

[95]The obvious first step is to ask if it is best to charge $16, which, after the 50 percent discount, retains the $8 price at the nursing home. This solution reduces quantity demanded in the outside world to just 4 cones. Profits fall to $48 in this market (4 cones times $12 each). Total profits are $88. Next try price of $15, which corresponds to 5 cones in the outside world but a price of $7.50 to the nursing home. Profits in the nursing home are $3.50 times 10, or $35. Profits in the outside world are $55 (5 cones times $11), for a total profit of $90. It turns out that the next lower price of $14 also gives $90 in profit, and thus the answer is $P = \$15$. At this price, the nursing home customers pay $7.50 and thus gain a total surplus of $5. The monopolist loses $14 in profits compared to the unfettered two-price scheme.

Using calculus, let x be fixed sales at the nursing home, p and q be price and quantity in the outside world, and c marginal cost. Note that the nursing home price must be $\frac{1}{2} p$. So profits $= pq + \frac{1}{2} px - c(x + q)$. Use the demand curve to express q in terms of p: $q = 20 - p$. Substitute $c = 4$ and $x = 10$. The control variable is p. Take the first derivative of profits with respect to p and set the result to zero. This gives $p = \$14.50$ and $q = 5.5$. Rounding the price upward to the nearest dollar gives $p = \$15$ and $q = 5$; hence, the nursing home price is $7.50.

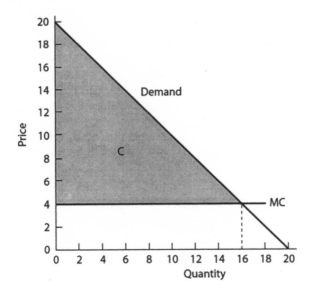

Figure 5-5. Perfect Price Discrimination

It is interesting to note that in a solution characterized by perfect price discrimination, there is essentially no consumer surplus, but there also is no deadweight loss. This latter loss is eliminated because the monopolist serves all consumers who are willing to pay a price in excess of marginal cost. That is, to reach consumers lower down on the demand curve, he does not have to reduce price for all other consumers. All efficient trades occur. Total profits are $128, which is twice as much as in the one-price solution.

Even though deadweight costs are zero, it does not follow that the social cost of monopoly is lower with perfect price discrimination compared to the one-price solution. The now higher excess profits are subject to rent erosion. Assuming that there are no rents accruing to inputs in the market for monopoly, then the social cost of monopoly under perfect price discrimination is unambiguously higher than under a one-price monopoly solution. The entirety of consumer surplus is converted to profits, which is converted to social cost in the market for monopoly.

C. OTHER WAYS TO EXTRACT CONSUMER SURPLUS

Tie-ins. How can firms try to extract consumer surplus that at least approximates the result generated by perfect price discrimination? Firms can try to accomplish this result in several ways. One way is to create a tie-in—that is, require buyers of product *A* to also buy product *B*.

Perfect price discrimination: Occurs when the seller knows each consumer's demand curve and sells its product or service at a different price for every unit purchased by every consumer, less one penny.

In this solution, the entirety of consumer surplus is converted into excess profits. Unless substantial economic rents are earned by some inputs in the market for monopoly, the social cost of monopoly is higher under perfect price discrimination as compared to a one-price solution.

A notable example is the case of IBM at the time that it had a virtual monopoly on computer mainframes. It recognized that heavy users of computing equipment are willing to pay a higher price for the mainframes than less intense users. If it charges a high price to the intense users, it forgoes the opportunity to earn profits from less intense users. If it charges a lower price to reach the latter market, it sacrifices large profits obtainable from the intense users.

One solution (the one that IBM devised) is to sell the mainframes for a relatively low price but to require users to purchase punch cards exclusively from IBM. The price it charged for these cards exceeded the competitive price of other similar cards in the market. One thought might be, "Hey, IBM is trying to extend its mainframe monopoly to the punch card market!" A more likely explanation is that IBM was trying to extract as much surplus from the monopoly it held on the mainframe market. By earning its excess profits in proportion to the number of cards used, intense users pay a higher price for the mainframe than the less intense users. Indeed, all users pay prices in proportion to their intensity of use.

Tie-in: A requirement to purchase product *B* as a condition of purchasing product *A*. Often a tie-in can help a firm with market power extract more consumer surplus.

Auctions. An alternative solution is to hold an auction. Consider the problem of the gas queue in chapter 4. In the queue solution to the maximum price problem, the most intense demanders of gasoline got the gas by waiting in line longer than those with a lower demand price. Suppose one person owned all the gasoline stations, or alternatively that all the owners agreed to the following scheme. Charge the regulated pump price (because the law requires it), but to create an "orderly" market, announce that only customers who hold green plastic cards issued by the station can purchase the gas. Each ticket gives the holder the right to purchase x gallons of gas per period, where the quantities written on all the cards, when summed, exactly exhaust the gasoline allocation each period.

If it were legal, the gas station owner can hold an auction, whereupon each driver submits a secret bid for a card. The bid specifies a request for x gallons of gasoline. The bid price is on a per-gallon basis. The cards go to the highest bidders. In this case, each consumer is fearful that his bid will be insufficient to obtain a card, and so his tendency is to bid an amount that cuts well into his consumer surplus. While the owner is unlikely to extract every penny of surplus, it would extract a good deal of it.

A good example of auctions is given by the practice of scalping tickets for a sports game, like the Washington Redskins. If you own a season ticket and a big game is coming up, would you be better off announcing an arbitrary price for the ticket or putting an ad in the paper asking for offers? Which way do you think you will get a higher price and still be sure to sell the ticket?

Another example is a typical auction held at Christie's. If you have a special painting by Renoir, do you announce a price or hold an auction at which collectors from around the world can meet and bid for the painting? The competition likely will successfully extract more consumer surplus than trying to guess about demand conditions.

> *Auctions* extract surplus from buyers in markets in which there is either one or just a few sellers.[96]

IV. Price Discrimination in Competitive Markets

While most students feel fairly comfortable with the intuitive notion that monopolists charge different prices, they often slip into a mistake. They think that if a firm charges two prices for what seems like the same product, it must mean that the firm has monopoly power. In fact, this is not the case. As long as there are fixed cost to production, price discrimination can occur in markets where there is no market power.

A. MOVIE THEATERS

To illustrate, I use a well-known case of movie theaters.[97] Consider the following stylized example. There are 100 theaters in some city, each of which has 100 seats. Assume that whenever a movie is shown all the

---

[96]The appendix to chapter 9 gives more information about auctions.

[97]This example is found in Harold Demsetz, "Joint Supply and Price Discrimination," *Journal of Law and Economics* 16 (October 1973): 389–405.

seats are taken, so that we do not have to worry about empty seats. Suppose further that the marginal cost of servicing customers is zero, but that there is a fixed cost of $1,000 to operate the theater each day (heat, air conditioning, investment returns to the investors, rent, etc.). At first, I suppose that people go to shows only in the evening. The demand for movies by these consumers is shown by the downsloping schedule appropriately labeled figure 5-6, panel (a).

The vertical axis is ticket price. The horizontal axis is number of seats. Owing to my assumption of full capacity, there is a one-to-one relationship between seats and movie theaters (the number of movie theaters equals number of seats, divided by 100). I assume that ticket prices are $10, so that each theater collects $1,000 per period. Hence, we know that $10 is a sustainable price because it is just sufficient to pay for average total costs. At this price, there are 100 theaters operating in the city, and thus, 10,000 moviegoers attending a show every day.[98]

Suppose now that while waiting to open for the evening customers, some enterprising theater owner notices that each afternoon there are hundreds of retirees, homemakers with children, kids who skipped school, and other assorted people all walking aimlessly around, obviously looking for something to do. After making some inquiries, she figures that many of these folks would be willing to pay up to $4 to see a movie in the afternoon. While she does not yet perceive total day demand, I depict the schedule that actually exists by the downward sloping schedule appropriately labeled in the figure. The owner gets the idea: why not open in the afternoon and present the movie a second time each day?

She decides to charge $4. Since she only needs 100 people to fill her theater, she finds at first that she can fill her theater at this price. She therefore earns $400 in excess profits. That is, in addition to the $10 ticket price she collects from the evening moviegoers, she now collects $4 from each of 100 people in the afternoon. Soon, as other theater owners notice, they too open in the afternoon to collect an extra $400. But as they add to the supply of afternoon seats, the afternoon price must fall. After all the theaters open in the afternoon, they find that the afternoon market clears at a $3 price, as shown in panel (a). Still, each owner is collecting an extra $300 in excess profits each day. What happens next?

In a word, *entry*. Excess profits attract entrants into the market who also want to earn excess profits. Thus, more theaters open. In the new equilibrium, what are the afternoon and evening ticket prices? How many theaters will operate? We know that in the new equilibrium, total revenues per period must be $1,000 because this is the cost of operating

---

[98]There are 100 theaters each with 100 seats. Since I assume full capacity, then there are 10,000 moviegoers each period.

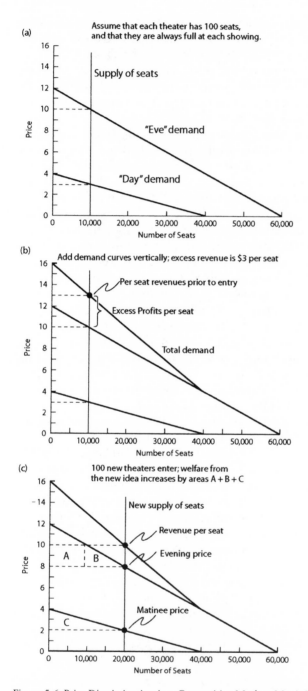

(a) Assume that each theater has 100 seats, and that they are always full at each showing.

Supply of seats

"Eve" demand

"Day" demand

Price

Number of Seats

(b) Add demand curves vertically; excess revenue is $3 per seat

Per seat revenues prior to entry

Excess Profits per seat

Total demand

Price

Number of Seats

(c) 100 new theaters enter; welfare from the new idea increases by areas A + B + C

New supply of seats

Revenue per seat

Evening price

A   B

Matinee price

C

Price

Number of Seats

Figure 5-6. Price Discrimination in a Competitive Market: Movie Theaters

the theater, including a competitive return. But how do we figure out the particulars of the solution?

The answer is simple. The trick is to recognize that the total demand for a movie seat each day is the *vertical* summation of the afternoon and evening demand prices. Why vertical and not horizontal? Adding demand curves horizontally implicitly assumes that if I consume ten gallons of gasoline, then no one else can consume the same ten gallons. But evening moviegoers do not preclude the afternoon viewers from using the same seats each day. Thus, the total demand for seats is the summation of the prices offered by afternoon and evening prices.

Panel (*b*) shows total demand for seats as the bold "kinked" downward-sloping schedule. It kinks at output 40,000 seats. This is the maximum number of afternoon moviegoers willing to pay a positive price. The panel shows equilibrium after all the existing movie theaters have matinee showings but before any entry of new theaters. The price of matinee tickets clears at $3. Existing theaters earn $3 in excess profits per seat.

Panel (*c*) shows equilibrium after entry. The equilibrium supply of seats is given where the total daily revenue per seat equals the sustainable price (namely, $10). Zero profits is reestablished when an additional 100 theaters enter. There are now 20,000 seats in the market. The additional supply reduces prices. The evening market-clearing price in the new equilibrium is $8. The matinee price is $2. The sum of these prices is total revenue per seat per day, which exactly equals the sustainable price.

Should the evening customers be mad that the afternoon customers pay a lower price? No. Because of the afternoon audience, the evening price *falls* from $10 to $8. So indeed the evening customers are *better off* because of the two-price scheme. Areas *A* + *B* in panel (*c*) measure these gains. Area *A* is the welfare gain to the old moviegoers who now pay a lower price. Area *B* represents the welfare gain to evening moviegoers who enter the market at the lower price. Matinee attendees gain surplus measured by area *C*. Thus, the welfare gain to the innovation is the sum of areas *A* + *B* + *C*.

If multiple prices are outlawed then 100 theaters go out of business, the evening price increases by $2, there are no matinees, and consumers lose surplus amounts denoted by areas *A* + *B* + *C*.

EXERCISE:
How does the movie theater pricing solution square with marginal cost pricing? Can you depict the cost structure of the movie theater? Do not forget that the fire code restriction limits seats to 100. Appendix B gives the answer.

B. OTHER EXAMPLES

Time-of-day pricing. Other time-of-day price discrimination is commonly found. For example, gourmet restaurants often serve lunch at substantial discounts from the evening price. Effectively, owners have figured out that while daytime diners are unwilling to pay the same price for gourmet food as evening diners, they are willing and able to pay a price in excess of marginal cost; hence, they are contributing something toward overhead. As a result, restaurants are able to offer their evening meals at a price lower than they would if they served only in the evening. Indeed, theater owners and restaurant owners who do not open during the day will find it difficult to compete with theaters and restaurants that do, because the latter can offer lower evening prices and still earn a competitive rate of return on their investments.

The airline industry offers another example. Some flights, say commuter flights from Washington, D.C., to New York City, predictably fly more or less full during the hours of 7:00 A.M. to 9:00 A.M. and from 4:00 P.M. to 6:00 P.M. Discount tickets usually are sold for flights with departure times less popular with businesspeople. As long as discount flyers on the interim flights pay more for their flights than the marginal cost of making these trips, it reduces the prices charged to the full-fare customers. There is a natural separation of the market because midday flights are not very useful for business travelers. Similar arguments apply to weekend flights until Sunday nights, when some business travelers return to the airports.

There are many other examples of time-of-day price differences. Golf courses often offer lower prices during off-peak times. Golfers who work usually cannot use the course during weekdays, especially during the middle of the day. If retirees are willing to pay a fee that exceeds the marginal cost of having them on the course, then the lower off-peak prices reduce the fees for full-fare golfers. Regular golfers cannot easily substitute into the low-price hours, and so the markets remain relatively insulated.

Perishable goods. Price discounting is common when a product is about to become valueless. For example, when produce and meats near their useful shelf life at the supermarket, they often are heavily discounted. If these products are not sold quickly, they are worthless. If the store can obtain some revenues from these products, then it is better off (and so are all other customers in the long run because competition among stores will translate these salvaged revenues into lower overall prices). Since most customers are willing to pay the higher price for produce and meat when fresh, it is likely that the buyers of the ripened produce and near-old meat are segmented from the regular buyers.

Airline seats also can have a perishable quality. If a plane departs an airport with an empty seat, it is essentially throwing away the seat for that flight. This is why airlines sell standby tickets at deep discounts.

Standbys risk unpredictable departure times. Most regular passengers have plans and are not tempted to shift to standby status. But if some students or retirees are willing to perform this function, then if they pay a fare in excess of the small marginal cost of serving them, all passengers ultimately benefit from their contribution to overhead.

Indeed, a newfound way for airlines to sell cheap tickets is through the Internet. If a day or two before flight time there are still twenty unused tickets for some particular flight, the airline often sells them through the Internet at a deep discount. As long as most passengers are unwilling to wait until a day or two before departure to obtain seats on a desired flight, it is likely that users of this service are segmented from regular passengers who are willing to pay a higher price in exchange for the certainty of flying at a particular time.

Common expenses. Another source of price differences is the existence of common overhead among many products. Grocery stores are an example. They sell thousands of products, all of which share the same overhead costs. How much overhead should be assigned to each item? If the store tries to assign too much overhead to products that have a high demand elasticity, it will lose lots of sales. Thus, it is more natural for them to attach a higher overhead rate to products that have an inelastic demand. Thus, even though there may be zero excess profits in the grocery business, pricing is done using a formula that closely resembles a monopolist (who also will charge a higher price to those who react less to price increases).

Moreover, since grocery stores in different parts of the city may have different clientele, they will not have the same mix of products, nor will the customers have the same set of demand elasticities. Thus, the overhead allocation may look quite different across grocery stores. Thus, one might observe the same chain charging $3 for a dozen oranges in store *A* and $4 in store *B*, giving rise to the impression that store *B* is "gouging" its customers. This does not mean, however, that excess profits exist in either store, when viewed from the perspective of total sales.

Price discrimination can exist in competitive markets under a variety of conditions as long as fixed costs are important relative to variable costs.

Common examples include time-of-day or time-of-week price differences (as in movie theaters, restaurants, golf courses, and airline seating), perishable goods (ripe produce and near-old meat in grocery stores, an airline about to fly with an empty seat), or joint supply conditions (as in the allocation of common fixed expenses in grocery markets).

Price discrimination in competitive markets always expands output and increases consumer surplus.

EXERCISE:
What is the dollar value of increased consumer surplus that results from price discrimination in the movie theater example illustrated in figure 5-6?[99]

Thinking about price discrimination. Price discrimination is a characteristic of markets where there is some element of monopoly pricing *and* in some markets that are perfectly competitive. In one case, the enhanced profits generated from separate pricing are "bad" because they generate higher profits and thus attract more rent erosion. In the other case, they are "good" in a Pareto sense because all consumers are better off and producers are no worse off. Hence, from a public policy perspective, price discrimination alone is insufficient to conclude that sellers have market power.

A PRICE DISCRIMINATION PUZZLE: WHY DOES HARVARD DISCOUNT TUITION?

It is apparent that Harvard University is deluged with applications from thousands of highly qualified applicants who can pay the full cost of tuition. So why does Harvard reject some of these applicants in favor of others who pay little or no tuition? Perhaps they are practicing charity, but suppose for the sake of discussion that they are not. Why would they *discount* prices when they could obtain full freight? Assume the following hypothetical facts: out of 1,000 students admitted to Harvard, 900 pay full price and 100 pay zero.

Because of the discounting of prices, we can pretty much rule out monopoly issues. If Harvard had market power, it would be thinking about obtaining higher prices, not lower ones. It cannot be an overhead argument. Unlike movie theaters, two students cannot occupy the same seat; they are mutually exclusive. Since every seat can be sold at full-price, the overhead explanation does not make sense; the

continued . . .

---

[99]Consumer surplus for evening viewers increases by areas $A + B$, which amounts to $30,000 (area $A = (\$10 - \$8) \times 10,000 = \$20,000$; and area $B = (\$10 - \$8) \times 10,000 \times \frac{1}{2} = \$10,000$). Consumer surplus for daytime viewers increases by the amount denoted by area C, which amounts to $20,000 (equal to $(\$4 - \$2) \times 20,000 \times \frac{1}{2}$). Thus, the matinee innovation increases consumer surplus by $50,000.

A Price Discrimination Puzzle *Continued*

full-price students cannot receive a lower price by admitting zero-price students. The answer must lie elsewhere. Several alternatives may suggest themselves. I offer two.

First explanation. If Harvard accepts only smart students, it might not have the most exciting class of students one could imagine. And indeed the 900 students and their parents would perhaps hope for an environment in which they could meet fun or interesting people on campus to make the educational experience more rewarding and enjoyable. Suppose that indeed these 900 full-price users would attain dramatically higher surplus from exposure to the 100 "interesting" students. Then presumably, they would gladly pay an additional 11 percent tuition to make up for the zero-tuition students. Indeed, if the educational experience is sufficiently rewarding, these 900 students could end up gifting more monies to Harvard as faithful alumni.

Second explanation. Perhaps the explanation lies not in the 900 other students but in the 100 that attend Harvard for free. Suppose that if these 100 were not accepted, another 100 smart kids would attend. Also suppose that these marginal 100 are not great prospects for future giving to Harvard. But each of the 100 kids who never would have attended Harvard *but for* the "gift" of zero tuition are incredibly grateful for the opportunity they have been given—so grateful, in fact, that if they are very successful later on, they might be happy to send large amounts of money to Harvard. If the tuition is $30,000 per year, then the total "gift" to these lucky 100 people amounts to $12 million over four years. But if Harvard is careful to choose promising candidates to award the zero-tuition prize, all it needs is a few successes to make up for the forgone tuition.

Other explanations? What ideas do you have that might explain this anomalous pricing pattern?

V. Competition of the Few

We have concentrated on two extreme forms of market structure: perfect competition and monopoly. What about all the variations in between? Do we need other models to try to characterize these outcomes? In some circumstances, it is important to learn more about the details of markets and to try to customize models to the situation at hand—for example, in the context of a particular antitrust case. For our purposes, however, and for most applications, the competition and monopoly models will suffice.

A. CHEATING

Consider the market that I portray in figure 5-7. Competitive price is $4. The optimal (single) monopoly price is $12. Suppose a dozen or more major firms in this market want to collude on price. For concreteness, consider OPEC,[100] the international cartel of many large oil-producing countries. While cartels are illegal in the United States, OPEC is organized in countries outside the United States, where cartels are legal.

Suppose that OPEC nations meet. Currently price is $4. They would like to raise price to $12 to earn maximum profits for the group. Each country is given a quota, so that total OPEC output is restricted to 8 billion barrels of oil per period. They all agree. Now consider a single country. It has a quota of 100,000 barrels per period, so that its share of excess profits is $800,000. When the representative returns home, he might figure that now that the price includes an excess profit of $8 per barrel, his country could earn even more money by producing a little more than its quota. Perhaps it sneaks out another 25,000 barrels in hopes of earning $1 million excess profits instead of $800,000.

This cheating tendency should not be very surprising. If a group of people is willing to get together to stick it to consumers, why is it not

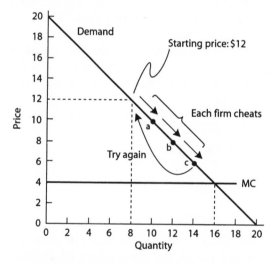

Figure 5-7. The Incentive to Cheat on Collusion

[100]Organization of Petroleum Exporting Countries. OPEC does not control all international oil, but I assume that they do for purposes of this example.

appealing to think that they also are willing to do the same to each other? Generally, the problem is considered under the heading of No Honor among Thieves.

The problem, of course, is that if one country is willing to cheat on the agreement, why not all countries? But if all countries cheat, the $12 price is not sustainable. Suppose that all the cheating results in a price of $11 at output 9 billion barrels (above point a in the figure). Now reconsider the country we earlier discussed. It thought it would earn $1 million in profits after cheating (that is, by selling 125,000 barrels). But at the $11 price, it earns only $7 excess per barrel for a total of $875,000. It then thinks, "Well, if I expand output by another 18,000 barrels or so, I can regain my target of $1 million in excess profits."[101] Besides, since it is apparent from the price movement that all his colleagues are cheating, why be a sucker by being the only one restricting output? But as all countries expand output, price falls, which begets more cheating (points b and c in the figure).

It is apparent that the process of cheating works to push price back in the direction of $4. I have shown some arrows to depict this process in figure 5-7. At some point, OPEC calls another meeting to try to reinstill some discipline. This effort may prop up price again, as indicated by the arrow returning to the pre-cheating target price. But then the process starts all over again.

If cheating is substantial, then the competitive model is probably a pretty good approximation to the oil market. In instances in which price is sticky at the monopoly level (say a group of firms has learned to police each other's output pretty accurately), then we can use the monopoly model as a good approximation. The point is that for most purposes, we do not add much to our understanding of the oil market by trying to understand the pattern of arrows that I have portrayed in the figure.

Cheating: The tendency of participants in a collusive scheme to violate their assigned output quota. While each hopes to earn more excess profits at the higher price, their collective action increases output and drives price back toward competitive levels.

B. PRISONER'S DILEMMA

It has become obvious to most students of price theory that we can find an analogy to the cheating phenomenon in the prisoner's dilemma.

[101]That is, at the $7 excess price, another 17,857 barrels would give the country the extra $125,000 in excess that it is looking for.

> *Prisoner's dilemma*: The general finding that when unable to explicitly collude, criminals have a natural tendency to cheat on each other, a process that tends to give these participants the worst outcome as a group.

The problem works in the following way. Two criminals have been apprehended with unlicensed firearms and burglary tools. The stolen items, however, are in the form of untraceable cash, and thus, on this evidence, the prosecutor figures she can obtain two-year sentences for each of them. However, if she could convince one of the prisoners to confess, she could use his testimony to obtain a burglary conviction on the second one, in which case she could win a ten-year sentence. She puts each in a different cell and offers each the following deal. *"If you both confess to burglary, then you will receive a five-year prison term. If you both do not confess, you will receive a two-year term. Finally, if you squeal on your accomplice and your accomplice does not squeal on you, then he receives a ten-year prison term and you receive a one-year sentence."*

These outcomes are shown in table 5-2. Along the side, I portray prisoner *A* and along the top prisoner *B*. Each has two choices: confess or not confess. The numbers in each cell denote years in prison. Prisoner *A*'s numbers are listed first in each cell, and prisoner *B*'s numbers are listed second. If one confesses, then he implicates his friend. What is the optimal decision for each criminal: confess or not confess?

Consider prisoner *A*. He figures that there are only two decisions that his friend could make: confess or not confess. What if *B* confesses? In this case, if *A* does not confess then he gets ten years; if he confesses then he gets five years; thus, if *B* confesses then *A* is better off confessing.

What if *B* does not confess? In this case, if *A* confesses, he gets only one year, but if he does not confess then he gets two years. Again, *A* is

TABLE 5-2. THE PRISONER'S DILEMMA

	Prisoner B	
Prisoner A	Confess	Do Not Confess
Confess	*A*: 5 5	*B*: 1 10
Do Not Confess	*C*: 10 1	*D*: 2 2

Note: Numbers include years in prison. The first number in each cell refers to *A* and the second to *B*.

better off confessing. *No matter what* B *does,* A *is better off confessing.* In the meantime, *B* is going through the same calculus and comes to the same conclusion; hence both confess and each goes to jail for five years.

The same logic applies to the previous OPEC example. The country I considered must have asked the following question: should I hold to my 100,000-barrel quota or increase output to 125,000? My conspirators can do one of two things: either comply with their quotas or cheat. If they all comply with their quotas, am I better off cheating? Yes because then I earn an $8 excess profit times an additional 25,000 barrels, or $200,000 in total.

What if they cheat so that price falls to $11, yielding $7 in excess profit? Am I better off producing 100,000 barrels or 125,000 barrels? The answer is 125,000 barrels. Thus, no matter what the others do, I am better off cheating. All other participants think in the same way, and so everyone cheats. As a result, they do not obtain the result most favorable to them as a group.

This general principle lies at the core of antitrust laws. No one thinks that antitrust laws alone will prevent attempts to collude to raise price. Instead, the antitrust principles make it more difficult for firms to execute any collusion agreements. Companies who write a collusion contract are in direct violation of the law and are almost surely to be convicted based on the written evidence.

Similarly, the laws make it difficult for officers of competing companies to meet and make oral agreements. Evidence of such meetings can be used against these firms in a court of law, and any party to the agreement is a potential witness against the others. Furthermore, the laws make it difficult for firms to merge for monopoly. Mergers that seriously threaten market domination by one or a few firms likely will be challenged.

This leaves open the possibility that firms can tacitly agree to maintain some agreed-upon price. But in this case, absent a direct way in which each firm can police the output of the others, it is likely that cheating will occur. By making cheating easy, the antitrust laws essentially tap the natural tendency of each conspirator to cheat his fellow conspirators, with the end result that consumers are not likely to pay too-high prices for any extended period of time.

EXERCISE:
Return to the earlier box entitled "Why Is Auto Theft a Crime?" If you understand that discussion, then you are doing well. If you want to see whether you are doing *very* well, see if you can follow the discussion about price discrimination in the milk market in appendix A.

Appendix A: Price Discrimination in the Milk Market

Price regulation in the milk market is quite complex. Thousands of federal and state workers help milk farmers conspire to increase the price of fluid milk, a process that generates additional rent to farmers at the expense of consumers of milk. I will abstract from most of the complexities of the program to illustrate the main results.[102] There are two uses of raw milk: fluid milk, which most people buy in jugs at the grocery store; and cheese and other related dairy products. The demand curve for fluid milk is more inelastic than the demand for cheese products in the relevant range.

A. HOW MILK REGULATIONS WORK

To simplify the characterization of the market, I make the extreme assumption that the demand for milk used for cheese is perfectly elastic at price P_c. In figure 5-8, panel (a), I show how this market would clear in the absence of coordinated federal and state regulation. The downward-sloping schedule curve is the demand for fluid milk; the flat schedule at price P_c is the demand for milk used in cheese. The upward-sloping schedule is the long-term supply of milk to the market generated by thousands of dairy farmers. In a competitive market, Q_T units of milk clear at price P_c; the quantity Q_f is devoted to fluid milk uses, and the remainder $Q_T - Q_f$ to cheese production. The area above the supply curve but below price P_c represents rents collected by farmers who own property that is particularly suited for milk production.

Panel (b) demonstrates the regulated solution. The federal government effectively announces a minimum price of fluid milk, which I denote as P_f

[102]This application is a simplification of a model of milk marketing orders that Rob Masson and I estimated based on data from the 1970s. Those regulations continue intact in today's market. See R. Ippolito and R. Masson, "The Social Cost of Milk Regulation," *Journal of Law and Economics* 21 (April 1978): 33–66.

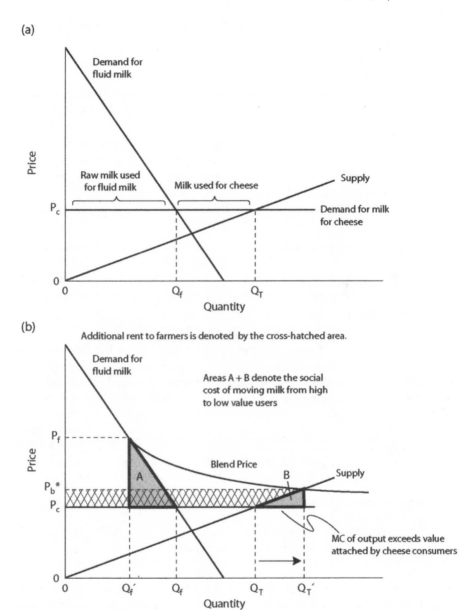

Figure 5-8. The Market for Milk

in the figure. At this price, the quantity of fluid milk demanded falls from Q_f to Q_f'.

EXERCISE:
Step 1: Fix the price of fluid milk to some level higher than the competitive price, thereby reducing the quantity demanded for fluid milk.

In the federal regulation scheme, there is no provision for farmers to restrict output to some quota. Instead, the regulation allows farmers to produce whatever level of milk they want. Simply put, any milk produced beyond quantity Q_f' is dumped onto the cheese market. Since demand in this market is quite elastic, it has little price impact. In my illustration, there is no price impact.

EXERCISE:
Step 2: Any production in excess of the restricted output used for fluid milk is dumped onto the cheese market with little consequent price impact.

What price do farmers receive for their milk? From the farmers' perspective, they simply deliver milk to cooperative collection points; they do not know or care which market ends up with their milk. In the meantime, the regulators calculate the average revenue collected per gallon of raw milk. They call this the "blend price." Simply put, it is the weighted average of the price collected for fluid milk and milk used for cheese production. In figure 5-8, panel (*b*), this blend is shown by the nonlinear schedule that starts at the point on the fluid milk demand curve corresponding to price P_f, and gradually falls to price P_c at higher levels of output.[103]

EXERCISE:
Step 3: Farmers receive the average price of raw milk, which is a blend of milk used for fluid milk and cheese.

Why does the schedule look this way? Suppose that only Q_f' units of milk are delivered to market. In this case, all the output is used for fluid milk, and thus the average price fetched for this milk is P_f per gallon. Any milk delivered beyond this level must be used for cheese, which

---

[103]In particular the blend price P_b is calculated as follows: $P_b = [P_f Q_f + P_c(Q' - Q_f')]/Q$, where Q is the total quantity of milk delivered to market. When $Q = Q_T'$ then $P_b = [P_f Q_f' + P_c(Q_T' - Q_f')]/Q_T'$.

EXERCISE:

Step 4: Find total milk output by setting the blend price equal to the supply price; Q_T' gallons of milk are delivered to market.

---

fetches a lower price, P_c. As an ever-higher portion of raw milk is used in cheese, the average, or blend price, falls toward P_c. Farmers receive the blend price for their output. They produce Q_T' units of milk under the regulatory scheme.

B. THE SOCIAL COST OF REGULATION

We can now characterize the main impact of the regulatory scheme. The quantity of milk sold in the fluid market falls to Q_f', and the price paid by fluid milk consumers increases from P_c to P_f. This reduction in milk sold in the fluid market is dumped into the cheese market. It is apparent that a deadweight loss arises. The quantity of milk equal to $Q_f - Q_f'$ is taken from fluid milk consumers who attach a price in excess of P_c to each of these units and is given to consumers who attach a value equal to P_c. This loss is measured by the shaded triangle A in the figure.

Total milk supplied to market increases from Q_T to Q_T'. Note that over this range of output, the value attached to the marginal units of milk is P_c; yet each of these incremental gallons cost more than this price to produce. Hence, we have the additional "triangle loss" measured by shaded area labeled B in the figure.

Finally, farmers receive the blend price P_b^*, which exceeds the free-market price. They therefore collect additional rent from the regulatory scheme equal to the crosshatched area in the figure. This is the "prize" won by dairy farmers. Forgetting about how we ended up with this regulation (it dates back to the Great Depression), it is apparent that dairy

---

Impact of Milk Regulation

The regulation reduces the quantity of raw milk supplied to the fluid milk market, which raises its price. The price paid to farmers increases above the competitive level, which leads to an inefficient expansion of raw milk production. Triangle welfare losses are generated because milk is transferred from high-value users to low-value users, and because the marginal cost of producing milk beyond the competitive level is higher than the value attached to it by consumers. In addition, dairy rents increase, creating an incentive for rent erosion both in the form of lobbying to maintain the regulations and by way of encouraging other lobbying activity by other industries to receive similar favors.

farmers are willing to expend substantial monies to ensure that the regulation is not eliminated. Indeed, they are willing to spend an amount up to the present value of the crosshatched area in the figure. Furthermore, the existence of these kinds of rents invites others to try to obtain similar favors from government. Hence, the crosshatched area is a part of the social cost of milk price regulation.

EXERCISE:

Suppose that the demand for fluid milk is described by $P^f = 20 - Q^f$. Let the demand for raw milk for cheese be perfectly horizontal at price $P_c = \$6$. Finally, let the supply of raw milk be described by $P = \frac{1}{4} Q$. Find the price and output in a competitive solution. How much raw milk is used for fluid and cheese purposes?

Now assume that a regulatory price scheme is imposed. Suppose that the regulated fluid milk output is set at the price that a monopolist would set. Determine the equilibrium blend price and quantity. Round down quantity to the nearest integer and solve for the blend price. What is output in the new equilibrium? How much milk is used for fluid and cheese purposes? What are the dollar triangle losses? How much additional rent do farmers collect?[104]

---

[104]The answers in the competitive solution are: $Q_T = 24$, $P_f = P_c = \$6$, $Q_f = 14$, $Q_c = 10$. In the regulatory scheme, the optimal monopoly price is found by setting marginal cost equal to marginal revenue. Be careful. The MC over the relevant range is $\$6$. Why? Because the opportunity cost of using milk for fluid uses is the demand price of cheese customers. $MR = 20 - 2Q$; $MC = 6$, and so $Q_f = 7$ and $P_f = \$13$. The blend price is $P_b = [\$13 \times 7 + \$6 (Q - 7)] \div Q$, where Q is total raw milk supplied. Set this price equal to the supply price ($P = \frac{1}{4}Q$) to find the equilibrium output. After rounding down, we have $Q_T' = 30$, and thus, $P_b{}^* = \$7.50$. Additional rent is $\$40.50$. The value of triangle A is $\$24.50$, the value of triangle B is $\$4.50$. Cheese users consume 23 units of the 30 units of raw milk delivered. Note: You need the quadratic formula to obtain the answer; that is, the solution to the equation, $ax^2 + bx + c = 0$, is $x = [-b \pm \sqrt{b^2 - 4ac}] \div 2a$.

Appendix B: The Movie Theater Cost Structure

The question posed in the text is simply put: how does the movie theater pricing example square with marginal cost pricing? Since marginal costs are zero, then unless price is zero, it seems like this cannot happen. In reality, the marginal cost is zero only for the first 100 customers. Once 100 people enter, then the fire code regulation effectively makes the marginal cost of adding one more seat to be infinitely large. So the trick is to recognize that the *MC* curve is vertical at 100 seats. Now you can see that no matter what the price, the movie theater always chooses to fill 100 seats. At any price above $10 the movie theater owner earns excess profits. The sustainable price is $10. Figure 5-9 depicts the solution.

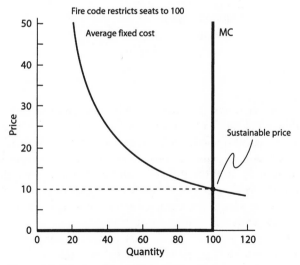

Figure 5-9. Solution: Movie Theater Cost Structure

Chapter 6

Public Goods and Common Resources

Toward Understanding the Economics of Property Rights

Main Economic Concepts	1. Public goods give rise to special problems because it is difficult for their producer to collect revenues from consumers who attach value to their product but are inclined to free ride.
	2. A patent monopoly is one way to award property rights to innovations, which are classic public goods. But the patent institution is imperfect because it gives rise to monopoly pricing and promotes rent erosion.
	3. The common resource problem is the flip side of the public good problem. In this case, some resource already exists, but it is overused because its use is perceived to be "free."
	4. The public good and common resource problems both stem from the poor assignment of property rights.
New Terms	1. Patent monopoly
	2. Free rider
	3. Public goods
	4. Common resources
	5. Contracts under duress

The subject matter raised in chapter 5 provides a natural setting to pursue the public goods and common resource problems. The theater example introduces the rationale for adding demand curves vertically; this is a classic characteristic of public goods. In addition, however, public goods share a common feature: the difficulty and perhaps impossibility of collecting revenues from users. Since producers naturally are reluctant to produce goods for which they cannot earn a competitive return, we have the potential for underprovision of public goods.

The market for innovation is a classic example of public goods. Patents are designed to establish property rights for new ideas as a way of defeating the natural tendency to free ride off someone else's research and development efforts. But patents raise their own set of problems, including deadweight losses and rent erosion, much like the market for monopoly.[105]

Common property issues are the flip side of the underprovision problem. Public goods, like innovations, are underprovided owing to the inability of producers to capture the benefits of their ideas. But resources that already exist, like fish, clean air, and so on, tend to be overused because producers view them as free goods. Both problems are diminished with better assignment of property rights.

I. An Introduction to Public Goods

Public goods have three features: (1) a large fixed cost, (2) the ability of consumers to enjoy a product without inhibiting someone else's enjoyment—the afternoon moviegoers do not prevent the evening attendees from enjoying the show—and (3) an inability to charge users a fee. The latter characteristic is clearly not applicable to movie theaters, since a viewer must pay to enter the theater. Hence, a movie is a private good.

Suppose that instead of viewing a movie, the issue is viewing a fireworks display as might occur in most American cities on July Fourth. In this case, as long as the display occurs high in the sky, then a large number of viewers can enjoy it for many miles around without affecting the enjoyment of others. Unlike the movies, however, it is difficult to imagine the private provision of fireworks because the producer has no practical way to charge viewers for the privilege of seeing the display.

A public good has three properties: Its production is characterized by lots of fixed costs; its consumption by one person does not affect the ability of other consumers to enjoy the same product; and it is difficult to collect a fee from consumers who enjoy the benefits of the product.

Fireworks shown at ground level inside a stadium satisfies the first two principles but not the third because the owner can charge admission. Fireworks shown one thousand feet in the sky above the stadium has all the characteristics of a public good. It can be enjoyed by a limitless number of people within sight of the fireworks without affecting the enjoyment of anyone else, and it is hard for the owner to collect a fee from all the individuals enjoying the show.

The city could ask the citizens to voluntarily pay an amount into city hall proportional to the value they attach to the show. But presumably,

---

[105]The potential for rent erosion in a patent system has long been recognized in the literature. See Arnold Plant, "The Economic Theory Concerning Patents and Inventions," *Economica* 1 (February 1934): 30–51.

many citizens would either free ride completely (claim the show was valueless to them), or partially free ride by underrepresenting the true value. In this case, the usual solution is for the municipality to pay for the show from tax revenues. Presumably, the city's elected officials try to offer a show consistent with the demands of the citizens. It solves the collection problem by using tax revenues. The implicit tax assessment may not directly match the beneficiaries of the show. Taxpayers who really do not attach much value to fireworks pay too much, and those who attach lots of value pay too little. But this is just a transfer from one citizen to another.

Free rider: One who reaps the benefits of someone else's investment without paying for it.

One cannot free ride on the purchase of a private good like an ear of corn because one needs to pay for it to have the opportunity to enjoy it. Taking corn without paying for it is a "crime," which means that the law protects the property rights to corn held by the producer. The term *free rider* normally is found in the market for public goods because consumption can occur without a payment. The term *free rider* has a tinge of thievery to it, except it normally refers to a legal activity.

To illustrate the optimum level of fireworks display, we need to express the fireworks demand curve for each citizen and then add his or her demand curves *vertically* to arrive at the market demand curve. Why vertically? The market demand curve for gasoline is the horizontal summation of individual demand curves. This is because if Ken buys 20 gallons of gasoline, then Jane cannot enjoy the benefits of those same 20 gallons without taking them from Ken. Ken's and Jane's consumption are said to be mutually exclusive: either Ken or Jane gets the gasoline, but not both. In the case of fireworks, consumption is not mutually exclusive. Ken and Jane can both enjoy them without interfering with the other's enjoyment. From the perspective of the city as a whole, the question is, how much are the citizens willing to pay to see a common fireworks display. To find out, sum the demand curves vertically.

Figure 6-1, panel (*a*), illustrates the process assuming that Jane and Ken are the only two citizens. Their demand curves are labeled P_J and P_K, representing their willingness to pay for various quantities of fireworks. Owing to diminishing marginal utility, each user is willing to pay more for the initial unit of fireworks than the second, and so on. Jane is willing to pay a higher price than Ken for the first unit, but diminishing returns set in faster. The total willingness of Jane and Ken to pay for fireworks is the vertical summation of these two curves, shown by the schedule labeled P.

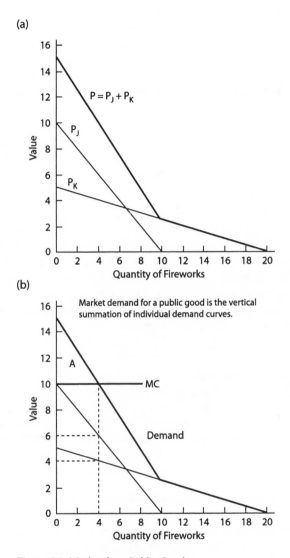

Figure 6-1. Market for a Public Good

Panel (*b*) reproduces these demand curves and also shows the marginal cost of providing more fireworks, which I assume is constant at $10 per unit. Four units of fireworks is the optimum amount. At this level, Jane is willing to pay $6 on the margin, and Ken $4. Together, they value the fourth unit as $10, which is just equal to the marginal cost of providing it. Joint surplus is measured by area *A*.

In a full information world, perhaps the city would assess these prices against Ken and Jane. In reality, it may effectively charge Ken and Jane

> *Market demand for a public good* is the vertical summation of individuals' demand curves. Each user can enjoy the good without interfering with others' enjoyment. An example is fireworks shown high in the sky.
>
> *The optimal amount of a public good* is determined by the equality of the aggregate value that users attach to the good and the marginal social cost of providing it.

through their income tax. If Jane or Ken ends up paying more or less than the values they attach to the fireworks, then this is just a transfer, which I do not concern myself with in this book.

> *Revisiting the Notion of Transactions Costs*
> In the absence of transactions costs all public goods are private goods as long as property rights are clearly assigned. Zero transactions costs means that the provider of the fireworks knows Ken's and Jane's demand curves, delivers 4 units of fireworks, then costlessly bills and collects $6 and $4 from Jane and Ken. There is no need for the public provision of these goods. The only requirement is that the government clearly assigns the property rights to enjoying the fireworks to its provider.

Figure 6-1 presumes that the government accurately assesses the demand for fireworks. More realistically, the city does not know the demand curves for fireworks for its citizens with precision, and so perhaps it offers either 3 units or 5 units, in which case the surplus from the show will be less than portrayed in panel (*b*). It makes sense to publicly provide fireworks if the total surplus derived by a show high in the sky exceeds the surplus available by a private showing (say, ground-level fireworks in a stadium).

> EXERCISE:
> The city may not know that 4 units is the optimum display quantity. If they offer x units, how high or low does x have to be in order to conclude that the citizens would be better off with no fireworks?[106]

---

[106]Any positive amount but less than 4 preserves some portion of area A, and so the only way for the city to make its citizens worse off compared to no fireworks display is to offer too much. This amount has to be such that they move sufficiently far to the right of 4 that the reduction in surplus from the oversupply of fireworks display equals area A. It is apparent from inspection that this amount is 8 units. Over the range 4 to 8, the citizens attach less value to the marginal unit of fireworks than to the marginal cost of producing it. Thus, as long as the city offers no more than 8 units, the citizens are better off with an imperfect amount of fireworks compared to having none.

Is Government Provision Optimal?
When assessing the benefits of government provision of a public good, it is inappropriate to compare the perfect outcome government can create with zero provision of the good in its absence. A better approach is to compare the underprovision of public goods versus the imperfect outcome that government generates.

In the case of fireworks, the private sector can offer ground-level fireworks at stadiums and other venues. The government can provide sky-high fireworks, but not necessarily the optimum level. The optimum solution is the one that gives the most surplus.

II. Innovations: Classic Public Goods

There are many examples of public goods. Everyone benefits from a national defense, and yet each individual has some incentive to free ride on its benefits. Similarly, everyone may benefit by attenuating the poverty problem, but perhaps many citizens would prefer that their neighbor pay for it, and so on. There is another class of public goods, however, where there are some prospects for collection but perhaps far below their value added. I refer to the market for innovation, which also goes by the loftier title "the market for intellectual property rights."

Ideas are public goods. If I discover the combination of chemicals that remedy migraine headaches instantaneously and without side effects, then many millions of people could potentially benefit from the new idea. The fact that Jane benefits from the idea does not prevent Ken from benefiting. Suppose that after incurring research and development (R&D) expenses of $25 million, it turns out that the formula is ½ teaspoon of salt, 200 mg of calcium and ¼ cup of vinegar. In this case, once discovered, everyone at home can implement the idea at almost zero cost, and there is no incentive for any user to pay for the idea.

If innovations lead to ideas that cannot be packaged in the form of a product (as in the prior headache remedy), it is hard to envision how the private sector can profitably pursue the idea. But if the innovation can be packaged—say the headache remedy is more complex than I describe and requires the facilities of a drug company for its safe production—then the prospects for collection become brighter. Indeed, a patent might be awarded for the idea, meaning that anyone manufacturing the pills that encompass the headache idea must pay a royalty to the innovator.

Before looking at the patent solution, I first look at the ideal solution, that is, the optimum delivery of innovations in a full information world (another mention of zero transactions cost). This gives us some benchmark to see how well we can do for any proposal to generate innovations in an imperfect world. I first describe the source of value added by new ideas, then consider the number of innovations that maximizes societal surplus.

A. THE SOLUTION IN AN IDEAL WORLD

A single new idea: A headache remedy. For simplicity, consider a three-period model. In period zero, an innovator engages in R&D efforts that lead to new products. During periods 1 and 2, consumers enjoy the benefits of the innovation. Figure 6-2 shows a demand for some product that is the subject of innovation in periods 1(panel [*a*]) and 2 (panel [*b*]). It might be a new drug to eliminate migraine headaches. The demand for headache *pills* is the *horizontal* summation of demand curves for each consumer; that is, the pills themselves are not a public good, only the idea that makes the pills effective.

The demand price for headache pills captures the value that consumers attach to their medical effects. The area under the demand curves measures this value, which amounts to $200 in each period.

We can think of the R&D process as one during which chemists and medical researchers figure out which combination of chemicals cures a migraine headache. Suppose the outcome is one in which a specific dose combination of fifteen cheap chemicals makes up the solution. Once known, pills that contain these chemicals cost practically nothing to produce. Suppose that the marginal cost of producing these pills is zero; hence, the only costs to recoup are those attributable to R&D. This means that there is a potential to realize as much as $400 in surplus from this idea, minus the cost of R&D.

It is useful to represent the surplus values from figure 6-2 in a different way. Think of panel (*a*) as a two-dimensional flexible container holding 200 units of water. Imagine squeezing the bottom until it is only 1 unit wide. To keep the same water in the container, stretch the container upward until it is 200 units high. Do the same for panel (*b*). Stack the rectangle from panel (*b*) onto the rectangle you made from panel (*a*) to create a single, thin, even more elongated container 400 units high. This merely puts the same water in a different-looking container. Finally, move the elongated container to create the first column bar in figure 6-3.

Thus, the $400 surplus in the first column in the bar chart in figure 6-3 is the same surplus as in the two $200 triangles from figure 6-2, expressed in a different way. The gray area at the bottom of the column is new information: it represents the $25 R&D costs of developing the headache remedy. Thus, the white portion of the column represents the societal surplus from generating the solution.

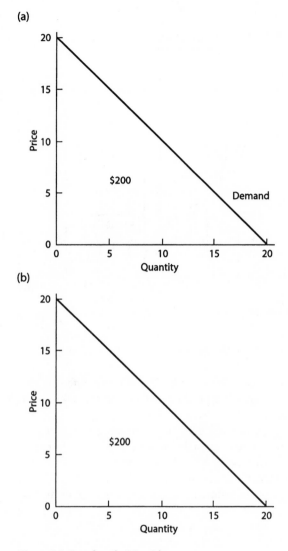

Figure 6-2. Benefits of a New Idea

Representing nineteen other new ideas. Suppose that there is a demand for nineteen other new drugs and that the demand curves for every one look exactly like those depicted in panels (*a*) and (*b*) in figure 6-2. Suppose that the marginal cost of producing these new products, once developed, is zero. Thus, the total value attached by society for each new idea is reflected by the area under the demand curves in both periods, an amount that equals $400. In figure 6-3, I array these additional innovations side by side

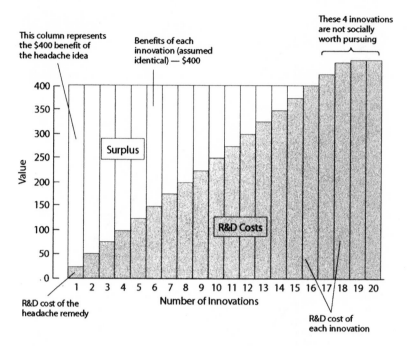

Figure 6-3. Number of Innovations: Benevolent Dictator Solution

and against the headache remedy that is represented by the first bar column. Each has the same height representing the $400 value that society values each idea.

Suppose that while the benefits of these innovations are identical, the R&D cost of developing each of these ideas is different. Suppose that the first innovation costs $25, the second $50, the third $75, and so on, where the sixteenth innovation costs $400 (inclusive of a competitive rate of return on investment). I portray these costs by overlaying gray columns onto the white ones. Thus, the white that still shows is surplus from each innovation after accounting for the R&D costs.

An all-knowing benevolent dictator would identify all new ideas for which there is a positive societal surplus. These include the first sixteen. The seventeenth idea confers $400 in benefits but costs $425 to develop. It is not worthwhile to develop. He then pays the R&D costs and makes the ideas freely available to the market. In terms of figure 6-3, he generates total surplus denoted by the white areas in the first sixteen columns, which are equal to the two surplus areas under the demand curves in figure 6-2, times sixteenth innovations, minus R&D expenses.

How does the benevolent dictator collect these amounts? In principle, he assesses lump sum amounts from the users of the innovation. As long as he compensates the innovator at least his R&D costs and leaves each consumer with some positive surplus from the innovation, then the innovation is Pareto superior.

Is the government the same as the benevolent dictator? Why not assume that the government is just like the benevolent dictator and let it do all the R&D work? The government does in fact engage in much R&D work. Even though most other antibiotics have been supplied by the private sector, penicillin was developed by the federal government during World War II to reduce deaths on the battlefield. It was never subject to patent. It sold for marginal cost from the first day of its production. The Internet is a creation of the U.S. Department of Defense and was never subject to patent. The National Institutes of Health fund large medical research projects and play an important role in advances in medicine. Many important innovations in agriculture are funded through the U.S. Department of Agriculture or performed directly at USDA research farms.

If the government can be successful in its efforts, there is obviously some room for substantial gain to society. But one is suspicious that, since the government is not influenced by the profit motive, it might not be as astute as profit-making firms in identifying and producing new ideas that have lots of potential for surplus. When one thinks of the hundreds of thousands of products on the market, and the millions of ways in which they can be made to give higher value to consumers, it is hard to envision a body of bureaucrats finding efficient ways to identify promising opportunities for advancement, where "promising" is measured to reflect what *consumers* find valuable.

B. PATENT AWARDS

Suppose we conclude that the profit motive is more likely to generate an inventory of innovations that give higher surplus than the government. Then we need to find a way to let private innovators recoup their investments in R&D. One way to do this is to award a patent on a new idea. A patent gives the owner a property right on the idea for some predetermined period of time. Effectively, the patent converts a public good into a private good. During this period of patent protection, the innovator has a monopoly on her idea, which gives her the opportunity to earn excess profits.

The profits opportunity it affords is directly proportional to value added. If consumers find little value in the idea, then the innovator earns little excess profits. If the idea has great value, then she earns large excess profits. Thus, the incentives provided by the patent system are in sync with the market value that consumers attach to the idea. This is the main attraction of the private provision of new ideas.

> *A patent is the award of property rights to a new idea for a limited period*. It allows the holder to set a price like a monopolist, the idea being that the excess profits can provide a way for the innovator to recoup its R&D costs.
>
> *A patent does not solve all public good problems, just those that can be embodied in a product that cannot easily be reproduced outside the factory*. If a person holds a patent on fireworks, he still cannot collect fees from everyone who enjoys his display. Record companies have been losing their ability to recoup their investments in songs because new technology facilitates copying music outside the factory.
>
> *The value of a patent is proportional to the value added by the idea*. Thus, consumer valuation is the driving force in the market for new ideas. This is the main attraction of the private production of new ideas.

C. HOW THE PATENT SYSTEM AFFECTS SOCIETAL SURPLUS

While the patent system has some attractions, it does not deliver an outcome that we might observe in an ideal world. By awarding legal monopolies, we end up with forgone triangles of consumer surplus and lots of rent erosion. To illustrate how patents affect the surplus from innovations, consider how it might work in our simple three-period example. Suppose that upon obtaining a patent, the innovator is entitled to hold a property right for one period, during which she can reap the benefits of monopoly pricing. In the second period she relinquishes her property rights, and the product becomes available at the marginal cost of production, which I assume is zero. I portray this problem in figure 6-4, which reproduces figure 6-2, except it shows the effect of monopoly pricing for one period (panel [a]).

For simplicity, assume that the monopolist can charge a single price. We know that this price corresponds to the quantity on the demand curve where marginal revenue equals marginal cost. In our problem, since marginal cost equals zero, it is apparent from panel (a) of figure 6-4 that the innovator chooses output of 10 units, which corresponds to price $10.[107] The patent holder earns $100 in profits. This is her reward for developing the idea. Consumers realize surplus denoted by the crosshatched area A in panel (a). The patent expires after one period. During the remaining period, price falls to zero. Consumers enjoy surplus of area C (panel [b]).

---

[107]Recall that when a linear demand curve is written with price on the left-hand side, the marginal revenue curve is the same except with twice the slope. Thus, since the demand curve is $P = 20 - Q$, it follows that the marginal revenue curve is $MR = 20 - 2Q$. Recall that $MC = 0$. Setting these expressions equal ($MR = MC$) gives us $Q = 10$. Plug this value back in to the demand curve to discover the price: $P = 20 - 10 = \$10$.

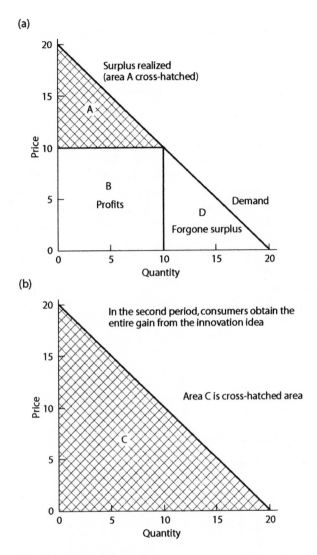

Figure 6-4. Patent Monopoly

As a result of paying for the innovation by monopoly pricing, consumers never realize triangle D in panel (a) of figure 6-4. These are consumers willing and able to pay a price less than $10 for the pills but more than zero, which is how much it costs to produce them. Surplus increases by area D if price is set equal to the marginal cost of producing pills. It is not realized, however, because the monopolist finds it privately optimal to set a higher price.

Compared to a solution that has marginal cost pricing, we can think of this triangle as a deadweight loss. It is surplus forgone owing to monopoly pricing. Thus, it is apparent that we have three kinds of areas to summarize in the case of the monopoly solution: consumer surplus realized (crosshatched areas), consumer surplus forgone (area D), and monopoly profits (area B in panel [a]).

It is again convenient to express these areas in a rectangle 1 unit wide and $400 in height, just as before. That is, we still need to account for the entire areas under both demand curves in figure 6-4, which tells us the maximum potential amount of surplus delivered from the new ideas. But now we need to account for three categories that describe the disposition of these potential benefits. To extend the water analogy, think of forgone surplus as oil, consumer surplus as vinegar, and profits as plain water. Water settles to the bottom, oil rises to the top, and vinegar occupies the space between.

I restack the areas with these three compartments in figure 6-5. Note that I only show the details for the first four innovations. Why are these four particularly important? They are the only ones produced when the reward is set to $100. R&D costs of the fifth idea are $125. It does not pay for a private innovator to pursue this idea if the reward is only $100. The four open rectangle areas at the top of each bar column correspond to the four triangles like area D in figure 6-4 (each is $50). The shaded rectangles

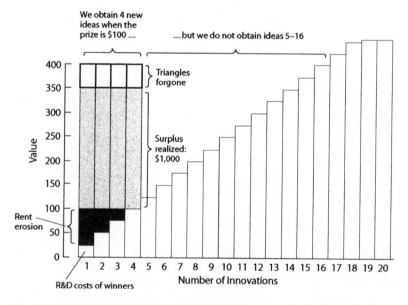

Figure 6-5. One Period Monopoly Property Right

correspond directly to the crosshatched areas $(A + C)$ in figure 6-4. They are each valued at $250. The bottom $100 of each column bar (black plus white) represents profits to innovators (the equivalent of area B from figure 6-4).

It is tempting to infer that the white portions at the bottom of these column bars are the R&D expenses and the black portion just above represents "surplus" to the R&D industry, that is, the portion of monopoly profits left over after paying the R&D costs. This condition describes the winner of the patent. It does not reflect the expenses for the R&D industry as a whole because it does not account for innovators who tried but failed to win the same patent. Consider the first innovation. It costs $25 to play the R&D game and the prize is $100. How can it be equilibrium for only one firm to try to obtain the patent? The answer—as you already know—is that it is not.

The formula we learned for rent erosion is $C = PRIZE / N$, where C is the cost of playing, which in our case is $25, and $PRIZE$ is the amount of profits from one period of monopoly pricing, which in this case is $100. Hence, viewed ex ante, it must have been true that there were enough firms competing for a patent, namely $N = 4$, to ensure that expected profits were zero. In reality, a patent is awarded to the first firm that shows up with the blueprints in hand. To adapt this idea to our application, suppose that if multiple firms deliver the formula for the new drug, the patent office simply puts their names in a hat and randomly draws a winner.

From our earlier discussion, we know that this process guarantees that the cost of the innovation is not $25 but four times $25, or $100. Similarly, the second innovation costs $50. Since the prize is $100, two innovators pursue the prize, and so on. This erosion means that we lose rectangle B in figure 6-4.

The black area in figure 6-5 shows rent erosion for all four innovations.[108] Note that owing to rent erosion, the R&D costs of winners and losers equal anticipated monopoly profits. This means that we can use monopoly profits as a shorthand way of expressing total R&D costs. *This is a startling result: to calculate total R&D costs from an innovation, we do not need to know anything about cost curves in the R&D business, only the expected monopoly profits it generates.*[109]

---

[108]Because of the "lumpiness" of my example, N does not always divide evenly into $100, but if I modified the model to make the probability of winning the prize a function of how much an innovator spent, then it is easy to envision how the prize will always be exactly exhausted.

[109]If there are some R&D inputs in scarce supply, some of the erosion will be diminished because some of the "cost" really is rent to inputs.

Surplus from innovation is denoted by the shaded areas in figure 6-5. It is apparent that the dollar value of these areas is $1,000. In terms of figure 6-4, the consumer surplus retained for each innovation is measured by area A in panel (a) plus area C in panel (b), for a total of $250 per innovation. This is less than the total amount of surplus obtainable in a perfect world but still more than we would have if we had no way to solve the collection problem.

> *The social costs of a patent monopoly equal the usual triangle welfare loss owing to restricted output, plus monopoly profits.* These profits equal R&D expenses incurred by the winners *and* losers in the patent race.

D. THE PATENT QUANDARY

I have illustrated the surplus forthcoming with a one-period monopoly price. If society is more generous in its willingness to pay for innovation, it could generate more innovations but not necessarily more surplus. Suppose that in our illustration, society awards patent holders two periods of monopoly pricing instead of one. Figure 6-6 depicts this solution. Profits, denoted by areas $B + F$, are twice as high as in the one-price solution. In addition, instead of losing only one triangle of forgone surplus from monopoly pricing (area D), we lose another of equal size (area G). Thus, it apparent that the surplus realized for each innovation equals the sum of areas A and E.

Figure 6-7 summarizes this outcome for all twenty innovations. The new policy awards $200 in profits, and so innovators now find it privately optimal to deliver eight innovations instead of four. But the policy carries significant costs. Triangle losses now amount to $100 per innovation, as shown in the white rectangle areas at the top of each of the eight innovations delivered.

In addition, the doubling of the patent prize increases the amount of rent erosion on all the inframarginal innovations. For example, for the first innovation that costs $25, society incurred $75 in erosion with one period of monopoly pricing. Now the prize is $200, and so the expected rent erosion increases to $175, and so on. The social cost of providing eight innovations is denoted by the combination of the black areas (R&D expenditures by the losers) and white areas at the bottom of the eight columns (R&D expenditures by the winners). The shaded areas, worth $800, denote net surplus in this approach. That is, for each innovation, consumers enjoy surplus denoted by triangle A in panel (a) of figure 6-6 plus a triangle E in panel (b). The surplus amounts to $100 per innovation, times eight innovations, or $800.

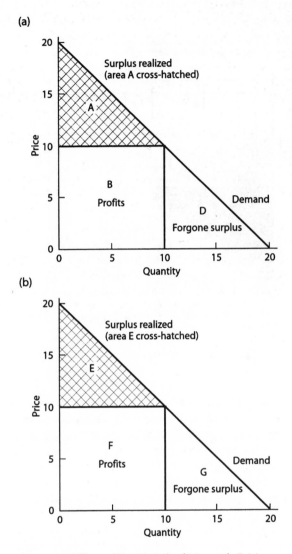

Figure 6-6. Effects of Two Periods of Monopoly Pricing

Thus, more generosity leads to more innovations but lower surplus per innovation, making it difficult to predict the net effect. Increasing the payoff from zero to $100 increases surplus. Increasing it further to $200 reduces surplus.

In the limit, if we award a monopoly for two periods and allow perfect price discrimination (assuming it is costless to effect); this eliminates all the triangles. The patent now awards $400 per innovation. This prize

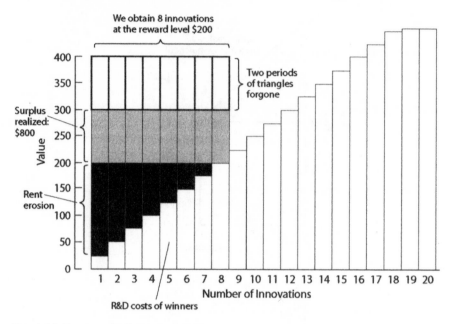

Figure 6-7. Two Periods of Monopoly Pricing

fetches all sixteen innovations to market. The entirety of societal surplus from innovation, however, is devoured by social costs, because all the benefits are subject to rent erosion. In this scenario, we are no better off as a society with the new ideas than we are without them! The only way in which any surplus is preserved in this approach is if some inputs to the R&D process are in scarce supply, so that they would capture some of the rents from this process (recall the example of litigation lawyers in figure 3-7).

Figure 6-8 gives a visual demonstration of the patent quandary. The horizontal axis measures society's generosity level toward innovators (percentage of total surplus given as monopoly profits). The vertical axis shows society's dollar level of surplus realized from new ideas. If it awards no benefits, society obtains (close to) zero innovations. If it allots all the surplus to innovators, then it has lots of innovations but no surplus per innovation, except for some rents that might accrue to R&D inputs.

At first, society gains something by paying more for the R&D because it overcomes some of the underprovision of public goods. But the patent prize creates a common resource problem that acts as a countervailing

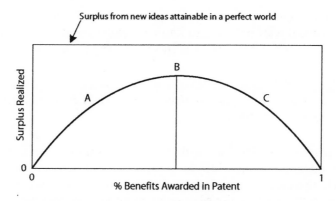

Figure 6-8. The Patent Quandry

force. Society hopes to find a policy that delivers as much net surplus as possible, but no one knows what this function looks like. It is just as likely that we are at points *A*, *B*, or *C*. In other words, either shortening or lengthening the patent period might increase surplus or reduce it.

If the costs and benefits of all new potential ideas were somehow known, one might think about paying the "right price" for each and thereby gaining more societal surplus. We not only could obtain point *B* but also could approach the maximum attainable surplus from all new ideas. The futility of this approach becomes apparent when we consider that there are thousands of firms working on thousands of new ideas, most of which the government has no awareness. Presumably, the existing system in the United States—twenty years from the time of patent

---

THE PROPERTY RIGHTS QUANDARY FOR PATENTS

If society is too generous in paying for new ideas, it encourages the erosion of more of the surplus from innovations in the form of wasteful competition. If it pays too little, it risks losing lots of innovations that confer large amounts of surplus to society. Owing to lack of information, we do not know which level of generosity toward innovators generates the most surplus.

A common pitfall in patent discussions is to misapply the "More is better" principle. That is, society is better off if it confers more monopoly profits to patent holders because it generates more innovations. The error in this thinking is that it ignores the fact that these policies foster more triangle losses and more rent erosion, which may reduce the surplus to innovation. More *surplus* is better, not more innovations.

application—delivers some significant surplus from innovations. There is no practical way, however, to know if surplus would be higher if the period were set to either five, ten, fifteen, or twenty-five years.

E. OTHER IDEAS ABOUT PATENTS

One can imagine other patent policies that could be competitive with the one now in existence.

No patent system. The idea is that some innovations would allow the owner to exploit the new idea for some significant period anyway, since it would take time for copycats to figure out how to replicate the idea. We obtain fewer innovations but retain more surplus from each, plus we save the litigation costs that surround the issuance of patents. The person who invented afternoon movies delivered large gains in consumer surplus in the movie market without the benefit of a patent (chapter 5). Coca-Cola's formula is sufficiently difficult to decipher that it never obtained a patent on its product.

Auction patent rights. If we had sufficient information about the potential for new ideas, we could eliminate some of the rent erosion by auctioning the rights to pursue innovations *before* any R&D costs are expended. For example, suppose that ex ante, we know about the potential to generate the sixteen innovations in the previous illustration. And suppose that we auction the rights to pursue each innovation to the highest bidder at the *beginning* of the R&D period. The winner has the exclusive rights to obtain a patent at the end of the period. Finally, suppose that we allow one period of monopoly pricing. Then four innovations are profitable.

In this solution, there is no rent erosion because property rights are awarded ex ante not ex post. Assuming a competitive market, the winning bid for the property rights to each of the four innovations ought to be pretty close to $100, minus R&D costs. For example, the winning bid for the right to pursue the headache remedy should be close to $75. In terms of figure 6-5, the government collects the equivalent of the black areas for the first four ideas. We still lose the equivalent of triangle D in panel (*a*) of figure 6-4 for each innovation.

Allow price discrimination. Earlier, I outlined the economic implications of allowing two periods of monopoly pricing, where I stipulated a single monopoly price. In the context of figure 6-7, this solution generates $200 of monopoly profits and eight innovations, where each innovation confers $100 in surplus for a total of $800.

Suppose instead that we allow monopoly pricing for only one period but allow the patent monopolist to practice perfect price discrimination (and suppose that it is costless to do so). Would we do better than the two-period single-price solution? Monopoly profits would be the same; that is, price discrimination for one period generates $200 in profits.[110] This tells us two things: (1) we obtain the same eight innovations, and (2) total R&D costs plus rent erosion is the same as the two-period, one-price policy.

In terms of figure 6-6, a perfect price discrimination scheme confers profits equal to areas $A + B + D$ in panel (a) to the patent holder, which ensures that this amount is converted to economic cost (through rent erosion). This leaves areas $E + F + G$ in panel (b) as consumer surplus, which is worth $200. In terms of figure 6-7, the price discrimination solution converts white rectangles at the top of each column bar to additional surplus.

Recall that when we awarded a patent holder the right to a single monopoly price for one period, we received four innovations worth $200 each (figure 6-5). When we award a patent holder two periods of a single monopoly price, we reduce surplus to $100 per innovation, which, even though multiplied by eight innovations, gives lower total surplus. But with perfect price discrimination for one period, we regenerate a surplus of $200 per innovation and yet retain eight innovations, giving a total surplus of $1,600, which is far better than the surplus we found when we allowed either one or two periods of a single monopoly price.

EXERCISE:

Suppose that the government allows patent holders to have two periods of perfect price discrimination, and suppose it is costless to discriminate in price. In the context of figure 6-4, this means that patent holders can collect the entire area under the demand curve in both periods. Assume that the government knows about all potential innovations and auctions the property rights ex ante to pursue each idea. Make the same assumptions as we did in the context of figure 6-3 (all innovations have the same value, but each one costs $25 more than the prior one to develop). How many innovations occur? What is the expected revenue from the auction? What is the surplus from innovations? Assume that all input prices are invariant to the amount of R&D and that the R&D market comprises many competing firms.[111]

---

[110]In terms of panel (a) of figure 6-4, perfect price discrimination confers the entire area under the demand curve, which amounts to $200.

[111]All sixteen innovations are developed. The government collects the amount denoted by area labeled Surplus in figure 6-3, which is also societal surplus. R&D expenses are limited to area labeled R&D Costs; *there is no rent erosion.*

An Occasional Good Guy
Dr. Jonas Salk (1914–1995), who discovered the vaccine for polio, arguably one of the most beneficial medical discoveries of the twentieth century, did not apply for a patent but made a gift of his idea "to all the children of the world."[112]

III. Contracts under Duress: The Common Resource Problem

I now turn to a related issue: the "common resource problem." This problem refers to the consequences that follow if property rights are not clearly assigned to a valuable asset. A common example is clean air. If no one owns the rights to clean air, then there will be too much pollution. Each individual polluter views the air as a free resource, which he can fill with particulates for zero cost. I return to more familiar applications of this idea in later chapters. For now, I develop the notion explicitly using the example of contracts under duress.

Common resource problem: The overuse of a valuable asset that has ill-defined property rights. If no one has property rights to an asset ex ante, then its value is driven toward zero because competitors erode resources as they try to attain the rights to the assets ex post.

Suppose that you have just been in an automobile accident and will die if not brought to the hospital within the hour. A car stops and offers you a deal: in return for signing a contract that awards all your assets to him, he will drive you to the hospital. Thus, if your wealth is $1 million, you just exchanged it for your life. Should the courts honor this contract?

One example that illustrates this problem is given by a hypothetical case of the oil ship in distress.[113] Suppose that we have the following facts. A ship has whale oil on board worth $100. It runs into some rocks. The weight of the oil makes it impossible to get off the rocks, and further, unless the weight is relieved, the wave action will tear apart the boat, which is worth $300. Assume that the ship owner has no way to communicate and, even if he did, it would take too long to get help. The owner has no way to pump the oil out of the boat without the help of the rescue ship.

---

[112]His vaccine was overtaken by an oral variety discovered by Albert Sabin, but the zero-royalty Salk vaccine put a strict limit on the amounts that anyone could collect for the vaccine. In 1956, Salk received the first Congressional Medal for Civilian Service, and in 1977, he received the Presidential Medal of Freedom.
[113]This example is given in Frank Buckley's Contracts class.

A rescue ship shows up. He sees the predicament of the captain and asks him if he would like to negotiate a price for the oil. Faced with disaster, the owner is willing to give up the oil for zero price; indeed, he is willing to pay up to $300 more than this to save his boat. What deal is struck is hard to say but, for our purposes, suppose that the rescue ship always gets the better of the deal; that is, it gets the oil for nothing plus a promissory note for $300.

When he arrives in port, the owner refuses to pay the $300, and furthermore, he wants his oil back, saying that he was "held up" at sea. The rescue ship shows the court the written and signed contract. The ship owner was not coerced to sign; he did so voluntarily. Should the court honor the contract? The rescue ship claims that the deal is good because, after all, it costs lots of money to float a rescue ship, and the fact that it was out there all year waiting for the chance to help someone provides consideration for an implicit contract. A deal is a deal.

The term *holdup* refers to the advantageous "taking" from others, even if not done at the point of a gun. The term *opportunistic behavior* often is used to reference the same phenomenon. Usually, the term arises after one actor irrevocably commits to an action, leaving himself vulnerable to subsequent exploitation. Fear of a holdup gives rise to a demand for contracts that enumerate each party's obligations when these circumstances can arise.

An example: Ken and Jane agree to start a law firm. Ken agrees to (irrevocably) obligate $100,000 to sign a one-year lease. Jane agrees to provide the clients. Ken and Jane agree to a 50-50 split of profits, which are expected to be $400,000 during the first year. (Ken and Jane do not need a contract because they are friends.) But after Ken commits $100,000 to the lease, Jane says, "I want 75 percent of the profits, or otherwise I will not deliver the clients and will take a job elsewhere." This is a "holdup" in economic parlance. It can be avoided by writing a contract with a penalty provision if either party does not perform according to the agreement.

THE SHIP UNDER DISTRESS PROBLEM

Here are the basic assumptions:

It costs $40 to float a rescue ship for a season.

Each season, one hundred ships pass through, and exactly one ship always runs up on rocks.

continued . . .

THE SHIP UNDER DISTRESS PROBLEM *Continued*

Its oil is worth $100, the ship itself is worth $300, and all is lost if the whale oil is not pumped out quickly.

If there is only one rescue ship at sea, there is a 50 percent chance that it will find the trapped ship in time; this probability increases to 75, 90, and 100 percent if a second, third, and fourth ship patrols the seas.

A "me first" ex post property rights system rules the seas; once one rescue ship shows up at the scene of an accident, no other rescue ship approaches.[114]

A. HONOR THE CONTRACT

First, consider the solution that arises if the courts honor such a contract. One approach is to think that the $400 gain to the rescue ship is just a transfer, and so while there may be an equity issue at stake, there is no economic harm. This answer is incorrect.

We know that one ship hits the rocks each year. Whichever rescue ship finds it first gets a $400 prize (there's the p word again). It costs $40 to float a rescue ship for the season. Let us suppose that there are four rescue ships at sea. Is this equilibrium? Use our formula to ask if expected gain exceeds expected cost. Assume that rocks are equally distributed around the sea and that the optimal search pattern is to simply divide the sea into N sections, so that each rescue ship has an equal chance of finding a ship in distress.

Once a rescue ship shows up at the scene of the accident, no other rescue ship approaches. This means that the expected gain from operating a rescue ship for the season is $(1/N)$ *PRIZE*. When the *PRIZE* equals $400 and four ships are at sea ($N = 4$), the expected value of the prize is $100. But it only costs $40 to float a rescue ship; hence, expected profits are positive. Should a fifth ship go out? Yes, because the expected gain is $80 compared to the $40 cost of floating the ship. How about the sixth? Yes, because the expected gain of $67 exceeds the cost of $40. In equilibrium, using our formula, we know that there will be ten rescue ships floating at sea every season.

The social cost of this rule of law is high. There are ten ships at sea, each costing $40 to float. The social gain is the rescue of one ship per season where the rescue is worth $400. Hence, there is no surplus from having rescue ships at sea. If we had no rescue ships at sea, we would lose $100 of oil plus one ship worth $300 per year (assume that all the people on board are in no jeopardy of harm). In the current solution, we save this

---

[114]I can generate the same solution if a different rule of sea obtained, namely, one in which all rescue ships that show up agree to split the revenues from the whale oil ship.

amount but spend an equal amount in the doing. We might just as well put up with occasional loss of ships as to enforce contracts in duress.

> The problem with enforcing contracts made under duress is that they encourage too many resources looking for a "ship in distress."
>
> *A common pitfall*: Many students think that if we have $400 worth of rescue ships, the net benefits cannot be zero because "at least we salvage the ship and its oil." But this ignores the opportunity costs of the resources devoted to the rescue business. The time and effort that goes into building and operating the rescue ships can be used to produce other things. For example, their time instead could be used toward building an extra whale oil ship per year!

B. NULLIFY THE CONTRACT AND IMPOSE A REASONABLE SETTLEMENT

Now consider a solution in which the court takes the other extreme position. It orders the owner to reimburse the rescue ship for the $40 that it cost its owner to float his ship for the season. What are the consequences of this rule? In this case, *no* rescue ships go to sea. Why? Suppose only one rescue ship goes to sea. The expected value is $20 (it has a 50 percent chance of finding a ship in distress, whereupon it can collect only $40). This expected revenue does not support the $40 cost of floating a rescue ship.

C. THE OPTIMAL SETTLEMENT RULE

The optimal reimbursement is one that delivers the socially optimal number of rescue ships at sea. Figure 6-9 provides the information to solve this problem. The number of rescue ships is shown along the bottom. The vertical axis measures value.

The dark bold line (that looks like steps) shows the marginal gain to each rescue ship at sea. The first ship contributes an expected value of $200 (it has a 50 percent chance of saving $400 of resources); the second ship adds an incremental value of finding the ship, which is valued at $100 (it adds an incremental probability of 25 percent of saving $400 of resources). The third adds $60 in value and the fourth $40.[115] The fourth ship makes the probability of success 100 percent. Additional ships add no value.

The marginal cost of floating a rescue ship is $40 (as denoted by the horizontal line at $40 in the figure). The socially optimal number of rescue ships is determined by the equality of *marginal* value added and marginal cost. If floating one more rescue ship adds more value than it

---

[115]Recall that the third ship increases the chance of finding the ship in distress in time from 75 to 90 percent, and that the fourth increases these chances to 100 percent. Multiply these incremental probabilities times $400 to obtain $60 and $40.

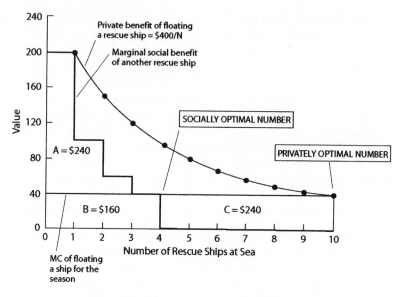

Figure 6-9. Contracts under Duress: The Common Resource Problem

costs, then it is socially advantageous for the ship to go out. If the value added is less than the cost of floating one more ship, it should not go out. Thus, the socially optimal number of rescue ships is either three or four; the fourth ship expends as many resources as he expects to save, and so it is a toss-up when he should go to sea. For our discussion, I will set the optimal solution at four ships. Total value added is $400 in this solution, and the costs of finding the ship is $160 (area B). Societal surplus is $240 (area A).

The *socially optimal number of rescue ships* is determined by the equality of the marginal value added to society from having one more rescue ship at sea and the marginal cost of floating one more ship. In our problem, the "correct" number of ships is four. Societal surplus is maximized in this solution. It turns out to be $240 (equal to the $400 saved resources less the cost of the four rescue ships, or $160).

Another common pitfall: Students have a tendency to fall into the trap of thinking that the socially optimal number of ships is whatever number generates a 100 percent chance of saving the prize amount. If the prize is $400 and three ships give a 95 percent chance of recovery, it is not socially desirable for the fourth ship to go out, even if it increases the chances of recovery to 100 percent. The value added is only $20 compared to the $40 cost of floating the fourth ship.

Note that the figure also portrays the private gain facing rescue ships under a system in which the lucky finder gets the $400 prize. This schedule, denoted by the closed circles connected by a solid line, is the *average* value of N rescue ships at sea, not the marginal value; each point corresponds to the chance that any given rescue ship is the lucky winner, 1/N, times the prize amount, times the probability that all N rescue ships find the whale oil ship. After four rescue ships are at sea, we know that the latter probability is 100 percent. For fewer ships, the expected prize equals $400, times the probability that the whale oil ship is found by anyone. Thus, if two ships are at sea, they have a 75 percent chance that one will find the ship and obtain the prize amount. Thus, the average expected prize for two ships is $300. Each of these two ships has a one in two chance of being the winner, which is an expected prize amount of $150. A similar calculation holds when there are three ships.[116]

In a free-for-all or first-come-first-served solution, we get ten rescue ships at sea because each rescue ship owner sets average value of rescue activity to its marginal cost. In so doing, six additional rescue ships go to sea, each costing $40. Since the oil ship already is assured of its rescue if only four ships are out, the extra six ships add no value, and thus their presence represents $240 of wasted resources (area C). This amount, not coincidentally, exactly offsets the surplus from the socially optimal solution. That is, area A equals area C in the figure.

Question 1: What remuneration can the court set to ensure a socially optimal number of rescue ships? We know that each rescue ship views the expected value of going to sea as (1/N) *PRIZE*. The cost of going out is $40. Thus, if the court wants the solution N = 4, what level does it set compensation upon a rescue?[117]

Question 2: Can you think of a contractual solution that would allow the whale ships themselves to solve the holdup problem?[118]

---

[116]Three ships give a 90 percent probability that someone finds the whale oil ship in distress, and so the expected prize is $400 times 90 percent, or $360. Each ship has a one in three chance of being the lucky winner, and so each views the expected value of floating a ship equal to $120.

[117]It should set this level equal to the total cost of floating the *socially optimal* number of rescue ships, which in this case is $160. In this case, four rescue ships will be at sea. Each ship has a 25 percent chance of finding a ship, whereupon it earns $160. The expected benefit is $40, which is the cost of floating a ship.

[118]Imagine that there are ten whale oil ships. An insurer might step forward and offer the following contract. In exchange for an insurance premium of $16, Rescue Inc. agrees to float four rescue ships under its flag and to provide rescues as needed at no additional fee. If a client's whale ship becomes distressed, then it knows that a rescue from Rescue Inc. is in the offing and so is not vulnerable to opportunistic behavior. Free riding is not a problem because one must have an insurance receipt to qualify for the free rescue. The premiums pay for the cost of floating the four ships.

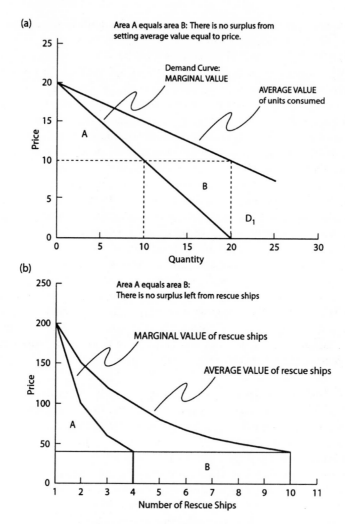

Figure 6-10. Setting Average Value to Marginal Cost

D. THE MAIN PROBLEM: SETTING AVERAGE VALUE TO MARGINAL COST

The problem that arises from setting average benefits to marginal cost in figure 6-9 is general; that is, it always leads to zero surplus. To show this, consider the demand curve we have oft used ($Q = 20 - P$), which I show in figure 6-10, panel (a). If price is $10, you know to choose 10 units because at this quantity, the *marginal* value of the tenth unit of consumption is $10, the same as the marginal cost of the unit (the price). You generate surplus denoted by area A.

If instead you keep track of the *average* value of all the units you consume, then you will find that the average value of consuming 10 units exceeds the marginal value of the tenth unit because every inframarginal unit from 1 to 9 delivers more marginal value than $10. I portray the schedule of average values at every quantity as shown in the figure.[119] Setting the average value equal to price generates negative surplus for all units beyond 10. Indeed, the eleventh to the twentieth unit each deliver negative surplus which, when summed, equals area *B*. Area *B* exactly offsets area *A*, which means that there is no consumer surplus from consuming 20 units.[120]

Panel (*b*) reproduces figure 6-9, except that I show the schedules as continuous lines to look more like panel (*a*). Opting for the number of rescue ships where the marginal benefits of floating a ship equals the marginal cost gives surplus measured by area *A*. Choosing the number of ships where *average* benefits equal marginal cost develops negative surplus for every ship beyond four. The negative surplus, measured by area *B*, exactly offsets the positive surplus given by area *A*. Ergo, there is no net surplus from rescue ships.

Another version of the delta-Q rule: Anytime quantity is not determined by the equality between marginal benefits and marginal costs, look for a delta Q and associated waste. In the case of common resources, the losses are always to the right of the efficient solution (these are the areas labeled *B* in both panels of figure 6-10).

E. ANOTHER WAY TO THINK ABOUT THE PROBLEM

Why does the common resource problem generate such an inefficient solution? In a nutshell, it is because each additional entrant who searches for the ship has two components to his perceived gain. One is the true social gain that stems from the higher probability of finding the ship, and the second is that he takes part of the gains already garnered by those already searching for the ship.

The first ship has a private and social gain of $200. So far, so good. But when the second ship enters, he perceives his gain to be equal to the value of the whale oil prize, $400, times the 75 percent probability that

---

[119]If you derive this schedule on a calculator, you will have a result a bit different because you are limited to whole numbers. To get the exact answer, integrate the area under the inverse demand curve, $P = 20 - Q$ to obtain total valuation: $TV = 20Q - \frac{1}{2}Q^2$. Divide by Q to obtain average value: $AV = 20 - \frac{1}{2}Q$, which has half the slope as the inverse demand curve; hence, intersects price at 20 units instead of 10 units.

[120]If average value equals price (which is the marginal and average cost of each unit), then total value equals total expenditures; ergo, there is no surplus of value over cost.

he or the first ship finds the booty, all times the one in two chance that the second ship is the lucky winner as compared with the first ship. This expected value is $150 (= $400 × .75 × ½). The first ship also has the same $150 expected value. But it had an expected value of $200 before the second ship entered; so $50 of the second ship's gain came at the expense of the first ship. In other words, the second ship sees the transfer as though it is a gain, which of course it is not (at least to society).

To find the social gain of entry, we need to add the changes in expected benefits for both ships. The second ship has a gain of $150 (compared to $0 before he entered). The first ship has a loss of $50 (compare $200 before entry with $150 after). The net change in benefits is $100. Indeed, this is the *social* gain from entry, even though ship 2 sees a *private* gain of $150. If one person has the property rights to the rescue ship operation, he takes into account the effects of entry on the expected values of ships already at sea, and so he treats these as transfers, as society does.

PATENTS, PART 2

Students often think that the rent erosion that surrounds patents somehow is ameliorated by the reality that multiple pursuers increase the likelihood that a new idea is discovered. In all likelihood this is true. But as the treasure ship problem shows, the rent is eroded anyway. Each patent entrant (at least for the first few entrants) adds something to the likelihood of finding the patent, but this just increases the overall likelihood that a prize will be awarded to someone (as in the probability of the whale oil ship increasing from 50 percent at first to 100 percent). In the end, the prize amount is burned up with the social cost of rescue ships, just as the prize from the now more certain patent is burned by excessive R&D costs.

IV. The Source of Rent Erosion: Poorly Defined Property Rights

We keep seeing the problem of rent erosion, and so it is time to nail down its cause. It turns out to be a faulty approach to assigning property rights. Whenever we award property rights on a first-come-first-served, or finders keepers basis, we essentially are saying that no one owns a resource until someone expends resources in order to lay claim to it. As long as it is costly to lay claim to "it," then the value of "it" will be eroded.

In the case of patents, "it" was the right to have a monopoly where the cost to play was R&D expenditures. In the case of wheat farmers, "it" was one or another scheme to generate more rent to farmers, where the cost to play took the form of lobbying expenses. In the case of gasoline, "it" was the scarce gasoline that was being sold at "below market" prices, the property rights to which required wasting time in line. In the case of rescue ships, "it" is the value of the saved ship and the costs are those to float rescue ships. In the case of the minimum wage, "it" is a supercompetitive wage, the rights to which were "auctioned" off to those willing to work hardest on the job.

Ex ante assignment of property rights solves each problem. The assignment can take the form of an auction or be done on a random basis. In the case of the gasoline queue, the government could have either auctioned the rights to purchase gas, mailed these rights in the form of coupons to taxpayers at random, or awarded property rights to random people that allowed them to set up tolls at gas stations. In the case of patents, drug companies' names could be put in a hat and each randomly assigned the exclusive rights to obtain patents on selected ideas. In this solution, property rights are assigned *before*, and not after, R&D expenditures are incurred.

Similarly in the rescue boat example, one solution is to auction the rescue rights to a single company to patrol the sea each season, regardless of the rule of law toward duress contracts. Suppose the court enforced contracts under duress, so that each oil ship caught on the rocks pays $400. If the state auctions the property rights, then assuming a competitive market, the winning bid will be close to $240, or exactly the amount collected in the "holdup," less the expenses of floating the optimum number of rescue ships. Four rescue ships patrol the waters no matter who holds the property rights.[121]

EXERCISE:
What if the court enforces contracts under duress, and the state awards exclusive rights to one rescue ship company but does not hold an auction. Instead, it awards the rights to the company that has the nicest-looking ships. Evaluate the efficiency of the outcome that will emerge from this rule.[122]

---

[121]Indeed, one possibility is that the state gives the auction amount ($240) to the ship that is held up.

[122]Four rescue ships will be at sea. The holdup will confer $400 to the company, from which the $160 cost is subtracted, leaving $240 as excess profits. However, this $240 would be eroded in the form of overinvestment in ships to win the bids. Presumably, in equilibrium, we would have four extraordinarily nice-looking ships making one rescue per year, where the social surplus in this activity would be zero.

This principle is general. If Florida announces the approximate location of a treasure ship with valuable jewels and awards the property rights to the first ship that finds the booty, then it generates wasteful expenditures on search. If the United States announces that land will be given away "free" to the first settlers in Oklahoma, then we can assume that settlers will engage in excessive resource expenditures (for example, overinvestment in fast wagons, bodyguards, guns, and so on) to get there first and ensure that no one can outmuscle them off the property. If gold is discovered on land with no clear property rights, then large amounts of resources will be wasted both defending and trying to steal each other's lodes. Hopefully, it is beginning to dawn on you that a clear and secure ex ante assignment of property rights is a cornerstone of an efficient economic system.

VOCABULARY REVIEW

Patents arise to solve a *public goods* problem. To give some incentive to overcome the *underprovision* of new ideas, innovators are awarded an exclusive *property right* to the benefits of their R&D efforts. This results in *deadweight losses* from *monopoly pricing*. *Expected excess profits* from a new idea attract *entry* of competing innovators, which ensures that the *patent prize* is fully eroded by resource expenditures. The only surplus that arises from the process is *consumer surplus* that survives during the patent period, plus consumer surplus after the patent period ends, plus perhaps some *rents* to inputs to the R&D process. In effect, the patent creates a *common resource problem* as a part of a solution to a public goods problem!

EXERCISE 1:
Suppose that it is announced that a treasure ship sunk one hundred miles from the coast of Florida in 1710 with jewels estimated to have a current value of $1 billion. It costs $50 million to mount a search mission. The first two ships generate a probability of discovery of 90 percent; the third ship increases the probability to 100 percent. Compare two rules of law: (1) the first search team that finds the ship has property rights to the booty; and (2) Florida announces that it owns the wreck and auctions the right to search for the wreck. How many search vessels go out in either case? What is the societal surplus in either case?[123]

---

[123]In the free-for-all solution, twenty vessels search and there is no societal surplus. In the second solution, three vessels search and the surplus is $850 million.

EXERCISE 2:

Suppose that in the ambulance situation discussed earlier, the average person in an accident has assets of $1 million and that fifty people would die each year along U.S. 404 but for a fast ambulance ride to the hospital. It costs $500,000 per year to keep an ambulance in service along the route. A benevolent dictator would put five ambulances in service, which would save all fifty victims.

Suppose now that there are no public ambulance services, only private ambulances. All are licensed for quality. Assume that the rule of law is: the first ambulance at the scene has the exclusive right to sign whatever contract it can on the spot. How many ambulances will patrol this route? What is the dollar value of waste compared to a system set up by a benevolent dictator?[124]

Often the common resource problem is referenced in environmental issues. For example, if the property rights to whale hunting worldwide were owned by one country or one firm, then employers have the incentive to hunt a sufficiently small stock so as to ensure a profitable hunting opportunity over the long run. But if no one owns the rights to whales—effectively property rights are awarded one whale at a time ex post as hunters kill them—then it is not hard to see why there is too much hunting at the expense of the long-term prospects. No individual or company or country internalizes the benefits of future large catches. Similarly, if no one owns the property rights to clean air, then it is not hard to envision that we will end up with too much pollution. I will return to this theme in chapter 7 when I discuss the Coase theorem.

Common resource: An asset that confers property rights ex post, that is, after market participants engage resources to lay claim to it.

Assigning property rights to fish on the basis of how many are caught, or patents on the basis of having spent resources to develop an idea, is the equivalent of assigning property rights ex post. It generates waste because no one takes into account the *marginal* benefits of their activity; instead, they consider only the *average* benefits.

The award of ex ante property rights to resources almost always yields higher societal surplus compared to a solution in which property assignments are assigned ex post.

[124]One hundred ambulances will be clogging U.S. 404, all looking for a victim. This is ninety-five too many, which implies a waste of $47.5 million.

Often the problem is diminished if competition for property rights can be channeled into a productive activity. We saw in the case of the minimum wage that the property rights to jobs paying a "too-high" wage ultimately were assigned by a competition to work harder. We ended up with an inefficient solution, but not the pure waste outcome we found in gasoline queues. Efficient solutions often are found in two approaches: auctions and random ex ante property rights assignments.

By auctioning quota tickets for gasoline, minimum wage jobs, White House tour tickets, the rights to pursue patents, rescue ship rights, and so on, erosion is replaced by a lump sum bid for the property rights. A similar outcome emerges if property rights are assigned randomly to knowledgeable parties and the rights are made transferable. In the latter case, the people who are the most efficient innovators, the ones who most want to see the White House, those who want the gasoline most intensely, those who most want to see the football game, will *find* those with the tickets and bid the highest amounts. Either way, the rights are auctioned off to the highest bidders.

A general solution to rent erosion problems is an auction, either one held directly or one that implicitly occurs after rights have been randomly assigned. The highest-value users will bid the highest amounts for the scarce resource and thus will maximize its asset value.

A Brief Review

This is a good time to pause and review some of the important concepts covered so far.

Consumer Surplus. Use the compensation principle to ask a simple question. Given an optimal allocation of income between x and all else, "How much more income does it take to agree to consume zero units of x?" The answer is the consumer surplus you have from consuming the optimal quantity of x. It is equivalent to the area under the demand curve above price. Alternatively, ask how much you are willing to pay for the first unit of x, how much for the second unit, and so on. Consumer surplus is the difference between these amounts and market price. A rational consumer does not consume any units of x for which consumer surplus is negative.

Entry and Exit. Resources naturally flow to their highest use. Entry of new firms occurs in industries earning excess profits. Exit occurs where firms are earning negative excess profits. It is equivalent

continued . . .

A Brief Review *Continued*

to the so-called Las Vegas rule: ignoring the cost of operating gambling casinos, gamblers gravitate toward games where the expected payoff is greater than the cost of playing, and vice versa. In equilibrium, there is no expected advantage in playing any particular game. Likewise, equilibrium exists when there are neither positive nor negative excess profits. Put simply, we have a sustainable price.

Rents. Whenever some input used in an industry has an upward-sloping supply curve, then there are multiple sustainable prices in the final market, one for each level of demand. The long-run supply curve in an industry is a schedule that connects each possible sustainable price. Every point along this supply curve is characterized by zero excess profits for producers. The area above the long-run supply curve but below price is rent to inputs.

Surplus from Trade. The forces of demand and supply determine price in any market. The gains from trade are measured by the total of consumer surplus plus rents. This is the dollar value of the net utility that consumers and producers enjoy from any market transaction.

Deadweight Costs. Interference with the market forces output away from its efficient level. The source can be taxation, government-sanctioned minimum and maximum prices, monopoly pricing, and so on. Policies that move consumers away from their optimum choices give rise to deadweight losses. The delta-Q rule locates the spot where these "triangle losses" develop. Deadweight losses represent lost opportunities for mutually beneficial trade.

Rent Erosion: The Common Resource Problem. Whenever property rights are ill defined, resources are devoted to obtaining them. These expenditures are pure waste. Resources used to seize property rights to a existing asset have an opportunity cost. They could be used to create goods and services. Rent erosion is a term of art that describes any situation in which surplus is replaced by resource cost. Rent erosion is akin to burning down a house. An asset that had value is no more. The common resource problem means that there is some asset to which property rights are not properly assigned ex ante, and thus resources are expended to claim property rights ex post. Waste always ensues.

Chapter 7

Externalities

The Coase Theorem

Main Economic Concepts	1. When the actions of one person affect another outside a contractual relationship, then we need to find a way to accommodate the externality in order to have an efficient outcome.
	2. One approach is to find redress through tort law, but here, we need to worry about the rule of law that delivers the socially efficient result. Issues surrounding asymmetric information and moral hazard affect the choice. Regulatory solutions might also work under some circumstances.
	3. The Coase theorem shows that if transactions costs are zero, which implies full information to market participants and costless bargaining, then the market will always find the optimum solution; there is no role for courts or legislative remedies. The theorem means that efficient solutions in the face of externalities must revolve around arguments involving transactions cost.
New Terms	1. Level of care
	2. Coase theorem
	3. Externality
	4. Spillover effect
	5. Private cost
	6. Corrective tax (also called a Pigou tax)

When two parties enter into a trade that has no substantial impact on a third unrelated party, then the outcome is expected to be socially beneficial. As we saw in chapter 1, Ken and Jane are expected to find a way to reach the contract curve, regardless of their starting position. Both are better off from trading, and no one is worse off. Thus, the transaction produces a Pareto efficient outcome. It is time now to pay closer attention to market transactions that affect third parties.

I. Why Externality Issues Are Different

As you will learn in subsequent chapters, problems can arise when parties in transactions do not face the true cost of their actions. "Moral hazard" and "agency costs" arise owing to the combination of asymmetric information and mispricing of some activity. When such problems arise within a private transaction, it is up to the parties themselves, not the government, to maximize surplus.

When transactions affect third parties, however, we need to worry about the "external effect," sometimes called a "spillover effect." If consumers pay airlines to transport them to their desired destinations, passengers and airlines gain from the transaction. In this case, however, third parties, namely homeowners on the airport flight path, absorb some of the cost of airport operations in the form of noise from takeoffs and landings. If the harm on homeowners is not reflected in the market, then we have too much noise.

A *spillover effect*, or *externality*, refers to an economic impact on a third party, or "stranger," to the primary transaction. Thus, passengers and airlines contract to maximize the surplus from air transportation, but may ignore the spillover effect on homeowners who are affected by airport noise.

In terms of market nomenclature you recognize, I am merely reciting the consequences of setting the price of making noise to zero. If airlines face a zero price to making noise, even though the social cost of noise is not zero, then airlines make too much noise. By convention, when a third party is involved, we deal with these problems under the heading "externalities." In these cases, it may be necessary to involve an agent to

---

Internalize is a term of art that means that a market participant who imposes some externality on others has been encouraged to take the cost of the externality into account in his own decision making. If a driver is made responsible through tort law for harm done to others, then this rule of law internalizes the harm imposed by a reckless driver on others.

Private cost distinguishes the costs that are realized by some market participants, from the "full cost" to society from engaging in some action. Suppose a firm can produce a product for C per unit in equilibrium. It imposes a negative impact on society in the form of air pollution that creates a health problem, which is valued at S per unit. The social cost of producing x is $S + C$, which exceeds the private cost C.

the transaction to represent the interests of strangers adversely affected by a transaction. This intervention can take the form of judicial rules, regulatory solutions, taxation of negative externalities, and so on.

In the context of externalities, we would say that airlines (passengers) react to the "private cost" of flying and not the full social cost because they do not account for the adverse impact of noise. The problem is solved if a way can be found to encourage the airlines to "internalize" the full cost of flying, inclusive of the cost of noise.

Ideally, we would like to set up a system in which parties to a transaction consider the entirety of the cost they impose on society. I explore the economics of one common externality, namely, airport noise, and show how various rules of law might be invoked to obtain the desired solution. It will become apparent that solutions involve trade-offs. While some market participants are willing to pay some positive amount for the right to impose an externality, others are willing to pay some positive amount for the rights to eliminate it.

The economics of externalities reminds us that every action has an opportunity cost. Within this constraint, the goal is to find solutions that maximize societal surplus, which often involve trade-offs between competing uses of resources.

II. Airport Noise

Airport noise is a classic example of externality because the primary participants engaging in a contract (airlines and passengers) have no natural incentive to consider the negative impact of noise from takeoffs and landings. We get too much noise. Homeowners around the airports are strangers to the primary contract, and yet are adversely affected.

A. SETTING UP AN EXTERNALITY MODEL

I first derive the socially optimum amount of noise (the beneficial dictator decision). I then consider mechanisms that might deliver this solution. In the course of that discussion, I present the **Coase theorem** and the notion of a "corrective tax."

1. Model Strategy

It is useful to articulate a model strategy when dealing with a "bad" like noise. If we define quantity on the horizontal axis in terms of units of noise pollution, then we have to start talking about the "demand for a bad," which twists our demand concepts around, forcing us to "relearn" those concepts backward, as it were. A better idea is to transform the problem to look like a typical demand curve. To accomplish this outcome, I define quantity along the horizontal axis as units of quiet. Rightward movements are units of noise removed from the air, or units of quiet acquired. Put simply, we transform the problem from one of evaluating units of "bad" to one involving units of "good." This puts us on familiar footing.

2. The Market for Airport Noise

Figure 7-1, panel (a), depicts the market for airport noise. Units of quiet are measured along the horizontal axis. For simplicity, assume that 1 unit of noise corresponds to 1 round-trip takeoff and landing, and that there are 100 flights per period. Thus, you can read the axis to mean that at quantity 100 units of quiet, there are zero flights per period operating from the airport, and that at zero units of quiet, there are 100 flights. In other words, units of quiet are read left to right, and units of noise are read right to left. For the first part of the problem, I assume that noise per plane is given; airlines can reduce noise only by flying fewer planes.

Model strategy when dealing with a "bad": Set the horizontal axis so that it measures units of improvement. If we are dealing with pollution, the zero axis represents zero quantity of clean air (relative to the existing pollution); movements to the right represent higher quantities of clean air.

By implication, movements from right to left on the horizontal axis imply more "bad," for example, more units of pollution.

As a general rule, when confronting a new problem, try to redefine the problem so that it fits into a model with which you have some familiarity and which has facilitated solutions to problems you have faced in the past.

3. Homeowner Demand for Quiet Also Is Their Supply of Noise

The downward-sloping schedule from left to right measures the amount that homeowners along the flight path, as a group, are willing to pay to rid themselves of the airport noise. Noise reduction is a public good. One homeowner on the flight path can enjoy more quiet, without interfering with her neighbor's ability to enjoy the same quiet. Hence, the social demand for more quiet is obtained from the vertical summation of each homeowner's demand for quiet. Given that there is lots of noise at the zero axis, homeowners are willing to pay a considerable amount to

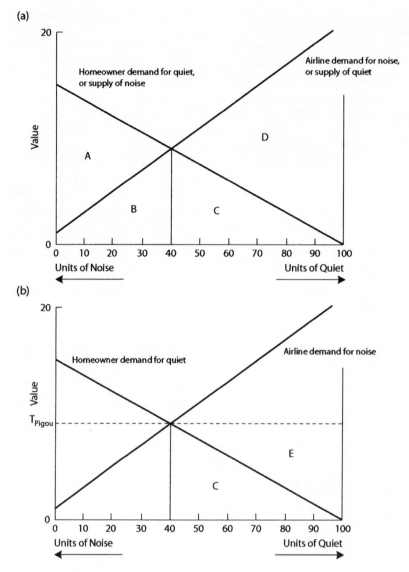

Figure 7-1. The Airport Noise Problem

purchase their first units of quiet. After most of the noise is eliminated, the marginal benefit of further noise reduction is near zero (at the horizontal axis point measured by 100).

We can read along the homeowner demand curve in two directions. From left to right, it is the amount that homeowners are willing to pay to obtain more units of quiet. From right to left starting at 100 units of quiet, it is the minimum amount of money that homeowners require to allow noise. *Put differently, read left to right, the homeowner schedule is a demand curve for units of quiet. Read right to left, the same schedule is a supply curve of units of noise permitted.*

4. Airline Supply of Quiet Also Is Their Demand for Noise

While homeowners attach a value to quiet, airlines attach a value to making noise. Implicitly, the passenger demand for travel means that passengers are willing to pay something for the right to make noise so that they can travel to their destinations on a frequent basis. The most that passengers on each plane are willing to pay to make noise is the vertical distance between their demand for air transportation and the airline ticket price (not shown). For example, suppose that each of 200 passengers on a plane is willing to pay $1,000 for a flight from X to Y. And suppose that the ticket price is $400. As a group, these passengers are willing to pay as much as much as $120,000 for the right to make noise. Thus, when I refer to "airline" demand, I really mean "passenger" demand, but since the airline is acting as an agent for its passengers, it is sensible to use these terms interchangeably.

In terms of figure 7-1, panel (a), the airlines' schedule sloping upward from left to right looks like a supply curve. Indeed it is: it is the minimum price that passengers will accept to provide each unit of quiet they supply. Put differently, it is the minimum price they will accept to refrain from taking a flight (which produces a unit of quiet). To look at the airline's schedule as a demand curve, recall that noise units are read right to left. So, starting at 100 units of quiet (no noise), the height of the airline schedule represents the maximum that passengers are willing to pay to have the first flight scheduled, which creates 1 unit of noise. Note that I line up the flights in order of the maximum amount that passengers are willing to pay to have that flight available each day. Flights that have the highest demand for noise are the first candidates to make noise, and subsequent flights are arrayed according to willingness to pay (read right to left).

B. THERE IS NO COSTLESS SOLUTION TO AN EXTERNALITY PROBLEM

There is an opportunity cost to the sound waves in the air no matter what policy is followed. The cost of quiet is the airline passengers' forgone flights. The cost of noise is the imposition of a negative externality on homeowners. If a zero noise solution is enforced, the homeowners receive surplus $A + B + C$ from 100 units of quiet, but airline passengers give up surplus from travel, as measured by areas $B + C + D$. At the other extreme, if airlines are allowed to fly as many flights as they please without consideration of homeowners, then reverse these surplus calculations: passengers gain $B + C + D$; homeowners lose $A + B + C$. There is no such thing as a free lunch.

There is an opportunity cost imparted no matter which noise policy is followed. If airlines have free use of the airspace, their passengers gain surplus but at the expense of a negative noise externality imposed on homeowners. If no flights are allowed, then homeowners gain surplus from quiet but at the expense of negative "quiet" externality imposed on air passengers who cannot use the airspace.

The homeowner schedule is a demand for quiet read left to right and a supply of noise read right to left. It represents the maximum that they would pay for each unit of quiet or the minimum amount they would accept to permit noise. The airline schedule is either a supply of quiet or a demand for noise, depending on which way the units are read, left to right or right to left. In either case, we are looking at a demand and supply schedule for quiet or, equivalently, a demand and supply schedule for noise.

C. THE SOCIALLY OPTIMUM LEVEL OF EXTERNALITY

Using the rule that a dollar is a dollar, it is apparent that 40 units of quiet maximize total surplus of air passengers and homeowners combined. Starting at the zero axis and moving rightward (more quiet), homeowners attach a higher value to eliminating the 100th flight than the value that passengers attach to taking the flight. The same condition characterizes the 99th through the 61st flight. Alternatively, the optimum amount of noise is 60 units.

Homeowners attach a value to 40 units of quiet measured by areas $A + B$. Airlines attach a value to eliminating this quiet denoted by area B. Hence, the delivery of 40 units of quiet confers surplus measured by area A. It does not make sense to cancel the 41st flight because passengers on this flight gain surplus from flying that exceeds the value that homeowners attach to one more unit of quiet.

Viewed from the other extreme (100 units of quiet, or alternatively, zero flights), airlines attach a value to make 60 units of noise, measured by areas $C + D$, whereas homeowners attach a cost to this noise measured by area C. Hence, the scheduling of 60 flights confers surplus measured by area D. In sum, flying 60 planes and grounding 40 produces the greatest amount of societal surplus, denoted by areas $A + D$.

The *socially optimum amount of noise* occurs when the marginal benefit of making more noise equals the marginal cost of permitting more noise. This is the level of noise that an all-knowing benevolent dictator permits in the airspace.

Strategy: Start by finding the socially optimum solution, even if it is entirely unattainable. When evaluating an inefficiency, start by determining where the socially optimum solution lies. Assume that there is an all-knowing benevolent dictator who wants to maximize surplus. Even though the approach often yields an unattainable solution, it gives you a baseline to compare against the various "real-world" solutions you consider. You are looking for a solution that gets you as close to the perfect solution as is economically feasible.

III. The Coase Theorem

In a famous paper, Ronald Coase shows that the market delivers the socially optimal amount of some externality without benefit of intervention under two conditions: transactions costs are zero, and property rights are well defined.[125] In the context of our noise problem, Coase argues that if homeowners and airlines have costless access to full information and can come together and bargain at zero cost, then the market will be characterized by 40 units of quiet, regardless of who owns the rights to make noise.

Coase theorem: If transactions costs are zero, and property rights are well defined, then the market delivers the socially optimal amount of an externality without outside intervention. It does not matter who owns the property rights; the socially desirable amount obtains.

In the airport noise problem, the optimum amount of noise is delivered whether the airlines or homeowners own the property rights to the sound waves over the flight path.

A. AIRLINES OWN NOISE RIGHTS

Suppose that airlines have the rights to make noise. The first reaction is to think that airlines will ignore homeowners' demand for quiet and

[125]Ronald Coase, "The Problem of Social Cost," *Journal of Law and Economics* 3 (October 1960): 1–44.

simply make 100 units of noise. In terms of figure 7-1, panel (a), this solution corresponds to the zero axis, where zero units of quiet are offered. To obtain the first 40 units of quiet, however, homeowners are willing to pay a sum equal to areas $A + B$; but it is worth only area B to airlines to make the noise.

Suppose that Ken is the agent for the airlines (and by implication all the passengers), and Jane is the agent for the homeowners. Jane could offer Ken an amount equal to area B to eliminate 40 flights, which fully compensates the passengers for their forgone surplus from these flights. Homeowners retain a surplus measured by area A.

What if Ken is a good bargainer and insists that Jane pay B plus some of A in order to give up these flights? As long as Ken and Jane can make a deal, it does not matter how the surplus A is split. Homeowners have to retain part of area A or else they will not make the deal. Airlines (passengers) have to receive at least area B or else they are unwilling to give up the flights. Both can be made better off by splitting the amount A; hence, we can assume that Ken and Jane can strike a deal.

Note that the homeowners cannot convince airlines to give up the remaining 60 flights. Beyond 40 units of quiet, it is apparent that the amount that airlines require to cancel the remaining 60 flights (areas $C + D$) greatly exceeds what homeowners are willing to pay (area C); hence, Ken and Jane cannot make a deal to reduce flights beyond the 40 flights now deleted from the schedule.

B. HOMEOWNERS OWN NOISE RIGHTS

Now suppose that homeowners own the rights to make noise in the airspace. Will they insist upon zero noise? Suppose they do, so that we are at 100 units of quiet. Airlines are willing to offer an amount equal to areas $C + D$ to homeowners to permit 60 units of noise; homeowners would be willing to accept an amount measured by area C to allow this noise. Area D measures the amount by which airlines and homeowners as a group are better off making a deal. Presumably, Ken and Jane can agree on 60 flights.

What about the remaining 40 flights? Airlines are willing to pay an amount denoted by area B to have 40 more flights, but homeowners require a payment equal to areas $A + B$ to permit the noise. It is apparent that Ken cannot succeed in buying the rights to the last 40 flights.

No matter who owns the property rights to make noise over the flight path, we end up with 40 units of quiet and 60 units of noise. The socially optimal solution results as long as transactions costs are zero and someone owns the property rights to the sound waves over the flight path. In general, the party that is awarded the property rights has more money in its pocket after the deals are done, but in Coase, equity issues are an irrelevancy. All that matters is the delivery of the optimal amount of the externality.

Equity issues are an irrelevancy in Coase. It is not productive to address externality issues by appealing to equity concepts. If my neighbor likes to do carpentry on weekends and I like quiet, why is my right to quiet more important than his right to pursue his hobby? Rather than taking sides, Coase merely says that if quiet is more important to me than making noise is to him, then quiet will prevail regardless of or who owns the property rights to making noise.

The party awarded the property rights usually has more money in its pocket at the end of the problem.

C. WHAT IF TRANSACTIONS COSTS ARE NOT ZERO?

What does it mean to say transactions costs are zero? In context, the meaning of this phrase usually is clear even if in general it is difficult (and usually not necessary) to define. In the airport problem, it means that agents for airlines and homeowners know the demand for quiet for each homeowner and passenger without incurring resource expense, can costlessly collect fees proportionally related to value attached to marginal units of noise/quiet, and can come to an agreement without eroding the surplus.

Transactions costs are real costs but different in character from production costs. Think of production costs as those that increase the utility of a good or service, or reduce its disutility. Think of transactions costs as resource expenditures that erode surplus. The costs of flying planes are production costs because they give rise to the utility from flying. Adding mufflers to reduce noise emissions reduces disutility to homeowners. These are production costs.

Transactions costs in the context of public goods and externalities usually are information-gathering costs. The information is the relevant set required to strike a deal. These costs in no way increase the utility of flying or reduce the disutility of noise. They are expenditures financed by the surplus availed from a mutually beneficial deal.

Invoking a solution in which an all-knowing benevolent dictator asserts an outcome is tantamount to announcing zero transactions costs. He knows all demand prices for all parties affected by a public good or externality, can discern the socially optimum deal, and can costlessly collect and disburse funds to finalize the agreement.

continued . . .

Continued

When transactions costs are zero, *all* the surplus from the optimum deal is realized. In reality, all solutions are imperfect, require resource costs to effect, and thus yield less surplus than the highest attainable. In general, we must look for the alternative that gives the best outcome.

Refer back to the discussion of patents. The patent solution ends up burning lots of the surplus generated by R&D expenditures. Put differently, they are laden with transactions costs and indeed may dominate the production costs required to develop the idea in the first place. Nevertheless, the patent system as we know it may still be the best attainable outcome given available technology.

1. Government Solutions

If transactions costs are not zero, can we find the optimum solution? The Coase theorem itself suggests that a solution might be found if some group can act as an agent for the parties affected by the externalities. In this context, it is useful to think of a role to be played by government.

For example, it is not a stretch to think that a handful of airlines might be pretty good representatives for travelers, particularly since it is part of their business to estimate passenger demand for travel. It is much more difficult for homeowners to come together. Given that there is a cost to negotiating with airlines in the real world, an incentive is created for each homeowner to free ride on the group—that is, to enjoy the benefits of reduced noise but refrain from paying the cost of negotiation.

As a practical matter, political representatives might play a role in trying to broker a noise deal for their constituents. Politicians might serve as reasonably good agents in this problem, if their constituents comprise both homeowners along the flight path and passengers using the airlines. Presumably, the large number of passengers and intense interest of the homeowners will translate into expected votes that might generate a reasonable approximation to the optimum solution.

There are many other examples of public solutions. If the majority of Americans want to have some thousand-year-old sequoia trees left standing, even if they themselves will never lay eyes on them, and if these demands are sufficiently intense, then the federal government will be able to outbid logging companies for the property rights to the trees. Alternatively, if most Americans want some bald eagles to survive, then the government can impose regulations restricting the use of pesticides and development in eagle habitat. This "regulatory" solution is less likely to deliver an efficient result, unless those adversely affected by fewer pesticides are heard (for example, food costs will be higher and mosquitoes will ruin more picnics).

As in the discussion of fireworks and innovations, there is no reason to believe that the government solution will be socially optimal. If it were, it would be purely by accident. The real-world question is whether a government-imposed solution is likely to generate more surplus than an imperfect free market that includes some externalities.

2. Vertical Integration

Coase might explain some "vertical integration" in markets. Vertical integration means that a producer buys an input into its process. Noise is part of the production process of creating flights. Put simply, the optimum amount of noise is more likely to be forthcoming if the parties who own the airport also own the property affected by the noise. In this case, the airport internalizes the benefits of the noise to their passengers *and* the costs imposed on home owners. The latter effect implicitly shows itself in property values: the more noise, the less that prospective home owners are willing to pay for the land and vice versa.

Suppose the airport owns the land along the flight path. Consider the following three options: (a) not build any homes, (b) build homes but make 100 units of noise, or (c) build homes but make 40 units of noise. To make the problem simple, assume that we have a one-period model. Also, assume that the airport is a perfect agent for passengers so that it fully values the surplus enjoyed by the travelers using the airport.

Policy (b) trumps (a) because the airport can sell the property for some positive value to people who are least affected by noise. But the airport can do better than this. If it builds homes and restricts noise to 40 units, homebuyers would be willing to pay an additional amount for the property equal to areas $A + B$. in figure 7-1, panel (*a*). Since this amount exceeds the surplus to passengers (area B), the airport has an incentive to restrict noise.

> *Vertical integration* often is motivated by the promise of reduced transactions costs, which in the context of the Coase theorem can offer a way to deliver the socially optimum amount of some externality.

3. Contractual Solutions

We often observe smaller-scale externality problems solved in a contractual context. A good example is an enclave of new homes developed by a single builder. As a part of the deed, buyers agree to a series of restrictions on their land; for example, they may not build additional structures, install pools, or paint their house without the approval of the homeowner's board (who presumably would veto paint schemes with shocking pink combined with lime-colored trim). In this way, the "look" of the neighborhood can be preserved, thereby preventing some owners from engaging in acts that devalue neighbors' property.

The contract also may include a tie-in sale. That is, in addition to buying the house, the owner agrees also to buy maintenance services with monthly fees to the homeowner's organization. In this way, all lawns and yards are nicely maintained, and the noise from lawn mowers and leaf blowers is restricted to one or two days per week, neither of which include weekends. They may also require trash pickup from the organization's vendor once per week. In this way, visual and noise externalities are controlled for the neighborhood as a whole.

Another example is the purchase of an apartment through a cooperative organization, or co-op board. Here, a purchaser buys shares in the building, which also gives her exclusive rights to apartment 2001 on the twentieth floor on Madison Avenue. She also agrees as part of the contract to buy other services including pest control spraying, common area cleaning fees, and so on. In addition, she agrees that she cannot sell her shares to a buyer without the board's approval. In this way, rock stars, who might have all-night parties, or opera stars, who make lots of noise practicing their parts, are excluded from the building.

Of course, the opera star can solve her own externality problem by purchasing a condominium on Eighth Avenue on the nineteenth floor and *also* buying the apartments on the eighteenth and twentieth floors for rental purposes. She then has an incentive to find a schedule to practice her singing that maximizes the joint value of her freedom to sing and the rent from her apartments. By fully disclosing that she is an opera star and contractually agreeing to a limited schedule, say during the daytime on weekdays, she can find tenants who work during these days and who might be willing to pay almost the full market rent for these apartments.

D. CORRECTIVE TAXES

Arthur Pigou made the simple observation that as long as the government needs to raise revenue, why not attach taxes on "bads" instead of "goods."[126] He had in mind taxes on noise, smoke, and the like. These are "corrective" taxes because they encourage polluters to internalize the full cost of their production; that is, they correct the bias of using too much of an apparently free resource.

---

[126] Arthur Pigou, *Public Finance* (London: Macmillan, 1928).

> A *corrective tax* is one that brings price *closer* to the social marginal cost of production and hence *improves* welfare. A synonym is a *Pigou tax*.

For corrective taxes to work, the government needs to be able to estimate the schedules in figure 7-1, panel (*a*). If the aggregate functions can be estimated, then the government can set the corrective tax at T_{Pigou}, which generates the optimum amount of noise. Panel (*b*) in figure 7-1 shows this tax. Faced with a tax of this magnitude on each unit of noise it produces, the airline makes 60 units of noise. It pays to make this noise because the tax is less than the amount that passengers are willing to pay to make this noise. Beyond this level of noise, however, the tax exceeds the value to airlines of making noise, and hence airlines offer 40 units of quiet. Of course, the authorities may know these schedules only with some error.

Such a tax might succeed in increasing total surplus compared to a world of unabated noise, though the amount of improvement depends on the accuracy with which the schedules in panel (*b*) can be estimated. As long as information is not free, it is almost never pays to be fully informed. The question is: can a tax or regulatory solution generate more surplus (inclusive of enforcement costs) than the free market left to its own imperfections? The answer of necessity depends on the particular problem at issue.

EXERCISE:

Question 1: What is the tax revenue in figure 7-1, panel (*b*), under the optimal corrective tax?[127]

Question 2: Suppose that the tax authorities have imperfect information, so that they might set the tax 10 percent too high or too low. Under what conditions will the amount of noise be closer to the optimum?[128]

IV. Allowing for Noise Abatement

It is important that a corrective tax be assessed against the externality itself, not some product that it correlated with the externality. In the case

---

[127]Tax revenue is T_{Pigou}, times 60 units, which is denoted by areas $C + E$.

[128]The social cost from choosing the wrong tax rate depends on elasticities of the airline and homeowner schedules. The largest triangle loss from errors in corrective taxes is expected when the elasticity of the airline's demand for noise is elastic (thus ensuring a large base to the welfare triangle), and the homeowner's supply of it is inelastic (guarantees a large height to the triangle). Try these schedules on a piece of graph paper and depict some error in picking the tax rate, and you will see what I mean.

of plane noise, for example, there might be a temptation to attach a tax on flights because flights are the proximate cause of noise. There may be other ways, however, to reduce noise pollution besides reducing flights. If so, a tax on flights eliminates the incentive to reduce noise per flight. The cost of abating noise might be lower than sacrificing the surplus gained by passengers from flying to their destinations.

A. STYLIZED ABATEMENT TECHNOLOGY

To keep the model tractable, suppose that planes can use mufflers. Assume that the muffler depreciates by some fixed amount per takeoff and perhaps causes the plane to use more fuel. I can represent the cost of noise abatement by some constant amount per flight, MC_A. Figure 7-2, panel (a), reflects the new information. In what follows, I discuss the solution that has the optimal amount of noise abatement.

Airline passengers gain from more (but quiet) flights. I first address the gain to passengers. Consider the 61st flight, which previously did not leave the ground. Passengers on this flight are willing to pay an amount that exceeds the cost of the muffler. So, flights 61–80 now depart but make no noise. Areas $B + I$ denote the value to airline passengers from the extra flights. Area I denotes the costs of abatement. Homeowners are indifferent as to the extra flights because they are silent. Silent flights are just as good to them as no flights. Area B measures the net social gain from these flights.

Homeowners gain from fewer noisy flights. The existence of the muffler technology means that it is socially optimal to eliminate the noise on at least some of the 60 flights that occurred even without the mufflers because over part of this range, homeowners attach a higher value to reduced noise than the cost of reducing it. By adding mufflers to the 33rd through the 59th flights, airlines confer a gain to homeowners measures by areas $E + H$. Area H measures the cost of abatement. Thus, for these flights, it is cheaper to abate than to expose homeowners to noise. Area E measures the net increase in surplus from changing these flights from noisy to quiet status.

Some planes continue to fly noisy. It is not socially optimal for airlines to add mufflers to its first 33 flights because over this range of noise, homeowners are not willing to pay the marginal cost of eliminating this segment of noise. That is, areas $F + G$ denote abatement costs over this range of flights. Area F denotes the value that homeowners attach to the reduced noise. It is socially optimal to retain 33 noisy flights.

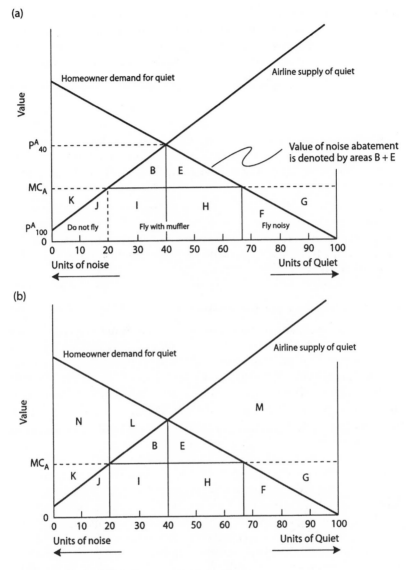

Figure 7-2. Optimal Flight Pattern with Noise Abatement

Some planes still do not fly. If only 33 flights fly noisy, then the home-owners' supply of noise has a discontinuity. At the 33rd flight, their marginal supply price for noise is MC_A. The next 47 flights fly quiet, and so the supply price continues its rise only at the 80th flight. But this means that the cost to homeowners of absorbing the noise from these planes exceeds areas $J + K$ in the figure. These areas measure the costs of abatement. So it is cheaper to abate than to ask homeowners to absorb the noise. Moreover, passengers on the 81st to 100th flights attach a value to flying measured by area J, which is less than the abatement costs; hence, they stay on the ground.

The introduction of noise abatement equipment changes the optimal amount of noise. It pays to expand the number of flights *and* reduce the total number of noisy flights. In our solution, it still is optimal to have some noisy flights and to have some flights stay on the ground.

EXERCISE:
Redraw figure 7-2, panel (a), placing the marginal cost of noise abatement, MC_A, below P_{100}^A. How does the solution differ from the one we just derived?[129]

B. A CORRECTIVE TAX WITH ABATEMENT

The way I have constructed the noise abatement technology, it is hard to find the optimal corrective tax. Consider figure 7-2, panel (b), which reproduces panel (a) but has additional labels. Suppose that transactions costs are prohibitively high, and so we look to a corrective tax to deliver the best solution. If the tax on a noisy flight is set to MC_A plus a penny, airlines will put mufflers on 80 of their flights, *including* the first 33 flights because it is cheaper than paying the tax on noise. This outcome creates waste measured by area G in panel (b).

If the tax is set to MC_A minus a penny, then the airlines will not attach any mufflers because paying the tax on noise is cheaper than eliminating it. Thus, we end up with 80 noisy flights, with a consequent reduction in welfare measured by areas $E + B + L$ in the figure. Put simply, a flat marginal cost of noise abatement maximizes the chances that the tax authorities deliver a socially inefficient solution.

If the tax authorities know all the schedules in figure 7-2, panel (b), then they can reproduce the optimum solution by attaching a tax equal to MC_A plus a penny for all but 33 flights. But they typically will not know these schedules with certainty and hence are prone to error. If they have a reasonable estimate of the various schedules, then given the asymmetry of losses in this problem, the best solution is to err on the side of too high a tax on noise (better to risk losing surplus G than surplus $E + B + L$).

---

[129]The key difference is that it now pays to have 100 flights, almost all of which will fly quiet.

C. COASE WITH ABATEMENT

Owing to the powerful assumption of zero transactions costs, which implies perfect information, among other things, the Coase theorem always works no matter how complex the problem. For example, in terms of figure 7-2, panel (*b*), suppose that airlines own the property rights to sound waves over the flight path. In this case, start at the left of the chart and work rightward. Homeowners are willing to offer airlines the amount denoted by areas $N + K + J$ to eliminate the last 20 flights. Airline passengers attach a value to these flights in the amount denoted by area J. Hence, homeowners can offer the airlines the amount denoted by area J plus something more to eliminate these flights. It does not make sense for airlines to fly silent because the costs of the abatement (areas $K + J$) are greater than the benefits (area J).

Homeowners are willing to pay an amount denoted by areas $I + H + E + B + L$ to attach mufflers on 47 flights from the 34th to the 80th flight. It cost airlines $I + H$ to attach the mufflers. The potential surplus, denoted by areas $E + B + L$, ensures that the parties can strike a deal to obtain this result. Thus, there are 47 silent flights.

Homeowners absorb the noise from the first 33 flights. Area F is the value of their disutility from this noise, which is less than the cost of noise abatement denoted by areas $F + G$. These flights fly noisy.

EXERCISE:

In terms of figure 7-2, panel (*b*), assuming that transactions costs are zero, confirm that if the property rights to making noise in the flight path are given to homeowners, we still end up with 33 noisy flights and 47 quiet flights. How much will homeowners collect from airlines in this solution?[130]

D. TRADABLE NOISE PERMITS

If it is optimal to have some pollution in the market, then if the cost of abatement is different across polluters, there is some social gain from allowing pollution permits to be traded. In the airport noise example, I

---

[130]Start from the right and work leftward. Areas $F + G$ denote the costs to airlines to eliminate noise on the first 33 flights, but homeowners attach a value of F to get rid of the noise. Hence, the airlines can offer homeowners F plus part of G to obtain permission to have 33 noisy flights. It is cheaper for the airlines to attach mufflers to the next 47 flights than to pay homeowners to absorb it. It does not pay for the airlines to try to bribe homeowners to take the last 20 flights because it costs more to attach a muffler than their passengers are willing to pay. Hence, the solution gives the same pattern of noisy, quiet, and forgone flights as when airlines own the rights. Homeowners collect F plus part of G.

assume that all the airlines serving the airport could abate pollution at cost MC_A. But suppose that there are two kinds of airplanes: type A and type B. Their planes are otherwise identical except that it costs more to attach noise mufflers to type B. Suppose that half the airlines use type A planes and half type B, and that the marginal cost of noise abatement is $1,000 for type A firms and $2,000 for type B firms.

Suppose that the airport issues 10 noise permits to the type A airline and 10 to type B. Each flies 20 flights per day, meaning that as many quiet flights must leave as noisy ones. If the permits are not tradable, then the cost of 20 units of quiet is $30,000.

Suppose now that the airport allows airlines to trade permits. In this case, type B airline is willing to pay up to $2,000 to type A airline to obtain one of A's noise permits. Type A firms are willing to sell their permits if the price exceeds $1,000. It pays for type A and type B airlines to strike a deal that ensures that all 20 permits are held by type B airlines; hence, type A airlines always fly quiet, and type B airlines always fly noisy. In this case, the same noise is abated at a cost of $20,000 instead of $30,000. The allocation of this savings between these airlines is not important to the solution.

E. WHAT IF HOMEOWNERS CAN ABATE SOME NOISE?

I have assumed that only airlines can efficiently engage in noise abatement. But homeowners also can reduce the impact of noise. Homeowners can install insulation and triple-pane windows, use air conditioning in place of open windows, stay indoors during peak flying times, and so on. Moreover, in the long run, the owners of houses along the flight path would drift toward people who were less aggravated by the noise, which would further ameliorate the effects. To keep the problem manageable, I ignore these factors. If I introduce them, however, the optimal amount of noise likely would increase.

Chapter 8

Pollution in the Workplace: Contract or Externality?

An Introduction to the Rules of Law

Main Economic Concepts	1. When serious information problems characterize a market with no apparent externalities, a debate sometimes arises about whether, in effect, public policy should regulate the level of harm *as though* it were an externality, in effect treating some participants in a contract as though they were strangers.
	2. Sometimes, any of several alternatives can yield the efficient solution, including buyer beware, strict liability, and contributory negligence rules.
	3. Torts are the flip side of contracts. Economic damages equal the ex post payment that exposed parties would have charged if they had the opportunity to contract ex ante per episode of harm.
	4. If courts award damages that are higher or lower than economic damages, then society ends up with too many or too few units of care.
New Terms	1. Buyer beware standard
	2. Strict liability standard
	3. Negligence standard
	4. Contributory negligence
	5. Comparative negligence
	6. Economic damages
	7. Value of life
	8. Learned hand formula

In this chapter, I address a contract that has no externalities, and thus, one that normally does not warrant intervention. In reality, there are many situations in which public intervention in markets is advocated on the argument that at least some participants are so ill informed about a hazard that we might just as well treat it *as though* it were an externality. The argument assumes that market participants cannot find an efficient solution without outside intervention. These debates often arise when workers are exposed to pollutants that contribute to adverse health after a long period of exposure.

I. Compensation for Exposure to Air Particulates

I consider the case of air pollution that characterizes many job sites, like coal mines, drywall production factories, or textile plants. For our purposes, I assume that pollution from production affects only employees and not parties outside the firm.

If coal mine dust merely is aesthetically unpleasant, then since this job characteristic is transparent, workers on their own volition would require a premium to tolerate the unpleasantness of dirty work. The public policy issue arises because of the possibility of less obvious long-term consequences of exposure to dust. Suppose we know that if employees are exposed to air particulates, a significant portion of workers will suffer varying levels of health problems in the long run. What is the efficient level of air particulate in the work environment?

As long as workers are informed about the hazards, the problem is resolved naturally through the emergence of a "compensating differential." In this case, the firm internalizes the total cost of the hazard and delivers the optimum amount of harm to workers. But if workers are uninformed, which often is an argument for external intervention, the efficient solution emerges only with the help of tort law, direct regulation, or a corrective tax.

Information almost always is a substitute for intervention in the form of either tort law or direct regulation or taxation.

"Lack of information" is the underlying rationale for intervention in private contracts; that is, the information problem is what triggers reactions like those observed when parties impose harm on a stranger.

Consider cigarette smoking. Smoking causes long-term health problems. If smokers are uninformed, then we have a problem closely related to an externality; that is, society is characterized by too much smoking. On this basis, one might try to justify intervention in the form of either regulation of nicotine and tar levels, cigarette taxes, or tort suits eliciting damages ex post from tobacco companies.

If smokers are informed, then the problem is simply a private transaction between "Ken and Jane." Just because smoking has ill effects does not

---

EXERCISE:
Think how to model the smoking decision. You need to show the full cost of smoking and be able to depict whether someone decides to smoke and, if so, how much to smoke. Show the solution before and after the arrival of health information about the hazards of smoking.[131]

---

[131]Appendix A gives the answer.

mean that all consumers find it optimal to refrain from smoking. After factoring in the health costs, some consumers rationally choose to smoke.

A. SETTING UP THE AIR PARTICULATE PROBLEM

When dealing with a "bad" like air particulates, employ the strategy by we used for externalities. Redefine the problem so that the horizontal axis measures more units of a "good," and thus, units of "bad" are read from right to left. I define quantity along the horizontal axis as units of clean air; that is, as we move rightward from the zero axis, we can think of either units of particulates *removed* from the air or units of clean air *obtained*.

Consider *figure 8-1*, panel (*a*). The zero axis represents the amount of air particulates if the firm makes no effort to clean the air. We can think of 100 percent clean air as the elimination of all the air particulates. I define units of clear air such that we have zero pollution when we have 100 units of clean air.

B. THE DEMAND FOR CLEAN AIR

The demand curve for cleaner air at work measures the added compensation that *fully informed* workers, as a group, require to accept the higher risk of each subsequent unit of air particulate. Since workers can take jobs that have no significant health hazards, then it follows that firms that expose workers to polluted air must pay some premium to attract workers from the labor market. The premium is the "compensating differential." The demand curve in figure 8-1, panel (*a*), tells us how much that premium needs to be as a function of the pollution level at the job site.

It is best to start at the point where there are 100 units of clean air (at the rightmost part of the figure). At first, workers do not require much compensation to absorb a little pollution, and this is why the height of their demand curve for cleaner air is close to zero around this point. As we move leftward, workers are absorbing ever-higher amounts of pollution, which makes marginal units of pollution even more dangerous. This concern translates to higher amounts of required compensation for each additional unit of exposure. If there is no abatement, workers require

---

The *"demand curve" for cleaner air at work* measures the amount that fully informed workers on the job site, as a group, require as compensation for absorbing each small increment of air particulate.

The area under the demand curve over the range of pollution that exists on the work site is the total amount of compensation required by workers to tolerate it. If the firm gives workers C_0 units of clean air, then $100 - C_0$ units of pollution still exist; workers require compensation to absorb this harm equal to area C in figure 8-1, panel (*a*).

(a)

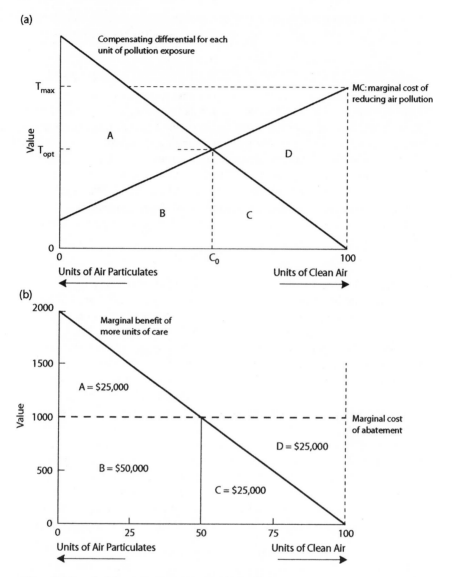

Figure 8-1. Level of Care: Air Particulates in the Workplace

a dollar compensation to accept this level of pollution at work, valued by areas $A + B + C$ in the figure. Put simply, *dirty air is not free*; firms must compensate workers to tolerate it.

C. THE SUPPLY OF CLEAN AIR

The upsloping schedule, labeled MC, describes the marginal cost incurred by the firm to rid particulates from the air. Starting at the zero axis (zero units of clean air), the first units of clean air are obtainable at relatively low cost, and so the height of the *MC* schedule is quite low. Further units of clean air are progressively more costly, involving more technology and so on. The schedule *MC* is the supply curve for clean air: it is the minimum cost of eliminating each unit of pollution. Put simply, *clean air is not free*; firms must expend resources to eliminate air particulates.

> *Every action has an opportunity cost.* Dirty air is costly to the firm in the form of higher wages. Clean air is costly to the firm in the form of pollution abatement costs. The firm's task is to find the solution with the least cost.

D. THE SOCIALLY OPTIMAL AMOUNT OF CLEAN AIR

It is apparent that the socially optimal level of clean air is given by C_0. It is worth cleaning the air to this point because over this range, workers attach a value to each marginal unit of clean air in excess of the marginal cost of providing it. Units of clean air beyond C_0 carry a marginal cost that exceeds the marginal benefit of further care. If the firm cleans C_0 units of air, it incurs pollution abatement costs measured by area *B*. The firm reduces its compensating differential payments by an amount measured by areas $A + B$. Hence, relative to zero pollution abatement, the delivery of C_0 units of clean air reduces the social cost of pollution by an amount denoted by area *A*.

Similarly, viewed from the perspective of 100 percent clean air, it is optimal to have $100 - C_0$ units of air particulates because over this range, workers require compensating differential measured by area *C*, which is less than the cost of eliminating the pollution, which is measured by areas $C + D$. Compared to 100 percent clean environment, the social gain from offering $100 - C_0$ units of dirty air is measured by area *D*.

Put a slightly different way, the dirty air generated by its production process costs the firm an amount measured by areas $B + C$. Area *B* denotes pollution abatement costs; area *C* denotes additional wages to compensate workers for accepting some dirty air. This outcome describes the optimum level of pollution at the work site.

II. How Do We Obtain the Socially Efficient Solution?

A. A CONTRACT SOLUTION (BUYER BEWARE)

How does the market deliver the optimal solution? We have just considered one way. If workers have full information, there is no reason to believe that private contracts will result in a suboptimum equilibrium. This solution is general. If either workers or consumers have full information about risks and are direct parties to a transaction, then the market will deliver the socially optimal number of care units. Under these conditions, there is no need for intervention. We therefore refer to this standard as **buyer beware.**

Buyer beware standard: As long as parties to a transaction are fully informed, we can expect the market to deliver optimum levels of potential harm.

There is no expected benefit from regulation or the judicial process. This outcome is no different from one involving Ken and Jane trading clothes and food; harm is just another commodity that trades at a market-clearing price.

In our example, competition in the labor market ensures that the compensating differential is such that the marginal worker is just indifferent to working at a lower wage in a cleaner environment or a higher wage in an environment that has some pollution. We can think of the analogy discussed in chapter 4. Suppose that in anticipation of a Van Gogh showing, the Smithsonian gives all the tickets to so-called street people so they can see the beautiful art exhibit. In all likelihood, few will choose to see it. Most will sell their tickets (clean air) for an agreed-upon price (compensating differential) to a higher-value user (the firm). Most things are worth giving up if the price is right. A "perfect" job site is no exception.

B. REGULATORY SOLUTION

The buyer beware standard serves to provide a benchmark for analysis. In reality, workers may be poorly informed about risk and thus may have difficulty formulating the proper compensating differential required to offset the health risks. The information argument is often invoked in these cases to justify government intervention.

If information is costly, we can think of workers hiring agents in the form of either Congress (or the regulatory agencies that administer legislation) or the judiciary to find the optimum solution. If they are perfect agents, they will effect the same solution as fully informed workers. We presume that before Congress enacts workplace health legislation, it collects expert information. Courts effectively do the same by ultimately delivering a judicial standard for evaluating cases that involve harm imposed by workplace exposure.

Zero harm is one obvious standard. A regulation can be issued that prohibits any measurable level of pollution at the work site. A prohibitive tax on air particulates equal to t_{max} in figure 8-1, panel (*a*), delivers the same result. Either way, the plant has no pollution. Relative to the optimum level of clear air, the compensating differential (area C) disappears owing to the cleaner air, but abatement costs increase by more than these savings (areas $C + D$). Social waste arises in an amount denoted by area D. The regulators or legislators are not representing society's interests. They have encouraged too many units of care.

> A *zero-harm exposure standard* assumes that workers and other market participants are unwilling to sell their exposure for a finite price. But this outcome is likely only in the most extreme cases. Generally, as we learned in chapter 1, Ken and Jane can strike a deal. In consideration of a sufficiently higher wage, most workers will accept some health risk and other risk of harm.

C. STRICT LIABILITY STANDARD

Suppose that workers are oblivious to the health hazards of air particulates on the job. They do not perceive the particulates as a "bad" and so do not demand compensation to tolerate the effects. Even if the firm knows about the health costs of the hazard and wants to compensate workers for these costs, the reality is that if workers across the industry do not perceive the costs, competition will drive the compensating differential to zero. Why?

Firms that do the right thing will be at a cost disadvantage to those who act *as though* they don't care, and ultimately the former firms will be driven from the market. Owing to asymmetric information (workers know less than firms about job-related health hazards), we end up with a corner solution: only firms that "don't care" survive. In this case, air pollution on the job site is akin to an externality. It imposes harm on workers in an amount denoted by the sum of areas $A + B + C$ in figure 8-1, panel (*a*) with no compensation. We end up with too much dirty air.

The optimal solution is to affix responsibility for health costs on the party that can discover and solve the problem at lowest cost. If workers can perform this function more efficiently, then a buyer beware policy is optimal. If firms can perform the function more efficiently, then a **strict liability standard** is optimal.

> A *strict liability standard* requires the party responsible for supplying harm to compensate victims for damages, regardless of fault.
>
> This standard applied against party A is more likely to be optimal if (1) information is poor to party B, (2) it is cheaper for party A to discover harm, and (3) the solution to harm is mostly in the hands of party A.

Assume that jurors are perfect agents for workers in an ex ante sense: they award judgments to workers equal to the amounts that workers *would have* solicited from the firm if they had full information. In terms of figure 8-1, panel (*a*), if the firm does not clean any air, then the firm absorbs judgments in an amount measured by areas $A + B + C$. By incurring C_0 units of care at a total cost measured by area B, the firm reduces judgments in an amount measured by areas $A + B$. The firm realizes the net savings measured by area A. Beyond C_0 units, it is cheaper for the firm to pay the judgments measured by area C than to eliminate the judgments by incurring abatement costs measured by areas $C + D$. Hence, we have the socially optimum result.

In effect, the judgments, denoted by area C, are a kind of stand-in for a compensating differential that workers would have charged the firm, had they been informed about the health hazards. It is worth noting that if strict liability is invoked, there is no compensating differential even if workers are informed. Workers, receive the differential later on (in an expected sense) in the form of judgments collected by victims of the pollution. Either way, the firm pays for the right to impose health risks on workers and delivers the optimal amount of pollution on the work site.

> *Strict liability* can deliver a socially optimum result if juries award damages that replicate the compensation that workers would have charged if they had full information.
>
> *Liability standards* are substitutes for compensating differentials. Assuming that courts can accurately calculate damages, then tort awards to harmed workers are the equivalent of a stream of compensating wage differentials. The standard can improve efficiency only if workers are uninformed.

III. The Compensation Principle and Economic Damages

We now are on the cusp of developing an important principle of law: torts are merely the flip side of contracts. What does this mean? You know that if contracts are feasible—which at least requires fully informed participants—optimal exposure to harm is delivered and workers are compensated an amount denoted by area C in figure 8-1, panel (*a*). If contracts are not economic—say because the cost of informing workers about the long-term health effects is too high—a torts solution can produce the same outcome ex post if it sets awards in the amount denoted by area C. Hence, torts merely accomplish ex post what would have been accomplished through contracting ex ante, had it been feasible.

> Torts accomplish ex post what is infeasible to accomplish ex ante through contracting.

A. TORTS ARE THE FLIP SIDE OF CONTRACTS

To develop this point more fully, I reconsider the plant pollution problem with a few more specific assumptions. In period 1, 100 workers are exposed to pollution at the work site. In period 2, they are either harmed or unharmed. If they are harmed, they incur $25,000 in health expenses, after which the health problem is fixed. The marginal cost of abating 1 unit of pollution is $1,000.

The benefits that workers attach to clean air are a function of the health implications of exposure. Suppose that if our 100 workers are exposed to 50 units of pollution, 1 worker is harmed. If pollution doubles to 100 units, 4 workers are harmed. These facts are consistent with the following demand curve for clean air (but you need not derive it yourself):[132]

$$MB = \$2,000 - \$20\,x,$$

where x is the quantity of clean air. This schedule is the vertical summation of each worker's demand curve for clean air. Workers as a group are willing to pay $2,000 for the first unit of pollution abatement and lesser amounts on the margin as they obtain more clean air.

1. The Contracting Solution

This demand schedule is shown as the downward-sloping line in figure 8-1, panel (b). Since the marginal cost of abatement is $1,000 per unit of pollution, then it is optimal to abate 50 units. Area B denotes the cost of abatement. Area C represents $25,000 in higher wages that the firm pays workers to compensate them for the harm that will come to 1 out of 100 workers exposed to the hazard. Each of 100 workers receives $250 to compensate them for exposure to a 1 percent chance of incurring a health problem that costs $25,000.

Suppose that each exposed worker is harmed with probability, p. The compensating differential, c, that *each* exposed worker requires to accept

[132]The underlying model can be specified as follows. The number of harmed workers, N, is a function of the quantity of pollution, Q. The number of harmed workers increases disproportionately with the square of pollution: $N = .0004\,Q^2$. Total health costs, say C, equal the number of harmed workers times the cost of dealing with the harm. Thus, total health costs are $25,000\,N$. Substituting N from above, this cost can be expressed in terms of the quantity of pollution: $C = \$10\,Q^2$. Taking the first derivative with respect to Q gives the marginal cost of imposing pollution: $MC = 20\,Q$. This is the supply of dirty air. The amount of clean air $x = 100 - Q$. Hence, the demand for clean air $MB = 20\,(100 - x) = 2,000 - 20x$.

the risk equals the economic cost of harm, H, times the probability that he will be harmed.

The compensating differential is the amount that a fully- informed person requires to accept exposure to harm that has economic cost, H, times the probability that exposure produces harm, p:

$$C = pH$$

Each worker receives a compensating differential of $250 to accept a 1 percent risk of incurring harm worth $25,000. In the aggregate, all 100 workers exposed to risk receive the amount $25,000, which not co-incidentally equals the amount of harm imposed on the one person who will realize the adverse outcome. Each worker could insure against this eventuality by purchasing an insurance policy, which in a competitive insurance market would carry a premium of $250 (ignoring the administrative cost of running the insurance company).

2. A Liability Rule

If workers have no information about health risk, then a contract solution does not prevail. In this case, a liability rule can generate the same outcome if the award is set equal to economic damages. In particular, using a strict liability rule, suppose that the court awards the amount, $H = \$25,000$, ex post to the unlucky worker who is harmed. Notice that the amount of the award equals the sum of compensating differentials that all 100 workers would have required in the form of a compensating differential ex ante had they had full information.

Awarding economic damages in a tort is akin to paying off the health insurance policy that each exposed victim in principle could have purchased ex ante with the compensating differential they would have received in a contract.

At this level the firm internalizes the full cost of employing workers in a dirty environment, which amounts to $25,000 per episode of harm. The firm has an incentive to limit pollution to 50 units, which reduces the number of harmed workers from 4 to 1.

A liability standard can deliver the optimum amount of harm as long as it delivers economic damages.

This means that upon encountering a harmed person, the correct question to ask to arrive at economic damages has two parts: (1) how much would *this* person have required in compensation to accept exposure to this harm, and (2) how many individuals are exposed per episode of harm? Economic damages are the product of these two numbers.

Suppose that air pollution from exposure to cotton produces about the same damages to lungs as exposure to coal dust. Suppose it has long been known that coal dust causes lung damage in 1 out of 20 workers exposed and that the law enforces a buyer beware standard in coal dust owing to its well-known dangers. A compensating differential develops. Suppose finally that economists estimate that wages among miners are higher by about $20,000 per worker over a lifetime of work to compensate for dangers of incurring a lung dysfunction. If cotton dangers are recently announced and the courts enforce a strict liability standard for harmed cotton workers, what are economic damages for harmed cotton workers?

Economic Damages
The economic cost of harm equals the compensating differential that a harmed person would have required ex ante to accept exposure (if he were fully informed), divided by the probability that exposure produces harm, p:

$$H = \frac{c}{p}$$

The probability of harm equals the number of episodes of harm, n, divided by the number of exposed workers, N. Thus, an equivalent formula is:

$$H = c \frac{N}{n}$$

which says that economic damages per episode of harm equal the compensating differential times the number of exposed persons, divided by the number of harm episodes expected for this population of exposures.

If we know the compensating differential for accepting risk and the probability that exposure yields harm, then we can infer the economic cost of harm.

If we do not know the compensating differential, then we can only try to replicate the components that exposed parties would have included in their calculus, had they been fully informed. Presumably, these components include medical costs, forgone wages, forgone leisure, pain and suffering, and so on.

We know that coal workers collect $20,000 *times* 20 workers exposed per episode of harm. So coal miners value harm at $400,000 per episode. Since cotton dust produces similar harm to coal dust, $400,000 might be a reasonable damage award per episode of lung damage to harmed cotton workers.

Recall from chapter 1 the example of an individual wrongly imprisoned in the District of Columbia for two years owing to an inadequate record-keeping system. We want to give the District of Columbia an incentive to engage in the optimal amount of care in its record keeping. While we need to use a liability rule in this case, we still are implicitly looking to replicate the amount that would have characterized a voluntary contract. What amount of money would the individual have required to accept the District of Columbia's "offer" of imprisonment under the agreed-upon conditions for two years? The answer to this question gives the amount of damages.

B. WHAT IF JUDGMENT AMOUNTS ARE NOT ECONOMIC DAMAGES?

Courts do not know the compensating differential that harmed individuals would have asked for ex ante and may not know the number of exposed persons to the risk that caused harm. Hence, courts try to capture economic damages ex post by considering factors such as lost wages, medical expenses, pain and suffering, and so on. But these may not represent the amounts that exposed parties would have required in the first place to be exposed to risk. Hence, court awards may exceed or fall short of economic damages.

If the courts award damages that on average are greater than economic damages, then firms react by engaging in too much abatement. Figure 8-2, panel (*a*), depicts this condition. The award of too-high damages is akin to the jury overstating the amount of the compensating differential that exposed individuals would have contracted for ex ante. The jury acts as though the workers' supply price of risk is given by the solid line starting at 100 units of clean air, which overstates the supply price that workers would have set if they had been fully informed (dashed line). The jury is not acting as a perfect agent for workers.

The chart shows the economic consequences of these errors. The firm increases the amount of clean air in the workplace to an inefficient level, C_1. Areas $E + G$ denote the additional abatement cost. But fully informed workers would require a lesser amount (area G) to absorb this amount of pollution. Area E measures the social waste. Areas $F + H$ denote future tort awards owing to remaining harm done at the higher level of care.

Panel (*b*) denotes the case when judgments on average are less than economic damages. In this case, firms abate too little pollution. They increase the amount of dirty air that imposes harm in the amount denoted

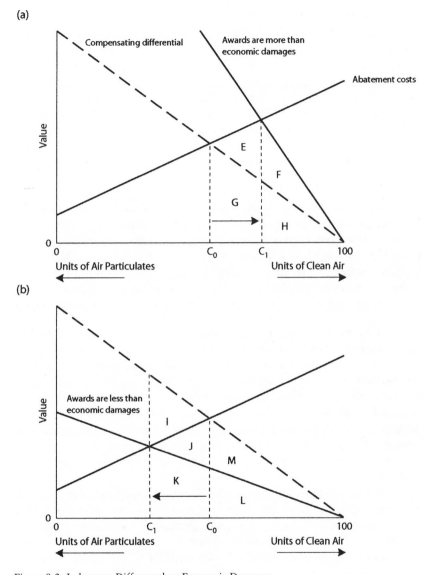

Figure 8-2. Judgments Different than Economic Damages

by areas $K + J + I$ but which costs an amount to abate denoted by areas $J + K$. Area I denotes social waste. Areas $K + L$ denote future awards. The question is not whether a liability rule gives the perfect outcome but whether it gives an outcome that is better than the next best (imperfect) alternative that we have at hand.

C. TRANSACTIONS COSTS AGAIN

The symmetry between torts and contracts raises the inevitable question about the role of transactions costs in the solution. The answer is another rendition of Coase: in the absence of transactions costs there are no torts, only contracts. Think about it. In the absence of transactions costs (the all-knowing benevolent dictator model), we know everyone who is exposed to risk and their requisite compensating differentials for risk exposure. Thus, any person wishing to engage in an activity that creates exposure does so only if he values it more than it costs. All compensating differentials are collected and distributed to the exposed population at zero cost.

In the absence of transactions costs, there are no torts, only contracts. Zero transactions costs means that all parties to exposed risk are fully informed, that payments are made ex ante from those imposing risks to those at risk, and that there are no costs to any of these transactions nor any costs of enforcing these agreements.

John Smith likes to drive fifty miles per hour through thirty-five miles-per-hour streets. He drives five thousand miles per year on these streets. It is economic for him to do so as long as all pedestrians and all motorists at risk are compensated their supply price of exposing themselves to this risk. If we can costlessly determine the compensation required by all exposed individuals and add them, we come to some aggregate required payment to permit excess speed. Let X denote this amount. Suppose that this number represents the expected costs of accident victims from the excess speed, taking account of lost wages, medical costs, pain and suffering, and so on.

If John is willing to pay the amount X for his "speeding permit," then it is economic for him to speed. As long as it is costless to determine this information and distribute the "speed premiums" to the exposed population, we have the right number of speed permits on the road. In this case, upon observing a predictable consequence of this speed (a pedestrian is hit, and so on), there is no tort action. All exposed parties already have been paid for exposure to this risk.

Obviously, the transactions costs of this contract are prohibitive. An alternative approach is to create a tort that pays damages upon observing an accident caused by excess speed. The court system will count as damages lost wages, medical expenses, pain and suffering, and so on, but of course these may not sum to X. They may be too high or too low. But they are an attempt to assess ex post an amount that in the aggregate would have been collected contractually ex ante in a world characterized by zero transactions costs.

D. VALUE OF LIFE IN A CONTRACT SETTING

Death is one outcome of a risky activity. The question naturally arises about the economic cost of this harm. Almost no one would exchange certain death for any amount of money. Yet, individuals often accept jobs that carry fatality risks. Presumably, they do not do so for free. For example, fire and police personnel, race car drivers, bodyguards, construction workers, and the like are exposed to some risk of death on the job. Since they could take jobs that carry virtually zero risk of death, presumably they take the more dangerous jobs only if adequately compensated.

Suppose that in the context of a two-period model, the probability that they will not live to enjoy period 2 is p. We observe by comparing wages for similarly skilled workers across occupations with zero fatality risk that the wage in a job with a p percent chance of fatality is higher by the amount c. Then we know that in order for this premium to develop, it must be true that workers are multiplying the probability of death by some number, say V, to convert a probability into a dollar value: $c = pV$.

The variable V is known in the literature as the "value of life." It is not the amount of money that a person would accept in exchange for certain death. Rather, it is that number, which when multiplied by the probability of death, gives the differential compensation required to accept some risk of death. For example, suppose that the probability of a fatality on some job is .001. Also, suppose that we observe that the wage differential in this job is $2,000. Then the value of life must be $2 million. That is to say, in return for a total payment of $2 million, 1,000 workers accept a job in which one is expected to die. One could imagine paying this premium either in the form of $2,000 per worker or as a $2 million life insurance policy payable for on-the-job deaths.

Panel (a) in figure 8-3 shows the market for risky jobs. The chart assumes a risk of death with a probability of 1 in 1,000. The supply prices of risk for all individuals is rising, reflecting the reality that some individuals sell their exposure at lower prices than others. The downward-sloping schedule is the demand for individuals willing to take a job with fatality

---

Value of life: That number, V, which when multiplied by the probability of death, p, gives us the observed premium required by informed participants to accept some risk of death, c:

$$c = pV$$

The value of c is the supply price of fatality risk, p.

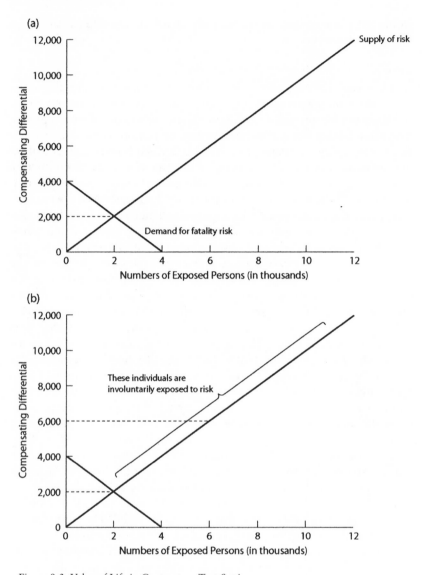

Figure 8-3. Value of Life in Contract vs. Tort Setting

risk. Only 2,000 individuals are in these jobs, each collecting a compensating differential equal to $2,000. The implied value of life is $2 million.

E. VALUE OF LIFE IN A LIABILITY SETTING

Now suppose that an automobile hits a pedestrian and a fatality results. The pedestrian had no opportunity to contract for a payment to accept the risk of death caused by speeding cars. In this case, a liability rule is used to compensate her family. From an efficiency perspective, society wants drivers to internalize the full cost of speed inclusive of dangers they pose to pedestrians. To determine the award, we can try to replicate the premium that a pedestrian would have required to accept fatality risk, had she had a chance to write a contract ex ante.

Even though this person did not have a chance to negotiate a contract, there are other opportunities to measure the premium from contracts that reflect overt fatality risk. Suppose that we discover through this process that observed risk premiums in these kinds of contracts imply that the value of life is $2 million. Then we might infer that such a number would be a good proxy to use in a case where we know that a contract is not possible, such as in a pedestrian fatality.[133] If we make this inference, however, we would have the wrong answer.

Panel (b) in figure 8-3 shows why. Whereas in a contract setting only the 2,000 individuals with the *lowest* supply prices take risky jobs, all 12,000 in the market might be involuntarily exposed to speed risk. This explains why economic damages in torts exceed the amounts implied by compensating differentials in contract settings. In the chart, the average exposed person requires a compensating differential of $6,000 to accept the risk, fully three times higher than those who voluntarily accept risks contractually.

To encourage an efficient amount of care in risky activities (say in connection with automobile driving), we need to convey the economic damages of the average exposed person to the tort, not the average exposed person to voluntary contracts exposed to similar risks.

The value of life in a tort setting exceeds the value in a contract setting. In the case of contracts, only those with the lowest supply prices work in risky activities, whereas in torts, exposure is involuntary and thus includes a cross section of individuals with supply prices higher than those who contract for risks.

Panel (b) also gives rise to another interesting phenomenon. In reality since fatality risk is only .001, then only 12 of the 12,000 individuals exposed to noncontracted risks are expected to die. The courts could try to figure out each victim's implied supply price of risk and then charge the

---

[133]In general, we would expect value of life estimates on the job site to be an underestimate for the population as a whole. If the value of life used in these calculations differs across the population, then one would assume that those with lowest values would gravitate to jobs with fatality risks (because to them the wage premium confers rent).

person responsible for his death the appropriate value of life. Over a period of time, these numbers would tend to average $6 million. Alternatively, if the court had some idea about the exposed population's average compensating differential, then it could simply assess a charge equal to $6 million per death no matter what the victim's particular value of life.

A court that assesses the right price upon each fatality creates an incentive for drivers to engage in the efficient amount of caution. Suppose it assesses damages of $6 million each time that a driver hits a pedestrian (strict liability). Suppose that insurance companies can perfectly monitor their customers' behaviors (imagine many monitors continuously scanning the bar codes on vehicles as they drive by, creating a record of speed and erratic driving) and can charge prices to each driver based on the probability that he or she will hit a pedestrian. If each driver is assessed a premium equal to the risk of fatality they pose to pedestrians, then drivers have the incentive to slow down to an efficient speed (one where the value of speed on the margin equals the full marginal cost of speed).[134]

The full cost of any activity that poses fatality risk must include the probability that the activity produces a fatality, times the average value of life of the *exposed* population.

Thus, it might cost the driver an extra $10 in private costs to operate his car twenty miles per hour over the speed limit for one hundred miles (in the form of higher gasoline consumption and the like). But suppose that there is a one-in-a-million chance that a stranger is killed as a result of this driver's excess speed. Then assuming that the value of life of the exposed population is $6 million, the full cost of this speed is $16 per 100 miles. This includes the private cost ($10) plus $6 for fatality risk (a one-millionth chance of incurring $6 million in damages). The full cost of speeding therefore depends on the value of life of the exposed population and the probability that speeding results in a fatality.

In reality, of course, courts do not calculate a value of life, nor do they estimate compensating differentials that the victim might have assessed ex ante. Instead, they look for numbers like forgone earnings, the value of lost companionship, and the like, which may approximate exposed

---

[134]In reality, insurance prices reflect imperfect information about behavior (the insurance can determine drivers' traffic records and accident records, and it also knows the history of accidents in certain automobile types, etc.), and so this cost is conveyed with a great deal of imperfection.

individuals' average value of life. Or it may not. There is either too much or too little care depending on whether judgment awards are too high or too low. In either case, predictable efficiency consequences arise (as demonstrated previously in figure 8-2). Appendix B demonstrates a model of speed in more detail.

EXERCISE:
Return to the workplace pollution numerical example shown in figure 8-1, panel (*b*). Suppose that workers can wear masks that reduce the number of harmed workers by 50 percent (but health costs per episode still are $25,000). Redraw the figure showing the new marginal costs of more pollution and determine the new optimal solution. Label all the areas and write the dollar amount that pertains to each. What happens to the amount that (1) the firm spends on abatement and (2) workers receive in compensation for accepting pollution? By how much does social welfare increase owing to the introduction of the masks? How many workers are harmed in the new equilibrium?[135]

A FEW FACTS ABOUT VALUE OF LIFE

1. Unbiased estimates put the value of life in the $5 million to $7 million range.[136]
2. Regulatory agencies use values of life in evaluating the costs and benefits of lifesaving regulations, though the values used are not necessarily consistent across agencies.
3. Courts do not use value of life concepts. Instead, they look for countable damages such as lost earnings and the like. Human capital measures (meaning the present value of wages) are less than value of life numbers and thus encourage too little care.

In the case of the Ford Pinto with its vulnerable gasoline tanks, it chose not to incur the expense of changing the location of the tanks because it was being billed in tort cases at roughly $200,000 per death, and so it was not optimal to move the tanks. The cost of moving the tanks was $137.5 million in exchange for saving 180 lives ($763,888 per life saved). A value of life concept would have generated the correction.

---

[135]Appendix C gives the answer.
[136]The summary information in this box can be found in W. Kip Viscusi, "The Value of Life in Legal Contexts: Survey and Critique," *American Law and Economics Review* (2000): 195–222.

CRIMES VERSUS TORTS

What is the difference between a tort and a crime? Both expose (mostly) strangers to risks without ex ante compensation. Both impose harm. Yet, "crimes" are treated differently than torts. How do we use economics to draw a distinction?

The willingness to settle up economic damages from harm is a key difference. In a tort, the person causing harm expresses a willingness to pay economic damages if held liable. In a crime, the one imposing harm usually has no intention of compensating victims.

The purpose of most crimes is to seize a valuable asset, and thus, by definition, the perpetrator is not willing to pay the victim's supply price. His "hiding" from the law merely underlies his intention to stiff his victim.

A tort often arises as an ancillary event to some other purpose as in a fatality during the course of driving, and thus, the principal purpose of the act is not to seize an asset.

As long as the one imposing harm stands ready to pay economic damages, he has an incentive to engage in due care. When individuals are able to pay economic damages but try to escape this responsibility, we can re-create appropriate due care by adding appropriate penalties to damages when they are caught. If they are unable and unwilling to pay damages, we need to find other ways to create care, as in, for example, the threat of incarceration.

Some examples to ponder (there are no answers, only questions):

1. If a person steals my car, we can presume he has no intention of compensating me, since that defeats the purpose of the theft in the first place. This seems like a crime. Alternatively, suppose someone notices that his car is missing at 2:00 A.M. Everyone in the neighborhood knows that anyone who calls the police never gets his car back. Instead, it usually shows up by 7:00 A.M. the next day with a $1,000 bill sticking out of the ignition. Is this a crime or a tort?

2. An individual in anger strikes another and causes some (fixable) damage. If the perpetrator immediately admits responsibility and offers to settle up with his victim, ponder whether anyone dials 911.

3. It is reputed that in a large metropolitan city in the United States, occasionally someone ends up "swimming with the fishes" (for good reasons we suppose). The following day, someone in a black suit shows up at the "swimmer's" house with a suitcase full of cash in "settlement money" for his widow (reportedly more than the bum was worth). These "fish events" are never reported to the police. Should they be?

continued . . .

CRIMES VERSUS TORTS *Continued*

4. A sober but negligent driver runs over a pedestrian and stays put to confront the consequences. He is likely to face the prospect of an adverse judgment in a tort. If the same driver "hits and runs" he commits a "crime." Is the distinction the willingness to settle up for economic damages?

IV. Negligence Standards

I have considered two liability standards: buyer beware and strict liability. In one case, the individual exposed to risk is liable for his own injuries. In the other, the one who supplies the exposure is liable for damages. A third standard introduces the notion of negligence. One who poses dangers is liable for damages from injury only if he is "negligent" in his acts. The immediate question, of course, is what constitutes negligence? In the plant pollution model used earlier, if the negligence threshold is triggered if there is *any* air pollution, then we have a strict liability standard. If the negligence threshold is triggered when pollution is almost completely unabated, then we have a buyer beware standard.

A. AN EFFICIENT NEGLIGENCE STANDARD

One obvious candidate for the negligence standard is one where the marginal cost of reducing harm is less than the corresponding benefits. This principle is embodied in the so-called *Learned Hand Formula*, which is simply a rendition of the marginal principles in economics. It says that the supplier of harm is not negligent (and hence, is not liable for harm) as long as he has produced the efficient level of abatement, for example, the delivery of C_0 units of clean air in figure 8-1, panel (*a*).

Learned Hand Formula: A person imposing potential harm is not negligent if he engages units of care such that the marginal cost of care equals the marginal cost of harm. In terms of figure 8-1, panel *a*, this standard is met as long as the firm offers C_0 units of clean air.

This standard also delivers the optimal amount of care. Firms know that if they do not deliver C_0 units of clean air, they are liable for damages. For example, if they fail to abate any pollution, then in terms of figure 8-1, panel (*a*), they are liable for damages measured by areas $A + B + C$. If they deliver C_0 units of clean air, then they are not liable for any damages. In the latter case, if workers are informed then they collect compensating differentials equal to the amount denoted by area C. If they are uninformed then area C denotes the health costs of exposure that workers themselves absorb in the future.

B. WHAT IF WORKERS CAN REDUCE HARM THEMSELVES?

A strict liability standard can discourage the market from finding cheaper solutions. Suppose that workers can reduce the health effect of air particulates by 50 percent by wearing a cheap paper mask. There is some disutility cost to wearing a mask, and so workers require a compensating differential for wearing one. Assume that in exchange for some aggregate amount, γ, the workforce is willing to wear masks. I do not portray this cost in the figure but refer to it later.

To see how this information changes the problem, consider figure 8-4, which replicates figure 8-1, panel (a), except it has one additional schedule. The new schedule denotes the marginal benefits of pollution abatement, *given that workers wear masks*. That is, if workers wear a mask, each unit of air particulate does less damage, and hence, workers' required compensating differential for health risk falls, even as a differential is created to compensate workers for wearing a mask.

If workers wear masks, the harm from exposure to $100 - C_0$ units of air particulates falls by an amount measured by area G. In addition, the optimal amount of clean air falls to C_1; that is, if workers are harmed

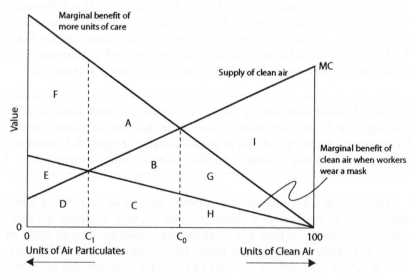

Figure 8-4. Reconsidering Risk: Facemask Use

less by pollution by wearing a mask, then the socially optimal amount of pollution increases by the amount $C_0 - C_1$. The harm from pollution for this additional exposure (area C) is less than the cost of abatement (areas $B + C$).

As long as the total savings from wearing a mask (areas $B + G$) exceed the cost to workers of wearing masks (the amount γ not shown), the optimal solution is C_1 units of clean air, and workers wear a mask.

If workers are *informed,* then a contractual solution delivers the optimum amount of pollution. Workers receive a compensating differential equal to areas $C + H$ to absorb the health cost of air particulates that penetrate their masks, plus an amount to compensate them for wearing the mask, γ. If workers are *uninformed,* then a strict liability standard delivers the optimal solution if the firm can cheaply monitor its employees to ensure that they wear the mask. In this case, the firm expects to pay judgments equal to areas $H + C$.

If, however, workers are installing wallboard off-site, so that the firm cannot determine if workers are indeed wearing a mask, then the mask solution may not work. That is, if damages under strict liability reflect observed health damage without regard to self-inflicted additional damages caused by failure to adhere to safety rules (like wearing a mask), then workers have no incentive to wear a mask. The firm is driven back to C_0 units of clean air. We do not have the efficient solution.

C. CONTRIBUTORY NEGLIGENCE

When masks are economical, C_1 units of care in figure 8-4 is the optimum solution. Under an efficient negligence standard, as long as firms engage in this level of care, they are not liable for harm. The optimum standard incorporates the efficiency of wearing masks. Will firms deliver this level? Yes, if the courts enforce a **contributory negligence standard.**

The concept of contributory negligence arises when workers can ameliorate harm more economically than the firm. In the context of figure 8-4, masks increase efficiency by areas $B + G$, less the cost of wearing the mask, which I have assumed to be small in relation to this gain. Workers who do not wear a mask are not entitled to damages from the health problems that develop from the exposure. Workers have an incentive to wear a mask, and firms have an incentive to provide the efficient level of care.

D. COMPARATIVE NEGLIGENCE

If the court enforces an efficient negligence standard, then the firm is not liable for damages as long as it offers C_1 units of clean air. Similarly, if workers do not wear masks under a contributory negligence standard, they are not entitled to damages regardless of whether the firm is negligent. What if both the firm and the worker are negligent? A comparative negligence standard can deliver the efficient solution.

A comparative negligence standard tries to divvy up damages according to whose negligence created which portion of harm. Under this standard, a firm that ignores pollution abatement is liable for damages in the amount limited to areas $E + D + C + H$ in figure 8-4. The firm is not liable for damages measured by areas $F + A + B + G$ because these incremental damages arise only if workers themselves are negligent. In this standard, workers have an incentive to wear face masks, and the firm minimizes its costs by choosing C_1 units of clean air. It later pays damages in the amount denoted by areas $C + H$.

E. STRICT LIABILITY WITH CONTRIBUTORY NEGLIGENCE

One can obtain a similar answer by combining strict liability with contributory negligence. In this case, the firm is liable for all harm done by exposure to air pollutants on the job site, but damages are limited to levels delivered by a nonnegligent worker. In terms of figure 8-4, workers have an incentive to wear a mask, and firms have an incentive to deliver C_1 units of clean air. The firm is liable for health damages in the amount denoted by areas $C + H$.

Contributory negligence: If a victim's own carelessness contributes to the accident that creates the tort action, he is not entitled to damages.

Comparative negligence: If both parties to a tort are negligent, the harmed party is entitled to the difference between actual damages and those that would have been sustained had he met his standard of care.

Examples of incremental damages include harm from an auto accident that stems from the harmed person failing to use a seat belt, head injuries that result because a motorcycle rider did not wear a helmet, a smoker who develops health problems because she continues her habit after the government announced health warnings, and so on.

A strict liability standard can be combined with a contributory negligence standard to produce an efficient result. In this approach, the firm is liable for harm imposed on workers, but only up to the amount of damages that would have been incurred by a nonnegligent worker. Thus, a driver that runs into another car for any reason is held liable for damages to the occupants of the car he hits, save for those incremental damages attributable to the occupants' failure to wear seat belts.

EXERCISE 1:
Apply the principles of this chapter to the case of automobile driving. More speed confers benefits to drivers in the form of saved time but kills more pedestrians. Think of the optimal tort standard in an environment in which pedestrians cannot affect the outcome. What are the implications of the courts recognizing contributory negligence when pedestrians can affect the fatality rate by engaging in due care?[137]

EXERCISE 2:
Return to the Tulips and Mums problem in figure 1-10, panel (*a*). Frank would have been at point *A* but ended up sat point *B*, whereupon Dick gave Frank $38 in damages the following year. This is a solution with a liability rule. How could you rephrase the problem to make it a contract solution?[138]

EXERCISE 3:
Two types of trespassers drown in backyard pools: toddlers wandering over from nearby houses and teenagers sneaking on the property when the owners are away. From the perspective of efficiency, which standard makes sense when considering backyard pools: strict liability or contributory negligence?[139]

---

[137]My solution is shown in appendix B.

[138]Before Frank buys any flowers, Dick (who likes mums better than tulips) says to Frank, "Hey, Frank! How much would I have to pay you to have a 125–25 mums–tulips split this year versus the usual 75–75?" Whereupon Frank figures that this contract puts him at *B* versus *A* in figure 1-10, panel (*a*), that is, on utility curve U_1 instead of U_2. He needs $38 to strike the deal. Hence, the liability rule we used to make Frank whole after Dick reneges is an ex post solution that replicates the contract price that would have prevailed had Dick paid Frank ex ante to plant the asymmetric garden.

[139]A strict liability standard might be more appropriate for children who drown in a neighbor's pool because they are too young to make calculating decisions. This may mean that three-foot fences are optimum. But it is doubtful that this standard is appropriate vis-à-vis teenage boys who jump over the fence to have a swim in the neighbor's pool at midnight after a few beers. If strict liability were applied in this case, we might end up with either no pools or pools with twelve-foot fencing around them, topped with barbed wire.

Appendix A: The Decision to Smoke and Rules of Law

This appendix addresses a question set out in the text. How do we model the smoking decision with and without information? I illustrate the problem under many simplifying assumptions. I abstract from any externalities about smoking—for example, secondhand smoke, deleterious effects of smoking during pregnancy, and so on.[140] I also assume away problems of addiction. In other words, I use a stylized example that helps raise some key legal concepts and some implications about information costs.

Consider a two-period model. In period 1, the consumer smokes C cigarettes. In period 2, he may or may not experience significant health effects. I assume that all smokers are alike in all relevant respects except that some are completely informed and others completely uninformed. The out-of-pocket cost per cigarette is P_0. The health cost per cigarette (which incorporates the dollar value of premature death plus other health-related expenses) is P_H.

Figure 8-5 depicts the smoking decision for an individual who finds it optimal to smoke with and without health information. The horizontal axis measures the number of cigarettes consumed in period 1, and the vertical axis denotes value. With no information, the individual perceives only the out-of-pocket cost of smoking, depicted by price P_0. He smokes C_0 cigarettes.

With full information about health hazards, he perceives the full cost as the sum of out-of-pocket cost plus the health cost of smoking, $P_0 + P_H$. He continues to smoke but reduces his intensity of smoking to

---

[140]I also abstract from the idea that smoking-related damages paid through health policies ought to be reimbursable. Insurance companies had the opportunity to charge risk-related premiums to smokers, and the fact that they did not make these assessments seems to preclude arguments about liability ex post.

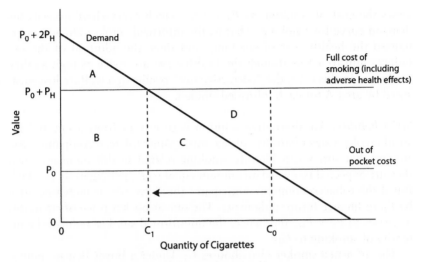

Figure 8-5. Reaction to Health Information about Smoking

C_1 cigarettes.[141] The consumer has found the optimum smoking level, taking account of the full costs of smoking. The informed smoker incurs health cost measured by area B and enjoys surplus measured by area A.

Now consider an identical smoker who does not process health information and hence smokes C_0 cigarettes with and without information. The uninformed smoker incurs a welfare gain from his habit equal to area A *minus* area D. If he had full information, he also would choose C_1 cigarettes and eliminate the reduction in welfare denoted by area D. Policy advocates assume that there are a nontrivial number of smokers who are in the latter category.

The problem that arises is that policy advocates only observe individuals smoking *after* information is available. They cannot tell whether the individual is informed and is smoking C_1 cigarettes, or is uninformed and is smoking C_0 cigarettes. These levels of smoking could be consistent with or without information, depending on individuals' particular demand curves for smoking.

A tax on cigarettes. Suppose that the advocate proposes a tax that is equal to the health harm of smoking, namely, P_H. If the smoker is uninformed, the tax encourages him to reduce smoking from C_0 to C_1, which improves his welfare by the amount denoted by area D. If, however, the smoker is informed, then the tax encourages him to quit because he

[141]Note that had I drawn his demand curve so that it intersected the vertical axis below $P_0 + P_H$, the smoker would have quit.

views the cost of smoking as $P_0 + 2P_H$, which everywhere exceeds his demand curve for smoking. That is, the informed smoker already internalized the health cost of smoking, and thus, the addition of the tax induces him to act as though the health costs are twice as high as they really are. In this case, the "corrective tax" results in a welfare loss measured by area A for each informed smoker.

Strict liability. An alternative solution is to refrain from a tax and instead invoke a strict liability rule ex ante against tobacco companies. Assuming that juries can identify smoking-related health damages, then they are expected to award an amount equal to P_H per cigarette smoked. But if the tobacco company anticipates these awards, it increases price by P_H to finance future judgments. The out-of-pocket price of cigarettes increases to $P_0 + P_H$, and hence, the uninformed smoker reduces the intensity of smoking to C_1.

The informed smoker also chooses C_1. Under a buyer beware policy, the informed smoker internalized the present value of health cost that he expected to pay later and thus perceived the full cost of smoking as $P_0 + P_H$. Under strict liability, he pays out-of-pocket costs, $P_0 + P_H$, now, but incurs no (uncompensated) health-related costs later on. Hence, he continues to choose smoking intensity C_1.

It is apparent that a strict liability rule works pretty well under the assumption that juries can decide at zero cost the marginal health effects done by smoking and correctly calculate damage.

Ex-post reneging. In reality, courts mostly have effectively enforced a buyer beware policy toward smokers, signaling to tobacco companies that P_0 is the appropriate price. Smokers nevertheless routinely have sued tobacco companies for damages, often involving cases of premature death occasioned by smoking. Since smokers had the opportunity to learn about the connection between lung cancer (and other ailments) and cigarette smoking since at least 1964,[142] the fact that they continued smoking suggests that they were willing to accept the possibility of lung cancer and early death in exchange for the benefits of smoking. Suing tobacco companies ex post is the equivalent of ex-post reneging. Ex ante, they accepted the risk of smoking. Ex post, they (or their heirs) wish to collect for damages from smoking.

Had tobacco companies anticipated strict liability, they would have charged price $P_0 + P_H$. In this case, smokers would pay for the awards made later to the victims of smoking. In a sense, the payment of P_H per cigarette is the equivalent to buying a life insurance policy against the

---

[142] The first surgeon general's report on cigarette smoking was released in 1964.

hazards of smoking. Changing rules ex post amounts to a transfer from tobacco company shareholders to smokers (or their heirs), which is tantamount to requiring an insurance company to pay a life insurance award to someone who never paid a life insurance premium.

Full information. Information provision is an alternative to strict liability. In the alternative, the government expends resources up front advising consumers about the health cost of smoking. This approach also involves the expenditure of resources, just as tort systems operate at a cost, but the policy increases the chances that each consumer will find the optimum level of risk. In this sense, information policies are substitutes for tort remedies. That is, government information programs signal a buyer beware standard.

Appendix B: Driving and Accidents

This appendix addresses the question set out in the text regarding the optimal speed of drivers. To make the solution tractable, I make some simplifying assumptions. Suppose that the only accidents are cars hitting adult pedestrians. Drivers are never pedestrians, and vice versa. Speed is monitored costlessly. There are 100,000 pedestrians, all of whom have the same value of life. There are 1 million drivers, all of whom attach the same value to driving faster. Pedestrian fatalities are spillover effects of driving. Drivers never drink and drive and are not reckless as such. The simple fact is that higher speeds kill more pedestrians. Accidents always kill pedestrians but never damage cars or their occupants.

Assume that one more unit of speed has a *marginal* benefit defined as follows:

$MB = \$120 - S,$

where S is number of speed units attained. This schedule says that the first whole unit of speed is worth \$119, the second \$118, and so on. Once speed is 40 units, the marginal benefit of the next unit is \$80.

Suppose that the *marginal* increase in pedestrian fatalities is described as follows:

$F = .4\,S.$

Thus, if cars are driving at 39 units of speed, then the next unit increases fatalities by another 16, and so on.

This is an externality problem. Pedestrians and drivers are strangers who have no opportunity to contract ex ante. Nevertheless, it is useful to think about the problem as if these two parties had an opportunity to contract ahead of time. Suppose that transactions costs are small and that pedestrians own the property rights to the streets. Drivers cannot drive unless they secure the privilege from pedestrians. Suppose that pedestrians could sell drivers permits that each allowed 1 unit of speed, so that 20 permits allow 20 units, 40 permits allow 40 units, and so on. Would pedestrians sell any permits?

One instinct is to think that pedestrians would not allow any driving, since it provides the safest outcome. But this means that they forgo some considerable income from letting drivers use the roads. Presumably, there is some amount of money that drivers could offer pedestrians to accept some small risk of a fatality in exchange for permitting them access to their roads at modest speeds.

Figure 8-6, panel (a), depicts the problem. The horizontal axis represents units of speed, where 100 is the maximum amount of speed. The vertical axis is millions of dollars. Assuming that there is no congestion effect (all 1 million drivers can use the roads without noticeably slowing down each other), then street access has a public good aspect to it, in the sense that we vertically sum the amounts each driver is willing to pay to use the roads. So the marginal benefits schedule is $120 million − S × 1 million.

The upward-sloping schedule denotes the amount that pedestrians as a group require to allow each incremental unit of speed. The function is upsloping reflecting the prior fatality function, which says that each additional unit of speed causes an ever-increasing marginal effect on the fatality rate. If drivers had the opportunity to make a deal with pedestrians, then it is apparent that the deal would stipulate 40 units of speed. Area B denotes the minimum amount of cash that drivers pay pedestrians for their permits. Societal surplus denoted by area A ensures that a deal can be made at this speed (because drivers will pay pedestrians the amount B and negotiate a payment of some portion of A).

Notice that this solution tells us the value that pedestrians put on a fatality. That is to say, we know that fatalities increase by 16 from 39 to 40 units of speed. They are willing to accept this increase in fatalities for $80 million. This means that for purposes of risk-taking decisions they are attaching a value to life in the amount of $5 million.

I can restate this in a kind of compensating differential format by supposing that there are 100,000 pedestrians. Drivers asking pedestrians to accept one more unit of speed (from 39 to 40) that will result in 16 additional casualties and asking how much payment they require. Assuming that all pedestrians are the same, they apparently answer $800 (because 100,000 pedestrians together, want $80 million to issue the last speed unit permit to all the drivers).

The formula for the compensating differential is:

$$c = p \, V,$$

where c is the amount of money that a person requires to accept a risk that causes harm valued at V and which occurs with probability p. In

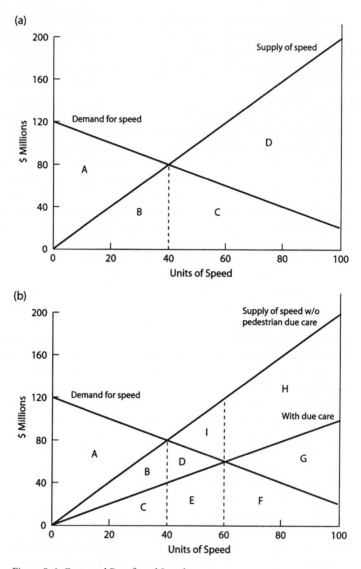

Figure 8-6. Costs and Benefits of Speed

this case, harm is death. Since pedestrians tell us they want $800 for the 40th speed permit, which imposes an incremental fatality rate of 16 out of 100,000 ($p = .00016$), then we can solve for V:

V = $800 / .00016 = $5 million.

How can society generate this level of speed if a contract solution is not possible? There are several possibilities. One is to regulate speed. In my problem, I suppose that monitoring is essentially free (think of electronic speed detectors reading speeds against bar code markers on each driver's windows that are mandated by law). Upon observing infractions above 40 units of speed, a bill is sent to offenders equal to $80 times the units of speed in excess of 40. We have the socially optimum level of speed.

Finally, we could rely on a tort system. Consider a negligence standard. Drivers pay a $5 million penalty if they hit a pedestrian at speeds in excess of 40 units. They pay no damages if a fatality occurs while traveling at lower speeds. Drivers have an incentive to limit speed to 40 units. Alternatively, if pedestrians can do nothing to avoid an accident, then a strict liability system can work, whereby each victim's family receives $5 million. Assuming each driver would obtain insurance (ignoring the administrative costs of insurance), and assuming that insurance companies can monitor speed, then the insurer would be willing to offer policies for higher-speed units at ever-higher prices. Drivers find it optimal to choose one that allows them to travel at 40 units of speed. There are 16 fatalities from the last unit of speed. But of course, there are some fatalities from all speed units below 40. It turns out that there are 320 fatalities.

In the latter case, the heirs of pedestrians collect $5 million after the fact. Families of victims receive $5 million times the number of fatalities for a total of $1.6 billion. Area B in figure 8-6 corresponds to these amounts.[143]

Panel (b) repeats the problem except this time allowing for the possibility that pedestrians can engage in due care (use crosswalks, look both ways before crossing, and so on) at some fixed cost Y (not shown), which is less than area B. An efficient contributory negligence standard yields an optimum speed of 60 units. If drivers do not exceed this speed, they are not liable for damages. Pedestrians have an incentive to engage in due care (because the cost of fatalities falls by areas $B + D + I$).

It is useful to compare this outcome to two extreme policies. If drivers are held harmless (a kind of buyer beware standard for pedestrians), pedestrians are cautious but drivers engage in 100 units of speed. Welfare falls by area G. If drivers are strictly liable for fatalities regardless of pedestrian behavior, then pedestrians do not exercise care and speed falls to 40 units. Welfare falls by areas $B + D$.

---

[143]The marginal fatality function is $F = .4S$. Use a spread sheet to add up the fatalities from each whole unit of speed up to 40 units. Alternatively integrate the function and confirm that total fatalities are 320.

Appendix C: Abatement
with Masks

This appendix gives the answer to the question: How does the optimal solution change if masks reduce the health impact of pollution in figure 8-1, panel (*b*), by one-half?

Figure 8-7 gives the solution. The masks reduce the number of health episodes by one-half, and so multiply each vertical segment on the demand for clean air by .5. This produces the lower schedule as depicted. Optimal abatement falls to zero. The costs of abatement fall by an amount denoted by $50,000 (areas *B* + *C*). The compensating differential

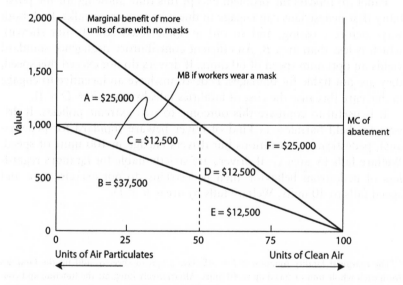

Figure 8-7. Introduction of Masks in the Workplace

increases from $25,000 (areas $E + D$) to $50,000 (areas $E + B$). Welfare increases by $25,000 as a result of the masks (areas $C + D$), minus the cost of wearing masks. Since total health costs are $50,000 (equal to the compensating differential for pollution), we know that two workers are harmed, each incurring $25,000 in health costs.

Lemons Markets and Adverse Selection

*Signals, Bonds, Reputation, and Tie-ins
as Solutions*

Main Economic Concepts	
Main Economic Concepts	1. Information is not perfect. This introduces some friction into the market that affects equilibrium. 2. When quality is not apparent at the point of sale, sellers must find ways to convince customers that they are offering high quality; otherwise, the market tends to degenerate into one characterized by low-quality goods. 3. When the seller has more information than the buyer, a so-called lemons market can develop. When buyers have more information, a similar problem arises in the sense that low quality drives out high quality, but is referred to as adverse selection.
New Terms	1. Lemons market 2. Reputation 3. Signal 4. Bonding 5. Quality assurance premium 6. Advertising 7. Warranty 8. Asymmetric information 9. Adverse selection 10. Specialized capital investments

I mostly have assumed that market participants have full information. In this chapter, I discuss some problems that arise from the absence of perfect information and show how the market finds solutions to these problems. Chapter 10 presents "sorting" solutions to poor quality. The most important lesson to learn in these chapters is not how imperfect information increases the costs of markets, but rather that clever and resourceful market participants find ways to overcome seemingly unsolvable problems that arise from poor information. Some solutions involve the use of contracts of one kind or another; others do not. The concept of reputation, which arose in the Dick and Frank Mums and Tulips problem in chapter 1, looms large in many solutions.

In 1961, George Stigler published a widely cited article entitled "The Economics of Information."[144] This piece introduced the idea that as long as consumers do not have perfect information, then even in a competitive market, different prices across firms could persist for the same goods. Since the cost of search is not zero, it is not optimal for consumers to find the lowest price, and hence even competitive markets are characterized by price dispersion. The problem might be especially large in markets where products do not cost too much and consumers do not often repeat their purchases, as for example in tourist areas.

The advent of better technology undoubtedly has diminished the magnitude of this problem. For example, while one once spent several hours on the phone discovering airline ticket prices, and seat availability, there are now sites on the Internet that list plane schedules, prices, and availability in a few minutes. Nevertheless, unless search costs are zero, every seller, and to some extent every buyer, has a small amount of market power, though it is doubtful in most settings that it will generate a solution markedly different from one that characterizes our model of perfect competition.

George Akerlof introduced a more problematic article about imperfect information in his famous article "The Market for 'Lemons'" in 1970.[145] Akerlof noted that the problem with poor information is not that prices might be somewhat disparate but that certain kinds of goods might not be produced. In particular, when sellers offer a product for sale that has two potential quality levels, high and low, and the consumer cannot tell the difference at the point of sale, the market can deteriorate to one in which only poor quality is offered.

I organize the discussion around the notion of **asymmetric information**, which means that one market participant in a trade knows more than his or her counterpart. I first discuss the problems that arise when the seller knows more than the buyer, which gives rise to the possibility of a so-called lemons market. I then discuss problems that arise when the buyer knows more than the seller, which gives rise to "adverse selection." A lemons market and adverse selection have a similar meaning: "bad drives out good," a concept that should be clear by the end of the chapter.

---

[144]George Stigler, "The Economics of Information," *Journal of Political Economy* 69 (June 1961): 313–365.
[145]George A. Akerlof, "The Market for 'Lemons': Quality Uncertainty and the Market Mechanism," *Quarterly Journal of Economics* 84 (August 1970): 488–500.

> *Asymmetric information* means that one party to a market transaction knows more than the other. For example, in the market for used cars, the seller usually knows more about the quality of a car than the buyer. In the case of health insurance, the buyer of the policy often knows more about his or her health than the insurance company selling the policy.

I. The "Lemons" Market Problem

A. HOW A "LEMONS" MARKET ARISES

Consider a used car market. There are two quality levels, "gems" and "lemons." Figure 9-1, panels (a) *and* (b), depicts the supply conditions for these two quality levels (over the relevant range of prices). Panel (a) depicts the quantity of gems for sale at various prices. Panel (b) depicts the supply of lemons. Owners of lemons generally are willing to sell at a lower price. The market supply curve of used cars in panel (c) is the horizontal summation of these two supply curves, labeled $S_L + S_G$.

Assume that both kinds of cars look identical to consumers so that, absent performing extensive tests and partially disassembling these cars, buyers cannot tell the difference in underlying quality. The sellers know the quality of their own used cars.

For the sake of argument, suppose that 50 percent of all used cars are gems and 50 percent are lemons. Suppose further that at first, potential buyers of used cars assume that 50 percent of used cars offered for sale are high quality and 50 percent low quality. Thus, they assume that there is a 50-50 chance that any used car they buy will be a "gem". On this basis, they form their demand for used cars, which is shown in panel (c) and labeled $D(50:50)$. Suppose that the equilibrium price turns out to be $5,500, as depicted in panel (c).

In evaluating the outcome in figure 9-1, it is apparent that lemons and gems are not availed on the used car market in equal proportions. The $5,500 price seems golden to an owner of a lemon. Not so to a gem owner, who views the price as pedestrian for a high-quality car. Indeed, in the illustration, about 90 lemons are offered at this price and only about 50 gems. Lemons now comprise about 65 percent of the supply of used cars, not 50 percent as buyers originally thought. Consumers come to realize these proportions, and so their demand curve falls to $D(65:35)$. The new market-clearing price is $5,000. But at this price, no owners of gems are willing to sell; hence, all used cars for sale are lemons, which means that the market demand falls to $D(100:0)$, which I do not show.

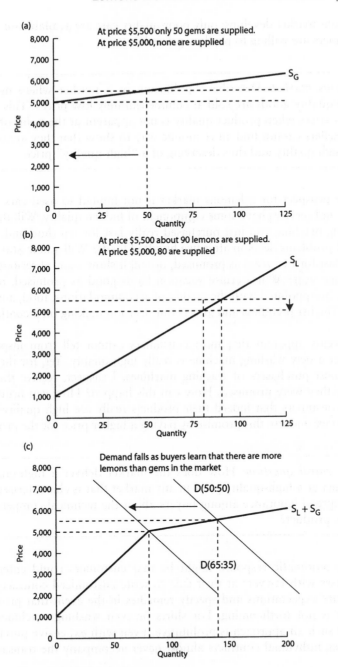

Figure 9-1. Market for Lemons

A lemons market develops: only poor-quality cars are available for which consumers are willing to pay low prices.[146]

> *Lemons market*: Describes equilibrium in a market where mostly poor-quality goods are sold at commensurately low prices. This situation arises when product quality is not apparent at the point of sale and sellers cannot find an economic way to show that they are offering high quality and thus deserving of a "high-quality" price.

The prospect for a lemons market is not limited to used cars. Most goods and services have some component of hidden quality. Will the new washing machine you just purchased really last for ten thousand loads, or will problems develop after five hundred loads? Will a new $60 jersey really last for five years as promised, or will it show signs of serious wear after one year? Will a cruise vacation be as good as promised, or will you be disappointed with the quality of accommodations, food, and port calls? The list is endless and affects our decision making on a continuous basis.

It seems apparent that most consumers cannot tell from inspection whether a new washing machine is really high quality. Yet, for the most part, most purchasers of washing machines, I suspect, receive the high quality they were promised. How can this happen? How can firms convince consumers that indeed their products really are high quality? And why do we endorse this promise by paying a higher price for the product?

> *The central question*: How does the market deliver a high-quality product at a high-quality price in any market that is characterized by widespread ignorance among buyers about the technical competence of the product?

One axiomatic response might be that customers could enter into purchases with lawyers at their side to write customized contracts that articulate expectations and specify remedies in the event that promised quality is not forthcoming. For shirts or even washing machines, the cost of such an approach is prohibitive. Even with expensive purchases, however, individual contracts almost never accompany the transaction.

---

[146]A lemons market does not necessarily refer to a corner solution. If the market predominantly comprises poor-quality products, then it is said to be a lemons market.

And so, implicitly, when we talk about solutions to product quality problems, we mean *economic solutions*, that is, ones where the cost of assuring quality is not "too high" in relation to the cost of producing and delivering the underlying product whose quality level is at issue.

B. A MARKET FOR INFORMATION

Where product quality is difficult to diagnose, we might think that a market will arise that delivers information to buyers at some reasonable price. One obvious solution is for consumers to use their *own experience* with the product to make judgments about quality. For example, if the product is gasoline, the fact that a consumer has paid weekly visits to a gas station for ten years without any problems caused by poor-quality gasoline may be sufficient information to make a judgment about high quality. This kind of information is less important when the same good is infrequently purchased.

Word of mouth is another partial solution. For example, suppose that MGM opens a movie on say December 1 touting it as a great film, well worth the $8 admission price and the three hours that it takes to see the film. If it turns out to be a lousy film, what will be the market for further showings say by December 20? Probably nil. Word spreads fast about bad films. Viewers in the initial weekends express disappointment to friends and colleagues, and demand slacks off considerably after only a few thousand viewers discover that they have wasted their time and money.

Another source is *expert information*. In the case of movies, independent critics abound, and soon after new movies are released, they are reviewed on television, in newspapers, and so on. Even in the case of used cars, one solution is to hire a trusted mechanic to take the used car for a day to drive and employ basic tests. A $300 expense may be well worth it in consideration of purchasing a $10,000 car.

Expert information also is available in other forms for most consumer goods. For example, *Consumer Reports* issues regular reports that compare performance across major consumer goods. J. D. Powell issues reports articulating consumer satisfaction with the performance of automobiles and conveying results of problems that develop with new cars. Many auto magazines like *Road and Track* evaluate the performance of new car varieties, and so on. Consumers collectively pay for these efforts through their magazine subscriptions, sometimes augmented by advertisers who buy space in these publications.

Businesses sometimes *self-regulate*. For example, the Better Business Bureau collects and disseminates information about consumer complaints against service providers. If most firms in an industry offer high quality, then they want to identify low-quality interlopers. Otherwise, sumers cannot tell who offers high quality and low quality, the for the industry's products falls.[147]

times, *direct quality regulations*, as for example in local building codes, help constrain the lower bound of quality offered in the market. For example, the existence of codes and inspections by local officials make it difficult for developers to build houses that violate explicit restrictions about foundations, support construction, electricity, and so on. Codes presume that almost no informed person would live in a house that could blow away in a seventy-mile-per-hour wind, heave six inches each winter, or ignite in flames because of a subpar electrical system. On this basis, it may be efficient for the code to eliminate some of the lowest quality levels from the market.

II. Bonding a Promise of High Quality

While these factors make important contributions to the market for information, it is doubtful that, by themselves, they are sufficient to deter the development of a lemons result in many markets, not the least of which is the used car market. The literature has concentrated on more durable institutions to address these problems. The central idea is that firms that produce high-quality goods will try to "signal" this quality level to consumers. To make this signal meaningful, they often implicitly "bond" their quality, giving rise to the notion of **bonding solutions** to problems that arise from uncertainty about underlying quality of merchandise.

A *signal* is any action designed to convey the idea that a product or service is high quality. A signal, however, is mostly talk and thus by itself is not sufficient to ensure the delivery of high quality.

A *bond* is any device that triggers a loss upon a seller that reneges on the delivery of a promised high quality.

All bonds are signals, but not all signals are bonds.

Bonds versus Signals. If a man tells a woman that he loves her and would like to marry her, he is sending her a strong *signal* that his amorous interests are long term. If he gives her an irrevocable gift of a $10,000 diamond ring and announces the engagement in the newspaper, he is *bonding* his promise of long-term interests. If he backs out, he not only loses the ten grand but also looks like a jerk in front of his family and friends.

---

[147]For example, if one insurance company invests in risky securities and is unable to pay promised annuities, demand for annuities from all insurance companies will fall, reflecting the uncertainty of collection. Insurance companies as a whole have a stake in the outcome, which may explain their support for insurance regulatory bodies in every state that, among other things, regulate permissible portfolios in insurance companies.

A. REPUTATION VALUE

It is useful to start with the commonsense notion that firms with "reputations" for quality can charge a higher price for their products. Ergo, many firms want to build reputation to be able to also charge a higher price. I want to develop more fully the concepts of *brand name*, or *reputation*. When we describe a firm as "reputable," we normally think that this firm has a reputation for delivery high-quality goods and that we have become convinced that the company will continue delivering high quality. If it does not, we reason, it will lose its reputation in the market, which again we presume is not in the self-interest of the company. What do we mean by reputation? What is the source of this value, and how does the value depreciate if promised quality is not delivered?

In an accounting sense, there is little doubt that there is value attached to the company "name." Table 9-1 shows a stylized balance sheet for some company. This is not a typical balance sheet developed by accountants. It is a balance sheet that reflects market values. Call it a market value balance sheet.

The idea behind a "balance sheet" is that, well, it balances: the assets that the company owns must be matched against the value of the securities issued by the firm that awards ownership claims to these assets (usually called liabilities). Assets are split into two main categories: physical assets and intangible assets. *Physical assets* comprise everything that we can observe, count, and attach a price to, like inventories, accounts receivable, machines and equipment, buildings and land, and so on. In table 9-1, I suppose that the market value of all these assets is $50.

On the right-hand side of the balance sheet are the ownership claims. These usually come in two varieties: bonds and stocks. Bonds are instruments that require the company to pay periodic interest until the maturity date when it pays off the principal. "Residual claimants" own stocks, meaning that if there are large profits, they enjoy substantial gains; but if there are losses, they may earn nothing. Shares of large companies normally trade on the New York Stock Exchange, and so its market price is transparent. The price of stock reflects investors' estimates of the present value of all future expected profits on existing investments,

TABLE 9-1. ABC COMPANY: MARKET VALUE BALANCE SHEET

Assets (Market Value)		Ownership Claims	
Physical assets	$50	Debt	$25
Intangible assets	$50	Equity (NYSE value)	$75
Total assets	$100	Total claims	$100

divided by all shares outstanding. If expected profits increase, so does the stock value and vice versa.

Notice that I attach a value of $25 and $75 on these instruments. How can this be? Physical assets are valued only at $50, implying that if bonds are worth $25, then equity should be worth only $25. Assuming that all physical assets have the proper market value, then this must mean that the market thinks that the firm has another asset that we cannot see or measure, namely *intangible assets* or *goodwill*. By inference, the value of these assets must be $50; hence, total assets ($100) now equal total ownership claims ($100). Economists often call intangible assets *reputation value*; businesspeople often refer to it as *brand name capital*.

Reputation value or *brand name* capital refers to the asset value of the company's name. It implies that the firm somehow has created a credible commitment to deliver high-quality products that consumers expect of the firm. In accounting terminology, this value is often referred to as an "intangible asset."

If the company reneges on promised quality, its reputation value is diminished. If so, it is apparent that its equity value will fall. Hence, stockholders have a stake in maintaining the reputation of the company. This means that reputation bonds the company's promised quality. If the firm reneges, it automatically imposes economic losses on shareholders.

Reputation is a bond. If the company reneges on the delivery of promised quality, its reputation suffers, which reduces stock value. Thus, shareholders suffer consequences in proportion to the firm's reputation value.

B. QUALITY ASSURANCE PREMIUM: WHERE DOES REPUTATION VALUE COME FROM?

Most large firms have substantial reputation value. Where does it come from? It is useful to discuss this idea in the context of a particular firm. McDonald's Corporation, a name undoubtedly known by all readers, started as a drive-in hamburger restaurant in San Bernardino, California. It now has thousands of franchises worldwide and is among the largest corporations in America. It is known for its famously consistent high-quality "fast" foods.

Historically, hamburger restaurants had difficulty establishing a reputation for good quality. It is hard to discern what exactly is in the "hamburger" from inspection, how long the meat has been hanging around, its storage temperature, and so on. Indeed, the nickname "greasy hamburger joints" conveyed the sense of low quality that consumers attached to these places.

McDonald's changed this perception. It established a production function whereby the famous "grease" used in making french fries was changed by prescription every x hours. Meat served to customers could not be older than y hours in the store, temperatures in the refrigerators were maintained at x degrees, french fries not sold within h hours were thrown out, rest rooms were checked every z hours, windows were washed every day, floors were mopped every h hours, and so on. This production function clearly is more expensive than the one used at Big Al's Greasy Spoon, which perhaps last changed its grease in 1983, about the same time it cleaned its front windows (no one ever had the courage to use the rest rooms at Big Al's, let alone discuss their current condition). But how was McDonald's going to convince customers that they should pay a price sufficiently high to pay for the quality it provides?

At first, this market seems similar to one that could, and arguably did, deteriorate into a lemons market. And it is reasonable to suppose that when McDonald's first started expanding, it faced a difficult hurdle: it had to convince customers that it really was a high-quality restaurant whose food parents could confidently give to their children. But how? In a well-known paper, Carl Shapiro proposed the following startlingly simply idea, often referred to as the **quality-assurance premium**.[148]

Suppose that we think about a two-period model in which the first period is now and the second period is the future. Figure 9-2 depicts these periods. The dashed-line schedules labeled C_L and C_H denote the marginal cost of serving low- and high-quality hamburgers. The horizontal axis measures the cumulative quantity of hamburgers served in both periods. Here is the key to the quality assurance premium model: *McDonald's does not try to get customers to pay high prices at first. It simply charges low-quality prices but delivers high-quality goods.*

In so doing, McDonald's incurs substantial losses measured by area A in the figure. But after customers visit the stores a few dozen times and hear about others' reactions through word of mouth, they begin to be convinced that this is not Big Al's. At that point, which may have been several years after McDonald's started expanding, consumers are willing

[148]Carl Shapiro, "Premiums for High Quality Products as Returns to Reputation," *Quarterly Journal of Economics* 98 (November 1983): 659–679.

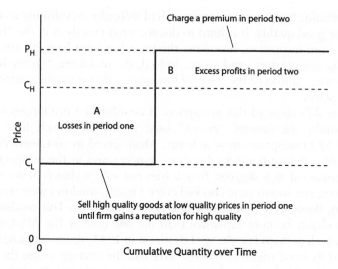

Figure 9-2. Quality-assurance Premium

to pay a higher price for McDonald's products compared to those offered at Big Al's.

To make everything work out, Shapiro posits that the period 2 price is just a bit higher than C_H; that is, that the high-quality producer earns a kind of "excess profit." The quality-assurance premium is the difference between the period 2 price, P_H, and the marginal cost of delivering high quality, C_H. The company is entitled to the premium only after it demonstrates through experience that it is a high-quality supplier.

Note that from the perspective of period 1, the model does not confer excess profits to a high-quality producer. Assuming a zero discount rate, competition requires that area B equals area A: the so-called excess profits in period 2 are offset by losses incurred during the first period. In this model, the period 1 pricing is a company's investment in its reputation as a high-quality producer. Area B is the value of the reputation it created. If companies expected abnormal profits from producing high-quality goods (area B exceeds A), then we expect entry into the high-quality market.

Why is the high price in period 2 referred to as a *quality assurance* premium? Because it is a bond: if the company reneges on its promise of high quality, consumers will begin to walk away from the company, which means that the company will lose its hard-earned opportunity to collect the premium. By maintaining its quality level, customers keep coming back, and the company gets to continue charging the high price. The value of B is the reputation value of the company and is an important ingredient in the brand name capital or intangible assets on the company's balance sheet.

> *Quality assurance premium* refers to an increment in price that a company is entitled to charge above its marginal cost to compensate its investment in establishing its reputation for high quality. If the firm reneges on promised quality, it loses the ability to collect the premium. This means that *the premium is a bond* whose value will be lost upon reneging on the continued delivery of high quality.

Viewing the solution ex post, that is, after the firm has built its reputation, it looks as though it earns excess profits because we see area *B* as future profits. But this situation does not invite entry because viewed ex ante, a new high-quality competitor must incur the costs of building reputation (area *A*). In equilibrium, this investment, together with the prospect of the future premium, reflects a competitive return in equilibrium even though ex post it looks like the company is earning excess profits.[149]

> *Quality assurance bonds are substitutes for contracts.* By bonding their quality, firms avoid the necessity of writing contracts specifying quality, terms and conditions that define reneging, remedies, and so on. A bond is a self-enforcing "implicit contract." It is implicit meaning that it is unwritten. Yet, the contract is credible owing to the bond.

C. SPECIALIZED INVESTMENTS

The quality assurance premium is not the only way that firms can bond quality. Another idea is **specialized capital investments**. Consider the case of McDonald's. It invests substantial additional monies in its famous golden arches and other characteristics that connote the idea that announces, "This building houses McDonald's." One interpretation could be that it just is a way to advertise that "the store is here." But one could

---

[149]There is an advanced topic embedded in this model that you do not need to worry about. Specifically, if the investment in reputation is a past cost, why does the market not revert to marginal cost pricing going forward, which means that the firm does not collect its return on reputation investment? One way to think about it is to imagine that the firm issues debt instruments up front that promise to pay interest forever. If the debt amount is D and the interest rate is i, then the firm must pay out the amount iD to debt holders every year forever. This amount must be paid contractually under the conditions of the loan, which converts the return into a recurring cost. No investors will invest in reputation up front without a contractual mechanism to ensure its repayment over time.

AN EXAMPLE OF A QUALITY ASSURANCE BOND: TENURE TRACK PROFESSORS

Most applicants to law school faculties have sound educational credentials, clerkships, and law firm experience. It is far from clear, however, that they will be successful either in scholarly work and teaching or in their role as "team player" in advancing the goals of the law school. To determine quality, a junior hire is required to work for six years at low pay as assistant professor or untenured associate professor. At the end of this period, if the faculty, dean, and provost agree that a junior faculty member is indeed a high-quality candidate, he or she is awarded lifetime tenure and a substantial increase in salary. Promotions to full professor and salary advancements depend on their continued delivery of high-quality work. This pay scheme sorts for high-quality individuals. Those of lesser quality are wasting their time working toward tenure that never will be awarded.

---

imagine McDonald's building facilities that had many general uses and simply attaching a nice sign denoting "McDonald's" that clearly identifies the store. Why spend so much more just to make the building unique? Taking into account wind and physics, it must represent a substantial expense for the company to build its "golden arches" above and beyond what it needs to spend to provide its high-quality hamburgers.

The cost takes on additional significance when one considers that, in contrast with a nice square nondescript building, the arches are of zero use to any other potential user of the site. Indeed, it is obvious that if anyone other than McDonald's occupies the lot, the arches and the funky looking building would have to be torn down to make way for a building with more general uses. *What information is conveyed when a company invests substantial additional monies to erect a structure that obviously is of little use to any other occupant?*

One answer is that it is sending a signal that the company is not going to fail, that is, the company is confident in the quality of its products. It erects an expensive and unique structure that will pay for itself only if the company is successful in garnering lots of repeat business over the long run. The specialized structure is a quality-assuring bond because if the company reneges on quality promised, it loses the value of its structure.[150]

---

[150]A well-known article with this theme is Benjamin Klein and Keith Leffler, "The Role of Market Forces in Assuring Contractual Performance," *Journal of Political Economy* 89 (August 1981): 615–641.

In this sense, the McDonald's arches do not so much announce *McDonald's is here* as they do *McDonald's is here to stay*.

> *Specialized capital investments* are quality assurance bonds because their value automatically falls when the company reneges on the delivery of promised quality.

D. ADVERTISING

Most consumers have the intuitive idea that the statement "I never heard of it" about a new product or firm, is an indictment of quality—that if one "knows" the brand, somehow it conveys quality assurance. I have already suggested a couple of ways in which consumers get to know producers, either because these firms have invested lots of time in building confidence, or because they have bonded quality in other ways by engaging in specific investments (or both). In a way, advertising is a special form of specialized investment. Indeed, *advertising is the quintessential example of a firm-specific investment.*

Return to the example of the MGM movie release. If the company believes that it has a good movie, then it is willing to pay substantial monies to advertise. It does this to attract a large "first wave" of viewers to see the movie. Suppose it spends $10 million advertising its new movie, *Raiders of a Lost Art*. Two outcomes are possible. The reviewers and first-wave moviegoers find the movie to be of low quality, in which case the market for the movie quickly evaporates. In this event, the company does not recoup its $10 million advertising expense: it becomes waste. Alternatively, the reviewers and first-wave moviegoers find the movie to be of high quality, in which case large numbers of subsequent viewers are ensured. In this event, the profits from the film easily pay for the advertising.

Consider these outcomes viewed from the perspective of MGM ex ante. Knowing ahead of time that they would not be able to recoup the $10 million advertising expenditures if customers did not find the quality high, MGM would not engage in the advertising. Hence, *the decision to advertise sends a signal to the market that the movie is high quality. The advertising not only lets the customers know about the movie, but also bonds its quality. If customers are disappointed, the advertising expenditure is lost.*

Put differently, if MGM ends up with a poor-quality movie, then if it advertises it to a wide audience, it merely informs more people of its low-quality production, thereby diminishing its reputation value as a high-quality producer. It is more likely that poor-quality movies will either not be released or released without much fanfare, and that high-quality movies will be more likely candidates for large promotion budgets. In this sense, MGM is providing a kind of *selection function* for the market; that is, it selects only its better films for release and its best films for large-scale promotion. MGM does this not because it cares whether consumers waste money seeing a poor-quality film, but because the reputation value of the company is maximized if it releases high-quality films and touts only its best films.

Advertising can be viewed in part as a quality assurance bond because if the product is not as good as promised, the seller cannot recoup its advertising investment.

It also is interesting to think about other ways in which producers bond movies not for consumers but for the purpose of attracting high-quality participants to its venture. Suppose MGM has a great script—so good that any talented actor and actress could make a great movie from it. But this fact may be hard to convey in a convincing way to other players in the movie business. One solution is for the producer to bond its confidence that the movie will be of high quality.

Suppose that MGM hires a star to be the lead actor, in exchange for a large sum of money. When MGM advertises that it is paying Jack Nickelodeon $20 million to do the film, it sends a signal to the movie making industry that MGM is committed to making a high-quality movie. If MGM subsequently does not succeed in making a high-quality film, then the $20 million up-front money is largely a waste. MGM recoups its investment only if it makes a good movie.

In this application, note that the consumers of the information mostly are other inputs into the movie, for example, potential directors, editors, supporting actors, costume people, special effects folks, and the like. Each of these players also has a reputation for quality that it wants to keep intact, starting with Jack Nickelodeon. Presumably, Jack, being a big star, is not interested in participating in a poor-quality movie, or else he will jeopardize his valuable reputation in the eyes of moviegoers. Presumably, Jack and his agent will look hard and long to make sure that they believe the prospects are bright for a successful film. Knowing that he will do this means that others who sign up for the film are partly depending on Jack's implicit bond of quality.

EXERCISE:

Question 1: What signal does it send to Jack Nickelodeon that instead of an offer of $20 million, MGM offers him zero salary but a 20 percent share of total revenue from the film?[151]

Question 2: Suppose that Jack, after considering the prior offer, decides that he will accept the 20 percent offer. What signal does this send to the other inputs considering joining the production team?[152]

E. WARRANTIES

Warranties are a more recognizable way to bond quality. Warranties must be credible to convey value to the market. For example, if some used car dealer leases a lot where everything on the lot is on wheels, including the trailer office, then it is unlikely that a sign on cardboard that reads Lifetime Warranty! conveys much meaning. It is taken for granted in warranty discussions that the companies that issue them have reputation value and other firm-specific assets to support a warranty promise.

What signal does a warranty send? To answer this question, consider a company, MyTag Washing Machines. It announces a new washer. Consider the two possibilities. The washing machine is low quality, in which case it requires lots of costly servicing. Alternatively, it is high quality, in which case it requires little servicing. Suppose MyTag guarantees to fix the washing machine free during the fist two years following purchase. This warranty sends a signal about high quality because if the new product turns out to be low quality, MyTag is going to incur large repair costs. The warranty is therefore a bond of high quality. It follows that customers seldom exercise their warranties.

Warranties bond high quality because if the company reneges on quality, it absorbs large repair costs. Warranties have value if they are issued by reputable companies.

True or false? Customers holding warranties seldom exercise them, and therefore, warranties have no value.[153]

---

[151]Jack would be suspicious that the anticipated film quality is low. He feels this way because the company is giving away a very big piece of revenue if it is successful but incurs no loss on his services if the movie is a flop.

[152]Presumably, Jack and his agent think that, despite the doubts of the producer, *Raiders of a Lost Art* likely will be successful, making other players more willing to sign up for the film.

[153]False. The value of a warranty is its signal value of high quality. Warranties are issued by firms producing high-quality goods that seldom require repair. In a sense, the value of a warranty to a consumer is the knowledge that they almost never will use it!

Other Examples of Contractual Bonds

Penalty clauses usually invoke an automatic financial loss upon failure to live up to a promise. If the ABA reserves five hundred rooms at the Holiday Inn in New Orleans on the nights of October 21–24, 2006, it is promising to show up with this many people on these dates. Its contract with Holiday Inn likely imposes a penalty if it reneges.

Performance clauses are close cousins of penalty clauses, except that a bonus is paid upon the successful delivery of a promised quality. If a contractor promises to deliver a completed building by October 21, 2006, then it is not unusual to find a contractual clause that pays a 10 percent bonus upon satisfying this pledge. If a football player promises high-quality play, his contract sometimes calls for bonuses to be paid upon successfully accomplishing the quality level he promises (for example, number of touchdowns or yards gained rushing, and so on). Upon signing these contracts, these sellers are bonding their promise of high quality to buyers.

Nonrefundable deposits also are close cousins to penalty clauses, except that the penalty amount is posted ex ante to guarantee performance. If a person promises to purchase a house and the seller takes it off the market in consideration of this promise, then a loss is imposed on the seller if the buyer reneges. When the buyer offers a nonrefundable deposit, she is bonding her promise to purchase the house.

REVISITING USED CARS: VERTICAL INTEGRATION OF NEW AND USED CARS

A trend in automobile sales is for new car dealers to vertically integrate into used cars. The used car lot is advertised under the same brand name as the new car dealership and often located next door, thereby exposing the dealer's reputation to the used car market. In addition, the used cars often come with a warranty for some significant period of time. How can the dealer be sure it is not going to damage its reputation and pay large amounts in warranty repairs?

The answer likely is found in the way most new cars are sold or leased. If leased, the contract often provides for regular servicing at the dealer as part of the leasing costs, and in addition, the leased car will carry a record of any repairs done under the warranty of the manufacturer. If sold, many manufacturers now offer "bumper to bumper" service and repair at zero marginal cost for up to four years of purchase. Owing to these institutions, the dealers know the quality

continued...

REVISITING USED CARS *Continued*

of most cars they sell or lease over the three or four years of the service warranty or lease period. Consequently, it knows which of the leased cars turned in at the end of the lease period are low quality and high quality. It also knows the quality of cars traded in for new cars by the segment of its buyers that are repeat purchasers of new cars every few years.

The dealer need only follow a simple rule: sell the high-quality cars under its brand name, and dump the low-quality used cars on the wholesale market, which find their way to Big Al's (its motto: You Ain't Never Seen No Cars Like This!). The dealer's used cars sell for high prices. Big Al's cars, notwithstanding his best efforts, sell for low prices.

This solution is composed partly of a reputation guaranty and partly of a contractual remedy through use of a warranty. But the key to the solution is that the dealer has found a way to acquire information by vertically integrating the sales, service, and used car functions.

III. Problems When the Seller Is Uninformed: Adverse Selection

I now turn to the other side of asymmetric information: the buyer knows more than the seller. In most industries, sellers do not care about the identity of the buyer. A gas station owner does not care about the customers at pump number seven today, as long as they are willing and able to pay for the gas they put into their automobiles. In some instances, however, it may matter, especially when the cost of the service being provided in part depends on the characteristics of consumers. For example, a one-price all-you-can-eat buffet likely attracts a disproportionate number

Adverse selection occurs when buyers select in on a basis that increases the cost of providing the product. The offer of an all-you-can-eat buffet is unusually attractive to individuals with large appetites; the offer of health coverage tends to attract individuals with unusually high health risks. While sellers might be able to observe some characteristics that affect costs, others are unobservable, which can make it difficult for some individuals to find the product at a price that is attractive to them.

of individuals with unusually large appetites, which works to increase the per-person cost of the buffet.

There are two kinds of adverse selection, one temporal (meaning "over time") and one cross section (meaning across individuals at a point in time).

A. TEMPORAL ADVERSE SELECTION

Temporal adverse selection arises most often in insurance settings and occurs when individuals purchase the insurance after the insurable event happens or is forecasted to happen. Examples include purchases of termite insurance after uncovering damage, hurricane insurance after a storm is forecasted, or signing up for health coverage after discovering cancer. This kind of ex post switching is not insurance but an attempt to take advantage of others who have been paying the premiums to insure against the *possibility* of incurring an insurable event.

Suppose that there are 2,000 people, 1,000 of whom decide to buy insurance against some malady. We expect 10 out of 1,000 to be diagnosed with this illness each period; it costs $100,000 to treat the malady successfully. Thus, total costs are expected to be $1 million (=10 × $100,000). The 1,000 insureds therefore pay $1,000 each to protect themselves against the financial burden of being the one diagnosed. The other 1,000 people also expect 10 to be diagnosed with the malady, but they do not purchase insurance.

Suppose, however, that upon learning of their diagnosis, the 10 victims from the *uninsured* group decide to purchase insurance *after* they are diagnosed. If the insurance company is unaware of the selection, then it charges each the $1,000 premium. Then the expected number of treatments is not 10 but 20, where the last 10 entrants each impose a $99,000 burden each on the rest of the insureds (that is, $100,000 in expenses, minus $1,000 in premiums). This implies that the insurance premium on the 1,000 who purchase insurance next year will be $2,000, not $1,000. But, of course, after everyone learns that they can buy insurance *after* they fall ill, then it is predictable that no one will purchase it while healthy.

Once it becomes apparent that you can jump in to the risk pool at any time, then all insureds have the incentive to become uninsured and to jump in upon diagnosis. In this case, the only people who purchase the insurance are the 20 workers adversely diagnosed. For the insurer not to lose money, he sets the premium upon entry to $100,000. In this case, the temporal adverse selection has completely degenerated the insurance function; that is, there is no insurance. We are just as well off to let each diagnosed person pay for his or her own expenses, without creating insurance in the first place.

Temporal adverse selection refers to individuals from a similar risk group entering an insurance risk pool *after* either receiving an adverse diagnosis or otherwise receiving information that increases the odds of having the malady that is the subject of the insurance.

A common contractual solution for this problem is a carve-out for *preexisting conditions* over some predetermined period following the issuance of the policy. In the example I discussed previously, if the insurer excludes insurance payments for maladies that existed at the time that the insured joined the risk pool, it could then charge new entrants a $1,000 fee without fear of temporal self-selection. The solution depends on the ability of the insurer to cheaply identify preexisting conditions that cause illness later; otherwise, the solution does not work.

Long-term contracting. Consider two alternative life insurance policies: term insurance and term renewable insurance. *Term life insurance* is operative for a short period, often one or two years. If the policyholder wishes to renew for another term, he must undergo a new health evaluation, which may mean a higher price, depending on the status of his health. For example, MGM might purchase a term life insurance policy on Jack Nickelodeon to cover the period he is filming *Raiders of a Lost Art*; the price depends on Jack's physical condition at the time the contract is signed.

Term renewable life insurance is one that keeps the insurance in force automatically as long as the insured continues to pay the premiums. Premiums cannot be increased if the individual is diagnosed with a malady but can reflect general increases in rates charged by the insurance company to all its life insurance policyholders.

Term renewable policies normally are quite inexpensive at young ages. To protect against temporal selection, the insurer might issue a relatively small life insurance policy, say in the amount $50,000, and then permit the insured to increase the amount gradually over time. At each step, the insured signs a contract certifying that an adverse event has not been

Some Solutions to Temporal Adverse Selection. Insurance companies protect themselves against temporal adverse selection by invoking preexisting conditions into their policies that rule out payments for maladies that have been diagnosed prior to joining the risk pool. Alternatively, they use long-term contracts, which offer lower premiums than term policies because they are less susceptible to adverse selection problems.

diagnosed as of that date. Once the contract is signed, the amount is locked in no matter what diagnosis he receives at a *future time*. Term renewable contracts receive the most favorable rates because they make it difficult to obtain substantial coverage after receiving an adverse diagnosis.

B. CROSS-SECTION ADVERSE SELECTION

Perhaps a more common problem is cross-section adverse selection. Some individuals are inherently more costly to insure. If these risk characteristics are observable, then in principle, they can be assessed different premiums. If the insurance company cannot fully observe these differences, however, it will experience adverse selection, meaning that it will find a disproportionate number of high risks in its buyer pool. If this problem is large, it can make it difficult for low risks to find insurance.

> *Cross-section adverse selection* occurs when individuals who are inherently high risk select themselves for insurance against that risk characteristic. Normally, the risk characteristic is at least partially unobservable. For example, smokers do not pose an adverse selection problem. Smoking intensity is easily inferred from a simple lung function test, and the insurer can set a separate sustainable price for smokers. But two persons who each show no symptoms of heart disease may differ in family histories of heart disease, which is not observable to the insurer. All else equal, the one with the more ominous family history will more often purchase a life insurance or health policy, and less often opt to purchase an annuity, thereby creating adverse selection.

Consider the classic example of health insurance. Suppose that there are two kinds of individuals: those at high risk of serious health problems and those at low risk. Assume that there is no way to tell by observation whether a particular individual is in either category. Other things equal, high-risk people presumably are willing to pay more for the insurance because they are far more likely to use it compared to low risk people. For the sake of the illustration, suppose that there are 10 high risks and 30 low risks.

1. Demand Conditions

Panel (*a*) of figure 9-3 shows the demand for health insurance for low-risk individuals. These individuals vary according to the amount each is willing to pay for an insurance policy. All are willing to pay at least $5, but none attach a value to the insurance in excess of $15. It costs $5 to provide insurance to these types, which I show in the figure.

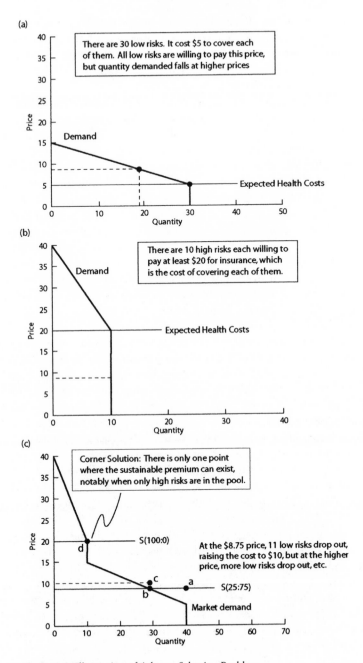

Figure 9-3. Illustration of Adverse Selection Problem

Panel (*b*) shows the demand curve for high risks. All are willing to pay at least $20, but none are willing to pay more than $40. In general, they are willing to pay more than low risks because they anticipate using the insurance more intensely. I assume that it costs $20 to provide a policy to these individuals, which I portray in the figure.

If the insurer can identify high- and low-risk individuals, then the low and high risks in the market have policies that cost $5 and $20 respectively. Thus, at prices that properly reflect risk, low-risk buyers represent 75 percent of the market.

Suppose instead that the insurer does *not* know the risk characteristic of the buyers. In this case, the insurer sets a single premium. Since both types pay the same premium, the first task is to horizontally sum the quantity demanded at each possible premium. The resulting market demand curve is shown as the "kinked" linear schedule in panel (*c*).

2. Supply Conditions

We know that the insurer must receive a premium that covers the health costs of the mix of high- and low-risk individuals at any quantity. Note in panel (*c*) that any given total quantity, Q, is the sum of Q_L low risks and Q_H high risks that want insurance at this price.

Suppose that the insurer anticipates that three of every four purchasers are low risks, which is their proportion in the population. In this case, the average cost of servicing the market is $8.75. That is, if 10 high risks and 30 low risks are in the market, then they incur a total health cost equal to $350 (=10 × $20 + 30 × $5). Spread over 40 insureds, the average cost is $8.75.

Note from panel (*a*), however, that at this price, 11 low risks are unwilling to buy the policy, leaving 19 low risks and 10 high risks. The weighted average cost for this pool, which is now more heavily composed of high risks, is roughly $10 ($20 × 10 + $5 × 19, all divided by 29 insureds). This means that the insurer needs to increase price to about $10, which encourages more low risks to leave the market, and so on. In this example, this process continues until all the low risks leave the market. The high risks have insurance at price $20. The low risks are unable to find insurance at sustainable price.

In terms of panel (*c*), the process is seen as follows. The insurer sets a price of $8.75 hoping to attract a pool of high and low risks in proportion to 25:75, which is denoted by point *a*. But at this price, 11 low risks depart the market, leaving only 29 individuals that want the insurance at this price (point *b*). This causes the insurer to increase price to about $10 (point c), which drives even more low risks from the market, and so on. He finally finds a sustainable solution when 100 percent of the insureds are high risks and the price is $20 (point *d*).

The high risks drive the low risks from the market for health insurance, just as lemons drive gems from the market for used cars. The process of high-cost buyers pushing low-cost buyers from the market is known as *adverse selection.*

By convention, when adverse selection is complete, we do not normally refer to it as a lemons market. One reason might be that we then have to label the high-cost buyers "poor quality," which sounds bad. Instead, we say that adverse selection eliminates low-cost consumers from the market. Or we say that adverse selection is complete, or adverse selection results in a completely degenerated equilibrium. Or, owing to adverse selection, we end up with a corner solution.

Markets characterized by unobservable high- and low-cost buyers do not always deteriorate into a corner solution. If groups either do not differ too much in the costs they impose, or if high risks represent a small portion of the pool, or if low risks are willing to pay high prices for insurance, the market can include both high and low risks at a sustainable premium. For example, in the previous illustration, suppose that I change the example so that it costs $4 to service the low risks. The price to service the high risks remains at $20, but assume now that instead of 10 high risks, there is only 2. Then the average cost of servicing the population is $5, (= [$4× 30 + $20 × 2] ÷32), which all 30 all low risks are willing to pay. Each high-risk participant receives a subsidy of $15 (= $20 cost minus $ 5 premium). Each low risk pays a $1 tax of sorts. Together, these "taxes" finance the subsidies to the high risks.

Another Lesson in Marginal Pricing The reason that "bad" drives out "good" is that, owing to poor information, prices do not distinguish the different costs of servicing the "bad" and the "good", but rather reflect the average of these costs. An "average" price of high- and low-risk consumers offers a subsidy to high risks, financed by a kind of tax on low risks, and hence, we end up with too many high risks in the market and too few low risks.

C. SOME MARKET SOLUTIONS

Cross-section adverse selection occurs when there are different risk profiles in the population—for example, smokers and nonsmokers. Even if both are in good health currently, smokers are expected to pose more health risks than nonsmokers. Other things equal, individuals who pose more risk are more likely to select into the insurance.

To the extent that risk attributes are observable, insurers might impose *risk-related premiums.* For example, auto insurers normally charge a premium to drivers under the age of twenty-five. Homeowners with brick structures and no smokers pay a lower fire insurance premium than those who live in wood houses populated by smokers. Life insurance quotes for racecar drivers are higher than those for law professors or the average policyholder.

Risk-related premiums can generate a sustainable set of insurance prices, but in many cases, differential prices are far from complete, even if risk differences are observed. It is costly to alter prices on the basis of attributes, and further, there are many variables that, if used, might be interpreted as violations of legislation that outlaw discrimination. For example, charging a premium to drivers over age seventy presumably incurs substantial resistance, either in the courts because it discriminates on the basis of age, or perhaps politically, as older drivers complain to their congressional representatives. Even different auto insurance rates on the basis of poor driving records is restricted in most states.[154]

Risk-related premiums reflect different costs of servicing the insureds based on observable differences in risk exposure. Women have lower mortality risks, and thus pay less for life insurance and more for annuities. Smokers pay more for health insurance than nonsmokers. But to the extent that differences are not observable, this solution is incomplete.

In many cases, risk-related pricing is not feasible because attributes that determine risks often are neither observable nor determinable at reasonable cost. For example, insurance companies that sell life insurance policies have discovered that customers who buy life insurance policies die with greater frequency than are implied by a normal mortality table. Insurers impose carve-outs for obvious temporal selection problems like suicidal motives and require new insureds to provide medical information and to [undergo] a medical exam. Notwithstanding these precautions, apparently purchasers know more about their likelihood of death than insurers.

Similarly, individuals who purchase annuities from insurance companies live longer than predicted by national mortality tables. That is, if an individual wants to buy an annuity of $200 per month starting at age

---

[154]Almost all states run assigned risk pools, which comprise drivers who would not be insurable at any rate they would be willing to pay. Most states, for whatever reason, set ceiling rates for these drivers and then require all insurers in the state to take an assigned proportion of the pool based on the portion of auto insurance policies that they write in the state.

sixty-five lasting until death, he or she can collect quotes from insurance companies. Each insurance company will quote the lump sum payment they require in order to guaranty the annuity starting at whatever date is stated in the contract. Individuals who either have lived healthier lifestyles or have genes amenable to long lives apparently are more prone to buy annuities. Annuity prices incorporate a "selection premium" to accommodate self-selection against the insurance company.

D. A "TIE-IN" CONTRACT

A solution to some information problems is a tie-in purchase. A tie-in requires the joint purchase of two products, x *and* y. In chapter 5, I noted that a *tie in* occurs sometimes when suppliers with market power want to price discriminate. Sometimes, antitrust authorities view a tie-in as a nefarious device used by a firm to "leverage" their monopoly in x to some other product, y, while in reality they merely are trying to extract as much surplus as they can from the power they have in x.

Similarly, in insurance, tie-ins might be viewed suspiciously in the sense that an insurance company is trying to force customers to buy product y when all they want is product x. In the context of adverse selection, however, consider another explanation. Assume that because of either costs, regulation, or both, insurance companies cannot determine the life expectancy of anyone who enters the door, and so use normal mortality tables. We already know that one solution is simply to anticipate selection in the premium structure. But is there another way the insurer can write a policy in which it could more confidently price according to population mortality tables, without fear of adverse selection?

Yes, by offering a tie-in contract, and specifically, offering a product that includes a life insurance policy *and* an annuity. If a fifty-year old person is willing to purchase an annuity starting at age sixty-five that has a present value of $100,000 *and* commit to purchasing a term renewable life insurance policy in the same amount, then the insurer can use average mortality tables to write the contract. Buyers with above-average life expectancy (according to their private information) see the annuity as a good deal and the life insurance as a bad deal, and vice versa for those with below-average life expectancy. The selection effects cancel.

A *tie-in* sometimes can provide a solution to an asymmetric information problem. A good example is a life insurance contract with an annuity contract. In this case, life insurance and annuities are expected to be priced using normal mortality tables.

E. THE EMPLOYMENT CONTRACT AS A TIE-IN

Most readers have by now figured out that many of the insurance contracts that I have mentioned are often provided in the context of the employment contract. Part of the reason for this may be attributable to tax laws.[155] Even if there were no tax bias, however, many of these contracts might be offered in the employment context anyway, owing to its natural defense against adverse selection.

Consider the case of adverse selection in health insurance in the private market. A retail insurance outlet finds that a disproportionate number of high-risk individuals purchase its policy. This process tends to drive up price for the low-risk individuals, who sometimes are "priced out of the market." This means that the majority of people who are low risk cannot find insurance because they cannot effectively convey their low-risk attribute (figure 9-3).

> *Priced out of the market* means that the market price exceeds the consumer's demand price at every quantity level. In the context of adverse selection, the premium for health insurance reflects not the marginal cost of servicing low-risk consumers but the weighted average of the marginal costs of providing insurance to low- and high-risk consumers. In this sense, if low-risk consumers could be identified, their premium would fall, in which case they might be "back in the market."

Adverse selection on health insurance is less likely to be important in an employment context. Unlike the insurance retail outlet where the *only* factor that determines demand for the product is a customer's expected use of the insurance policy, there are many attributes to a job. Individuals do not have access to an infinite number of jobs. Among the firms they consider, many factors enter into the calculus of choosing a job, including travel, overtime, wage level, type of work, other benefits, and so on. If there are many factors that affect these decisions, then it is likely that demand for health insurance is not a dominant consideration.

Suppose there are a sufficient number of factors influencing an employment match that for all intents and purposes, the applicants have the same health risk characteristics as the general population. We have one constraint to remember: firms will not pay workers more than the value they add to the firm on the margin. If they pay workers in the form of health insurance, then they must reduce cash wages by a corresponding amount. Similarly, the implicit premium charged to employees for their

[155]For example, health insurance offered through the employer is never taxed. Employer contributions are tax deductible to the firm and are not taxable income to the individual.

insurance coverage (in the form of lower wages) reflects the average of the costs of providing coverage to workers who are low- and high-risk health insureds in the employment pool.

Suppose that applicants to some firm are composed of high and low risks in proportion to their numbers in the population. Thus, for every 10 high risks that enter, there are 30 low risks.[156] Figure 9-4 reproduces the demand curves from panels (*a*) and (*b*) of figure 9-3.

The employer can increase employee surplus without expending any resources. It can do this because it can offer health coverage without fear of adverse selection. Based on the mix of risks among its workers, the firm can find an insurer to offer coverage at the premium of \$8.75. In consideration

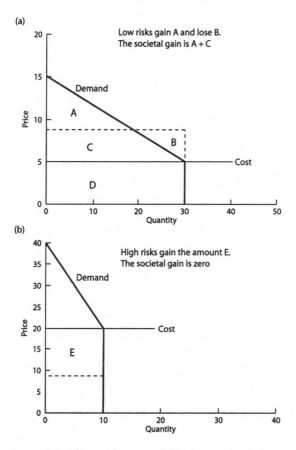

Figure 9-4. Adverse Selection with Employment Tie-in

[156]This ratio of entrants makes the problem easiest, but most of the results would hold if workers entered in somewhat different proportions from this.

of offering the health policy, it reduces cash wages by \$8.75 for each worker.[157] At this price, the firm does not fear entry of high risks or exit of low risks because too many other factors influence job decisions.

In addition, notice that low risks transfer some monies to high risks. This transfer (the cross subsidy) is measured by area E in panel (b), which is the same as areas $C + B$ in panel (a). The amount of the subsidy to the high risks must equal the amount of "taxes" assessed against the low risks. Assuming that a dollar is a dollar, this transfer does not convey any change in societal surplus. The transfer obviously makes high risks better off, but importantly, even after making this transfer, most low risks are net better off from the tie-in. The way I have drawn demand in panel (a), about 18 low risks are better off in the amount denoted by area A. The remaining 12 low risks that are net worse off by area B in panel (a). It is important that most low risks are better off from the tie-in, net of the subsidy, because otherwise they will not support the tie-in.

Cross subsidy is a term that often arises in an insurance context. It means that low-risk insureds pay more than it costs to service them, and the high-risk insureds obtain coverage at a price lower than the cost they impose on the system. Sometimes, cross subsidies arise because they are the only feasible solution in the presence of poor information. Sometimes they arise by fiat; for example, in most states, regulators force insurance companies to offer subsidized coverage to high-risk drivers, financed by the imposition of an excess charge on low-risk drivers. Similarly, taxpayers as a whole are required to pay a cross subsidy against natural disasters to those living in floodplains via a federal flood insurance program.

The solution provides a good exercise in evaluating social surplus. Note in panel (b) that the same 10 high risks receive insurance as would receive it in the retail market; the value they attach to the insurance and the social cost of providing it are the same as they were in the corner solution that prevailed in the figure 9-3. In contrast, 30 low risks portrayed in panel (a) now receive insurance, which they value by areas $A + C + D$. But society can provide this insurance at a cost denoted by area D. This leaves the gain in societal surplus equal to areas $A + C$.

An alternative (or at least the way to find the whereabouts of the gain or loss) is to use the delta-Q rule. Find the change in quantity from the policy,

---

[157]If the insurer knows that 30 workers are low risk and 10 are high risk, then the total cost of servicing this group is $\$5 \times 30 + \$20 \times 10 = \$350$. Since there are 40 workers, this translates to a charge of \$8.75 per worker. I ignore administrative costs of insurance.

which in this case is positive, and look up and find the triangle gain. In this problem, the quantity change is for low risks only. Thirty low risks now receive the insurance. Look upwards the triangle gain is $A + C$.

The gains and losses to each group can be used to double-check that the gain in social welfare is equal to an amount denoted by areas $A + C$. Net of the transfer, low risks gain area A minus area B, and high risks gain area E. So, the change in societal surplus is $\Delta S = A - B + E$. But the amount of the subsidy to high risks must equal the amount given up by low risk, which means that area E equals areas $C + B$. If we make this

---

How to Find the Change in Social Welfare

There are three ways to find the welfare change from a change in polic:

1. Social gains versus resource costs: Identify the valuations consumers attach to any changes in quantity and compare them to the resource costs of delivering these values. It is helpful to strip any transfer from the figure because it makes it easier to see the changes in welfare. Remember that the cross subsidies are just transfers.

2. Delta-Q rule: Find the changes in quantities that result from the change in policy. Look up and find the triangle gain or loss. It is easier to identify the correct triangle if you strip away the transfers.

3. Summing-up rule: Leave the transfers in the figure. Add up all the changes in welfare for each group affected by the changes including the pluses and the minuses. The result is the net change in welfare. Make sure you do not forget any group. For example, in chapter 4, the taxpayers funded all the price support payments, and so not just the consumers and producers are affected.

VOCABULARY REVIEW

Adverse selection can price low-risk individuals *out of the market.* Firms can offset this problem by offering health insurance as a *tie-in* to the employment contract. Low-risk workers provide a *cross subsidy* to their high-risk colleagues, proving that *there is no such thing as a free lunch* but still gain substantial *consumer surplus,* proving the idiom that *you have to give something to get something.* The firm's use of the tie-in improves welfare of the employees; otherwise the firm would not use it. While not every worker gains by the tie-in (hence not a *Pareto* improvement), we have a clear increase in *social welfare* in a *Kaldor-Hicks* sense.

substitution for E, we obtain $\Delta S = A + C$, which verifies our earlier conclusion.

The employment tie-in can be combined with a product tie-in. For example, it is common for large firms to offer pension annuities. The latter benefit requires workers to implicitly sacrifice their wages throughout their lifetimes in exchange for an annuity that is tied to their service level and wage at retirement. In this way, the firm employs various tie-ins across the benefit package. To the extent that some workers have relatively poor health, then this may increase health costs in the firm, but to the extent that less healthy workers have higher mortality risks then the firm pays out less in pension benefits. In this sense, if the firm is careful in

---

EXERCISE:

Can you explain these observations using adverse selection?

1. Compared to menu prices for individual meals, the average diner views the price of the all-you-can-eat-buffet as relatively high.[158]

2. Credit card interest rates seem high in comparison to rates charged by banks, say for auto or house loans.[159]

3. Auto insurers charge high premium rates for liability coverage on Corvettes.[160]

---

setting up its benefits package, it might be able to offset any systematic adverse selection of less healthy individuals.

The use of the word "selection" in economics does not necessarily connote *adverse* selection. Every time a transaction occurs, we observe a selection effect. At $1 per apple, those who buy apples have selected themselves into the market; those who think the price is too high have selected out. Individuals who select themselves into litigation work are those who attach most value to the prospects of winning a case relative to the cost of anxiety inherent in the work. These are desirable sorts that work to increase surplus. Adverse selection is characterized by a

---

[158]Folks with big appetites dominate the buffet line, which tends to drive up the price. To them, the price seems fine. To folks with modest appetites the price seems high; hence, the market degenerates so that mostly big-appetite folks eat at all-you-can-eat buffets.

[159]Individuals with assets like houses or cars, stock certificates, or excellent credit risk histories can obtain a loan at the bank at favorable rates; those who cannot tend to borrow from their credit cards. Credit card defaults are much higher than bank loan defaults—hence, the higher rates on credit cards.

[160]People who like to drive fast and live a "full life" gravitate toward fast cars; old fogies that drive at fifty-five miles per hour gravitate towards Eldorados. Insurance companies discovered long ago that selection factors into claims across car types, and charge accordingly.

reduction in surplus for some segment of the market, notably low-cost buyers.

IV. Adverse Selection in the Job Market

While adverse selection is a problem in insurance markets, it is equally troublesome in the labor market. Firms hire workers on the expectation that they will stay with the company for some reasonable period. Moreover, once the firm converts an applicant to an employee, they face the prospects of substantial firing costs. Yet, worker quality is not readily observable at the time of hire, and hence, firms worry about adverse selection.

Perhaps the best way to describe the problem is by asking the question that all employers ask when confronted by an applicant. Why is this person in the job market? If she is good quality, why does she not already have a good job, and why is her employer unwilling to promote her to the level she is seeking here? A firm needs to have an adequate answer to the question before making a job offer.

Workers show up more or less as blank slates as job applicants. While they have a list of places that they attended school, selected clubs and organizations they joined, and the positions they have worked in the past, this information tells an employer almost nothing except that broadly speaking, the person is adequately trained to be an economist or a lawyer or a bricklayer. But what kind of worker is she? Is she trustworthy? Can she get along with coworkers? Can she write? Is she a good team player? Will this person be willing to work overtime or be willing to travel as needed? Will she be reliable? Will she work hard, or will she tend to talk with colleagues and take long lunch breaks? None of this information is availed in a vita.

Moreover, owing to fear of litigation exposure, past employers are reluctant to provide an honest reference about a job seeker's past performance. Normally, there is no payoff for an honest evaluation but lots of potential exposure. This payoff structure produces very little useful information to prospective employers.

1. Networking
One common solution to poor information in the job market is the concept of networking. An employer is more likely to obtain honest information about an applicant if past employers are personally known to the new potential employer. In this setting, he or she can be more confident that upon the assurance of confidentiality and no written notes to file, he or she will get an honest evaluation about the applicant. Similarly, from the perspective of the applicant, if she knows lots of people

in the market, she can ask colleagues to make calls for her to introduce her without the implication of adverse selection coloring her application. This approach is akin to the word of mouth solution used by consumers in trying to evaluate restaurants or movies.

2. Hire Only at Entry Level: How Adverse Selection Arises

Adverse selection is dramatically reduced at entry level. When the class of 2006 hits the market for lawyers, every one of these applicants has a good excuse to be in the market: they are scheduled to complete law school and are now looking for an entry-level job. No one is in the market because they left their last job. This fact dramatically tilts the odds in favor of a good hire, as compared to hiring individually from a pool of applicants who have quit their last jobs.

In addition, workers quit their jobs much more frequently when they are at the start of their careers. Once a worker attains journeyman status, he or she is much less likely to leave. Junior lawyers quit frequently; partners almost never do. Thus, if a law firm makes a mistake in a junior hire, it can simply delay promotions and give undesirable assignments. Most of the "problem" hires will "pick up" the negative signal and leave on their own. A partner hired at the most senior level is unlikely to leave on his own, and hence, a hiring mistake can be very costly at the top.

If junior hires turn out to be exceptional, then it is predictable that the firm does whatever is required to retain them. Hiring predominantly at the entry level diminishes selection problems. Problem hires usually leave on their own volition, and the best prospects are pursued vigorously for retention. Note the selection problem this creates from the other side of these transactions. Anyone leaving a law firm after the first tour almost certainly is not "star potential," and some are almost certainly among the worst of the junior class.

Universities do almost all their hiring in this way. Junior faculty normally are hired after law school, clerkship, and law firm stint. They then pass through a six-year period as an untenured faculty member. If they are not offered tenure, they depart and suffer the stigma of having been rejected at law school x, after which they almost certainly land at a lesser institution owing to adverse selection. The best prospects are offered tenure, and the dean makes sure through salary policies that the best are paid their full opportunity wage. Hence, the best professors almost never leave. Rarely do universities hire directly at the senior level.

Knowing ahead of time that an early departure from the initial job evokes a self-selection suspicion, it becomes important for students to find a job at an institution that they think will work out for the long run. Thus, interviews for junior-level positions take on a much more important flavor than they would if information about job applicants were transparent. In one sense, an efficiency is conferred on the market. New graduates tend to self-select from the get-go into firms and other institutions that they think will be compatible with them over the long term.

3. Signaling

Workers know that adverse selection characterizes the market and expect employers to be looking for clues that answer the "why on the market" questions. Thus, workers that are part of a broad layoff at a major company will signal that they were not singled out for layoff. But of course, employers know that layoffs do not affect random workers and that all employers try to target layoffs to select out their worst workers. Others may signal that they have been out of the workforce for personal or family reasons, and thus, their entry is not related to being fired or laid off. But employers wonder what kind of worker selects himself out of the workforce for long periods of time. And so it goes. A better signal is one that carries a bond for quality, an issue that I develop more fully in the next chapter.

Appendix: Auctions as Applications of Demand Theory and Bonding

Auctions are trades that involve one seller and more than one buyer, or vice versa. Often, auctions involve a unique product or service that comes up for sale periodically. This makes the problem different than a single seller of a reproducible homogeneous product, like gasoline. It could, for example, describe the sale of a Renoir painting. One could imagine a seller individually negotiating with each potential buyer to determine who is willing to make the highest bid. This sometimes happens. If a baseball player becomes a free agent, meaning that he is contractually free to bargain with any baseball team, his agent likely will negotiate individually with several teams. This approach is costly because it involves lots of transactions. Since these costs are netted out of the deal, buyers and sellers have an incentive to try to minimize them.

An auction often is a more efficient mechanism to help the seller obtain the highest price for his product or service. There are at least three types of common auctions—the English, Dutch, and sealed bid—though in practice, these can be modified in any number of ways. An English auction is one that most people are familiar with. They take place at Sotheby's and Christie's, where results are often reported in the press. Here, potential buyers assemble and engage in continuous bidding. The highest bidder wins the property rights to the auctioned item. In a Dutch auction, the seller starts with a high price and gradually reduces it. The first bidder to raise his hand wins the prize. In a sealed bid auction, there is no assemblage of buyers. Each buyer independently submits a bid to the seller's agent. The winner is the highest bidder, but often, the price he pays is not his bid but the *second-highest* bid.

We normally think of auctions involving unique objects like art. In exchange for a portion of the selling price (often 10 percent), a reputable auction house like Sotheby's or Christie's arranges to sell say a Renoir painting. As a part of their function, they advertise to buyers who are

An *English auction* is one in which buyers assemble and engage in continuous bidding. The highest bidder wins.

A *Dutch auction* is one in which the seller announces a high price and gradually reduces it until a buyer accepts the offer.

A *sealed bid auction* is one in which buyers submit secret bids for some prize. The highest bidder wins, but often the winner gets the prize at the price offered by the second-highest bidder.

likely to be interested in bidding. They also ensure that the painting is genuine and has the proper ownership credentials, and so on. Put simply, when buyers show up at one of these premier auction houses, they know that the painting is a Renoir. The only question is what the painting is worth to each. And it turns out, as I show later, that we discover the answer to this question for everyone *except* the person who wins the bid.

The function of the "house." The guaranty function provided by the "house" is valuable. If buyers did not believe the auction house's assertion that the painting is a Renoir, then each bidder, or perhaps several bidders together, would have to find experts and arrange for them to vouch for the painting's authenticity and provenance. These expenditures, often duplicative, erode buyers' resources without benefiting the seller. To the extent that the auction is costly, it is natural to expect that the net price that buyers are willing to pay the seller for some painting must be discounted by the cost they incur to engage in the auction. Thus, it is in the seller's interest to minimize buyers' outlays to participate in an honest auction.

Given the importance of reputation in this market, we should not be surprised to find evidence of quality assurance premiums collected by well-known auction houses; these premiums assure buyers of the economic stake that the auction house has in maintaining its high-quality reputation. We should also not be surprised to find evidence of firm-specific investments by these firms, like advertising in swanky magazines to also convey the impression of permanence.

Auction houses also perform a function for *sellers* beyond finding willing buyers. That is, the auction house can certify the ability of various bidders to pay the prices that they offer. Most bidders for a Renoir already are well-known in the art world and themselves have reputations to protect. Bidders that are less well-known may be asked to either bond their bids, to alternatively, to find an agent represent them that the auction house knows to be reputable.

Why an English Auction? In principle, we should expect the Renoir painting to sell for about as much whether the seller uses an English,

Dutch, or sealed bid auction. First, I show why we expect this result, and then I show some practical reasons why English auctions might deliver the best result to buyers and sellers.

English. In an English auction, bidding starts low and proceeds upward until the next to last person who wants the painting drops out. Figure 9-5 helps us think about this process. Think of lining up the bidders according to the price that they are willing to pay for the painting. The result looks like a demand curve as illustrated in the figure. I draw it as a continuous line but show that in reality, there are a finite number of bidders at the auction, which I denote by closed circle marks along this schedule. Each of these points represents the reservation price of each of the bidders. It is apparent that person A is willing to pay the most for the painting.

A reservation price is the maximum that a buyer is willing to offer for some good or service. A seller also has a reservation price: it is the minimum that she is willing to accept for the product or service she is selling.

All demand curves and supply curves are schedules of reservation prices of buyers and sellers. We invoke the nomenclature in bargaining problems because often there are only two players who must find the price that makes a deal, whereas in competitive markets, the forces of all the buyers and sellers generate an equilibrium price. But the concept itself is not unique to bargaining situations.

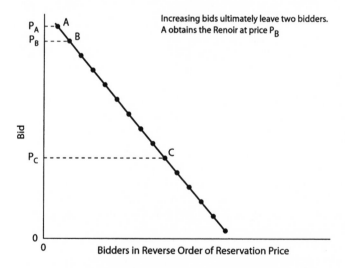

Figure 9-5. Results of English Auction for Renoir Painting

When the auctioneer starts the bidding, suppose person C bids P_C. Anyone with a reservation price less than P_C remains silent. As the bidding escalates, person C drops out, conveying his reservation price to other bidders. Other bidders drop out one at time as the price escalates beyond ones they are willing to pay, until there are only two bidders left, A and B. Assuming that the bids escalate at relatively modest increments, person A simply matches person B's offer plus something. Once the bid exceeds person B's reservation price, P_B, person A gets the painting. Hence, the winner obtains the painting at the highest price that the *next highest* bidder is willing to pay. The winner's reservation price is never discovered. He will walk away from the auction with the Renoir, plus some surplus, measured by the difference between his reservation price, P_A, and the reservation price of the next highest bidder, P_B.

Seller's reservation price. Sometimes, the seller reserves the right to refuse the highest offer. This can occur if the highest price falls below the reservation price of the seller. This will seldom happen, however, in a reputable auction house, unless there is a great deal of uncertainty about bid prices. Otherwise, bidders incur the cost of attending the auction without any benefit conveying to any of them. The auction house can minimize this problem by discovering the seller's reservation price beforehand and declining to auction the piece if this price exceeds those that at least some bidders are willing to pay.

Sealed Bid. A sealed bid auction delivers the same result as long as the winner pays not the price he bid but the one offered by the *second-highest* bidder. By awarding the prize in this way, each bidder had no incentive to disguise his reservation price. If the buyer bids more than his reservation price to increase his chances of winning the bid, he risks the possibility that the next highest bid will exceed his true reservation price. He has no incentive to bid something less than his reservation price, since he does not have to pay this price if he wins. Hence, we expect that the results of a sealed bid auction would be that person A wins and pays price P_B, as shown in figure 9-5.

Dutch. A Dutch auction starts at a high price, and the auctioneer gradually reduces the asking price until someone accepts it. In the case of the Renoir, person A is unlikely to raise his hand when the price hits P_A, hoping that he can snare the painting for a lower price. In fact, it is worth something to person A to invest some resources to find out something about other bidders' reservation prices. If he has zero information, he will have to bid something like P_A, which conveys zero surplus to him. If some expenditures help him discover what the demand curve looks like in figure 9-5, then he may be able to increase his expected surplus by figuring out the best price at which to raise his hand.

Practical problems. The latter discussion raises some practical issues with the Dutch auction. The seller might think that a Dutch auction delivers a better price, since the tendency is for the highest bidder to raise his hand when the price is just below P_A. In practice, the approach may encourage bidders to expend monies to discover other bidders' reservation prices. In this way, bidders along the top portion of the curve can better "game" the process. In the end, sellers do not expect a price much higher than P_B. Yet, by encouraging bidders to expend monies for information that would be conveyed freely in an English auction, they reduce the expected value of participating in the auction in the first place.

From a broader perspective, the auction house is trying to "make a market" (find a buyer for the sellers' pieces at agreed-upon prices) at the lowest cost. Moreover, the house does not want sellers to squeeze bidders for every ounce of their surplus. If somehow sellers could figure out a way to award zero surplus to every winning bidder, then one has to consider why bidders would ever show up for an auction. If sellers and winning bidders walk away from the transaction with surplus, then this improves the prospects for the house to make markets for other objects in the future.

The sealed bid auction suffers none of these problems, and in principle, offers a competitive alternative to an English auction. In practice, however, even though auction houses are reputable, bidders need to be convinced that the bidding process is not rigged. That is, bidders may feel vulnerable to a "ringer" (a dishonest person hired by the house or the seller to try to capture more of person A's surplus). If so, they will be discouraged from participating in a market because it reduces the expected surplus from participating. This fear is allayed when everyone is in the same room and can see who is bidding, and particularly if all the agents and other bidders are well-known to the house.

In a sealed bid, it is not easy for person A who "wins" the bid to know that the house did not submit a phony bid $1 less than his bid, in which case he cannot gain any surplus. While one can imagine safeguards to try to prevent this from happening, the perception that bidders are vulnerable to a phony second bid will make them reluctant to play this game. The house knows this, and neither it nor the seller loses anything by using an English format. A complex building proposal might be a better candidate for a sealed bid.

Chapter 10

Sorting as a Solution to Asymmetric Information

Coaxing Market Participants to Divulge Valuable Information

Main Economic Concepts	1. Information enhances the efficient allocation of resources. Sorting vehicles encourage participants to voluntarily divulge information about themselves to others involved in the transaction.
	2. It may be costly to disengage from an inefficient contract ex post, and this makes it important to reveal information ex ante.
	3. All opportunities that provide a choice result in sorting. All sorting yields a self-selection that confers information.
	4. The labor market lends itself to many sorting models because firms (the buyers) have little information about new hires (sellers) and yet, owing to numerous discrimination laws, firing workers gives rise to substantial litigation exposure.
	5. The Becker-Stigler "police model" is a good illustration of bonding, sorting, and self-selection. It also introduces the "economics of crime."
New Terms	1. Sorting
	2. Becker-Stigler police model
	3. Defined benefit pension
	4. Defined contribution pension
	5. High discounters
	6. Low discounters
	7. 401(k) pension
	8. Efficiency wage
	9. Self-selection
	10. Indenture premium
	11. Spence education bond model

Sorting is a mechanism that allows market participants to discover information before they engage in a transaction. Usually sorting is observed when information is asymmetric. Often, sellers have the informational advantage over buyers, but not always. If sellers have more information, then buyers sometimes can set up a "sort" that encourages sellers to divulge valuable information and, in so doing, improve the efficiency of the trade. If the sorting is effective, it does not matter whether sellers know that information is being pried from them.

Anytime market participants make a choice, a sorting function is performed and information is conveyed. For example, if an ice cream stand sells vanilla and strawberry, then every time a customer chooses one or the other, he divulges his tastes in ice cream. In this example, the information is productively used to ensure that the ice cream vendor orders the proper amounts of vanilla and strawberry to service its flow of customers. Presumably, all customers know which flavor they like; they divulge their preferences when they order ice cream. The vanilla lovers self-select into the vanilla line; the strawberry lovers self-select into the strawberry line. In a more complex setting, Ken either does not know or is trying to disguise his own attributes, and Jane sets up a sort to encourage Ken to divulge them.

An example from law firms. Consider the market for new lawyers. Many lawyers think that they would like a high-paying job with a large well-known law firm, say Jones, Dorr, and Porter. But most do not have very good information about what constitutes life at Jones, Dorr. The law firm needs lawyers who are unusually committed to work. They choose entry-level lawyers on the basis of performance in school and other factors that they think are most likely to predict success in the firm. The firm, however, knows from experience that many entrants will not be happy with the kind of intensity that exists at the firm.

Hence, Jones Dorr sets up a "sorting function" to discover which entrants are most likely to survive the firm's work ethic. They assign a myriad of cases to junior lawyers that require commitments to travel, work during nights or weekends, and so on to meet court deadlines, even if it occasionally means one-hundred-hour weeks. Junior associates who either cannot handle this pace or do not care to make this kind of commitment, *self-select* for an early departure from the firm. We have an efficient solution. The law firm ends up with workers most suited to its kind of work. Individuals who do not care for this kind of life find an alternative career path that is more consistent with a balance of work and nonwork activities.

Example of a sorting function. Many high-quality investment firms, law firms, accounting firms, dot-com firms, and so on are looking for workers who are supercommitted to the job and are willing to put the firm ahead of all other commitments in their lives. To get an efficient solution, firms often set up sorts on commitment early on. Those not cut out for this kind of life self-select for early departure from the firm. Those who stay comprise higher concentrations of highly committed workers who form the pool eligible for high-level positions. The voluntary nature of the departures ensures little litigation exposure.

An example from courtships. Suppose that Jane is equally smitten with Dave and Bing. She could envision being married to either. There is only one thing: Jane hates obesity. While Dave and Bing are both thin now, she is fearful of the possibility that at age fifty, her then-husband might be obese. If this happens, she knows that a divorce will be in the offing with all its consequent costs. So, she sets up a kind of test to encourage Bing and Dave to divulge more information about their likely future weights.

She invites each to a series of fancy restaurants (on her tab) where meals have lots of calories. She makes a point of leaving portions of each meal segment on her plate, thereby sending her dinner partner a signal that she wants to remain thin. She declines dessert but encourages her partner to choose from the dessert tray. Bing declines dessert. Dave chooses three

SOME GENERAL PRINCIPLES ABOUT SORTING

Choice implies sorting. Every time a choice is made, a sort occurs and information is conveyed.

A *sorting mechanism* encourages a productive separation of individuals on the basis of hidden attributes.

A *sort always produces self-selection.* If a law firm creates demanding jobs for new lawyers, those who do not want this pace of work self-select out of the firm.

Individuals subject to a sort always send signals, either knowingly or not. For example, Bing (he's the one who wins Jane's heart) may truly have an absence of a sweet tooth. Alternatively, he may have figured out Jane's sort and is conveying the idea that she is sufficiently important to him that he will conform to eating habits that maintain a weight that is important to her. Either way, Bing is sending favorable signals to Jane.

desserts, thereby divulging a sweet tooth—a bad omen for prospects of a thin waistline in middle age. Jane has created a *sorting function*. Dave and Bing *self-select* either into or out of a marriage. The solution is efficient. It is more likely that her marriage to Bing will survive midlife.

I. Bonds That Also Perform Sorting: The Becker-Stigler Police Model

Many sorting models are found in the labor market. Information in that market often is poor, and the consequences of bad matches between workers and firms can be considerable. I start with sorting functions that normally fall out of bonding solutions to quality assurance problems. I emphasize two well-known models in this chapter. One shows how a carefully constructed pension plan can reduce malfeasance among police officers (the Becker-Stigler police model). The other posits that schools of higher learning do not confer learning but instead are sorting devices to identify more capable candidates for the labor market. Michael Spence wrote the seminal work on this model, and so it is referred to as the "Spence sorting model." I show other examples of sorting along the way.

A. A BECKER-STIGLER PENSION BOND

The Becker-Stigler pension bond model is tailored for law students.[161] First, it confers an opportunity to study an application of bonding. Second, it shows how a bond performs a sort. And third, it introduces the notion of the economics of crime and deterrence.

A Becker-Stigler bond is the value of a deferred pension for law enforcement workers. Upon being caught in malfeasance during his career, a police officer loses the pension. The bond is intended to alter behavior—that is, to create a situation in which crime does not pay. But it also sets up a sort: given the pay structure, dishonest individuals self-select out of the queue of applicants.

Police officers are subject to temptation to engage in crime. The police department wants to encourage honest people to become police officers, or else the police function is of dubious value. So, it arranges compensation that requires its officers to bond their honesty. The existence

[161]Gary Becker, and George J. Stigler, "Law Enforcement, Malfeasance and Compensation of Enforcers," *Journal of Legal Studies* 3 (January 1974): 1–18.

of this bond acts as a sort: given the nature of the compensation arrangement, only honest individuals find it advantageous to apply.

Police officers in almost all jurisdictions are covered by a "defined benefit pension plan." This kind of pension typically pays a life annuity to a worker who has attained retirement age, based on service level and pay.

A typical police compensation package includes a modest cash wage, with a large payoff at the end of a twenty-year career in the form of a pension annuity often equal to 50 percent of final wage. Given that twenty years of service is attained usually around age forty, this amounts to an annuity collected for over forty years on average. It is apparent that a large portion of the payoff from being a police officer is the pension. What is unique to police pensions, aside from retirement so early in life, is that they "vest" only after twenty years, which means that if an officer is fired or quits after nineteen years, he or she gets nothing. *The property value of the pension annuity is conferred to the police officer only upon the successful completion of twenty years of service.*

A *defined benefit pension* pays a lifetime annuity starting at retirement age based on salary and service. Corporation *XYZ* pays employees a pension annuity starting at retirement age equal to 2 percent of final salary times years of service.

A *police pension* pays a lifetime annuity often equal to 50 percent of final wage after twenty years of service. It vests at twenty years, meaning that police officers gain the property rights to it *only* if they successfully complete twenty years of service. If they quit or are fired during their tenure, they lose their pension. This is the pension studied in Becker-Stigler.

I present a model that has the same features of Becker-Stigler but differs in some of the details to make it easier to explain. I assume that the alternative wage of an officer is $10,000 per year. That is, given the ability and training that a police department is looking for, they would need to pay $10,000 per year. For simplicity, I assume that wages are flat over the career and also that the interest rate is zero so that we do not need to bother with discounting. In other words, a dollar received ten years from now is equally valued to a dollar today.

Suppose that instead of paying $10,000 per year, the police department pays $5,000 in cash wages and promises to pay $100,000 at the end of twenty years in the form of a pension benefit. We can think of the $100,000 as the value of the promised annuity as of the retirement date.

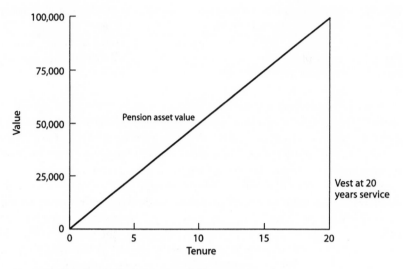

Figure 10-1. Becker-Stigler Pension Bond for Honesty

Effectively, $5,000 of wages are held back each year and returned to the officer at the end of twenty years if he or she successfully completes the contract.

Figure 10-1 shows this compensation schedule. The upsloping solid linear schedule shows the cumulative value of wages forgone in expectation of the pension. Thus, after ten years of service, the value of the "pension asset" is $50,000 because the police officer has sacrificed ten years of cash income at the rate of $5,000 per year. *The pension asset is a bond because the police officer retrieves it only upon successfully completing his tenure; else, the value is zero.*

Becker and Stigler assume that, if caught, there is insufficient evidence to obtain a conviction. In addition, we may assume that the evidence is insufficient to defend a charge of libel if the police department tells future potential employers why service was discontinued. Let us suppose that if caught, the officer typically voluntarily quits in lieu of being fired. This means that the sole cost of engaging in malfeasance is the loss of the pension benefit.

In the Becker-Stigler model, each police officer effectively posts the $100,000 bond at the beginning of tenure. This simplification needs to be modified. In reality, police officers pay for their pension gradually, by sacrificing cash wages. This means that early in tenure, police officers do not have as much to lose from malfeasance as older police officers. Hence, it is apparent that the police department ought to devote more of its internal affairs resources toward watching newer police officers and less on older police officers.

We can see this problem more clearly by writing a simple equation that depicts the "economics of crime." Suppose that if an officer engages in crime, he gains the amount C in criminal income, which I assume is a constant. There is some chance p that he will be caught in the year in which he commits the crime. Assume for simplicity that if he is not caught this year, he is never caught. Hence, a decision about crime next year is independent of this year. If caught, he keeps the income from crime, but is fired from the police force. Assuming that all police officers care only about maximizing their income. They engage in crime if the payoff exceeds the expected loss. Thus, the police department wants to maintain the following inequality at every year of tenure:

$$C < p_t B_t,$$

where B_t is the pension bond at tenure level t, and p_t is the probability that the crime will be discovered at tenure level t. The bond and the probability of detection are set by the police department. It wants to set these values such that the expected costs of engaging in crime are at least as large as the payoff from crime. Since the bond, B_t, is smaller at lower levels of t, then it is apparent that the police department should set the probability of getting caught so that it is higher for young police officers.[162]

A Key Equation in the Economics of Crime

Income-maximizing potential offenders do not engage in crime if and only if crime doesn't pay

$$C < pB,$$

where C is the payoff from crime, p is the probability of getting caught, and B is the loss imposed on the offender if caught. A profit-maximizing offender engages in crime if the payoff from crime exceeds the expected costs. In Becker-Stigler, the only penalty is loss of pension. The equation abstracts from many complications and qualifications but gives the essence of the problem. The main point is that offenders are assumed to be driven by economic calculations and not by antisocial attributes.[163]

---

[162]Since the expected cost of crime equals pB, then if this cost is to remain constant at all tenure levels, it follows that as the bond increases in value, the probability of getting caught can be reduced to maintain the same expected cost of malfeasance.

[163]Gary Becker, "Crime and Punishment: An Economic Approach," *Journal of Political Economy* 76 (March 1968): 169–217.

If all individuals are identical in their attributes, then we can view the police bond as a vehicle that affects behavior. This is the sense in which Becker-Stigler viewed the bond. If, however, individuals differ in attributes that might affect their propensity to engage in a crime, then the bond acts as a sorting device to encourage individuals to apply that are prone to honesty. I explore one such attribute next.

B. AN INDENTURE PREMIUM

In the pension solution I posit in figure 10-1, I am somewhat at odds with a fair characterization of compensation in equilibrium. If workers can collect $10,000 each year for working in some alternative occupation, why accept a pay package where much of the pay is tilted toward the end? There is some chance that individuals will quit the police force for reasons other than malfeasance (for example, they may not like doing all the paperwork, or they might find some situations too anxiety ridden, or their spouse might accept a job with Jones, Dorr, and Porter in San Francisco). Thus, the expected wage is less than $10,000 per year.

In reality, the policy department needs to pay some compensating differential to accommodate the severe tilt toward later tenure in its pay package. One might refer to this differential as an indenture premium because it compensates individuals for committing to a job for twenty years to obtain much of the benefits. One feature of the compensation package, however, is that it clearly is more inviting to individuals who think that they will want to stick with police work for the full twenty years; else, they stand to lose substantial monies if they walk away early.

> *Indenture premium*: A wage premium collected by workers because they have to wait until later in their careers to collect a large portion of their lifetime pay. The pay structure provides an incentive to stay in the police department for twenty years and to avoid episodes of malfeasance. It also attracts applicants who are most likely to stay with police work for the full twenty years.

C. HOW DOES THE BOND CREATE A SORT?

In Becker-Stigler, all applicants for police work are identical in all relevant attributes. But suppose that some people are honest and others are either honest or dishonest depending on which is more profitable. Put simply, suppose that an honest person would attach a high disutility to being caught in malfeasance and separated from the police force.

Suppose that using the compensation principle, this disutility is worth some dollar amount G.[164] Thus, if an honest person contemplates crime, he views the benefits as C but the cost as G. Assume that G exceeds C so that even without a bond, an honest person does not engage in crime. In contrast, suppose a dishonest person is characterized by a zero value of G.

To see the value of setting a wage system that creates a desirable sort, let me first consider one that does not work. In fact, it creates a perverse incentive for honest individuals to *avoid* police work. Suppose that the income from crime, C, is $20,000. The police department pays a salary of $10,000 with no pension. If the chance of detection is zero, then which type would self-select into police officer jobs?

Honest workers view the wage as $10,000. But dishonest workers view the wage as $10,000 *plus* the income from crime, $20,000. Indeed, the dishonest applicants would be willing to work for a zero wage because the $20,000 income from crime swamps the income from a non-police job ($10,000). Gradually, this competition for police work drives the wage to zero. The compensation system invites adverse selection of dishonest people for these jobs.

Suppose alternatively that the police department defers part of the wage. It pays a $5,000 cash wage plus $5,000 in the form of a deferred pension. Assume for simplicity that the indenture premium is zero. Suppose also that the police department sets the bond and the probability of getting caught in any tenure year t so that the expected penalty from engaging in crime is zero even for dishonest applicants; that is,

$$p_t B_t = C.$$

Crime does not pay for either honest or dishonest applicants. In this case, the dishonest people no longer dominate the applicant pool.

Notice that the bond and probability of detection are inversely related. To illustrate, suppose that the benefits of crime, C, are $15,000. If the profits from crime are not confiscated upon being caught (which I assume) then the bond from the pension is insufficient to deter crime in the first two years because even when the probability of detection is 100 percent, the bond is less than the proceeds from crime. In year 3, a 100 percent detection probability is sufficient to deter crime. By the time the bond reaches $45,000 (in year 9), the detection probability can be set to 33.3 percent, and so on.

---

[164]Recall that the compensation principle requires us to ask: how much income would I have to pay you to compensate you for the reduction in utility caused by the embarrassment of being involuntarily separated from the police force in front of your family and friends?

> The probability of detection needed to deter malfeasance in the police force is inversely related to the bond. All else equal, older police officers require less monitoring than younger officers.

The compensation level inclusive of the pension value is stable at $10,000; honest applicants no longer self-select out of the applicant pool. Dishonest people still apply, but the bond controls their behavior so that they do not engage in crime. Thus, the pension bond corrects the adverse selection problem by sorting in a representative number of honest people in the applicant queue and by controlling the behavior of dishonest people. Effectively, it erects a system in which it pays for officers to act *as though* they are honest. The pension bond also works to select in applicants who are "stayers," meaning that they are more likely to anticipate wanting to stay in the police department for the full twenty years.

D. AN ALTERNATIVE BOND: AN EFFICIENCY WAGE

The pension solution is not the only bond that works in this environment. Suppose that instead of paying a pension, the police department continues to hire workers who have a $10,000 alternative wage, but now instead of offering a pension, they simply pay them a $15,000 salary. In this alternative, police officers are deliberately paid more than their opportunity wage, so as to give them an incentive to want to stay employed. This bonus is called an **efficiency wage** because it is designed to encourage workers to comply with the implied employment contract with less monitoring.

The police department must resist the temptation to hire more skilled workers at the higher wage; otherwise workers will not view the wage as "special," which defeats the purpose of an efficiency wage. That is, at the $15,000 wage, workers with an opportunity wage of $14,000 apply and are more "qualified" than the $10,000-per-year applicants. Nevertheless, it is optimal to hire the latter because, to them, the "bonus" is special, and hence, they will value staying on the job. Workers that are more skilled will view police work as "just another job."

Certain lucky workers obtain these jobs. Suppose that the police department picks names out of a hat full of applicant names, all with a $10,000 alternative wage. Upon being chosen, new hires are presented with an asset of considerable value, namely, the property right to collect the bonus over the next twenty years if they are honest. On the first day of the job, this asset is worth $100,000.

> *Efficiency wage*: A premium that an employer deliberately pays to workers to give them an incentive to stay in employment and to perform according to the specifications in the employment contract. In a police model, the contract calls for honest enforcement of the laws.
>
> *Corollary*: In an efficiency wage arrangement, the firm *cannot* hire more skilled workers at the higher wage; else, the "bonus" from the perspective of employees disappears.
>
> The efficiency wage solution has the odd feature that the firm (or police department) deliberately hires lesser qualified applicants in the queue.

The police officer loses her property right to this asset if she is caught in a crime; otherwise, she retains it. Note that after she collects the $5,000 in the first year, she has only nineteen more years to collect the bonus; hence, the asset value of her property right in year 2 falls to $95,000. After she collects the bonus for two years, she has eighteen more years of the bonus. Her asset now is worth $90,000. It gradually falls by $5,000 per year until it reaches zero at year 20. Figure 10-2 shows this bond as a downsloping schedule. The pension bond is shown for comparison.

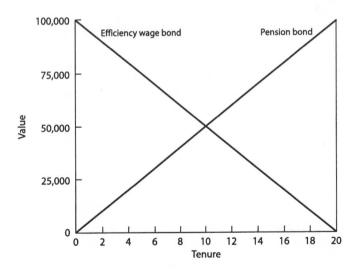

Figure 10-2. Efficiency Wage Bond for Honesty

EXERCISE:

Question: Note that efficiency wages create a queue of applicants who have lower opportunity wages. Assume only applicants who earn $10,000 are allowed in queue. Suppose that those chosen are those who either call more times to check on a job, take the personnel director to lunch, cull the favor of the union boss, and so on. How many resources will be expended to win each $100,000 prize?

Answer: You know the answer by now, and so I will not repeat it.[165] Incidentally, the efficiency wage works just as well whether or not it is subject to rent erosion. Fewer resources are wasted, however, if names of qualified applicants simply are picked from a hat.

In my example, the efficiency wage amounts to an extra $100,000 in compensation for each career. But the police department has a bond that penalizes young police officers more than older police officers. Hence, in the efficiency wage solution, the police department allocates more internal affairs resources to monitoring older police officers, since older officers have less to lose. This solution might be more attractive if young police officers, for other reasons, are more prone to crime than older police officers, and/or if the cost of monitoring older police officers is lower.

E. PUTTING THE TWO BONDS TOGETHER

A third solution is to combine the bonds. That is, suppose that the police department offers compensation equal to $15,000 per year, reflecting a $5,000 efficiency wage. But suppose it pays $10,000 in cash and $5,000 in the form of a pension. In this case, there is no indenture premium because the cash wage matches the alternative wage. The entire efficiency wage is paid in the form of the pension.

From the perspective of the first day on the job, the new entrant views the $5,000 bonus as an efficiency wage, with a value of $100,000. This bond falls to $95,000 after the first year because he has effectively deposited the money into his pension. Now his pension asset is worth $5,000. The pension asset bond plus the asset value of the efficiency wage equals $100,000. We now have a constant bond over tenure equal to $100,000, at a total cost of $100,000.

Notice that the cost of this solution is the same as the pure efficiency wage solution. In the combined bond solution, however, the internal

---

[165]OK, I will repeat it one last time. Suppose that an expenditure of K dollars gets your name in the hat. The number of names that will be put in the hat is N, where N satisfies the equality: *(1/N) PRIZE = K*, where the prize is the amount of the wage in excess of the opportunity wage. Ergo, applicants spend the amount NK, which equals the amount of the prize which in this case equals $100,000.

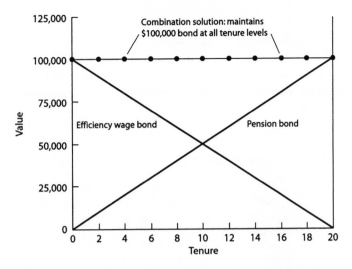

Figure 10-3. Combining an Efficiency Wage and a Pension Bond

affairs department can be smaller because the bond is $100,000 in every year. Previously it was only $50,000 on average, when only one or the other bonds were used. This tells us that if an efficiency wage is used, it is optimal to pay it in the form of a pension. That is, a solution that pays the efficiency wage in the form of a higher pension trumps a pure efficiency wage solution because it gives a higher bond at all tenure levels without imposing any additional costs. This solution is shown in figure 10-3. Note that this solution is identical to offering police recruits a signing bonus equal to $100,000, payable if they still are on the force in twenty years.

Other Applications of Becker-Stigler Bonds
Federal Judge Pay. The cash compensation for federal judges is approximately $150,000. But when the sum of service on the bench plus their age reaches eighty, they are entitled to retire on full salary, which they continue to collect until death. If they are impeached, they lose the pension.

Military pay. Military personnel have pensions almost the same as police officers; they receive 50 percent of their final pay after twenty years, where vesting occurs in year 20. If caught in malfeasance, they are stricken from the roles, meaning that even if they have attained
continued . . .

> *Continued*
>
> twenty years, they lose their pension. Lesser issues not involving felony-like malfeasance or those occurring outside the military often result in a "voluntary retirement" if twenty years has been attained or a "voluntary quit" if lesser service has been attained. In the latter case, there is no pension.

II. The Spence Model of Sorting

The Becker-Stigler model provides an excellent illustration of a bond that can provide a sort, though it is interesting that the authors did not pursue the sorting effect in their original model. In contrast, the Spence model, while it includes a bond, specifically envisions an efficient sorting mechanism.[166]

A. THE IDEA IN BRIEF

Michael Spence published an article in 1974, advancing the then-startling idea that higher education did not confer learning, as such, but acted as a sorting device. In a nutshell, the idea is that the market is looking for able individuals to perform more important jobs. But it is costly to discern which prospects have the ability to perform these functions. Ability is interpreted broadly so that it encompasses intellectual power but also other attributes necessary for success in important jobs, such as those that are demonstrated in a successful college career.

In effect, college students post a bond, in the sense that they spend four years of their lives, plus out-of-pocket expenses, to make it to graduation. Able people with good work habits view the education process as fairly easy to get through. The cost of doing well is higher for less capable individuals or for those with less zeal for work, less organizational skill, and so forth. Hence, only the most able students apply to college. The very fact the students show up as freshmen conveys the idea that

> The *Spence education bond model* portrays schooling as a kind of hurdle system in which students are required to divulge information about the attributes that likely will affect their performance in the job market. More able individuals can clear these hurdles at lower cost than those who are less able. The system forces self-selection up front: more able students are more likely to select themselves into the pool of applicants.

[166]Michael Spence, *Market Signaling* (Cambridge, MA: Harvard University Press, 1974).

they must think they can survive the process at a relatively low cost; else they are wasting their time and money.

B. APPLICATION TO LAW SCHOOL

We can view law school from the perspective of Spence. Suppose that that most law school graduates will specialize in some aspect of the law and that they will spend their first three years of employment learning that law. Suppose that law school merely erects a series of hurdles and that to clear these hurdles, a student must possess various attributes that are valued by law firms. These might include the ability to assimilate a large volume of material, cope with simultaneous and competing demands, maintain a disciplined study regimen, tolerate seventy-hour work weeks, handle the pressure of single final exams that carry all the credit, and so on.

Among college students contemplating the prospects of attending law school, the cost seems highest to those who have a comparative disadvantage in this kind of study, are insufficiently capable to handle intellectual challenges, and are unsure whether they are committed to a career in law. Moreover, students are required to put up substantial out-of-pocket monies and devote large amounts of their young adult lives to study.

For those who think that the work is doable without a "too high" cost in terms of work, money outlays, and anxiety, law school seems like a good deal. The very fact that students have selected into law school means that they are far more likely to be successful lawyers than those who do not attend, quite apart from learning anything about the law.

C. PURSUING THE MODEL ONE STEP FURTHER

We can take the Spence model one step further. Among students that make up the entering class at some law school, some are better prospects for law firms than others. But assuming that most entrants to a particular law school evince similar outward qualities, like LSAT scores and the like, the attributes that define law career promise within this group are largely unobserved. The law school must sort these students further by ranking, so that those most successful in accomplishing the goals that require the desired attributes are rated highest, the second best next highest, and so on.

The law school essentially delivers the market a "bottom-line" index that incorporates the end result of student attributes, both observable and unobservable, in the form of a grade sheet and class ranking. Future employers therefore learn a great deal about potential applicants: in this model, grades do not reflect the knowledge of materials but rather reveal information about hidden attributes.

Prospective students who have the attributes to perform well in the legal environment see lots of payoffs to a law degree with a high ranking.

Those who view themselves as unlikely to attain a relatively good position in class ranking view the cost of the process as very high in relation to the payoff from a poor showing. Hence, students self-select into law school on the basis of expected performance level. The "hurdle system" effectively improves the quality level of the incoming pool and helps ensure that, within this pool, the proper hierarchy of likely success is conveyed to prospective employers.

Sorting continues via the grade system. From the pool of promising entrants, law schools and other institutions of higher learning sort among the able group to ensure a proper hierarchy. Class ranking is a kind of summary measure of student attributes that reflect their likelihood of success in the labor market. The ranking conveys essential information about relative performance to the market that helps ensure an efficient allocation of graduates to available jobs.

III. Other Sorting Devices in the Labor Market

There are many other sorting devices. I already have mentioned the sort for commitment in large law firms. I now give further illustration of the wide variety of functions that these devices can play. I choose examples from an environment in which information plays an important role in guiding the allocation of resources toward their highest-value uses, namely, the labor market.

A. THE NOT-SO-FREE FREE SICK LEAVE

Why do firms offer sick leave? When you think about it, those who take the leave are effectively getting paid more than those who do not use it because they work fewer days for what seems like the same pay. But can this be so?

EXERCISE:

Question: Suppose that a firm offers twelve use-or-lose sick days each year (beyond regular vacation time and holidays). If they announce the policy that those who take all their sick leave are paid the same as those who take none, what will be the result?

Answer: The policy will result in adverse selection. Less reliable workers select themselves into the firm and use all their sick leave. Reliable workers avoid the firm and instead work for one that rewards the "reliability" attribute that distinguishes them.

It is pretty well known in the labor market that especially for young workers, and except for clearly identified uses like maternity leave, most workers use sick leave as annual leave. Most evening students who are over age thirty already know what some younger students will come to know: *most sick leave (gulp!) is not used by workers who are sick.* Many workers simply call in sick on Mondays and Fridays to enjoy a long weekend, or take Wednesday afternoon off to go skiing midweek, to see little Johnny play soccer, or catch an afternoon game at the ballpark. From the perspective of the employer, workers who are unreliable are less valuable than those who show up on a routine basis.

Suppose that sick leave is not a "free benefit" but a sorting device. It is offered not to allow time for sick employees with the flu to stay home with pay but to encourage workers to divulge their propensity to take time off if it appears free. By offering the time off, firms allow workers to self-select into two groups. Employees in one group cannot resist the offer of free time off and so use sick leave as though it were an entitlement. Members of the other group are loath to take sick leave except in emergencies, for fear of sending a signal that they are unreliable employees. Put simply, employers view frequent and cavalier use of sick leave as a signal of poor quality and view the abstention of its use as a signal of high quality. Workers who use sick leave earn a reputation for unreliability. Those who eschew it gain a reputation for reliability.

We can view this sorting in the same way as a quality-assurance premium. Recall from chapter 9 that consumers refused to pay a premium until the firm had supplied high-quality products at the low-quality price for some substantial period of time. After they demonstrated their high quality, consumers were willing to pay a high-quality price to these firms but not to firms who offer low-quality goods at low-quality prices. Sick

---

Paid sick leave is a sorting device. It sorts on the basis of reliability. Reliable workers pass up the opportunity to take "free" time off and thus send a signal of high quality to the firm; their continued abstention from using the time off creates a reputation for reliability.

A reliability wage premium develops. When firms fill more important jobs, they select candidates from the pool of reliable workers, leaving sick leave users in less important jobs, thereby creating a wage differential. In equilibrium, reliable workers work more and get paid more; unreliable workers take more time off and get paid less.

Related Idioms You get what you pay for; There's no such thing as a free lunch; When a deal seems too good to be true, it usually is.

leave policies are very much like the test of time in the quality model. If workers can reject the use of apparently free sick leave for a sufficiently long period, they are judged to be high quality and thus become eligible for a higher-quality wage.

Viewed more broadly, it is apparent that the firm incurs little or no cost from offering sick leave. That is to say, when job openings arise for important jobs, they select from the pool of reliable workers. Over time, reliable workers are assigned to higher-paying jobs. Unreliable workers are left with less important, lower-paying jobs. Thus, in the long run, reliable workers get paid more than unreliable workers. Indeed, the latter workers pay for their own sick leave by getting paid less over their career.

B. SORTING ON THE BASIS OF DISCOUNT RATES

Thus far, I have shown how sorting is done on the basis of honesty, ability, and reliability. I now consider sorting on the basis of a worker's "discount rate." By discount rate, I mean the degree to which workers value the future versus the present. Why does a worker's discount rate matter?

Suppose that there are two kinds of workers: high discounters and low discounters. Low discounters attach lots of value to the future. They work hard because they value the prospect of a promotion. They are careful with the company equipment because they do not want to be viewed as a high-cost employee. They are reluctant to take sick leave for fear of the signal it sends. They are natural savers in a financial sense because they value the future security implied by a growing portfolio. In contrast, high discounters think less about the future and so work less hard, call in sick, and spend now. What matters to them is leisure and consumption today; hence, they do not value investments in the future.

Low discounters attach value to consumption today *and* in the future. They work hard because they can see the future benefits in terms of promotion and so on. They also are savers because they can perceive the importance of having resources to buy goods and services in the future, like a house, car, college education for their children, a secure retirement, and so on.

High discounters attach disproportionate value to current consumption and leisure and care little about the future. They do not work hard because they value taking it easy today more heavily than the repercussions on their career path in the future. Similarly, they save little because they attach more value to consumption now than higher consumption in the future. Put simply, they highly "discount" future values.

In a nutshell, a firm values low discounters more than high discounters because it knows that low discounters are self-motivated to work hard to win the benefit of future promotions. In order to get the same level of work from high discounters, the firm must expend more monitoring resources, which is a drain on the firm's productivity. The problem from the firm's perspective is that at the time workers apply for a job, it is not obvious which are low and high discounters. Thus, we can presume that high discounters sometimes are hired. How can the company encourage them to select themselves out of the firm without imposing firing costs on the company (including the cost of litigation exposure)? One possibility is to offer a deceptively simple defined contribution pension plan.

In a "plain vanilla" defined contribution pension plan, the firm does not promise an annuity at retirement but instead builds a tax-preferred savings account for the employee. The firm might contribute 10 percent of every worker's salary into a pension account. The account has the worker's name on it. The balance accumulates with interest. Assume that the pension awards immediate vesting, as it often does, meaning that the worker owns the property rights to the pension account and so can take the balance of the account with her upon departure.

Tax rules require that if workers stay with the company, they must maintain the balance intact until they retire (or until they quit). Upon quitting, they can either roll their balance into an individual retirement account without tax consequences, or they can cash it out. In the latter case, unless they are at least fifty-nine and a half years old, the amount cashed out is assessed a 10 percent tax penalty and becomes immediate taxable income.

A *"plain vanilla" defined contribution pension* is one in which the firm contributes some percentage of pay into a worker's account; the account accumulates interest. Upon vesting, which often is immediate, the worker can take the value of the account upon quitting but must leave the account untouched until retirement if he stays.

A low discounter attaches equal value to the pension as he does to his cash wage because he values the future security implied by the pension. A high discounter attaches little value to the pension because it represents future spending, which he does not value. Other things equal, he wants to spend those monies now. The problem is that he cannot access monies in his pension while he is working for the company.

There is one way in which the high discounter can access the balance in his account immediately: *he can quit*. Thus, if a worker earns

$30,000, his plan accumulates $3,000 during the first year plus interest. The highest discounters will be unable to leave that money unspent and will be tempted to depart after the first year to gain access to those monies. Now suppose the second-highest discounters can ignore the $3,000 plus interest. After the second year, there is $6,000 plus accumulated interest, and after three years, $9,000 plus interest. Sooner or later, and mostly sooner, all the high discounters will select themselves out of the workforce in order to obtain access to the value of their pension accounts. This is a classic sorting device.

A defined contribution plan sorts on the basis of workers' discount rates. By effectively forcing each worker to save some of his compensation in a pension account, the firm sets up a choice: either stay with the firm and continue to accumulate a larger pension account, or quit and obtain access to pension monies immediately. High discounters self-select for early departure from the firm, leaving the firm's workforce dominated by low discounters.

Workers who quit for pension lump sums leave a tell-tale sign of their discount rate. They tend to gravitate toward firms that have no pensions and pay compensation in the form of cash wages. In the latter firms, compensation levels are lower because high discounters are worth less and hence are paid less. In this sense, the pension sorting is efficient: high discounters are allocated to jobs designed to accommodate low-quality workers, are paid an appropriately lower level of compensation, and receive their pay in the form that is of most value to them.

EXERCISE:

Questions: In the context of this discussion, why do firms often check to see if applicants have a history of credit problems?[167]

Can you think of other questions you could ask in a job interview that do not violate discrimination laws but might help discern whether a person is more likely a high or low discounter?[168]

---

[167]One explanation is that low discounters are not expected to overspend and thus are unlikely candidates for a list of bad credit risks. The list more likely is made up of high discounters who tend to spend their income as fast as, or faster than, they earn it.

[168]If the applicant has been in the workforce for a few years, some questions might be: Have you purchased a house? Do you have any savings in an individual retirement account (a tax-preferred savings vehicle availed to workers)? Have you worked for a company that offers a defined contribution plan and, if so, did you roll over the balance into an individual

C. 401(K) PENSION PLANS: ANOTHER SORT ON THE BASIS OF DISCOUNT RATES

A 401(k) pension also can effect a sort on discount rates. These plans do not force workers to save but instead give them a choice. In a typical 401(k) plan, a worker can save up to *x* percent of pay in the pension, *and* the firm promises to match these contributions *y* cents to the dollar. For example, suppose *x* equals 10 and *y* equals 50. If a worker contributes 10 percent of pay to his 401(k) plan, the company contributes 5 percent. The worker gains the property rights to the employer contributions upon vesting, which often is immediate. Can this plan perform a sort? Indeed, it can.

A 401(k) plan is a special kind of defined contribution plan. Workers choose to contribute a portion of their pay, and often the employer matches these contributions up to some percentage of pay. For example, Corporation *ABC* matches 50 percent of employee contributions up to 8 percent of pay. Often, employees can direct the investment choices in their 401(k), often choosing among mutual fund options.

Consider the reaction of low and high discounters to the offer of a 50 percent match on the first 10 percent of pay contributed to the 401(k). Low discounters save 10 percent of their pay and receive the 5 percent match. They value the saving anyway and attach substantial value to the match. High discounters do not save any portion of their cash wage because they want to spend it now. So, they pass up the 401(k) offer. Upon so doing, they reject the 5 percent bonus offered by the company as a match. The fact that they refuse to save in the face of an immediate 50 percent return identifies them as likely candidates for high-discounter status.

The net result is that low discounters receive a 5 percent pay increase, and the high discounters receive nothing. If the company had assembled all the employees in the gymnasium and formed two lines, one labeled "Volunteers to receive a 5 percent raise here" and the other "Volunteers for zero wage increase here," how many would fall into the second queue? Presumably, the answer is zero. Yet, by asking the same question

---

retirement account upon quitting? Did you buy your automobile outright? Do you maintain a balance on your credit card, or do you pay it off each month? Using information from the next section in the text, you could ask: Did your last job offer a 401(k) pension and, if so, did you make any contributions? Did you spend those monies upon departure? To ensure compliance with various discrimination rules, the best defense is to ask these questions of some of your current employees, then do a statistical test to see if performance is correlated with the answers. If so, then these are questions you want to ask and ones that you can defend as relevant to productivity in the event of a challenge.

but imposing a time dimension to it, the firm succeeds in getting its workers to self-select their wage on the basis of their expected quality level. *The 401(k) match sorts on the basis of discount rates and encourages high discounters to self-select for a wage discount.*

> *A 401(k)-pension plan is a sorting device.* By offering a matching amount on worker contributions to a pension plan, the firm encourages workers not only to divulge their discount rates but also to adjust their *own* pay on this basis. By divulging their lower quality, high discounters receive an immediate wage penalty.

Sorts are used in lots of employment settings to encourage an efficient allocation of workers both across and within firms. Workers' value added is highest if they match up early on with employers that value their particular attributes. Those firms who deal with the lower-quality workers, like high discounters, for example will set up a production function that is more tolerant of below-average work ethics, or will use more supervision so as to encourage more work through monitoring, with more immediate rewards for good work.

D. A POSTSCRIPT ON BECKER-STIGLER: ROLE OF HIGH DISCOUNTERS

It is interesting to revisit the Becker-Stigler bond in light of my discussion of high and low discounters. Consider the key equation in the economics of crime: engage in crime if the income from crime, C, exceeds the expected penalty, namely, the product of the probability of getting caught, p, and the penalty, B, if caught, where B is the accumulated value of forgone wages in consideration of the "twenty-and-out" pension promise. My calculations assumed that only low discounters were hired. What if high discounters enter the police force? This creates a serious problem for the police department. The pension payoff is so far in the future that a high discounter attaches practically a zero value to the bond. In this case, unless he has the "honesty" attribute that I discussed earlier, it pays for him to engage in crime: he perceives the benefits C, but the expected penalty to him is zero.

In this case, it becomes important for the police cash wage to fall below alternative job options. That is, a high discounter will view the *cash* wage as disproportionately important compared to a pension, and thus, it becomes important to offer an abnormally low cash wage especially during the first few years of tenure. In this way, high discounters are dissuaded from entering the applicant pool.

For example, in the combined bond solution, whereby a pension plus an efficiency wage were employed, I posited a $10,000 cash wage plus a

$5,000 per annum pension accrual, for total compensation worth $15,000 per year. A high discounter would perceive compensation to be $10,000, but since this is the same as the cash wage in an alternative job, he still might enter. If he does, he becomes a good candidate to develop into a "bad cop." In consideration of this factor, perhaps paying a cash wage of $5,000 in the first three years and then reverting to a $10,000 salary might be a better choice. The $15,000 in cash held back during the first three years could be added to the pension, so that we might set the pension at $115,000 after twenty years, instead of $100,000. In this approach, high discounters would tend to self-select out of the queue of applicants.

Additionally, if high discount rates pose a special problem, the police department could be especially rigorous in seeking out evidence of low discount rates. For example, college-educated recruits would be better candidates, since high discounters are unlikely to be willing to forgo four years of immediate income in exchange for higher future income. They might prefer nonsmokers, since they are more likely to fully value the future costs of smoking versus the current benefits. And they might be especially disinterested in applicants who show evidence of substantial debt or bad credit ratings, since this might suggest a high discount rate.

EXERCISE:

Can You Make Sense out of the Following
Compensation Packages?
A cosmetics retailer offers its employees a fairly low cash salary but substantial discounts on expensive perfume and other products sold in the store.[169]

A dot-com firm offers a pay package that has no provision for health insurance and pays its workers partly in the form of company stock options.[170]

A national law firm decides after one year that 50 percent of its new associates will not work out, but it allows them to use office facilities and time to search for a new job at full pay for one year after it sends them a signal that they will not make the cut.[171]

---

[169]The retailer is sending a signal that it prefers workers who attach lots of value to products sold in the beauty store. These workers will be more informed than others and will be walking advertisements for the store because they will use the products when working, and when not working, hopefully they will elicit questions that will stimulate more sales.

[170]The firm may want lots of young, unattached people who can work long hours and who are free of health problems. The stock options are designed to keep these workers at the firm until products of substantial value have been developed. Both policies tend to repel risk-averse types, suggesting that the company favors risk takers in its employment pool.

[171]Presumably, the firm is wary of gaining a reputation as a risky place to start as an associate. Effectively, by offering this kind of job, the applicant knows that if she is unsuccessful in

IV. More Examples of Sorts and Bonds

Finally, I review two additional sorting devices to give a somewhat broader view of their uses. I use one example from the grocery industry and one from the market for interviews at law firms.

A. SLOTTING ALLOWANCES

Slotting allowances are fees charged by grocery stores to producers who want to put their products on the grocer's shelf. Thus, a store in Washington, D.C., might charge $50,000 as a kind of entry fee to stock x square feet of shelf space. Assuming a competitive market, what might explain this practice?

One function seems apparent. Assume that producers with thousands of new products besiege grocers each year, all wanting shelf space. The store could try to figure out which products its customers most want. But the grocery manager presumably has little knowledge of all the varieties of products presented as candidates for shelf space. One easy solution for the grocer is to set a fee, which forces producers to divulge information; that is, it forces producers to sort on the basis of product quality.

If a producer thinks that its product will be attractive to large number of customers who will return many times to repeat their purchases, then presumably it would be willing to pay the fee. Another producer that thinks that its product might attract a modest quantity of sales would be reluctant to pay the fee. In effect, *a slotting allowance is a bond on a producer's promise that the grocer's customers will be happy with the product.* Producers with products most valued by the customers self-select for shelf space; the rest select themselves out of the queue for shelf space.

EXERCISE:

Question: Since consumers must pay for the slotting fee, are not consumers worse off by the amount of slotting fees?[172]

Think of a world in which slotting is outlawed; that is, either the Federal Trade Commission or the U.S. Congress declared slotting as a

---

the firm, she will be given generous amounts of time to "land softly" at another law firm more suited to her talents and job preferences. By generously treating the nonstayers, the firm gets a larger flow of promising lawyers to "try out" for more senior positions.

[172]No. In a competitive market, the grocer is richer by the amount of the slotting fees, but just like the first theater owner to discover the matinee market (chapter 5), excess profits are dissipated in the long run. Competitive pressures mean that the store's overhead charges to customers will fall by the amount of the slotting fees. Consumers pay a little more for the product to pay the slotting fee (now part of the cost structure of the producer) but pay lower overhead costs. Consumers are no worse off than before, but they are ensured that shelf space is stocked with the goods that they want.

barrier to entry for a new product. This policy says that every producer of every good has a right to shelf space in the grocery market! In other words, the property rights to shelf space do not belong to the grocer. This creates a common resource problem. If no one owns the shelf space, then how is shelf space allocated? First come first served? Do individual producers simply enter the store and move other goods off the shelf to replace them with their own?

One solution might be for the grocer to double or triple the size of the store and stock all merchandise that any producer wants to stock. In this case, shoppers have to spend twice or three times as long roaming half mile-long aisles trying to find the products they want. Any of these solutions imply large inefficiencies.

Considering the alternative, the idea that grocers own the property rights to their own shelves seems pretty attractive. Presumably, the grocer wants products on its shelves that its customers want and does not want to clutter the store with items that do not sell. The slotting allowance bonds quality. Only producers that are confident that their products will be attractive to consumers put their products on the shelf. Customers have the benefit of a more efficient shopping trip. The size of the grocery store is no larger than necessary to satisfy the customers.

VOCABULARY REVIEW

The slotting fee *bonds* quality. The fee *sorts* on the basis of products' attractiveness to store customers. Producers who have products that promise lots of sales *self-select* as candidates for shelf space. All others select themselves out of the queue for space. This solution is *efficient* because it ensures that the consumers get the products they most want and still economize on their shopping time, which carries an *opportunity cost*. Put differently, by *assigning property rights* to shelf space, the store prevents the creation of a *common resource problem*, with all the attendant *waste* generated by that solution.

B. PREPARING FOR A JOB INTERVIEW

Another good example of sorting is the interview process conducted by law firms for entry-level talent. Some law school graduates may be tempted to take fifty interviews. If each takes only two to three hours, then it might be economical to spend a couple hundred hours taking a quick look at a bunch of firms. But interviewing from the perspective of firms is costly. A law firm does not want to devote its valuable resources interviewing hundreds of students who are only marginally interested in employment in their firm. It prefers to spend more time with fewer students who are seriously interested in employment and think that they have a good chance of attracting an offer from the firm.

How does Jones and Dye figure out which prospects are both interested in and capable of filling its job openings? Presumably, all applicants show up in dark suits and show some evidence of recent grooming. This "presentation look" sends a signal that the applicant is a serious person, but unless it takes lots of time to acquire the "look," it is not a bond. If it does not cost much to present oneself, then the applicant does not lose much by dressing up for the interview. Jones and Dye wants applicants to bond their interest in the firm.

One time-honored way is for the firm to ask some probing questions designed to see how much the student knows about the firm. Most large firms have literature describing their operations, policies, compensation packages, and so on. Most have Internet sites that articulate information including major cases, business ventures that are on the horizon, and so on. Suppose that it takes fifty hours to assimilate this information, at least to the point of carrying on a conversation with someone from the firm. What signal does it send to Jones and Dye that the student arrives ready and prepared for the interview?

By engaging in the preparation, the student conveys the idea that she must be interested in employment with Jones and Dye; otherwise she wasted fifty hours of preparation. In this sense, *interview preparation bonds an applicant's interest in the job.* By making it known that no one makes it past the first interview without evincing extensive knowledge of the firm, Jones and Dye forces applicants to self-select on the basis of their interest in the firm. Only applicants seriously interested in the job end up on Jones and Dye's interview list; the others self-select out of the queue.

Suppose that other large law firms insist on similar preparation. Then the solution has the nice characteristic that fewer students interview with each firm. The interviews that occur are more likely between students and law firms that are seriously interested in each other. Fewer interview hours are wasted in the process.

ANOTHER VOCABULARY REVIEW

Showing up for an interview in a dark suit sends a positive *signal*. If the applicant shows up in a dark suit *and* makes it apparent that he has read extensively about the company prior to the interview, he *bonds* his interest in the firm. By making it known that applicants make it into a partner's office only if they bond their declarations of interest, the law firm sets up a *sort* that forces applicants to *self-select* on the basis of their interest and likely chances of hire in the firm.

A SPECIAL BOND

A student who performs well in lots of quantitative courses in law school bonds her interests and ability to deal with clients involved in business transactions, and to deal in complex contractual and tort matters. If she is not interested in these aspects of the law, then she has wasted lots of time taking courses that are of no relevance to her future career.

Chapter 11

Moral Hazard
and Agency Problems
When Mispricing Affects Behavior

Main Economic Concepts	1. Sometimes when the cost of obtaining information is high, mispricing occurs. In chapter 9 we learned that this can result in selection effects, notably a lemons market or adverse selection, depending on whether asymmetric information favored the seller or buyer.
	2. Mispricing also encourages an inefficient use of resources for any given individual; that is, it affects behavior. Moral hazard arises when the price of some resource has been set below its marginal cost of production, encouraging too much use. This hazard normally arises in an implied or explicit contractual relation between a buyer and seller, as for example between insurer and insured, or car rental company and customer.
	3. Moral hazard increases the cost of some contracts, but the potential for mischief owing to the hazard is not unlimited. The market can take steps to diminish its importance. One self-correcting mechanism is the concept of reputation. Market participants who act *as though* the price they pay is equal to the social cost of their actions can gain a reputation for honesty, consideration, and trustworthiness, traits that are valued in the market.
	4. When a principal hires an agent and information is costly, the compensation mechanism may encourage the agent to act in ways that are misaligned with the interests of the principal. The relation can be formal as between employer and employee, or more tenuous as between stockbroker and investor or lawyer and client. This divergence gives rise to agency costs. Often, these costs are attributable to moral hazard but normally are described as agency costs in the context of a contractual relation.

New Terms	1. Moral hazard
	2. Principal-agent problem
	3. Agency costs
	4. Reputation for avoiding moral hazard
	5. Precommitment
	6. Coinsurance

In the last chapter, I discussed sorting and selection issues at some length. I supposed that worker or product attributes were given, and that the problem for the market was to devise methods to identify either low or high quality. In this chapter, I turn to a discussion of "moral hazard." In general, the "hazard" arises in instances in which some product or service is underpriced. Price is set below the marginal cost of production, thereby encouraging too much use. The flip side is to view overuse as a kind of reckless behavior, which is why the problem sometimes is described as "too little care."

I start with a review of some terminology. Moral hazard, agency costs, and externalities are close cousins, and it is important to get the nomenclature straight. I then discuss some problems and solutions for moral hazard, followed by principal agency problems.

I. Nomenclature

Moral hazard is a term of art used often though not exclusively in the context of a buyer-seller relationship. Agency cost is used in the context of an employer-employee relationship—that is, between a principal and an agent. Finally, when mispricing affects parties *outside* an implied or explicit contract—that is, it affects "strangers"—then it falls under the category "externality." Thus, a moral hazard problem sometimes is described as agency costs or externality, depending on the context. All terms describe market situations in which some resource is mispriced, which in turn causes either "too much" or "too little" of some activity, compared to a perfect world characterized by zero transactions costs.

I addressed externalities and related materials in chapter 7. I also addressed the case where information in implied contracts is so poor as to give rise to an argument that the contract can be treated *as if* it were an externality, thereby creating an argument in the eyes of some for government intervention in private contracts. In the usual discussion of moral hazard and principal-agent problems in a contractual context, a role for government intervention does not typically arise.

KEEPING THE NOMENCLATURE STRAIGHT

Moral hazard, agency costs, and externalities all are close cousins in the sense that they involve altered behavior of some party caused by the mispricing of a resource.

Moral hazard and agency costs both arise in an implied or explicit contractual context when information is costly and often asymmetric. Externalities arise outside a contractual context—that is, when "strangers" are affected by the behavior of others. Sometimes, externality problems are rooted in information problems but often also reflect poor assignment of property rights.

Moral hazard is the term of art used when behavior is altered when mispricing arises in a buyer-seller contract. For example, if a car rental company sets a daily rate that does not change over a wide range of driving behavior, renters likely use too little care because they face a zero cost of driving in a way that lessens the useful life of the car.

Agency costs or principal-agent problems are terms of art applied when behavior problems from mispricing arise in the context of an employment context, either in a formal contract between firm and employee or in a quasi-employment context, as between a stockbroker and client. Sometimes, agency costs include a moral hazard but often are swept under the rubric of agency cost in this context.

Externalities often reflect a moral hazard but where the affected party is a stranger to the transaction. If the price of noise to airlines is zero, then they make too much of it. Externalities involve tort law and thus are best kept in a separate category (and are discussed in chapter 7).

Level of care is a reference to the flip side of moral hazard. If a person is using "too much" of some resource, it can be said that he is acting recklessly or using "too little care."

II. Moral Hazard

Rational producers do not deliberately set the price of some resource too low. But when transactions costs are high, it might be more efficient overall to set a price lower than the social marginal cost of producing it. When this occurs, a "moral hazard" arises, meaning that individuals use "too much" of some resource, or equivalently, engage in "too little care."

A. A SIMPLE WATER METER EXAMPLE

Suppose that some locality does not have water meters at every house owing to the cost of installation and the recurring costs of reading the meter each period. Instead, it uses a one-price policy for water use, like x dollars per month. In this case, each household acts *as if* each gallon of water is "free," even though the cost of purification and pumping is positive. Each household has an incentive to use water to the point where the marginal benefit is zero, instead of where the marginal benefit of its use equals the marginal cost of its production. The overuse of water is referred to as moral hazard.

B. THE MORAL HAZARD OF INSURANCE

Moral hazard is a fixture in the insurance industry. Consider a simple house fire insurance policy. Assume for simplicity that if a fire occurs and is not discovered quickly, the entire house and contents are ruined, but no one is hurt. There is no chance of fire spreading to a neighbor's house. The owner needs to rent a house while his house is being rebuilt and also needs to replace its contents. Suppose that H denotes the total cost of the fire.

1. Care without Insurance

A homeowner can take several steps to reduce the chances of a fire in her home. She can install lightning rods and smoke alarms, refrain from smoking in the house, ask guests to refrain from smoking, update and inspect the electrical system periodically, and so on. Conditional on C_i units of care, the probability of a house fire is p_i. Assume that there are lots of small steps that the owner can take to reduce the chances of a fire; call these steps "units of care."

Suppose that at zero units of care, the probability of a house fire is p_1. If the owner engages in the first unit of care, then the probability of a house fire falls by the amount $p_1 - p_0$. Since damage from fire is H, then the marginal benefit of this unit of care is $(p_1 - p_0)H$. As further care units are expended, the marginal effect on the probability of fire falls. I assume that if the owner engages in the last unit of care, the probability of fire is zero. Figure 11-1 shows the marginal benefits of care units as a downsloping function.

It is not costless for the homeowner to engage in care. Fire extinguishers and electrician services are costly, and so is the implied cost of the inconvenience of smoking outdoors, remaining awake until all the embers die out in the fireplace, and so on.[173] Some of these costs may be

---

[173]This is an application of the compensation principle. How much would a smoker pay in order to have the freedom to smoke indoors instead of retreating outside for each smoke? The answer to this question is the cost of smoking outdoors.

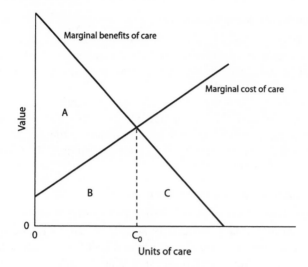

Figure 11-1. Level of Care with Fire Insurance

small, like refraining from using candles or the fireplace unless someone is directly monitoring the flames. After these basic units of care are used, however, further steps like installing a sprinkler system are more costly. For simplicity, I draw figure 11-1 as though units of care are homogeneous, so that we do not have to worry about identifying the marginal benefit and cost of a particular step to take.[174]

Without insurance, the homeowner would engage in C_0 units of care, which is the point at which the marginal cost of more care equals the marginal benefit. Area B measures the cost of engaging in this care level. Areas $A + B$ measure the benefits in terms of reduced likelihood of fire. Area A measures the net surplus from this level of care. Note that the owner accepts the expected loss measured by area C because the cost of reducing the probability of fire to zero is not worth the cost of prevention on the margin.

2. Care with Insurance

Suppose that the homeowner purchases fire insurance. The demand arises from the homeowners' concern that a fire would eliminate a large portion of her wealth position. She is willing to pay some relatively small

---

[174]In reality, each step is distinct and identifiable. We would model these steps in the following way. Identify the marginal benefits and marginal costs of the ith step, say B_i and C_i; then calculate the net surplus, $S_i = B_i - C_i$. Then line up all the steps in order of the size of the surplus, and take all the steps for which $S_i > 0$.

premium in exchange for insuring against the possibility of a catastrophe. Assuming a competitive insurance market, the premium for this policy equals the expected cost of fire, denoted by area C, plus some assessment to cover the administrative cost of insurance. Suppose that the insurance is complete in the sense that upon a fire, the house is rebuilt exactly as it was before, with all its contents replaced in the exact condition they were prior to the fire (including family photographs and heirlooms, etc.). The homeowner is put up at a nearby house at zero cost while her own house is rebuilt. That is, the full amount of the loss, H, is covered. Will the homeowner engage in the same care level with the insurance as before?

Presumably, the answer is no because now a fire imposes no cost on the homeowner. Hence, each homeowner enjoys her fireplace, smokes indoors, uses candles, spends less on electrical systems, and so on. If the insurance is complete, the cost of a fire to each homeowner appears to be zero. Hence, why should a homeowner incur the cost of prevention when he or she does not receive any benefit? Put simply, the insurance creates a moral hazard.

The moral hazard of insurance: Insurance conveys value to consumers because it rids them of the worry of losing a significant portion of their wealth position to some event, like an automobile accident or house fire. But once the insurance is in place, insureds lose some incentive to exercise proper care, thereby increasing the likelihood of losses. Insureds act *as though* more risk is costless, even though it is not.

The insurance does not in fact change the marginal *social* benefits of care units in figure 11-1. It changes the *private* benefits. Homeowners act *as though* the benefits of care are zero. The socially optimal level of care still is C_0, but homeowners engage in zero units of care. This means that there are more house fires, with incremental expected losses equal to areas $A+B$, which must be reflected in a higher insurance premium. We save prevention costs denoted by area B. Hence, the cost imposed by

---

EXERCISE:

Question: Can you think how to alter this model if insurance did not cover all the losses of a fire? Suppose that the homeowner faced a cost equal to, say, one-third of the value of the house upon a fire. How does the model change? What level of care is undertaken? How does it change the cost of moral hazard?

Answer: The answer is given later in the chapter.

moral hazard is measured by area A. If homeowners attach a high value to insurance, then they still might purchase the insurance despite the extra costs, but the surplus from the insurance is lower than it would be if there were no moral hazard.

C. THE PROVERBIAL FREE LUNCH

Moral hazard arises in many settings besides insurance. Almost all professionals know the drill when restaurant checks are shared equally among colleagues who go to lunch together. For a reference point, we might want to think of two businesspeople, Ken and Jane. When they lunch together, each pays his or her check. Ken gets a hamburger; Jane has a salad. Each pays the full cost of his or her own food, and so both order more food until the marginal cost just equals the marginal benefits. So far, so good.

Now suppose that they notice that Jack and Jill are usually at the next table. Jack has two hamburgers every day, and Jill has the same thing as Jane. So one day, they figure, why not all four sit together to have lunch? Owing to the cost of separate checks and keeping everything straight, the restaurant has a one-check-per-table policy. The customers themselves can figure out who owes what. When just two sit at a table, this is pretty doable, but with four it gets to be a grind.

One day, Jack (the one who has two hamburgers) suggests splitting the bill four ways, thereby saving the time and aggravation of figuring out separate bills. They all agree. But now a moral hazard problem creeps in. Every food item on the menu that has a price P_i now carries a cost to each person ordering of $\frac{1}{4} P_i$. Thus, the lemon pie that costs $4 still costs $4 (there's no such thing as a free lunch), but each individual diner *perceives* the private cost to be $1. So Jack switches from hamburgers to cheeseburgers. Jane and Jill now have the Caesar salad. Dessert is more often ordered.

After the new system settles in, the cost of lunch is noticeably higher. Too much food is consumed because the private cost is less than the true marginal cost; the diners eat "too much" food. This is a moral hazard problem that arises from assessing a diner the *average* cost of lunch across four people instead of the *marginal* cost of each item he or she individually orders. (Notice that *average* cost pricing gets us into trouble every single time we encounter it.)

It should be apparent that the larger the lunch group sharing the check, the higher the per capita lunch bill; this is because the perceived cost of the ith item is P_i/n, where n is the number of diners. The higher n, the lower the apparent price of food, which increases the quantity of food ordered. For example, if ten people split the lemon pie, the private cost falls to 40¢.

The problem can escalate over time. Suppose that a common office lunch occurs every Friday. All the diners at the lunch split the bill evenly. Over time, you might notice that those attending the lunch skip breakfast on those mornings, so as not to be "taken for a ride" by bigger

---

FEDERAL FINANCING OF LOCAL PROJECTS

A common practice is for the federal government to finance 90 percent of state and municipal projects. Suppose that Californians assess the benefits of building another dam on the Colorado River, with another aqueduct to service Los Angeles, at $10 billion. Then they will favor the project as long as the benefits exceed the private costs they face. If the project costs $90 billion, they perceive a clear private gain from the project, even though it implies a waste of resources to the tune of $80 billion to society as a whole.

Not to be outdone, the citizens of Boston get the feds to pay most of the cost of the "Big Dig," communities along the Mississippi River use federal funds to build more levees, Wyoming obtains funds to build more highways that almost no one uses, and so on.

If each state and local community had to pay for these capital projects themselves, then only those projects that conferred benefits in excess of social costs would be built.

The moral hazard problem is distinct from adverse selection. When the same people change their behavior in response to the underpricing of some resource, it is *moral hazard*. When the mispricing affects the composition of consumers, it is *adverse selection*.

Because mispricing of resources causes both moral hazard and adverse selection, the problems often show up together or are not very far apart.

AN ALL-YOU-CAN-EAT BUFFET

Access to a buffet for a lump-sum price will cause most individuals to overeat because the marginal cost of each unit of food has been set to zero (the moral hazard problem). The existence of this buffet attracts big eaters (adverse selection problem). Gradually, the price increases until big eaters dominate (a corner solution). Even then, each big eater will eat even more than he or she would if the dinner paid the true marginal cost of the food (the moral hazard problem persists).

eaters at lunch. Over the even longer haul, however, an adverse selection effect evolves. Small eaters find an excuse not to attend lunch on Friday. More big eaters find themselves available for lunch. Even after adverse selection settles in, however, the moral hazard problem persists. Big eaters eat even more than usual because the private marginal cost of food is set too low.

D. LIMITS ON MORAL HAZARD

1. Coinsurance
Moral hazard does not imply an absence of control over the "overuse" problem. In insurance markets, insurers often impose a **coinsurance** feature. For example, in health insurance, the insured may be responsible for 10 percent of medical bills. To illustrate the importance of coinsurance, reconsider the house fire insurance illustration in figure 11-1. Suppose that the insurance covers *two-thirds* of all losses, meaning that the homeowner absorbs *one-third*. The coinsurance mostly takes the form of the inconvenience of living in a hotel suite or rented house during construction, the loss of family photographs and heirlooms, the loss of souvenirs when the children were growing up, uninsured items like cash, and so on. To model the coinsurance, I reproduce the problem in figure 11-2 but show one additional schedule that depicts the private benefits that accrue to the homeowner of engaging in more units of care.

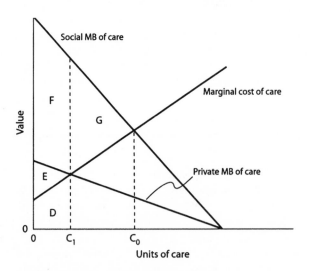

Figure 11-2. Level of Care with Coinsurance

Since the homeowner absorbs *one-third* of the cost, he perceives the marginal benefit of engaging in the ith unit of care not as the total benefit B_i but one-third of this amount, $\frac{1}{3} B_i$. The private benefit schedule is *one-third* of the height of each point along the marginal social benefit curve, representing the homeowner's share of the benefits of care. The vertical difference between the two downsloping schedules shows the benefits of care that accrue to the insurer. The latter benefits ultimately show up as reduced premiums for *all insureds*, and so each individual homeowner ignores these benefits in his calculation.

In this modification, it is now privately optimal for the homeowner to engage in C_1 units of care. The homeowner sets the marginal *private* benefit equal to the marginal cost of care. We still have too little care, but the solution reduces the cost of moral hazard. In particular, in exchange for preventive costs denoted by area D, the expected cost of fire falls by areas $D + E + F$, which will be reflected in the form of lower premiums in the same amount. The societal welfare gain is denoted by areas $E + F$, which equals the reduction in insurance premiums, minus the cost of prevention. The social cost of moral hazard is reduced to the amount denoted by area G.

2. *Pricing*
The insurance premium sometimes can be tailored to reflect different levels of risk exposure across the insureds. In this way, the insurer forces covered individuals to internalize the benefits of more care. For example, an insurer can set a higher price for a death or health policy for smokers compared to nonsmokers, a lower price for house insurance if the insureds have smoke detectors or burglary alarms, and a higher prices to drivers who collect numerous driving citations or who have had multiple accidents.

It is perhaps helpful to ponder situations in which differential risks are *not* priced. These examples come almost exclusively from insurance offered by the federal government. For example, houses covered by federal flood insurance typically are those found in areas *prone* to flooding, namely, floodplains, riverbanks, the seaside, and so forth. Private insurers are willing to write these policies only at premiums that reflect the expected value of losses. If homeowners had to face these market prices, they would face the *full cost* of living in proximity to water. As a result, population density in these areas would fall.

The federal government, however, offers flood insurance at prices that are less than the expected losses. By subsidizing the insurance, the government encourages moral hazard. Homeowners gain the benefits of having homes at water's edge or farmlands in fertile floodplains, but taxpayers absorb the flood costs. Homeowners continue to build and maintain homes and farms prone to flooding, even though the social benefits are likely exceeded by social costs. Private homeowners act in this way because the government suppresses the pricing that would force homeowners to internalize the full costs of their decisions.

Similarly, it is commonly expected that the federal government will absorb a large portion of damages that result when a catastrophic earthquake hits San Francisco. San Francisco is a pretty city with lots of nice views from the various hills. It is easy to see the benefits that citizens attach to living there. But would they make this decision if they had to face the *full costs* of living on a known fault line? Currently, the city's residents enjoy the benefits of their location decision, but U.S. taxpayers as a whole absorb the costs in the form of an implied bailout if a disaster occurs. A moral hazard is introduced: too many people build too many buildings on fault lines.

Without the promise of federal subsidies, density along the fault line would diminish, and homes would be built so as to reduce the damage of the quake. But since taxpayers as a whole will absorb most of the cost when the quake occurs, the incentives to reduce exposure to earthquake risks are diminished. As a result, the expected losses from earthquakes will dramatically exceed damage that would occur if the city's residents had to absorb the full costs of their decision to live on a fault line.

3. Reputation Value

A more subtle control over moral hazard is reputation value. Consider a person that can restrain herself from succumbing to the temptation of overusing a resource even if the cost is set to zero. We might think of this person as conscientious or considerate. In either case, she is a person that is considered trustworthy because others can depend on her to engage in an efficient level of care even if the cost of detection is close to zero.

For example, suppose that Jane will not exceed the speed limit of sixty-five miles per hour even if there is no chance of detection because she does not want to cause harm to others, even if her insurance would exonerate her from financial responsibility. Upon evincing this kind of behavior over a period of time, Jane accumulates a reputation for honesty. As we saw with Frank and Uncle Dick in chapter 1, trustworthiness has an asset value. Market participants find more value in engaging in transactions with Jane as compared with Uncle Dick.

In a long-run sense, the moral hazard problem in many situations may be diminished owing to the reputation value gained by agents who act *as though* the price equals social cost. Consider the example of sick leave in chapter 10. The firm sets the apparent price of taking a day off on a whim to zero. Workers who take advantage of the situation accumulate a reputation for unreliability or untrustworthiness. Those who act *as though* they recognize the social cost of taking time off (whether the cost is absorbed by themselves or someone else, namely their employer) gain positive asset value. In this case, the rewards accumulate over time in the form of promotions for workers who have substantial reputation value.

Jane employed a moral hazard "trap" to sort for a beau (chapter 10). She provided two suitors, Dave and Bing, with "free meals" that included "free desserts." In this case, Jane wants information about underlying susceptibility to eating high-calorie desserts, and so she does not want her suitors to be influenced by a positive cost of the dessert. In the face of zero marginal cost, Dave has three desserts while Bing has none. It is interesting to add at this point that perhaps Jane could continue the test by letting her beau buy a meal.

After her initial experiment, Jane knows that Dave has a serious sweet tooth, but she also knows that he is willing to stick her with a three-dessert tab when she offers to pay at an expensive restaurant. She receives two bad signals from him. But she does not yet have full information about Bing. It could be, for example, that he has a sweet tooth but is mindful of the cost he imposes on Jane if he opts for an expensive dessert.

This possibility also sends a positive signal to Jane because it suggests a quality of consideration and trustworthiness. But if Jane is committed to her preference for "thinness for life," then she should also observe whether Bing orders dessert when he is paying the bill. If Bing is trustworthy and considerate but has a wicked sweet tooth, he might buy dessert on his own dime. If so, he may have to find another marriage prospect because Jane is looking for someone who is trustworthy, considerate, *and* not plagued with a sweet tooth.

Reputation value as a constraint on moral hazard. Market participants that repeatedly engage in socially optimal behavior even in the face of moral hazard gain a reputation for trustworthiness.

In a way, this idea is an application of quality assurance premiums in chapter 9. By resisting the temptation of moral hazard (akin to offering high-quality service) even when "everyone else" is engaging in the hazard (akin to low-quality service), the "high-road" types create a reputation for trustworthiness, which is an asset because it permits its holder to receive a premium relative to her less trustworthy colleague.

4. Tie-ins

Tie-in sales also can play a role in reducing moral hazard. For example, when purchasing a new car under warranty, it is easy to see that some motorists may have some temptation to drive with less care than otherwise, knowing that most problems that might arise will be paid for by the warranty. One way to reduce this problem is to simply package the cost of all servicing in the price of the new car. Hence, when you buy a new car, you also must pay for the service cost for the next few years (it is part of the quoted price on the car). Why? One reason is that the auto company knows that if faced with a zero marginal cost of service, customers are more likely to bring the car in at regular intervals. To the extent that car problems arise because of inadequate servicing, many problems that might arise will be forestalled, thereby reducing warranty costs.

Service tie-ins are common in industrial machinery. When machines costing tens of millions of dollars are installed, it is common for the price to include on-site supervision of the use of the machine for some significant period. In addition to providing advice and training, the manufacturer wants to ensure that the customer is properly using the machine and giving it proper service. By bundling the service, the manufacturer expects lower warranty costs. In addition, the tie-in helps the manufacturer maintain its reputation for quality because it diminishes the chances that customers' complaints might be made publicly about a machine malfunction that might be the fault of the customer, not the manufacturer.

E. MORAL HAZARD IS NOT NECESSARILY A "SHOWSTOPPER"

The presence of moral hazard and its cousin, adverse selection, does not doom a market. Markets with these problems can exist, albeit with some imperfections. For example, the restaurant owner that operates the all-you-can-eat buffet presumably knows that his policy leads to adverse selection and moral hazard. But the one-price policy reduces the costs of service and billing substantially, so that his big-eater customers end up with more consumer surplus. Otherwise, the buffet would not survive.

The moral hazard problem often is controllable. The existence of moral hazard means that the market outcome differs from one that would exist in a perfect world. But in a world of imperfect information and significant transactions costs, it is often optimal for some moral hazard to persist. Participants may still earn substantially more surplus by controlling moral hazard than they could by trying to eliminate it.

The fact that a buffet for small eaters is not sustainable (owing to adverse selection) does not mean that the market cannot work for big eaters.

Similarly, most insurance policies carry some risk of moral hazard. For some lines of insurance, the problem is small. For example, few insureds will cut off an arm or otherwise maim themselves to collect on a policy that pays for a lost appendage, lost sight, and so on. Business insurance, on the other hand, is more expensive owing to moral hazard. If a firm is insured for its profits in the event of a business downturn, it will not expend as many resources to ensure continued success. This is why bankruptcy insurance for firms, though occasionally tried, has failed. The benefits of the insurance are swamped by moral hazard.

It is important to realize that the "market works" phrase conveys the idea that the market has attained the best possible solution, meaning that the highest amount of surplus is realized, *given all the costs of operating the market*. In reality, information is not free, and so the cost of obtaining information (like reading meters in the water use problem, keeping track of homeowners' use of their fireplaces in the case of fire insurance, etc.) needs to be incorporated into the market. An efficient solution does not refer to the perfect-world solution but rather to the allocation of resources that produces the highest amount of surplus, given all the costs of producing and delivering a good or service.

The *"market works"* does not mean that the market is perfect in the sense of conferring the maximum surplus obtainable in a world with full information and zero transactions cost. It means that the market has found the optimum solution, given all the costs of operating the market inclusive of the costs of obtaining information. When information is costly, it may be optimal to have some moral hazard and some adverse selection. Sometimes, the market will not survive these problems, meaning that given current technology, it is not optimal for these markets to exist.

AN EXAMPLE FROM BORDERS BOOKS

Historically, bookstores seemed to be wary of moral hazard problems. Reading books in the store was not allowed, attendants would fetch books for you, and food was not allowed in the store. For many buyers it was kind of a stuffy, off-putting experience.

Borders introduced a novel idea that seems to invite moral hazard. It created big stores with lots of tables and chairs, opened coffee shops

continued . . .

An Example from Borders Books *Continued*

inside the store, and encouraged patrons to read materials without first buying them. There is no direct supervision of the customers, so the customers are not discouraged from tearing the plastic wrapper off a new book to peruse it.

One would think that a serious moral hazard problem would arise. That is, since Borders sets a zero cost to customers who settle in and use their space, one could imagine customers responding with the queries: Why ever *buy* a book? Why not read it there and save the dime? Similarly, who cares if you spill coffee on the new book? It's not yours, so the heck with it. Pull the wrapper off the book and then not buy it? So what?

In reality, *despite the moral hazard*, Borders found the net result to be profitable. By encouraging lingering, the store creates the feeling for all customers that it is OK to hang around and look at books, to peruse them, and to have coffee over them. In the end, the store generates more customer sales per square foot than the stodgy competitors (allowing it to allocate its overhead over more customers). It turns out that lingering customers end up buying more books.

III. Precommitment as a Solution to Ex Post Moral Hazard: The Case of Health Insurance

Sometimes, moral hazard is handled with a precommitment contract. A good example is health insurance. Once the insurance is in place, each insured faces a zero price of using services (or a near-zero price in the event of modest coinsurance clauses). This means that even though all insureds up front might want to limit care, each individual insured, once afflicted with a serious health problem, knows that he will want to invoke every conceivable medical procedure that confers any benefits, regardless of costs.

A. THE MORAL HAZARD PROBLEM

Consider a stylistic example, which highlights the underlying economic decisions of patients and doctors. Suppose for simplicity that all employees in Firm X have the same preferences for medical care. Ex ante, all workers are equally likely to be afflicted with a serious disease and are willing to spend the same amounts to insure against medical expenses. Suppose that the odds are such that 100 out of 10,000 employees will be diagnosed with a life-threatening illness during the insurance period.

Technology makes available many different procedures to combat the illness. In table 11-1, I list five hypothetical procedures. Each is performed sequentially; thus, if procedure 1 fails, procedure 2 is tried, and so on. Procedure 1 is applied to all 100 workers diagnosed with the malady (column 3); the cost per treatment is $10,000 (column 4), resulting in a total cost of $1 million (column 5). This procedure saves 5 lives (column 2), which translates to a cost of $200,000 per life saved (column 6). *Notice that the process of deciding on willingness to pay for higher probabilities of living yields information about the value of life.*

The second procedure, which costs $20,000, is tried on the 95 workers who do not respond to the first treatment and is expected to save 4 additional lives, implying a cost of $475,000 per life saved, so on.[175] Finally, procedure 5, which we might think as highly experimental, costs $50,000 and saves 1 life out of 86 applications, implying a cost of $4.3 million per life saved.

Ex ante, workers must decide whether they want a policy that covers one, two, three, four, or five procedures. This decision depends on a comparison of expected medical outcomes and the implied premiums for each policy.

To determine premiums, cumulate the cost of sequential treatments (which I show in column 7) and divide by 10,000 participants in the plan (column 8). If workers as a group decide that they want "best care" (save the 15 lives that technology makes possible), then the premium per participant is $1,345. If they decide on a policy that covers the three most cost-effective procedures, which saves 12 lives, they pay a

TABLE 11-1. EFFICACY OF MEDICAL PROCEDURES TO CURE A LIFE-THREATENING MALADY

Sequential Procedure (1)	Lives Saved (2)	Eligible for Procedure (3)	Cost of Procedure (4)	Total Cost (cols. 3 × 4) (5)	Cost per Life Saved (cols. 2 × 5) (6)	Cumulative Costs (7)	Cumulative Costs (7)/10,000 (8)
1	5	100	$10,000	$1.0M	$0.2M	$1.0	$100
2	4	95	$20,000	$1.9M	$0.475M	$2.9M	$290
3	3	91	$30,000	$2.73M	$0.910M	$5.63M	$563
4	2	88	$40,000	$3.52M	$1.76M	$9.15M	$915
5	1	86	$50,000	$4.3M	$4.3M	$13.45	$1,345

Note: The example assumes 10,000 insureds with a 1 percent chance of having the malady.

[175]That is, applying a $20,000 procedure to 95 patients costs $1.9 million. Since 4 patients are saved, then the cost per life saved is $475,000.

premium of $563. Assume that every worker decides that the latter policy represents the optimal trade-off between costs and benefits.

In making this decision, workers implicitly decide to limit the amount they spend to reduce the probability of dying from some malady. Indeed, they reveal that collectively, they are willing to pay $910,000 per life saved (column 6) but not $1.76 million, which is the cost of the next highest option.

B. CONSUMER SURPLUS

Demand for health care. To show the solution in terms of a conventional measure of consumer surplus, I convert the information in the table to portray the demand and supply prices of additional units of care. The price that workers are willing to pay for the *j*th procedure, P_j^d, equals the number of lives saved by the procedure, S_j, times the implied value attached to each life saved by these workers, V. To express this premium on a per-participant basis, I divide by the number of workers, N, covered by the insurance.

$$p_j^d = \frac{1}{N} S_j V$$

We know that N is 10,000, and S_j is given in column 2 in table 11-1. For illustration, I assume that the value of life, V, is exactly $910,000.[176]

Supply of health care. The supply price of each procedure, P_j^S, equals the cost of the procedure C_j, (column 4) times the number of afflicted workers not yet cured, A_j (column 3 in the table), divided by the number of workers, N:

$$P_j^S = \frac{1}{N} C_j A_j$$

Optimum care. Figure 11-3 depicts these schedules. In reality, many incremental units of medical care could be undertaken, not just five discrete procedures. Hence, I can portray these schedules as continuous. Consumers in my example opt for care level $Q_{optimal}$, where the marginal

[176]Because I have a "lumpy" example, with only five procedures, I only know that workers are willing to pay at least $910,000 per life saved but less than $1.76 million per life saved. If I included many more units of medical care, I could derive a closer estimate of the true value of V.

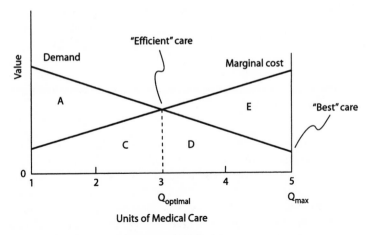

Figure 11-3. Demand and Supply of Medical Care

benefit attached to health care equals marginal cost. The cost of providing this level of care is denoted by area C.

While further units of care from $Q_{optimal}$ to Q_{max} confer benefits (as measured by area D), the cost of incremental care (as measured by areas D plus E) exceeds these benefits, and so consumers opt for an intermediate care level. This outcome $Q_{optimal}$ maximizes their consumer surplus from care (equal to area A), even though it does not provide the maximum care available given existing technology. Consumers have decided that their marginal dollars are better used elsewhere.

Ex post reneging. If insureds cannot contract for limited care, it is difficult to imagine that they will in fact receive care level $Q_{optimal}$. The existence of the third-party payer means that insureds, *once they become patients*, have an incentive to demand all care that confers positive benefits. Neither the doctor nor the hospital has an incentive to deprive the patient of higher levels of care. The patient faces a near-zero price of further care; the physician and other caregivers earn more fees by providing more care.

Without some contractual mechanism to prevent it, "best-care drift" will ensure that the result is Q_{max} level of care. This means that the cost of care increases from an amount denoted by area C to one denoted by the sum of areas $C + D + E$. In effect, though insureds agree up front to a limited policy, they can only credibly contract for best care because it is predictable that they will renege on the contract ex post once they become patients.

> A health insurance contract, even if it calls for limited care, is plagued with the problem of ex post reneging; that is, the tendency of insureds to demand higher care than they paid for, once they segue from insured to patient status. Without a control, best-care drift dominates health care, which increases premiums in amounts that are undesirable to insureds.

Put in a slightly different way, physicians and other caregivers are acting as the patients' agents in the function of providing health care. In this dimension, their interests are more or less aligned with the patients' interests. But in being vigilant agents for their patients in their role as caregivers, they are not performing a very good job of acting in the financial interests of the insureds. The challenge in obtaining an efficient solution is to find a way for caregivers to replicate the combination of price and service desired by the insureds.

C. CONTRACTING FOR EFFICIENT CARE

The tendency for units of health care to drift toward Q_{max} creates the market for managed care, notably health maintenance organizations (HMOs). An HMO vertically integrates the insurance and health functions. In this way, the HMO eliminates the agency problem that exists when physicians and caregivers act so as to ignore the financial implications of their actions on premiums for the insureds. By vertically integrating, the HMO can credibly offer a contract that generates maximum surplus to insureds.

In effect, the HMO contractually agrees to deliver $Q_{optimal}$ units of medical care. They resist delivering Q_{max} units, even though each individual insured knows that upon incurring a malady, he has an incentive to obtain a higher level of care. In this sense, it is rational and predictable that some insureds that become sick will be "dissatisfied" in an ex post sense, even though they opt for lower coverage ex ante.

There is a commitment problem, however, with this solution. Once they are afflicted, it is predictable that patients will try to force managed care companies to provide Q_{max} units. If juries are sympathetic to plaintiffs whose family member died but *might* have been saved with procedures 4 and 5 in table 11-1, then managed care contracts might be difficult to enforce.

In the case of insurance, a 1974 law, the Employee Retirement Income Security Act (ERISA), provides the necessary element to create a credible precommitment. ERISA specifically precludes patients from bringing suit under state tort laws against health plans offered by their employers. Upon a "denial of care" claim, patients or their families can sue the managed care company only under ERISA in federal court, and then only for the amount of money they expended on some procedure that is in dispute. Thus, if the court finds that the plan provided for procedure 4 in table 11-1 but delivered only procedures 1 through 3, then the court can order the plan to reimburse the participant or his heirs for the fourth procedure, if they opted for this treatment. There are no provisions for damages beyond this amount.[177]

ERISA creates the possibility for insureds to sign credible precommitment contracts with HMOs. In signing these documents, the insureds' agent (their employer) precommits to specified limits on care. The commitment is bonded by their forfeiture of the right to sue in state courts for denial of care.

Patients' rights bills give more freedom for patients to demand more units of care but create less freedom for insureds to opt for levels of care that maximize the surplus from insurance.

D. WHAT HAPPENS IF THE ERISA PREEMPTION IS ELIMINATED

It is useful to imagine the repercussions of eliminating ERISA protection against HMOs for denial of care. In this case, juries make decisions about level of care that is appropriate in a given medical situation. If juries are perfect agents for insureds, then presumably they will read the contractual language as the insureds did ex ante and enforce $Q_{optimal}$ level of care. If, however, juries are perfect agents for "harmed" patients or their heirs, then we can expect that care levels will drift toward best care. Suppose that juries are better agents of patients than insureds, so that they have a tendency to impose financial harm on caregivers that use care levels lower than harmed patients feel is appropriate, in an ex post sense.

Figure 11-4 depicts this outcome. This figure is the same as figure 11-3, albeit with a different scale. It has one additional schedule, appropriate labeled, that represents the expected judgment from engaging in various levels of care. I presume that if best care is offered, juries set damages to zero, since the caregivers used all available procedures to try to save the patient; hence, the schedule is zero at Q_{max} level of care. At lower levels of care (reading right to left in the figure), the expected judgment becomes ever higher as juries become progressively perturbed that HMOs use care levels progressively further away from best care.

---

[177]ERISA permits participants to sue particular caregivers like a surgeon if the issue is not denial of care but improper execution of a plan procedure. These suits follow ordinary malpractice law.

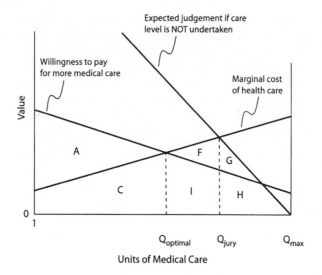

Figure 11-4. Social Cost of Excessive Judgments

In this case, rational caregivers set the level of care to Q_{jury}. Over the range of care, Q_{jury} and $Q_{optimal}$, caregivers are induced to provide more medical care because it is cheaper than the expected judgments that result from less care. Beyond Q_{jury}, the marginal cost of further care exceeds the expected judgments from denying best care, and so it pays to stop short of providing best care. The area denoted by areas $I + F$ is referred to as the cost of "defensive medicine" because it is driven not by the contractually efficient result but rather by the fear of adverse judgments. In this solution, juries have encouraged caregivers to incur a waste in the amount denoted by area F in figure 11-4.

Additionally, caregivers expect to incur adverse judgments. That is, as long as they stop short of offering best care, they expect to be sued successfully. Areas $G + H$ in the figure measure the dollar value of these judgments. Thus, the total cost of allowing juries to serve as agents for

---

True or false: The cost of excess litigation awards is measured by the cost of malpractice insurance.

False. The cost is measured by the sum of malpractice insurance *plus* the cost of defensive medicine.

A better measure of excess cost is the impact of litigation exposure on health care premium levels because these reflect both malpractice exposure and the cost of defensive medicine.

insureds is measured by the sum of defensive medicine plus medical malpractice awards. The premium increase implied by jury verdicts is measured by the sum of areas $F + G + H + I$.

IV. Agency Cost: A Close Cousin to Moral Hazard

A. WHAT ARE AGENCY COSTS?

Agency costs arise in an employment contract, either in a long-term employer and employee relationship or a shorter contractual relationship as in broker and investor or tort lawyer and plaintiff. When a principal hires an agent, owing to imperfect and asymmetric information, combined with a mispricing of some resource, the agent may be encouraged to pursue actions that are not in the best interests of the principal. In general, agency costs can take the form of moral hazard, but sometimes they show up in other ways. In any case, they are labeled **principal-agent problems**. As in moral hazard, in a world of costly information, the optimal level of agency costs usually is not zero, but can be contained by various schemes.

Agency costs refer to problems that arise when the financial interests of the person selling his services (the "agent") are not aligned with the interests of his employer (the "principal"). Often, the problem results in the agent engaging in too little care for the client.

Sometimes agency problems are attributable to mispricing a service or good, oftentimes because of poor information but sometimes because property rights are set up incorrectly.

B. EXAMPLES OF AGENCY COSTS

1. Employment Context

Common employment situations have lots of examples of agency problems. For example, consider the use of the office printer in any firm. If a manager is writing a memo at home using his own printer, printer ink, and paper stock, he might do more editing on the computer screen and conserve the printing costs by, say, printing three drafts during the day. In contrast, at work the private cost of printing ink and paper to him (though not to his employer) is zero, and so he might print six draft copies. The marginal cost of the additional three copies has some value to him, but the value is not as high as the cost of printing; otherwise, he would have printed six copies at home. The extra printing that he does at work constitutes a moral hazard.

In this context, the worker is the agent, and the employer is the principal. By setting the price of printing to zero, the principal has encouraged his agent to act in a manner that is at odds with the best interest of the principal. We might also refer to the waste encouraged by "free" printing as a moral hazard problem or simply sweep it under the rubric of agency cost. Either term might be used in this context.

Similarly, office staff is less careful about spilling coffee on the rug because the company pays for the cleanup. They never check the level of engine oil in the company car. Who cares if engine damage occurs? They use fifty new pens a year at work, whereas they might use six if they had to buy them. The company does not want its employees to waste paper and pens, but it is too costly to price out each pen to employees. The company accepts some inefficiency caused by underpricing supplies, in exchange for the overall benefits that come about from having the firm produce some product or service.

Indeed, some people explain the existence of firms or other organizations like universities using this kind of theory.[178] In principle, each student could fashion his or her own law education outside a law school context. Teachers could offer courses individually. Students could arrange to take a course by one person to teach contracts, another for civil procedure, and so on. While each teacher would waste fewer pens and paper, the transactions cost would be high. Each individual teacher would have to assemble a group of students, who in turn would have to organize a schedule. The coordination costs would be particularly daunting, since each student presumably would take classes at different locations from different teachers around town, and so on. In addition, some other person would have to act as a kind of quality-control evaluator. How does a B grade from Joe Smith offering contracts in the Bronx compare to a B grade from Jane Doe offering torts in Jersey?

Presumably, by having a "law school" gather able faculty and students, conduct an orderly set of courses, and retain a rigid grading system, the product of a "legal education" is provided at a lower cost. In short, a "law school" exists because it reduces the transactions costs of attaining a legal education.[179] Consistent with this purpose, the law school eliminates transactions costs that swamp the benefits of controlling moral hazard (like pricing out pens and paper). In this context, the agency problems that arise between the law school and its employees may be small in comparison with the overall gain of a law school versus a freelance method of education.

---

[178]Ronald H. Coase, "The Nature of the Firm," *Economica* 4 (1937): 386–505.
[179]This is Coase's theory of the firm, ibid.

It is useful to recall, however, that *wherever a moral hazard exists, the opportunity to build reputation for trustworthiness also exists.* Office secretaries notice when Professor Smith fills the printer with his fourth ream in a day, that hundreds of unused pens are strewn around his office, that he puts personal mail in the "To be franked" mailbox, and so on. A reputation is created that assigns a low trustworthy coefficient to this person. Those who use due care in the face of moral hazard build reputation value.

Perhaps the most everyday kind of agency cost is the moral hazard incurred by providing office supplies at a zero price to employees. The cost of pricing out each box of paper clips and pencils would exceed the value of less waste, and thus, it is optimal to incur some moral hazard.

In this environment, individual employees have an opportunity to distinguish themselves by using office supplies *as though* they paid the full cost. In so doing, they build a reputation for honesty and trustworthiness in the firm, a desirable trait from the perspective of an employer looking for the best individuals to promote into more responsible jobs.

---

2. Stockbroker

Agency problems often arise in the context of brokerage services. A broker earns commissions each time he trades a stock for a customer. The customer would like to rid herself of a stock that her more-informed broker thinks might fall in value; otherwise, her interest is in maintaining her stock position because sales of stock often trigger capital gains taxes. If the broker were a perfect agent, in the sense of aligning his interests with hers, he would trade only when it was in his client's best interests. But since he earns commissions only when he trades, he has an incentive to trade her stocks "too much."

Part of the problem is attributable to poor information. If the client had all the information that the broker does about all opportunities to trade stocks profitably, then first, she may not need a broker's advice, and second, even if she used the broker to trade stock, she would make the decision when to trade. The other part of the problem is attributable to poor pricing.

By compensating the broker on the basis of trades, she creates an incentive for her agent to act contrary to her interests. The combination of poor information and mispricing causes an agency problem, which results in too much trading from the perspective of the principal. There may be no good solution. If she compensates her broker by a monthly flat fee, then since collecting information about good trades is costly, he now has an incentive to trade too little. Given the nature of asymmetric information, we seem to be stuck with an agency problem.

> Owners of stock (the principals) do not always understand the underlying factors that affect stock value, so they hire brokers (the agents) to advise them about what stocks to buy and sell. All else the same, the owner has a tax incentive to "buy and hold" stock but wants to sell a stock if conditions warrant it. The broker is paid on a commission basis each time he trades. Thus, his interests are not aligned with the owner. A likely outcome is for the broker to engage in "too much" trading.
>
> His fear of earning a reputation as a "churner" will temper the broker's inclination to trade "too much."
>
> Changing the fee structure to compensate a flat monthly fee gives the broker an incentive to trade too little because under this system, the broker maximizes profits by engaging in a "buy and hold" strategy for his clients, regardless of economic conditions that might warrant a sale.

3. Firm Ownership

A common venue of "agency costs" is in the corporate finance literature. Ownership of most large firms is widely dispersed across thousands of shareholders, most of whom own small amounts of stock.[180] This makes it difficult for stockholders as a group to ensure that the managers of the firm expend resources to maximize the stock value of the corporation. For example, managers might like to have private jets, fine antiques in their offices, company-paid memberships at golf courses, and so on. Since the stockholders essentially pick up the tab for all these expenses, managers may engage in some moral hazard.

The board of directors controls the managers, but the chief executive officer of the corporation often chooses members of the board. Thus, he picks his own monitors! It is easy to see at least the potential for managers to try to fool the stockholders into thinking that the jets and golf memberships are important, instead of trying to maximize the value of the firm. If the board was a perfect agent for stockholders, the problem would diminish. If managers themselves were perfect agents for stockholders, the problem would not exist.

---

[180]For a review article of agency problems in the finance literature, see D. Bruce Johnsen, "The Quasi-Rent Structure of Corporate Enterprise: A Transaction Cost Theory," 44 *Emory Law Journal* (1995): 1277–1356.

The crux of the problem is asymmetric information. The managers know more about the corporation and the optimal use of its resources than either the board or stockholders individually. The board often addresses this problem by giving stock options to high officers in the company. Thus, if the company stock performs well, managers are paid more. But this creates its own set of agency problems. Managers might then take steps that appear to make money in the short run, even though they know (but perhaps others do not yet know) that their actions might diminish profits in the long run. This is a particular problem, since most high officers achieve their position late in their career and retire within a few years of attaining the top jobs.

It is easy to imagine that a corrective force in this market will once again find its root in the notion of reputation. If the board is careful in approving top officers that have a long history of demonstrating restraint in the face of opportunities to waste money, the problem ought to diminish. If middle managers know that top officers will be chosen in part because of their reputation for making sound profit-making decisions over many years and consistently courting a reputation as careful spenders, then this selection criterion creates a climate that discourages wasteful behavior.

The separation of ownership and control of most major corporations represents an important potential source of agency problems. Managers know more about the opportunities in the firm than either stockholders or the board of directors, giving rise to the possibility of managers engaging in activities that overcompensate managers instead of maximizing firm value.

Boards often award stock options to provide an incentive for managers to care about maximizing profits, but paying too much compensation in this way might create another problem. That is, as long as executives have more information about their company than others, then they might be tempted to take actions that sacrifice larger long-run profits in exchange for short-run gains that boost profits now.

Presumably, the characteristics of managers selected for promotion in the firm, particularly those rising to the level of board oversight, will evince characteristics that suggest that they are more likely to be faithful agents of the stockholders.

---

4. A Royalty Problem

Consider another agency problem depicted in figure 11-5. An innovator holds a patent for a new product idea. The patent lasts for one period. He leases his idea to a manufacturer in exchange for an $8 royalty per unit

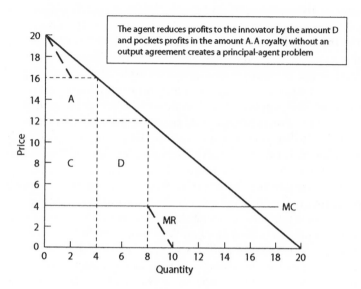

Figure 11-5. The Royalty Problem

sold. The marginal cost of production is $4. If the manufacturer were a perfect agent, he would set price to $12, sell 8 units. The manufacturer earns a competitive return, and the innovator collects $64 for his idea (areas $C + D$).

Instead, the manufacturer views the $8 as another marginal cost of production. Thus, his total marginal cost is $12. He sets this number equal to marginal revenue and thus sells 4 units at $16. In so doing, he reduces the innovator's profits by the amount D in the figure and appropriates the amount A. By setting a royalty fee without an output agreement, the innovator creates a principal-agent problem.

The innovator could solve the problem by vertically integrating into the production business, auctioning his idea to the highest bidder (in which case the winning bid should be close to $64), enforcing a minimum output restriction, or perhaps using a contract with a "best efforts" clause and relying on litigation later on if it looked like the manufacturer deliberately reduced output below the level that maximized the innovator's profits. In reality, if the idea is not that important compared to all the other things that the relevant manufacturers produce, the royalty may be the only practical solution, in which case the innovator lives with lower profits, and the market enjoys less surplus from the idea than it would otherwise.

V. Agency Costs and Rent Erosion: The Case of Tort Lawyers

A. THE REIMBURSEMENT SYSTEM

The relationship between tort lawyers and plaintiffs also gives rise to a classic agency problem but one that also is characterized by the possibility of rent erosion, which gives rise to a more interesting outcome. Specifically, consider the case of torts in which lawyers incur the costs of the suit and are compensated by one-third of any judgment they win for their client.

In a real-world model, it might be important to specify a full set of cost curves for the law firm and recognize the "discreteness" of care efforts that pose themselves to lawyers handling a case. To keep the problem simple, however, I assume that there are no fixed costs to running a law firm, though I will show later how they would alter the nature of the problem.

The lawyer must decide the quantity of legal services to devote to the case. I refer to these as units of care. For simplicity, I assume that "care" is a homogeneous measure of "things to do" to enhance the client's chances of winning a sizable judgment. More "care" could mean expending more time to enhance his chances of winning a case for a client or employing higher-quality legal personnel. In the latter case, the use of an hour of legal time in his firm might be worth 2 care units compared to some other firm that used less skilled lawyers. In this sense, we can think of care units as quality-adjusted units.

The uniqueness of the tort lawyer problem is that on the one hand, the one-third sharing formula encourages lawyers to engage in too little care for their client. But the requirement of zero excess profits will generate a competition among law firms for clients that works in the direction of providing too much care. The two problems superimposed can give a reasonable solution to the agency problem under some conditions.

B. THE PRINCIPAL-AGENT PROBLEM

I first consider the agency problem. Figure 11-6 depicts the model. The horizontal axis measures units of care used by the lawyer to win the case; the vertical axis measures value. The marginal benefits schedule labeled MB describes the change in expected judgment amount from one more unit of care. As more care is expended on the case, both the size of the judgment and the likelihood of winning increase, but at a diminishing rate, which explains the downward slope. The area under the curve is the summation of all the marginal benefits of further care; hence, for example, areas $C + A + E$ is the expected judgment from devoting C_1 units of care to the case.

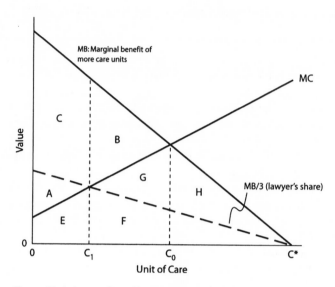

Figure 11-6. Agency Cost: Tort Lawyers and Clients

The lawyer receives one-third of any judgment, and so the dashed line labeled *MB/3* depicts his payoff schedule. It is one-third of the height of the schedule *MB*. Finally, the schedule *MC* reflects the marginal cost of further units of care, which is borne by the lawyer, not the client. I depict it as a rising schedule, but the outcome works just as well if marginal cost is flat. Thus, for example, the total cost of providing C_1 units of care is represented by area E.

If the client had all the legal knowledge to make decisions, she might finance the case herself. She would expend C_0 units of care. In this solution, she would expect a judgment represented by areas $C + A + E + B + G + F$, from which she would subtract expenses in the amount denoted by area $E + F + G$. Areas $A + B + C$ denote her surplus, which is the maximum attainable. But the client does not have sufficient information to know how many units of care to use on the case and cannot assess the likely benefits of these actions. Her lawyer acting as her agent is in a better position to make informed decisions about case strategy.

Notice, however, that an agency cost arises. From the lawyer's perspective, he maximizes the firm's profits by setting marginal cost equal *not* to his client's marginal benefits but rather to the law firm's marginal benefit schedule (that is, he sets the equality, $MC = MB/3$). Thus, his incentive is to expend C_1 units of care, where he incurs expenses E and expects revenues $A+E$. At this level of care, the *agent's surplus* is maximized (measured by area A). His client expects to earn a judgment, net of legal fees, measured by area C. The agency cost is measured by area B. This is the amount of surplus forgone by choosing too little care to win the case. The agency problem is attributable to the method of payment. Because the lawyer is compensated by some amount that is less than the marginal benefits of more care, he engages in "too little" care.

Tort lawyers receive one-third of judgments won by the plaintiff but finance all the legal expenses to bring the case. This pricing arrangement misaligns the client's best interest with her lawyer's interest. Tort lawyers engage in an effort level that falls short of the level that maximizes the expected net gain from the case for the client.

C. IMPLICATIONS OF RENT EROSION

The problem that arises in the previous solution is that the tort lawyer expects to earn excess profits measured by area A in figure 11-6. As we learned in chapter 3, excess profits attract entry. In the absence of fixed costs, law firms will compete for these cases in an attempt to gain this surplus. Area A is the prize of winning the rights to pursue the case. Put differently, no one owns the property rights to bring a promising case ex ante, and so resources must be expended to win these rights (as in a common resource problem). What form does this competition take?

One possibility is to imagine a solution characterized by pure waste: lawyers spend time hounding potential clients in an attempt to acquire more business. A more likely form of competition, however, is one in which law firms compete on the basis of expected awards for the client. That is, over time, firms that gain a reputation for more often winning large amounts for clients will improve their chances of attracting cases in the future. In my simple model, this competition takes the form of using more units of care.[181]

I show the outcome in figure 11-7. Competition drives units of care to a level that ensures zero profits, which corresponds to level C_2. At this level, area A equals area J, which denotes zero profits.[182] This

---

[181]If the competition takes the form of aggressive marketing of services instead of on the basis of improving the odds of winning cases, then the prize denoted by area A is eroded but units of care remain at C_1.

[182] For every unit of care to the left of C_1 the law firm obtains an expected revenue greater than marginal cost, but the opposite is true beyond C_1, units. To obtain a zero profits solution, expand care past C_1 until traingle J has the same area as traingle A.

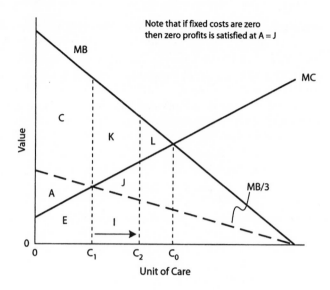

Note that if fixed costs are zero
then zero profits is satisfied at A = J

Figure 11-7. Agency Costs: Recognizing Rent Erosion

competition diminishes the principal agent problem (indeed under some circumstances, it could overcompensate for the problem by encouraging more than C_0 units of care).[183] Normally, we think of rent erosion as waste. In this case, however, assuming that tort awards are consistent with social efficiency, the imposition of a "wasteful" activity on top of a second source of inefficiency can improve welfare.

> Rent erosion works to diminish agency costs in the case of tort reimbursement and other shared payment schemes. The outcome illustrates how two sources of inefficiency can sometimes come together to provide a superior result.

If law firms have fixed costs then the prior solution is modified, but the nature of the problem remains. Assume that all potential cases have the same benefits and costs as those depicted in figure 11-7, each firm can bring one case per period, and fixed costs per period are F. Then we know from chapter 3 that C_1 units of care represent equilibrium output

---

[183]This outcome depends on the way in which the cost and benefit schedules are constructed.

if fixed costs F (not shown) equal excess revenues measured by area A in figure 11-7.

If fixed costs are lower ($F < A$), then rent erosion will take one of two forms: firms will compete on the basis of using more units of care, and so we will find a solution somewhere between C_1 and C_2; or firms will invest in more fixed costs on the idea that these expenditures will increase the benefit functions in the figure. Either way, the rent erosion will work to reduce the principal-agent problem.[184]

[184]If fixed costs are less than A, then either these cases will not be filed, or firms need to find a production function that has lower fixed costs, or they need more than a one-third sharing formula. In a more general model, cases have different payoffs. Those that promise too small a contribution to fixed cost will not be filed; competition will take the form of chasing after cases that are more lucrative. Thus, in a more general model, some cases are not filed, lucrative cases are filed, and rent erosion forces higher levels of care on the cases that are brought.

Game Theory and Related Issues

Strategic Thinking When Players Are Few and Information Is Poor

Main Economic Concepts	1. Game theory is an umbrella term that incorporates models that help players think about strategic choices when their actions affect the behavior of another player.
	2. Under certain conditions, it is often profitable to anticipate responses rather than to treat the world as indifferent to your actions.
	3. When striking deals with imperfect information about others' responses, it is useful for a player to sometimes put himself in his adversary's proverbial shoes.
New Terms	1. Dominant strategy
	2. Mixed strategy
	3. Tit-for-tat strategy
	4. First-mover advantage
	5. Coordination game
	6. Reaction function
	7. Cooperative game
	8. Noncooperative game
	9. Nash equilibrium
	10. Credible signal
	11. Reservation wage
	12. Maximin strategy
	13. "Vigorish"
	14. Cournot model
	15. Stackelberg model

Game theory is an area of study that broadly includes strategic behavior between two (or a few) actors. Usually, either party does not *know* what action the other party will take in the game but can sometimes predict his actions based on available information. In this sense, game theory is a tool to help make decisions under conditions of imperfect information. In almost all game theory models, one party makes a move, *taking into account the possible reactions of some other player*. If I engage in action *A*, what are my adversary's possible responses? If I engage in action *B*, what are his possible reactions? Thinking this process through can often help me figure out my best course of action. Often the "game" is played with two adversaries and poor information.

Game theory: A tool that allows players to improve their information by putting themselves in the other players' shoes and then choosing their optimal action. In this way, player *A* can take actions with more confidence about how player *B* will react. We also call this process *strategic planning*, conveying the idea of others' reactions to our choices.

Solutions to game theory modeling are highly dependent on assumptions, and so there seldom is a "right" answer except within the narrow confines of the assumptions of the model. The broad lesson to take away from this chapter is that, under certain conditions, it is often profitable to anticipate responses rather than to treat the world as indifferent to your actions.

I. The Dating Game: Basic Concepts in Game Theory

Game theory is used in many settings. The signaling and sorting models in earlier chapters are versions of game theory solutions. When a firm offers sick leave to set up a sort on workers inclined to engage in moral hazard (call in sick), one could think of this as a game. It sets up incentives that are attractive to unreliable workers but not to reliable workers. The sort is effective whether or not workers know the firm is playing a game. For example, if unreliability comes about because some workers have a high discount rate, then they might realize that the firm makes long-term promotion decisions based on current behavior in the "calling in sick game," but cannot resist the temptation of immediate paid leisure as compared to the long-term benefits of higher pay.

A. HOW THE GAME WORKS

The dating game is a good venue for illustrating game theory concepts. Shawn and Mary are in high school. They like each other but are too shy to explicitly reveal their interests. All high school students hang out either at the movies or bowling alley. Shawn attaches a value of one to seeing a movie and zero to bowling, whereas Mary attaches zero value to seeing a movie and one to bowling.

This problem has two choices, movies or bowling, and so it naturally fits into a neat two-by-two decision matrix. This kind of game is often referred to as the *normal form*, which first showed up as the prisoner's dilemma problem in chapter 5. In these problems, one player is arrayed

TABLE 12-1(A). MARY AND SHAWN DO NOT KNOW
EACH OTHER

	Mary			
Shawn	Movies		Bowling	
Movies	A: 1.0	0	B: 1.0	1.0
Bowling	C: 0	0	D: 0	1.0

Note: Numbers in the cells measure the dollar value of the
utility of movies or bowling.

along the side and the other on the top. The two choices define the two
columns and two rows. The payoffs from these choices are written in
each cell. The leftmost number pertains to the player along the side and
the second number to the player along the top. The payoffs assuming
that neither player attaches a value to being with the other, are shown in
table 12-1(*a*).

The *normal form* that the game takes is a simple decision box (often
a two-by-two). This form is used to illustrate a game in a simplified
way. In prisoner's dilemma, a 2 × 2 was natural because there were
only two discrete decisions. In the dating game, there are only two
places to choose. Decision boxes are *one way* to illustrate a game
theory solution, but often models are more complex than this.

In the decision boxes, the first number *always* refers to the party
along the side of the box; the second number always refers to the
party along the top.

In cells A and D, Shawn and Mary choose the same venue. In cells B
and C, they choose different venues. Since they do not know each other
yet, the only payoffs that appear reflect their intrinsic interests in going
to the movies or the bowling alley. Shawn prefers the movies regardless
of what Mary chooses. In either case, he prefers to go to the movies. He
has a **dominant strategy**. Similarly for Mary, she prefers to go bowling
regardless of Shawn's whereabouts. She also has a dominant strategy.
They end up in cell B.

A *dominant strategy* is an action that always is optimal for one
player no matter what the other player might do.

In playing a game, it is important to get the assumptions straight, as well as the rules of the game. The dating game is a **noncooperative game** because each player is making a decision independent of the other. In a **cooperative** game, Mary and Shawn would talk to each other and agree to go to the movies or bowling together.

A *cooperative game* is one in which both parties find a solution through an agreement, either implied or contractual. A cooperative solution often yields a payoff to both players that is higher than what noncooperative solutions would yield. Most of the games I consider are noncooperative solutions.

A *noncooperative game* is one in which the parties do not enter into formal agreement but rather make strategic moves based on their estimates of payoffs and rational decisions by the other player. In a noncooperative problem the players usually do not communicate with each other, but the problem can be modified to allow some signaling.

The dating game is characterized by *simultaneous* decisions. Shawn and Mary each make independent simultaneous decisions to go to the movies or bowling. In a *sequential* game Mary chooses where to go, and Shawn can use this information before deciding his move. We can play the dating game once or many times over several nights. In the latter case, it is a *repeated game*. Solutions in these games can sometimes differ from non-repetitive games because information unfolds from previous "plays."

Finally, we need to make an assumption about knowledge of the payoffs in the decision box. Often, a game assumes that players know each

---

Some Key Game Characteristics
Simultaneous or sequential decisions? Do both players make a decision at the same time or does one go first? In the latter case, the second mover has the information revealed from the first player's move.

One-time game or repeated game? If the game is played once, each player acts solely from knowledge of the payoff structure. If played many times, players can use information revealed in previous renditions.

Know the payoffs or not? Often, it is assumed that each player knows the other's payoff structure. The game, however, can be played with either imperfect knowledge or no knowledge of the other's payoffs. In the latter case, decisions are based on less information, but this problem can be attenuated if the games are repeated.

other's payoffs. But one can play a game in which each player knows only his own payoffs. The dating game always has simultaneous decisions. I assume initially that the game is played once and that both players know the payoffs, but I modify this assumption as we proceed.

Mary and Shawn like each other a little. Now assume that, independent of the values they attach to going to the movies or bowling, Mary and Shawn each value being with the other in an amount equal to .5. Think of this as the amount that each would pay in order to have the opportunity to be with each other (the compensation principle). The new payoffs are given in table 12-1(*b*).

The only difference in payoffs is that Shawn and Mary attach an extra .5 to being where the other is, which means that the payoffs in cells A and D all increase by .5.

Shawn goes through the following calculation. If Mary goes to the movies, then he is better off going to the movies (compare a 1.5 payoff to zero). If she goes bowling, he still is better off going to the movies (compare a payoff of 1 to .5). Shawn still has a dominant strategy: go to the movies. Similarly, Mary still has a dominant strategy: go bowling. This puts them in cell B. Mary and Shawn do not see each other.

Importantly, the outcome does not depend on whether each player knows the other's payoffs. The outcome is the same. Neither has an incentive to do something different given what the other is doing. Essentially, they are more interested in movies and bowling than they are in each other. Given this outcome, neither has an incentive to make a different decision if the game is repeated the next night. When each player is doing the best he or she can, given what the other player is doing, it is said to be *Nash equilibrium*.[185]

TABLE 12-1(B). MARY AND SHAWN LIKE EACH OTHER A LITTLE

		Mary			
Shawn		Movies		Bowling	
Movies	A:	1.5	.5	B: 1.0	1.0
Bowling	C:	0	0	D: 0.5	1.5

Note: Numbers in the cells include the dollar equivalents of the utility of being together.

[185]This solution is named after Nobel laureate John Nash.

> *Nash equilibrium* is one where neither party in a game has an incentive to move. Put somewhat differently, each party is doing the best it can, *given* the choice made by the other party in the game.

B. OUTCOMES WITH DIFFERENT PAYOFFS

It is useful to play the dating game with alternative assumptions about how much Mary and Shawn like each other. The results in this section change solely because of the different payoff structures, not because of an alteration in the nature of the game. I look at four alternative payoffs. Each is a separate problem.

Shawn Likes Mary More than Mary Likes Shawn. Suppose Shawn attaches a value of 1.5 to being in the same place as Mary (he really is smitten with her). Otherwise, all the other payoffs are the same. The payoff matrix changes to that shown in table 12-1(*c*).

In this case, Shawn does not have a dominant solution. If Mary is at the movies, then he prefers the movies (compare 2.5 to 0). If Mary is bowling, then he wants to go bowling (compare 1.5 to 1.0). But Mary has a dominant solution: go bowling. If Shawn knows the payoffs, then he knows Mary is going bowling. It is optimal for him to go bowling. Nash equilibrium is found in cell D. Each is doing the best he or she can, given what the other is doing.

If Shawn does not know Mary's payoffs, then he is not sure where she will go. If he thinks that she is equally likely to go either place (which is reasonable if he is agnostic about her payoffs), then he might choose the movies. The reason is that the average payoffs are higher than going bowling (compare 2.5 and 1.0 in the first row to zero and 1.5 in the second row). In this case, they will end up in cell B. If the game is repeated in subsequent nights, Shawn discovers Mary's location and also goes bowling.

TABLE 12-1(C). SHAWN LIKES MARY MORE THAN MARY LIKES SHAWN

	Mary			
Shawn	Movies		Bowling	
Movies	A: 2.5	0.5	B: 1.0	1.0
Bowling	C: 0	0	D: 1.5	1.5

TABLE 12-1(D). SHAWN AND MARY LIKE EACH OTHER
A LOT

Shawn	Mary			
	Movies		Bowling	
Movies	A: 2.5	1.5	B: 1.0	1.0
Bowling	C: 0	0	D: 1.5	2.5

Mary and Shawn Both Like Each Other a Lot. Suppose Mary feels as strongly about Shawn as he does about her. She attaches a value of 1.5 to seeing Shawn, and otherwise the payoffs are the same as in panel (*c*). The payoff matrix changes to that shown in table 12-1(*d*).

Even if the two players know the payoffs, neither has a dominant strategy, and hence, it is unpredictable where each will go on the first night. For example, if Mary goes to the movies then Shawn wants to go to the movies, but if Mary goes bowling, than Shawn wants to go bowling. This is an example of a **coordination game** because neither has a dominant strategy, and it pays both players to coordinate their actions to find an optimal solution.

One might argue that the solution on the first night is described by cell B. The reason is that Shawn expects a higher payoff from going to the movies versus bowling (compare 2.5 and 1.0 in the first row to zero and 1.5 in the second row). Mary expects a higher payoff from going bowling. Of course, each might anticipate the other's thinking, in which case they end up in cell C. Neither of these outcomes is Nash equilibrium. Both have an incentive to move, given what the other is doing. If they end up in either cell A or D, neither has an incentive to move (Nash equilibrium). They prefer being together. If they are apart, they want to move.

If the game repeats many nights, one assumes that sooner or later they will be in the same place, in which case the game finds equilibrium. One player, say Mary, can adopt a simple "stay put" strategy: always go bowling. If Shawn knows Mary's payoffs, he will find her soon. If he does not know her payoffs, he likely will find her within a few nights. Of course, one could imagine some solutions that keep them apart for many nights.[186]

---

[186]What if Mary *and* Shawn adopt a "stay put" strategy? Then she is waiting at the bowling alley while he is waiting at the movies. Alternatively, what if both adopt a simple "switch" strategy: go to the other place the night following a failed meeting. If they start at different spots the first night, they will not find each other until one changes strategy.

A *coordination game* is one in which neither player has a dominant strategy, and it pays both players to coordinate their actions to find an optimal solution.

Suppose that Mary does not know all Shawn's payoffs, particularly whether or not he likes her. She can set up a simple sort. First, always go bowling. If Shawn always shows up, he might be interested in her or may just like bowling. She can then switch to movies. If he follows her, then she infers that Shawn is smitten with her. Incidentally, when each discovers that the other likes the opposite activity, then each knows that the other bonded his or her signal by engaging in their least-favored activity.

Shawn and Mary Hate Each Other. Suppose instead that Shawn and Mary hate each other. He attaches a negative 1.5 to being in the same spot with her, and she feels the same way about him. The payoffs in this game are shown in table 12-1(*e*).

Both are happy if the other is *not* there. Nash equilibriums are in cells B and C. If the game repeats, one cannot imagine a stable solution in cell C because cell B improves welfare for both players. If they find themselves in cell C, Mary can adopt a simple strategy: go bowling. Shawn sees her and goes to the movies the next night.

Shawn Likes Mary but Mary Hates Shawn. Finally, consider the tragic case when Shawn is smitten with Mary but Mary hates Shawn. Shawn attaches an incremental value of 1.5 to being in the same place as Mary, but Mary attaches a negative 1.5 value to being in the same place. The payoffs are shown in table 12-1(*f*).

No cell is Nash equilibrium. If Shawn and Mary are in the same place, Mary wants to be somewhere else. If they are apart, Shawn wants

TABLE 12-1(E). MARY AND SHAWN HATE EACH OTHER

	Mary			
Shawn	Movies		Bowling	
Movies	A: −0.5	−1.5	B: 1.0	1.0
Bowling	C: 0	0	D: −1.5	−0.5

TABLE 12-1(F). SHAWN LOVES MARY BUT MARY HATES
SHAWN

	Mary	
Shawn	Movies	Bowling
Movies	A: 2.5 −1.5	B: 1.0 1.0
Bowling	C: 0 0	D: 1.5 −0.5

to be somewhere else. In a repeated game, Mary's best strategy is to follow a random pattern. If her whereabouts are predictable, Shawn ex-
ploits it and increases the chances of their being together. A random
strategy is called a **mixed strategy**.[187]

A *mixed strategy* is one in which the player is best off by altering his
actions unpredictably. It does not have to be a 50-50 strategy. It is to
be distinguished from a *pure strategy*, in which one or the other action is optimal.

There are many examples of mixed strategies. In boxing, for example,
it pays for both fighters to move in unpredictable ways. As soon as an
opponent detects a pattern of movement, he will exploit it. Hence, the
only equilibrium is one in which both fighters move randomly. In baseball, batters exploit a pitcher who always throws the ball at predictable

---

[187]If you know a little calculus, you can solve these mixed strategy games regardless of the
payoff numbers in the cells. The general way in which you would write this is as follows.
Let y be the probability that Shawn goes to the movies, and hence $1 - y$ is the probability
that he goes bowling. These same probabilities for Mary can be denoted x and $1 - x$. Represent the payoffs for Shawn in the table as follows: P_{MM} is the payoff to Shawn if he goes
to the movies and Mary also goes to the movies, P_{MB} the payoff for Shawn to attend the
movies if Mary goes bowling, and so on. The expected payoff to Shawn from going out
tonight can be written as follows: $E = y[xP_{MM} + (1 - x)P_{MB}] + (1 - y)[(1 - x)P_{BB} + xP_{BM}]$.
Since y is Shawn's control variable, take the first derivative of E with respect to y and
set the result equal to zero. This gives you the condition: $x(P_{MM} - P_{MB} + P_{BB} - P_{BM}) +
P_{MB} - P_{BB} = 0$. Solve for x. Given the payoffs in panel (f), you will discover that $x = \frac{1}{6}$.
The problem for Mary is exactly the same, except that you differentiate with respect to x,
and thus, the condition shows y as the variable, and, of course, the payoffs are Mary's and
not Shawn's. You will find that $y = \frac{1}{6}$. These conditions tell us that if Shawn and Mary go
to the movies one in six nights randomly, then both are doing the best they can, given
what the other is doing. If the payoffs are different, so are the equilibrium values of x and
y. For example, if Mary and Shawn were indifferent to bowling or movies, then the optimal probabilities would be $y = x = \frac{1}{2}$. Furthermore, in general, the values of x and y do
not have to be the same.

speeds and locations. Hence, successful pitchers follow a mixed strategy. If submarines always patrol the same routes at the same times every month, then it is trivial to defeat their defenses. A more effective strategy is to alter patterns randomly.

C. WHERE IS COASE? THE ROLE OF THE COOPERATIVE SOLUTION

It is natural to ask why the players often end up in a cell that does not yield the highest welfare. Why not? In a nutshell, it is because the players are not cooperating. If Shawn and Mary communicate with each other, then they will agree to be in a cell that yields the highest total welfare. In this case, we have a cooperative solution.

Does a cooperative solution make sense even if one of the players is worse off? Yes, because a cooperative solution assumes that side deals are possible, as in the Coase theorem. For example, consider the last dating game in which Mary is trying to avoid Shawn and Shawn is trying to find Mary. Cell B is the cooperative equilibrium because the total payoff is 2, which is higher than any other box. How can they get there?

If they are in cell C, then both are better off going to cell B. If they are in cell A, then Mary is better off in the amount 2.5 from a move to cell B, and Shawn is worse off in the amount 1.5. But Mary can fully compensate Shawn for his loss and still be better off. Similarly, if they are in cell D, Shawn loses .5 by moving to cell B, but Mary is better off in the amount 1.5. She can compensate him for his loss and still be better off.

In short, in the absence of transactions costs, the cooperative solution always prevails. This is just another rendition of the Coase theorem. In the case of Mary and Shawn, they are so bashful that the transactions costs of cooperating are not zero. In relation to the game depicted is table 12-1(f). Perhaps Mary should ask her friend to give Shawn a bunch of movie coupons!

A *cooperative solution* is one in which the players arrange a way to end up in the cell with the highest total payoffs. In many cases, side payments are required to make it in everyone's best interest to move from a Nash equilibrium to the cooperative solution.

II. Beyond the Dating Game: Other Practical Applications

The dating game introduces many of the concepts in game theory, including some hints about the role of information. Lack of information is at the core of many game problems, and it is interesting to consider a few ways in which players try to deal with these problems.

A. GAMES IN THE HIRING PROCESS

When applicants interview firms for jobs, the firm is not sure if the applicant is seriously interested or qualified for the job, and the applicant is not sure that the firm is seriously interested in her. Hence, both send signals and look for signals from the other in the job matching game. A law partner sends a strong signal to an interviewee when he spends three hours wining and dining a law student at an expensive restaurant. The student in turn sends a strong signal by making it apparent that she is well versed in the particulars of the firm.

Each could have simply *said* they were interested in each other. But these signals cost nothing to send and thus are not credible. They are made credible when time and money spent impressing each other are wasted if their interest is not genuine. When signals are bonded, they are credible.

A *credible signal* is one that is bonded. In the case of the job interview, both the applicant and the firm are wasting their resources *unless* they are interested in pursuing a job match.

Consider the larger problem of salary negotiation. When a firm is hiring a specialized labor input—that is, a person who does not have a large number of near-perfect substitutes—there is some range of salary over which a deal can be made. When Ken and Jane were at the tip of a "cigar" in the Edgeworth box (chapter 1), we said that one way or another, they would find their way to the contract curve. Some outcomes, however, are more favorable to Jane and some more favorable to Ken. We did not worry much about how this bargain would occur. Perhaps now is a good time to revisit this issue.

Suppose that Jane now is dean of Jane's Law School and Ken has become a distinguished law professor. Jane has determined that Ken would be a perfect fit for her school because his unique talents are consistent with her curriculum and approach she has worked to set up at the law school. She could hire other candidates, but none are as good as Ken, meaning that she envisions gaining some surplus from hiring Ken.

In the meantime, Ken is thinking that he very much would like to work with Jane at the law school. In addition, the school is located in the city where his children live and where he does consulting. In other words, while he might have some options at other law schools, Ken envisions some significant surplus from obtaining a position in Jane's Law School.

Suppose that Jane and Ken send strong signals to each other that a job match is desirable. The question, is at what salary will the deal be done? And can the negotiation kill the deal, even though both have potential surplus? Assume that while Jane and Ken may know each other casually, Jane wants to maximize the surplus from the school and Ken wants to maximize his surplus.

Figure 12-1, panel (a) portrays the problem. The vertical axis measures surplus. The horizontal axis measures wage offer. The downward-sloping schedule labeled J_0 measures Jane's surplus from doing a deal at wage rate

(a)

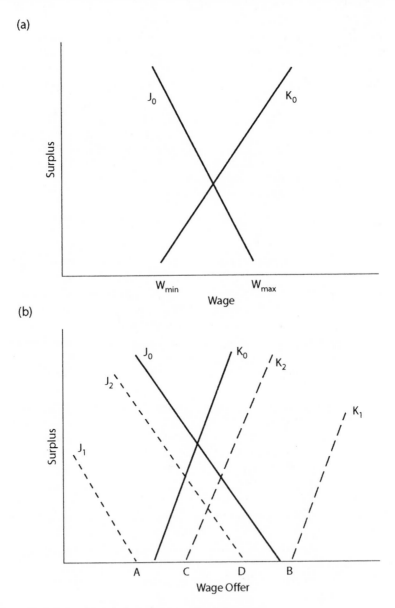

(b)

Figure 12-1. Salary Negotiations with Imperfect Information

W. Obviously, the lower the wage at which she can strike a deal, the higher her surplus. The upward-sloping schedule labeled K_0 measures Ken's surplus from a deal. His surplus increases with the wage at which he can strike a deal. It is immediately apparent that a deal cannot be done below W_{min} or above W_{max} because outside these limits, one or the other's surplus is zero.

We can think of the segment along the horizontal axis between W_{min} and W_{max} as the contract curve. Each knows that the other has some surplus from a match, but neither knows the location of the other's surplus curve. A cat and mouse game occurs between the two in an attempt to learn something about the other's schedule. In economic parlance, we would say that W_{min} is Ken's reservation wage and W_{max} is Jane's **reservation wage**.

A *reservation wage* to the seller is the minimum wage offer at which he is willing to strike a deal. A reservation wage to the buyer is the maximum wage at which she is willing to strike a deal.

Panel (*b*) shows this process visually. While Ken would like to maximize his surplus, he is reluctant to announce a wage as high as one labeled B on the horizontal axis because he is afraid of communicating to Jane that his surplus curve looks like K_1 in which case she will infer that a deal that gives her surplus is not possible. Moreover, he is afraid of conveying a signal to Jane that he will try to bleed her for every ounce of her surplus at every turn, making Jane wonder whether a long-term deal with a hard bargainer is worth it.

Jane is reluctant to offer Ken a wage denoted by point A, for two reasons. She fears signaling Ken that her surplus function looks like J_1, in which Ken may be discouraged from further considering the deal. She also may fear sending Ken a signal suggesting that she will try to minimize Ken's surplus if she can get away with it, which may make Ken leery of joining an association with Jane. Better to associate oneself, thinks Ken, with someone willing to share surplus, rather than with one who tries to squeeze him dry at every opportunity.

So rather than Ken announcing a wage demand or Jane making a job offer, each dances around the issue. Ken makes mention of other offers he is considering, perhaps trying to make Jane think that in consideration of other offers, his surplus from coming to Jane's Law School looks more like K_2. Jane talks about other candidates she is considering, making Ken think that perhaps her surplus schedule looks like J_2.

Notice that to the extent that both believe each other, the contract line looks like it shrinks to something like the segment CD along the horizontal axis in panel (*b*). Both make their orations credible by actually engaging in other interviews. Jane spends some monies to bring in candidates, and she openly suggests to Ken that Bing (who Ken hates) also wants the job. Ken talks to Dave's Law School (Jane's major competitor) to try to attract an offer from them, in hopes of scaring Jane into thinking she will lose all her surplus.

At some point, Jane breaks the deadlock and announces a wage offer: "Ken, we are going to offer you the salary C, and we would love for you to take the job." Ken responds, "No thanks. I have higher offers elsewhere. But if you increase your offer to $C + d$ (where $C + d > D$), I might be willing to make some sacrifice in wage to come and work at a wonderful place like Jane's Law School." At this point, both know a fair amount about where the other's surplus curve lies. If both are convinced that the other has willingly given up some surplus, so that both take away a feeling of a good deal, then in all likelihood a deal will happen. *Deals are more likely to be killed if one or the other party insists on iterating to the edge of the contract curve.*

More generally, if there are many buyers and only one seller, then it is more likely that the deal will minimize the surplus of the buyer, and vice versa. In a litigation context, however, there are two adversaries, both afraid that a jury will milk one or the other dry in their decision. So, it is in their interest to see whether a deal can be done outside court. A deal is hard to envision if the case seems open and shut. That is, if the verdict is almost certainly going to favor party A, then it is unlikely that party B is going to gain much surplus at the expense of B in a deal done in the corridor. But if the case is a toss-up, a deal seems much more likely assuming that both parties are willing to leave the other with some surplus.

B. IRRATIONAL BEHAVIOR: WHAT IF SIGNALS ARE CROSSED?

I have assumed thus far that players are rational and that both know the parameters in the decision boxes. Suppose, however, that I relax this assumption by introducing some sense of irrationality. Either one player is irrational or somehow is valuing the parameters in the problem in an asymmetric way. To be concrete, suppose Dean Jones of Macon Law School is considering hiring Professor Smith from South Law School.

1. Wasted Interview Costs

The law school anticipates net benefits of a hire equal to $1,050, but it costs $1,000 in plane fares and faculty time to pursue this faculty applicant. If the applicant is interested, they gain surplus $50; if the faculty member is uninterested, Macon is out $1,000. Once he commits the $1,000, Dean Jones immediately conveys a credible signal to Professor Smith that he is interested. But before committing, Dean Jones asks himself: is Professor Smith really interested? Dean Jones figures that since Professor Smith will have to spend time coming to the Macon campus and talking over the phone to pursue this job, Professor Smith must be interested, or otherwise Professor Smith is wasting his time. Dean Jones commits the $1,000. Both infer that the other is interested and that a match is imminent.

This is the end of the problem if both are rational. But suppose that unbeknownst to Dean Jones, Professor Smith finds utility in being wined and dined by others pursuing him as a faculty member, or perhaps he is trying to give the impression that he is about to leave South Law School, thereby signaling for a raise in his current job. Indeed, the ego gratification of being "stroked" is easily worth the time that he takes to come to Macon and to talk with an eager dean over the phone. In this case, to Dean Jones, it might seem as though Professor Smith is interested in the job, since expenditures of his time would seem to be wasted otherwise.

Dean Jones, of course, is not irrational. Since he is aware of the possibility of being "used" by Professor Smith, it is easy to imagine that Dean Jones will not commit the $1,000. That is, if Dean Jones is ahead $50 if Professor Smith is interested, as he calculates he must be, based on Dean Jones's evaluation, he still knows that if there is a small chance that he is misinterpreting the signal sent by Professor Smith, then he is out $1,000. Even if there is a 10 percent chance that Dean Jones is reading the signal wrong, the expected cost of a mistake (10 percent times $1,000) exceeds the value of a match ($50). Hence, to avoid the possibility of a large loss, Dean Jones does not commit to the $1,000.

EXERCISE:
Question: Can you think of a strategy that Dean Jones could follow to mitigate this problem?[188]

In general, when there is a large asymmetry between the gain and loss from a decision, then sometimes a rational player will choose the strategy that maximizes his chances of incurring the minimum cost from an error. This kind of problem often is referred to as a **Maximin strategy.**

---

[188]Dean Jones could commit to paying, say, 50 percent of the airfare, with the proviso that Professor Smith gets full payment if a match occurs. Or else he could ask Smith to pay the full airfare, with full reimbursement if the deal goes through.

> A *Maximin strategy*: A decision by a rational player that avoids the possibility of a large loss instead of one that generates a small gain. This solution often arises when there is an asymmetry between gains and losses and there is some chance that one player is not interpreting the other's payoff matrix correctly.

C. DICK GETS MUGGED IN THE PARK

Another Maximin example is suggested by a mugging. Suppose that Dick confronts a thug with a gun on the way to the subway after work in the park after dark. The mugger says, "Give me your money, or I will shoot you." Dick could observe that there are witnesses all around the park and that there is zero chance that the thug will avoid arrest and conviction. He presumes that the thug sees the same witnesses. Suppose that the cost to Dick of being shot is $1,000. If the thug shoots him, he takes the $300 out of Dick's pocket. I write his payoffs as the first entries in table 12-2(*a*).

The thug does not announce his payoffs, but Dick surmises them, *assuming* that the thug is somewhere near Dick's definition of rational. If the mugger does not shoot, he gets $300 if Dick is cooperative and zero if Dick is uncooperative. If he shoots, he gets $300 whether Dick is cooperative or not, *minus* some large number in the form of certain jail for a long time, say L, which is a number, we presume, that is far in excess of $300. I write his payoffs as the second numbers in each cell.

This is a sequential game. Dick gets to make the decision to say yes or no. Then the mugger reacts to Dick's decision. The process unfolds.

Dick has to be thinking: What if the thug does not see all the witnesses around the park and puts the probability of being caught far less than 100 percent? What if the thug has a very high discount rate, so that a prison term in the future is not important as compared to the immediate gratification of $300? This could especially be a problem if the thug is looking for a drug fix. Since the cost of being shot is higher than $300, Dick likely will figure that, despite his calculations from what he *thinks* is the perspective of the thug, there is some chance that Dick gets

TABLE 12-2(A). DICK GETS MUGGED IN THE PARK

	Mugger	
Dick	Shoot	Do not shoot
Give over the money	A: −1,300 300 − L	B: −300 300
Do not give over the money	C: −1,300 300 − L	D: 0 0

Steps in a Sequential Game

1. Dick first thinks through each decision using the payoffs in panel (*a*). If he gives over the $300, the mugger will not shoot. If he does not give him the money, he will not shoot. Dick infers this behaviour because the payoffs to the mugger are always higher if he refrains from shooting.

2. Dick knows that the thug has a dominant strategy: the thug will not shoot no matter what Dick does.

3. Dick therefore knows he effectively can choose whether to be in cell B or cell D. Since cell D has zero cost and cell B has a minus $300 outcome, Dick says no.

4. Once Dick says no, the mugger's optimal strategy is to leave empty-handed.

. . . Or is it?

it wrong, in which case he pays a large price. Suppose that the thug puts the cost of getting caught at only $100 (that is, L = $100). This gives us the payoff matrix depicted in table 12-2(*b*).

These payoffs give Dick pause, and his process of reasoning is as follows. Recall that it is a sequential game. Dick gets to say yes or no, whereupon the mugger reacts.

Sequential Decision with the New Payoffs

1. Dick figures that if he gives over the money, it is optimal for the mugger not to shoot. But if Dick says no, it is optimal for the thug to shoot.

2. Dick therefore knows that the two possible outcomes are cell B and cell C.

3. Based on this information, Dick wants to be in cell B over cell C because the latter imposes a $1,300 cost and the former only $300.

4. To obtain this result, Dick says yes, whereupon the mugger does not shoot.

TABLE 12-2(B). DICK GETS MUGGED IN THE PARK—DIFFERENT PAYOFFS

		Mugger			
Dick		Shoot		Do not shoot	
Give over the money	A:	−1,300	200	B: −300	300
Do not give over the money	C:	−1,300	200	D: 0	0

A seemingly irrational player affects decision making. Sometimes, it is to the detriment of both parties to a transaction. In the Professor Smith-Dean Jones example, Dean Jones's suspicion of seemingly irrational behavior on the part of Professor Smith means that Professor Smith does not receive a job offer, even though both might have benefited from a deal. In the mugging example, the thug is at a distinct advantage compared to a victim walking across the park. If Dick was sure that the mugger was rational and fully informed, then he could have walked out of the park with his $300.

III. Institutions and Cooperative Outcomes

The role of institutions oftentimes is to change the rules of the game so that the players can attain the cooperative solution. The Mafia is one (hypothetical) illustration of the roles that institutions can play to improve outcomes. Rules of law work in very similar ways.

A. THE PRISONER'S DILEMMA RECONSIDERED

I introduced the prisoner's dilemma in chapter 5. The decision matrix in table 12-3(*a*) reproduces the payoffs.

If both prisoners do not confess, they each receive only two years in prison. If one confesses while the other does not, the prosecutor cuts a deal for the former to serve only one year but uses his testimony to get ten years for the other. If both confess, they each receive five years. The dominant solution for both players is confess; hence, both receive five years. The cooperative solution is in cell D, where each receives two years in prison.

The Mafia can solve the problem by changing the payoffs. In particular, change the payoff in the "Confess" option to read "100-year prison sentence." The new payoff matrix is shown in table 12-3(*b*).

The dominant solution now is "Do not confess." The Mafia members choose the solution that minimizes their joint sentences.

TABLE 12-3(A). THE PRISONER'S DILEMMA

	Prisoner 2	
Prisoner 1	Confess	Do not confess
Confess	A: 5 5	B: 1 10
Do not confess	C: 10 1	D: 2 2

Note: Numbers in the cells are years in prison.

TABLE 12-3(B). THE PRISONER'S DILEMMA WITH NEW
PAYOFFS

	Prisoner 2	
Prisoner 1	Confess	Do not confess
Confess	*A:* 100 100	*B:* 100 10
Do not confess	*C:* 10 100	*D:* 2 2

Note: Numbers in the cells are years in prison.

A joint defense agreement (JDA) can accomplish the same result, albeit less dramatically. Suppose that prisoner 1 hires the law firm of Jones White to represent him. Jones White cannot also represent prisoner 2 owing to the possibility of a conflict of interest, but it can refer this business to John Smith, a former associate now at Case Howell. Importantly, Jones White can pay Smith's fees. Jones White and Case Howell can then enter into a JDA in which they agree to share information and design a common strategy to defeat the prosecution's case. It is easy to imagine that a JDA can generate a result in cell D.[189]

B. SOLVING THE COMMON RESOURCE PROBLEM: HOLDUPS IN THE BUILDING TRADES

In a major metropolitan city, a common event is the building of a new skyscraper. The investors putting this deal together need to follow a tight schedule to earn money. They borrow to finance the construction phase and begin to receive positive cash flow once tenants are in the building. Suppose that the building costs $10 billion. The investors earn $500 million in returns on their investments if the project is completed on time.

Consider their daunting task. They must arrange for dozens of unions to come together on the job, along with hundreds of suppliers. Since inventorying parts in the city is not possible, each day's supplies must be trucked in every night for work the next day. This means that any one of hundreds of "players" can "hold up" the investors. That is, by threatening to stop work or miss delivery deadlines, they can milk the investors for the entirety of their $500 million profits. Anticipating this "holdup" game, no investor commits to building a skyscraper.

---

[189]For a detailed discussion, see Craig S. Lerner, "Conspirators' Privilege and Innocents' Refuge: A New Approach to Joint Defense Agreements," 77 *Notre Dame Law Review* 1449 (2002).

To illustrate the nature of the problem, suppose that there are only two suppliers, table 12-3(c) shows the payoffs. Assume that $500 million is up for grabs. If one supplier conducts the holdup, then he gets the entire amount; if both hold up the contractor, they split the booty. It is apparent that cell A represents the predictable outcome: a holdup is inevitable. No developer is interested in playing this game.

It has been alleged that the Mafia has found a solution. It assesses a "fee" from the investors equal to 10 percent of the total cost of construction, in this case, amounting to $1 billion. The Mafia allegedly divvies this sum out to all the players in the game. In return, all the players relinquish their "rights" to a holdup. The Mafia seizes the property rights to a holdup and gives all the players their fair share. In other words, the Mafia overcomes the common resource problem and arbitrarily allocates the shares in the holdup enterprise on an "equitable" basis. After the payments are made, all players must cooperate to build the skyscraper on time.

Table 12-3(d) shows how the stylized solution looks. Notice the unattractive payoffs along the column and row that pertain to the holdup option. Cell D is the predictable outcome. The skyscraper is constructed with another on-time delivery, or so it is alleged.

The fee that facilitates this transaction can be called **vigorish**. It is a cost of doing business. In the building example, the "fee" is reflected in

TABLE 12-3(C). THE HOLDUP PROBLEM

	Supplier 2			
Supplier 1	Holdup		No Holdup	
Holdup	A: 250	250	B: 500	0
No Hold	C: 0	500	D: 0	0

Note: Numbers in the cells are years in prison.

TABLE 12-3(D). THE HOLDUP PROBLEM RESOLVED

	Supplier 2			
Supplier 1	Holdup		No Holdup	
Holdup	A: −∞	−∞	B: −∞	50
No Hold	C: 50	−∞	D: 50	50

Note: The symbol ∞ means and infinite amount.

the rents assessed tenants once the building is complete. The investors receive their $500 million required return. An efficient solution to an intractable problem has been found.

Vigorish: A term of art that means a cut or a piece of the action collected by the house. It is the difference between monies paid in and monies received by suppliers of the product. It is the difference between amounts gambled and won in Las Vegas, the legal fee to write a contract, the broker's fee for doing a stock trade. It is the proverbial middleman payment.

C. SOLVING THE PUBLIC GOODS COLLECTION PROBLEM: PROTECTION FOR THE NEIGHBORHOOD

Suppose that some street in Brooklyn suffers a high rate of crime that threatens the continued viability of the stores on this street. To make the problem susceptible to a two-by-two matrix game problem, suppose that there are only two stores. It costs $12 per period to eliminate crime by creating a roving team of private enforcers. Each store would gain $10 from these efforts. It clearly makes sense to engage in this action because it promises surplus equal to $8. But it will not happen.

The enforcement action is a public good. Once the enforcers are in the neighborhood, I get the protection whether or not I pay my share of the costs. Table 12-3(e) summarizes the problem. Neither store can earn positive surplus from paying the enforcement cost itself (cells B and C). If both stores split the costs, both earn positive surplus (cell A). But neither has an incentive to contribute. Each wants to take the free ride. Cell D is Nash equilibrium. Both stores free ride and enforcement does not happen.

It is difficult within normal constraints to force fellow storeowners to pay for a public good like enforcement. The Mafia has found a solution, or so it is said. It provides the enforcement services. Effectively, the word is out: criminals who trespass this street face infinitely large negative

TABLE 12-3(E). THE ENFORCEMENT PUBLIC GOODS PROBLEM

	Store 2			
Store 1	Pay		Free ride	
Pay	A: 4	4	B: −2	10
Free ride	C: 10	−2	D: 0	0

Note: Numbers in the cells are dollars.

TABLE 12-3(F). THE ENFORCEMENT PROBLEM SOLVED

Store 1	Store 2			
	Pay		Free ride	
Pay	A:	4 4	B:	4 0
Free ride	C:	0 4	D:	0 0

payoffs (this game box is not shown). The criminals do the calculations. They do not trespass. To solve the collection problem, the Mafia changes the payoff structure. Stores who do not free ride are asked to pay only their fair share. Those that refuse discover that their trash is not collected. City inspectors begin citing them for sanitation violations. In the end, the garbage, it seems, is picked up. Enforcement happens. Surplus is enjoyed. Some people call this outcome "extortion." Others call it the efficient solution of a free rider problem.

Table 12-3(f) shows the solution (where the cost of trash buildup is counted as −10). Cell A is the predictable outcome. The payoff from free riding was $10 before but zero afterward owing to the $10 trash noncollection citation costs.

IV. How Legal Standards Change the Payoffs

A. DRIVERS AND CYCLISTS

Consider a similar solution to a "level of care" problem. Suppose that it costs a driver the amount 10 to go slow as compared to driving fast. It costs a motorcycle rider 10 to wear a helmet. Suppose that the driver goes slow. Then the costs of head injuries are zero if the cyclist wears a helmet and 20 if he does not. If the driver goes fast, then the cost of head injuries is 50 if the cyclist wears a helmet and 100 if he does not. There are no damages to either the car or its occupants if an accident occurs.

Consider a rule of law that holds drivers blameless regardless of their speed. The payoffs to this game are shown in table 12-4(a).

The dominant solution for the driver is to go fast (he faces no cost and gains the value of his time). The dominant solution for the motorcyclist is to wear a helmet. Cell B describes the solution (which is Nash equilibrium). Note that the lowest total cost of accidents and accident prevention costs is found in cell D. A hold blameless law does not generate the efficient solution.

Now invoke a strict liability standard. The driver pays all damages regardless of fault. In this case, the payoff matrix is as shown in table 12-4(b).

TABLE 12-4(A). DRIVER IS BLAMELESS REGARDLESS OF SPEED

Driver	Motorcyclist			
	No helmet		Helmet	
Fast	A:	0 100	B:	0 60
Slow	C:	10 20	D:	10 10

Note: Numbers in the cells are costs.

TABLE 12-4(B). DRIVER IS STRICTLY LIABLE

Driver	Motorcyclist			
	No helmet		Helmet	
Fast	A:	100 0	B:	50 10
Slow	C:	30 0	D:	10 10

Note: Numbers in the cells are costs.

TABLE 12-4(C). DRIVER IS LIABLE ONLY IF CYCLIST WEARS A HELMET

Driver	Motorcyclist			
	No helmet		Helmet	
Fast	A:	0 100	B:	50 10
Slow	C:	10 20	D:	10 10

Note: Numbers in the cells are costs.

The motorcyclist has a dominant solution: do not wear a helmet (why pay the cost when the other guy pays full damages?). The driver has a dominant solution: go slow. We have found another suboptimal solution in cell C.

Finally, consider a rule of law that requires the driver to pay damages only if the motorcyclist wears a helmet (contributory negligence standard). This payoff matrix is as shown in table 12-4(c).

The motorcyclist has a dominant strategy: wear a helmet. Given this decision, the driver has an incentive to go slow. They have discovered the optimal solution in cell D. If the proper incentives are reflected in the rule of law, an efficient outcome is inevitable. The same problem is demonstrated in chapter 8, appendix B, using a more familiar continuous speed model.

B. A NOISE PROBLEM

Consider a simple noise problem. Assume that at current flight levels, airplane passengers enjoy surplus from using the airwaves by the amount 150. Homeowners attach a value to the noise externality of −100. By installing mufflers, the airlines can reduce the cost of noise to homeowners by 75 percent. Homeowners can obtain the same result by installing triple-pane windows. The mufflers cost 30 and the windows cost 60. There is no noise if both mufflers and windows are installed. To keep all the numbers positive, I index homeowners' valuations so that with full noise, they have zero utility but value full quiet in the amount 100. Table 12-5(a) shows the payoffs.

The airline payoffs are either 120 or 150 depending on whether or not they install mufflers. In cell D, homeowners enjoy zero value because they incur full noise. In cell A mufflers plus triple-pane windows reduce all the noise, which homeowners value in the amount 100, from which they subtract the cost of windows (60). In cell C, homeowners enjoy a surplus of 15, which equals the value added by the noise reduction from windows alone (75) minus the cost of window installation. In cell B they enjoy 75 units of surplus because they obtain the noise reduction from the mufflers and save the window installation costs. In cell D, no one abates noise and so homeowners have no change in surplus.

If airlines are not held responsible for noise, then Cell C is Nash equilibrium. Airlines have a dominant solution: do not install mufflers. Given this decision, it is optimal for homeowners to install triple-pane windows. This is not the socially optimum solution. Cell B clearly awards higher surplus (it is the cooperative solution). The reason is that it is

TABLE 12-5(A). A NOISE ABATEMENT PROBLEM

	Homeowners Install Windows			
Airplanes Use Mufflers	Yes		No	
Yes	A: 120	40	B: 120	75
No	C: 150	15	D: 150	0

Note: Numbers in the cells are positive net payoffs.

TABLE 12-5(B). A VERTICAL INTEGRATION SOLUTION

	Homeowners Install Windows	
Airplanes Use Mufflers	Yes	No
Yes	A: 160	B: 195
No	C: 165	D: 150

Note: Numbers in the cells are positive net payoffs.

cheaper for the airlines to abate noise than homeowners. Yet, it is not in the interest of airlines to incur this expense.

How can we get from cell C to cell B? In a Coase world of zero transactions costs, homeowners can offer to install the mufflers. This action costs the homeowners the amount 30, but they save the window installation costs (60). An alternative solution is to effect a noise tax. If airlines fail to install mufflers, they are assessed a tax equal to 31. This tax reduces the payoffs to airlines in the last row of the table from 150 to 119, which delivers the outcome in cell B.

Alternatively, consider a vertical integration solution. Suppose that the airlines own the airport and the land within the range affected by its noise. Assume that the negative externality shows up in the form of lower home values. The airlines want to maximize their total surplus. This solution collapses two players to one. Hence, simply add the payoffs in each cell as shown in table 12-5(b). It is apparent that airlines maximize their joint surplus by choosing to install mufflers instead of windows. They end up in cell B, as shown in the table 12-5(b).

An alternative solution to arrive at the same results is to hold airlines responsible for their negative noise externality. One could estimate this value by evaluating land value discounts in the vicinity of the airport.

EXERCISE 1:
A student does not know if the teacher is going to ask a question about patents on the final exam. He hates to study for "nothing." He figures his payoffs in the following way: If he studies he gains 10 if the question is on the exam and −5 if it is not. If he does not study, he gains zero if the question is not on the exam and −5 if it is. From the teacher's perspective, if he puts the question on the exam, he finds out information worth 5 if the student studies and 10 if he does not study.
continued...

EXERCISE 1: *Continued*
If he does not put the question on the exam, he obtains information worth zero no matter what the student does.

Should the teacher ask the question on the exam? Should the student study for this question? Does each player have a dominant solution? What is the Nash solution?[190]

EXERCISE 2:
Consider a simple noise problem. Assume that at current flight levels, airplane passengers enjoy surplus from using the airwaves by the amount 150. Homeowners attach a value to the noise externality of -100. By installing mufflers, the airlines can reduce the cost of noise to homeowners by 50 percent. Homeowners can obtain the same result by installing triple-pane windows. The mufflers cost 20 and the windows cost 10. There is no noise if both mufflers and windows are installed. To keep all the numbers positive, I index homeowners' valuations so that with full noise, they have zero utility but value full quiet in the amount 100.

What are the payoffs in this game if airlines are held harmless for noise? [191]

continued . . .

[190]The payoff box is as follows:

		Student	
Teacher		Study	Do not study
Ask the question		A: 5 10	B: 10 -5
Do not ask the question		C: 0 -5	D: 0 0

The student does not have a dominant solution, but the teacher does, and thus he asks the question. The student knows that the teacher has a dominant solution, and thus he studies for the exam. Cell A is Nash equilibrium.

[191]When airlines are blameless for noise, airplanes fly noisy and homeowners install windows:

	Homeowners Install Windows	
Airlines Install Mufflers	Yes	No
Yes	A: 130 90	B: 130 50
No	C: 150 40	D: 150 0

EXERCISE 2: *Continued*
What are the payoffs and Nash equilibrium when airlines are strictly liable for noise?[192]

How does the solution change under a contributory negligence rule?[193]

EXERCISE 3:
A firm wants to assign a reliable worker to an important job. I label her a worker bee. It decides to sort for reliability by offering "free" sick leave. The "good" job pays $10 more than the regular jobs that are currently occupied by candidates.

There are two candidates. One is a leisure lover and one a worker bee, but we do not know this by inspection. The firm decides to give the job to the one who does not take sick leave. If both do not, or both do, then it picks one for the job randomly. Everyone knows that the sick leave benefit is a test. Leisure lovers attach a $6 value to taking the sick leave, whereas worker bees attach zero value to time off.

What are the payoffs in this game?
Is the firm certain to get a worker bee in the job?[194]

How does the solution change if leisure lovers attach a $4 value to free time off?[195]

[192]When airlines are strictly liable to pay for noise externalities, airplanes fly quiet and homeowners do not install windows:

	Homeowners Install Windows	
Airlines Install Mufflers	Yes	No
Yes	A: 130 90	B: 80 100
No	C: 100 90	D: 50 100

[193]With contributory negligence, airlines are responsible for noise costs unless homeowners install windows. Cell A is Nash equilibrium.

	Homeowners Install Windows	
Airlines Install Mufflers	Yes	No
Yes	A: 130 90	B: 130 50
No	C: 100 90	D: 150 0

V. Applications to Quasi-monopoly Markets: Some Simple Game Theory Models

Game theory has found frequent application in markets that are neither a monopoly nor perfectly competitive. If two competing firms cannot cooperate owing to antitrust laws, can they find a noncooperative solution that generates excess profits? Since firms have many output choices, the game lends itself to a mathematical treatment, but the essence of these solutions can be illustrated in decision boxes.

We normally think that game theory concepts do not apply when markets are characterized by either competition or monopoly. In reality, game theory concepts arise in both markets. Consider the case of *perfect competition*. Even though the farmer responds to market prices, the

---

[194]The payoff box is as follows:

	Leisure Lover	
Worker Bee	Take sick leave	Go to work
Take sick leave	A: 5 11	B: 0 10
Go to work	C: 10 6	D: 5 5

The worker bee sees a payoff of $10 if he alone goes to work and $5 if both he and the leisure lover show up; he gets nothing if he takes sick leave and the leisure lover does not. The leisure lover has the same payoffs from going to work, but adds $6 to payoffs in the take sick leave column. Cell C is Nash; the firm gets the reliable worker in the job.
[195]The new payoff box is as follows:

	Leisure Lover	
Worker Bee	Take sick leave	Go to work
Take sick leave	A: 5 9	B: 0 10
Go to work	C: 10 4	D: 5 5

The change in payoffs changes the solution. Now, the leisure lover does not value the time off so highly that he is willing to jeopardize his chances of getting the good job. He does not take sick leave. Neither does the worker bee. Cell D is Nash. The firm has a fifty-fifty chance of hiring the leisure lover into the good job. This might not be a problem if the required reliability on the job is met by someone who values leisure at $4 but not $6.

market does not respond to anything the farmer does, and so the game has a trivial solution. Each wheat farmer individually is playing a game vis-à-vis a "market." The farmer can, and presumably does, think through his optimal reaction, given different market prices. He has a dominant strategy: no matter what price is announced, he sets output to the point where his marginal cost equals price.

Similarly, in a *monopoly*, there is only one player, which makes it unnatural to think about him playing a game. But consider the agglomeration of consumers as the "other party," and think of the monopolist playing the "monopoly game," which involves a strategic decision. He chooses price, taking into account the actions of his adversary (the consumer). In this case, the consumer's reaction function is the demand curve. The monopolist has a dominant strategy: given any demand curve, set output where marginal cost equals marginal revenue. Since consumers cannot act in concert, they cannot coordinate an optimal response, which makes the game uninteresting.

While game theory nomenclature can be applied to monopoly or competitive decisions, we usually do not encumber the discussion with a new vocabulary, since the second party is not also acting strategically. Just as we can describe the marginal revenue schedule for any demand curve in a competitive market, we do not normally do so unless the supplier uses this concept to set price, which happens in monopoly but not competition.

A. THE COURNOT MODEL

Many times, game theory discussions of markets with a few producers start with a presentation of the Cournot model, which has been in the literature for over 150 years.[196] It is a simple model that determines market price and quantity in a market that has only two producers.

Suppose that there are only two producers of some product and no possibility of entry. There are no fixed costs. Marginal cost of production is constant, but different, for each firm. Firm 1 holds a patent on a cheap process to produce some good. Firm 2 has figured out a different way of producing the product without infringing on firm 1's patent, albeit at a higher marginal cost.

In consideration of antitrust laws, the firms cannot find a cooperative solution by merging or engaging in a contract that sets price and output. Assume that they do not communicate. They simply observe each other's output and choose their own output based on the other firm's choice. Ergo this a noncooperative game.

---

[196] Augustin Cournot, *Recherches sur les principes mathématiques de la théorie des Richesses* (*Researches into the Mathematical Principles of Wealth*) (Paris, 1838).

Assumptions. I assume a linear demand curve and constant marginal cost schedules. The key assumption in the Cournot problem is that *each firm takes the other firm's output as a given.* He then considers himself a monopolist with respect to the market that remains. He takes into account the effects of his output on market price and chooses his optimal output, assuming that the other firm does not change its output. The particular demand curve and the constant marginal costs for both firms are given in the following box.

Assumptions for the Cournot example:
　1. Two firms. No fixed costs to production. Marginal cost is zero for firm 1 and $4 for firm 2.
　2. The demand curve is $P = 20 - Q$, where P is price and Q is quantity.
　3. Output can be produced only in whole units.

Firm 1's optimal output depends on firm 2's output, and vice versa. Since the solution to the problem requires some tedious math, I solved the problem for you. Firm 1 produces 8 units and firm 2 produces 4 units. The two firms together produce 12 units, which corresponds to price $8.[197]

Even if you cannot solve the problem mathematically, you still can find the answer in a decision box, except you need more than a two-by-two matrix. Because I already know the answer, table 12-6 presents a three-by-three matrix centered around the correct answer. In principle, one could create a much larger matrix with all possible output combinations between the two firms. Here is how to complete all the numbers in the cells.

Consider cell A. Firm 1 produces 9 units and firm 2 produces 5 units. This gives a total output of 14. The demand curve ($P = 20 - Q$) tells us that at this output level, the market price is $6. Since firm 1 produces output at zero marginal cost, it earns $6 times 9 units, or $54. Firm 2 has a marginal cost of $4 and thus earns $2 in profit times 5 units, or $10. Proceed in a similar way to complete all the cells in the box.

---

[197]Using calculus, simply define profits of firm 1 as $\pi_1 = Pq_1$ (recall that marginal cost is zero). Substitute for price P using the demand curve $(P = 20 - Q)$, and remember that $Q = q_1 + q_2$; so, $\pi_1 = Pq_1 = [20 - (q_1 + q_2)]q_1$. Multiply out to get: $\pi_1 = 20q_1 - q_1^2 + q_1q_2$. Take the first derivative with respect to q_1 and set the result equal to zero: $\pi_1 = 20 - 2q_1 - q_2 = 0 \Rightarrow q_1 = 10 - 1/2\ q_2$, which gives us firm 1's reaction curve. Remembering that $c_2 = 4$ then proceeding similarly, you should be able to verify that firm 2's reaction curve is $q_2 = 8 - 1/2\ q_1$. You have two equations and two unknowns, which give the solutions $q_1 = 8$ and $q_2 = 4$.

TABLE 12-6. COURNOT AS A PRISONER'S DILEMMA

Firm 1	Firm 2					
	5 units		4 units		3 units	
9 units	A: $54	$10	B: $63	$12	C: $72	$12
8 units	D: $56	$15	E: $64	$16	F: $72	$15
7 units	G: $56	$20	H: $63	$20	I: $70	$18

Note: The first number in each cell corresponds to firm 1; the second number refers to firm 2.

The Cournot model assumes that each firm makes a move assuming that the other maintains its output level. This makes it amenable to the usual way in which we find solutions in a decision box. Firm 1, for example, asks which output it should choose, given firm 2's choice. Suppose firm 2 chooses 5 units. Firm 1 is indifferent to producing between 7 or 8 units (profits are $56) but rules out producing 9 units (profits are $54). Thus, we know that cell A cannot be the solution.

The easiest way to find the Nash equilibrium is to eliminate all the cells that cannot be the solution. We can have a Nash equilibrium if *neither* firm has an incentive to move. If firm 1 finds itself in cell A, it has an incentive to increase output, meaning that cell A cannot be a Nash equilibrium. If firm 2 produces 4 units, firm 1 wants to produce 8 units, meaning that cells B and H cannot be Nash. Similarly, if firm 1 produces 7 units, then firm 2 will not produce 3 units, which rules out cell I. Proceeding in this fashion, it is apparent that cell E (and no other cell) is Nash equilibrium.

Notice that cell E does not produce the highest level of profits for both firms taken together. The comparative solution is given by cell I, which gives a total of $88 in profits. Compared to the noncooperative solution in cell E, the solution in cell I gives firm 1 an additional profit of $6 and firm 2, $2. If both firms cooperated, they would each agree to reduce output by 1 unit and both be better off. But they do not cooperate in a Cournot model. We have rediscovered the prisoner's dilemma: both firms are better off in cell I, but they end up in cell E.

The matrix also makes clear why an attempt at a cooperative solution is hard to maintain. Suppose that there are only two oil-producing countries that make up the international cartel, OPEC. They discover that the optimal solution is cell I, and thus, agree to quotas of 7 and 3 units. Once the quotas are established, both countries have an incentive to cheat by 1 unit.

EXERCISES:

Questions:

1. Can you think of a cooperative solution that improves on cell I?

2. Assuming a one-period model, in comparison to the Cournot solution, what is the maximum that firm 1 is willing to pay for firm 2's patent?

3. What is the least amount that firm 2 will accept?

4. If the two firms merge, what is consumer surplus in this market?[198]

B. SEQUENTIAL DECISION: STACKELBERG

Cournot assumes that firm 1 and firm 2 enter the market at the same time. But suppose that firm 1 obtains its patent first. Firm 2 is about to receive its competing patent and go into production soon after. Given that firm 1 gets there first, will it choose the same output as before? No, because it knows that firm 2 will choose an output that maximizes its profits, *given* the output chosen by firm 1. Since firm 1 can predict firm 2's response to its decision, why not take this into account? The sequential problem is called a Stackelberg model.[199]

The solution is straightforward. All we need to do is expand table 12-6 to show more output choices, as shown in table 12-7. The numbers in each cell are created as before. Since firm 1 chooses first, it is natural to consider each possible output choice it has, then look for the optimal reaction from firm 2.

If firm 1 produces 8 units, firm 2 chooses 4 units because it gives the highest profits ($16). If firm 1 chooses 10 units, firm 2 produces 3 units. Continuing this exercise tells firm 1 that the feasible set of solutions is described by the cells outlined in bold. Notice that some of the outlines incorporate two merged cells. These are cases in which firm 2 is indifferent to choosing between one of two output levels.

---

[198]The best cooperative solution is for firm 1 to produce all the output because its marginal cost is zero. This means that the firms can split total profits of $100 instead of $88. In comparison to the Cournot solution, which is depicted in cell E, firm 1 is willing to pay as much as $36 for firm 2's patent (since monopoly profits are $100 with firm 2 out of the market); firm 2 is willing to accept anything above $16. Thus, we can assume that a deal can work at a price somewhere between $16 and $36. After the buyout, price is $10 and output is 10. Hence, consumer surplus is ½ ($20 − $10) × 10 = $50. The model is named after its creator Heinrich von Stackelberg (1905–1946). See *The Theory of the Market Economy*, trans. A.T. Peacock (New York: Oxford Univ. Press, 1952).

[199]We know from note 197 that firm 2's reaction curve is $q_2 = 8 - 1/2q_1$. Firm 1's profits are $\pi = Pq_1$. But we know that $P = 20 - Q$ and that $Q = q_1 + q_2$. Making all these substitutions gives us $\pi = [20 - q_1 - (8 - 1/2q_1)]q_1$, which simplifies to $\pi = 12q_1 - 1/2q_1^2$. Take the first derivative with respect to q_1, which gives the solution $q_1 = 12$. Using firm 2's reaction function then $q_2 = 2$.

TABLE 12-7. THE STACKELBERG SOLUTION

Firm 1	Firm 2					
	5 units	4 units	3 units	2 units	1 unit	0 units
13 units	A: 26 −10	B: 39 −4	C: 52 0	D: 71.5 2		E: 91 0
12 units	F: 36 −5	G: 48 0	H: 60 3	I: 72 4	J: 84 3	K: 96 0
11 units	L: 44 0	M: 55 4	N: 71.5 6		O: 88 4	P: 99 0
10 units	Q: 50 5	R: 60 8	S: 70 9	T: 80 8	U: 90 5	V: 100 0
9 units	X: 54 10	Y: 67.5 12		Z: 81 10	a: 90 6	b: 99 0
8 units	c: 56 15	d: 64 16	e: 72 15	f: 80 12	g: 88 5	h: 96 0
7 units	i: 59.5 20		j: 70 18	k: 77 14	l: 84 8	m: 91 0

Note: Numbers are profits ($ omitted); demand curve is $Q = 20 - P$, where Q is the sum of outputs of firms 1 and 2. Marginal cost for firm 1 is zero and 2 is $4. There are no fixed costs to production and no entry.

For example, when firm 1 produces 9 units, firm 2 earns $12 whether it produces 3 units or 4 units. Firm 1 prefers firm 2 to produce 3 units in this case (because the lower output increases price), but it cannot affect firm 2's behavior, and so I write the average of firm 1's profits from both cells, which is $67.50 in this case. This is firm 1's expected profit level if it produces 9 units. Which output choice delivers its highest profits?

Output 12 units is its best choice. Given this output, firm 2 chooses 2 units. Cell I is the solution. Total output is 14 units and price is $6. Firm 1 earns $72 and firm 2, $4. The cell also is Nash equilibrium because neither firm has an incentive to move.[200]

Notice that in comparison to the Cournot solution in table 12-6, firm 1 is better off and firm 2 worse off. Total profits are lower in this solution,

---

First-mover advantage refers to any solution in which the first to make a decision nets some advantage over the second. In Stackelberg, there is a first-mover advantage. This is not always the case in game theory models.

---

[200]At first, it looks like 13 units is the best choice because if firm 2 produces 1 unit, firm 1's profits are $78, which is higher than it can earn in any other bold-outlined cell. But there is an equally likely chance that firm 2 will choose to produce 2 units, in which case firm 1's profits are only $65. If there is a 50-50 chance that firm 2 chooses either 1 or 2 units of production, then firm 1 expects to earn the average of these two numbers, or $71.50.

TABLE 12-8. WHY FIRM 1 ACCOMMODATES FIRM 2

Firm 1	Firm 2			
	2 units		0 units	
16 units	A: $32	−$4	B: $64	$0
12 units	C: $72	$4	D: $96	$0

but firm 1 earns *higher* profits. It earns $72 compared to $64 in Cournot; firm 2 earns only $4 in comparison with $16 in Cournot. Clearly, firm 2 is worse off. In a one-period game, however, this is clearly the best it can do. This solution has a **first-mover advantage**.

It is reasonable to wonder why firm 1 does not set price so as to *eliminate* firm 2. Firm 1 has a cost advantage, and so why not exploit it to get rid of the second firm? Here, we need to make an assumption. Suppose that if the price falls below $4, it is costless for firm 2 to simply halt production and start up again as soon as the price increases above $4.[201] This means that to eliminate firm 2, firm 1 must set output equal to 16 units, which drives price down to $4 for the duration of its patent (suppose it sets price at $3.99). In this case, firm 1 earns approximately $4 over 16 units for a total profit of $64. This is less desirable than the outcome depicted in cell I in table 12-7. For convenience, I depict these two choices in table 12-8.

Firm 1 sets output to either 12 or 16 units. Depending on which choice firm 1 makes, firm 2 sets output to either 2 or zero units. Since firm 1 goes first, it is better off choosing 12 units and accommodating firm 2.

C. A TIT-FOR-TAT STRATEGY

If the game will last many periods, firm 2 might be able to encourage firm 1 to share profits in the market more equally. One way to accomplish this outcome is for firm 2 to adopt a simple tit-for-tat strategy. Whatever output firm 1 chooses, firm 2 chooses the same output or sufficient output to push the price to zero, whichever output is lower. If firm 1 chooses 12 units of output, firm 2 chooses 8 units, which pushes price to zero. Neither earns a profit. Firm 2 incurs a loss of $32. It is worse off compared to cell C in table 12-8 in the amount $36.[202] But firm 1 is worse off by $72.

---

[201]In a different problem, we could suppose that firm 2 has some fixed cost that needs to be covered, in which case firm 1 might be able to put firm 2 in bankruptcy if he held the price below $4 for any period. This is called predatory pricing, which I will not cover here.
[202]It incurs a loss of $32 on the 8 units it produces, as compared with a $4 profit in cell A.

If firm 1 becomes convinced that firm 2 will match its output, its optimal strategy changes. It is intuitively obvious that firm 1 is better off by splitting the maximum attainable profit rather than splitting some lower amount. Hence, firm 1 is led to choose output 5 units, which is matched by firm 2. At this level of output, price is $10, firm 1 earns $50 per period, and firm 2 earns $30.[203]

This, of course, may not be the final solution. Firm 1 may anticipate firm 2's actions and find a different strategy other than one that accommodates firm 2 in hopes of altering firm 2's behavior. Moreover, there is a tendency for these strategies to unravel when the end point of the game can be anticipated, as in my patent case. For example, in the final year of patent protection, firm 1 does not care what firm 2 does in the following year, and so firm 1 will act in a way that ignores firm 2's reaction. But knowing what happens in the last year can affect the optimal decisions in the penultimate year of patent protection, and so on.

EXERCISE:

Problem: Suppose that the New York port will be closed for three months, giving rise to surprise business for Philadelphia, worth say $1 billion in rent for the latter port. One firm controls the Philly port; all the workers are in the same union. The union wants part of the action for its workers. The firm would prefer to pocket the extra billion. The union refuses to unload any diverted New York–bound boats until they have a revised contract for the next three months. If Philly refuses to admit the boats, then they will divert to Boston as a second choice.

For simplicity, instead of considering a continuum of bargaining, suppose it takes three distinct phases. The firm offers the union a deal to split the $1 billion. If the union rejects the deal, it can make a counteroffer, but this takes one month, during which time $200 million of rent is lost, leaving only $800 million to split. If the firm refuses, it can make another offer, but this takes one month, during which time another $200 million in rent is lost, leaving only $600 million to split.

continued . . .

---

[203] You can show this by expanding table 12-7 to include more rows. You will discover that if firm 2 commits to matching firm output then firm 1's best output choice is 5 units. To show this with calculus, write the profits for firm 1 as $\pi_1 = Pq_1$. We know that $P = 20 - Q$ and $Q = q_1 + q_2$. If firm 2 sets its output so that $q_2 = q_1$, $Q = 2q_1$. Making these substitutions, rewrite firm 1's profits as $\pi_1 = (20 - 2q_1)q_1$, and multiply out: $\pi_1 = 20q_1 - 2q_1^2$. Take the first derivative with respect to q_1 and set the result to zero, which gives $q_1 = 5$.

EXERCISE: *Continued*

If the union refuses, by the time it comes up with another counteroffer, the three-month period is over, at which point New York reopens and there is zero rent.

Assume that this is a one-time event and that in fact the Philly harbor will fall into the ocean after three months and everyone knows it. Also assume that settlements must be made in $100 million units; that is, the firm offers either $100 million, $200 million, and so on, which rules out offers like $50 million or 50¢.

How much does the firm offer in the first instance? How much rent will the firm and union split? Under the conditions of the problem, is there a first-mover advantage? What if I changed the problem to allow two more rounds of bargaining, where the rent fell to $400 and $200 for the last two rounds?[204]

---

[204]The strategy to follow in this problem is to think backward. Where is this negotiation going if an agreement cannot be made? Well, we know one thing. If the matter deteriorates until the third and final offer is made, there is only $600 million to split. The firm will offer the union $100 million and keep $500 million. If the union is rational, it will accept this amount because the alternative is zero and because this is the last chance for an agreement.

But both the union and the firm know that this solution is the inevitable result if they get to round 3. So, if the two antagonists found themselves in the second round, both would be looking for a solution that beats the third-round result. The union makes the offer in the second round. It needs to offer the firm an amount that exceeds the third-round number to discourage the firm from pursuing the third round. The union can do this by offering the firm $600 million, which beats the $500 million they will earn in the third round. Since there is $800 million to split in the second round, this means that the union keeps $200 million, which beats the $100 million it would earn in the third round.

But the firm and the union can figure this out ahead of time. They know what will happen if they get to the second round. So the firm figures that it needs to make an offer to the union in round 1 that beats the amount that they could earn if the game proceeded to round 2 or 3. They can do this by offering the union $300 million in round 1, which beats the $200 million that the union could earn in round 2. The firm keeps $700 million, which beats the $600 million it could earn in round 2.

If the union is rational, it accepts the $300 million. There is a first-mover advantage. If the union went first, it would have earned $700 million and the firm $300 million. If I allowed two more rounds, then the union and the firm would each get $500 million in the first round.

Index